SHANGHAINESE

DICTIONARY
&
PHRASEBOOK

SHANGHAINESE

DICTIONARY
&
PHRASEBOOK

Richard VanNess Simmons

Hippocrene Books, Inc.
New York

For information, address:
Hippocrene Books, Inc.
171 Madison Avenue
New York, NY 10016
www.hippocrenebooks.com

Library of Congress Cataloging-in-Publication Data

Simmons, Richard VanNess.
 Shanghainese dictionary and phrasebook / by Richard Van-
Ness Simmons.
  p. cm.
 Includes bibliographical references.
 ISBN-13: 978-0-7818-1261-0 (pbk.)
 ISBN-10: 0-7818-1261-5 (pbk.)
1. Chinese language--Dialects--China--Shanghai. 2. Chinese
language--Conversation and phrase-books--English. 3. Chi-
nese langauge--Dictionaries--English. I. Title.
 PL2065.S56 2010
 495.1'71303--dc22

                                          2010041395

to my dad
Robert Harrison Simmons
who taught me to pursue my interests

ACKNOWLEDGMENTS

I am delighted to have had the opportunity to produce this volume. Having worked for many years researching the history and relationships of the Wu dialects in and around Jiangsu and Zhejiang along the Yangtze Delta, I am greatly pleased now to have a chance to share the fruits of my study and research with a more general audience interested in learning something of the colorful and fascinating language of Shanghai, that region's most widely spoken and vibrant dialect. My gratitude toward those who made this possible is wholehearted and everlasting.

While the process of compilation has been thoroughly rewarding, it has also been heavily demanding of my time and attention. I could not have managed to see it through without the devoted support and gentle patience of my wife Zhu Lihui, who enthusiastically encouraged me from the first conception of the project through to the end, and generously endured the inconveniences that the writing and compilation demanded of my life and time. I wish here to express my most heartfelt thanks to her for so lovingly standing beside me throughout all.

I would like to thank Qian Nairong for guidance and answers he provided to me during a visit I made to Shanghai in the summer of 2009 as part of my research for this volume. In addition to his advice, Qian Nairong's many excellent studies of Shanghainese have been invaluable in helping to round out my knowledge of the dialect and its history. I also wish to extend special appreciation to Huang Xiaodong, who carefully read through the whole manuscript, providing many valuable suggestions and catching many serious errors. Lacking his sharp eye and discerning knowledge, this volume would be far less reliable for reference.

Finally, I would like to thank the editors I have worked with at Hippocrene Books in compiling this book and preparing it for publication. Monica Bentley, to whom I am deeply indebted for originally suggesting the idea for this *Shanghainese Dictionary and Phrasebook*, worked closely with me in the early stages as I developed the Shanghainese Romanization used herein. Her guidance was instrumental in coming up with what I believe is a highly workable system. Monica also provided much valuable advice during the process of compilation and offered numerous useful comments on the initial drafts of the manuscript. The final draft of the manuscript has benefited from the keen eye of Barbara Keane Pigeon, who brilliantly polished the organization of the Phrasebook section and cleaned up many errors of style, substance, and spelling. Barbara's editorial expertise also has helped to ensure that the parts of speech identifications are rigorously accurate for both the English and the Shanghainese in the Dictionary section.

I am extremely grateful to all of these people for their assistance and support. This dictionary and phrasebook could not have been completed without it. Of course, any errors, inaccuracies, shortcomings, or omissions that remain in these pages are entirely my own.

Richard VanNess Simmons
Changchun, China 8/11/2011

CONTENTS

INTRODUCTION:
THE CITY AND ITS LANGUAGE

As China has followed a course of explosive development to enter the new global era as an economic pow-
erhouse and factory to the world, the city of Shànghǎi
has held a position at center stage, in the vanguard of
building and modernization. The city's skyline has
sprouted a thicket of tall new buildings of dazzling design that sparkle on the banks of the Huangpu River,
and serve collectively as a symbol of twenty-first-cen-
tury China. But in this country, where just about every
resident will remind us of China's long and grand three-
thousand-year history at just about every opportunity,
Shanghai is a relatively brash young newcomer.

A little over one-hundred and fifty years ago, Shanghai was a quiet riverside town, not much different from
the many other water and canal towns that dot this
broad flat Yangtze delta region. The region's main cultural centers for most of imperial China's later history
were south and west of Shanghai—in the cities of
Hángzhōu, Sūzhōu, Nánjīng, and Yángzhōu. Only following the tumultuous events of the mid-nineteenth
century did Shanghai emerge as the most prosperous of
the ports that Britain had demanded China open up to
foreign access and shared control. With that, Shanghai's
population began an explosive growth that has hardly
slowed in the ensuing century and a half.

The language that is spoken today in the city, a Chinese dialect of the Wú 吴 variety, evolved through those
years, following a dynamic course of development
along with the city's growing and ever changing population. The Shanghai dialect took shape in the cross cur-
rents of immigrants and locals, ever changing,
constantly absorbing new influences, and always subject to the forces of the latest cultural trends and contemporary social tides.

The land upon which Shanghai sits was formed of
silt deposited by the Yangtze River at its entrance to the

Yellow Sea. The river's delta had pushed far enough east just under a thousand years ago that in the mid-eleventh century we find the first historical and administrative record of a market site for a population that had moved on to the fertile tidelands. These people, most of whom were probably from the surrounding Wú-dialect-speaking region and who had likely been attracted by the potential of this new land, made their livelihood farming, fishing, and brewing rice wine. Many of them settled on the banks of the Wúsōng River 吴淞江 (now also known as Sūzhōu Creek), which cut through the delta on its way to the sea.

One of the earliest villages in the area was known as Hùdú 沪渎 'fishing basket channel', named for bamboo traps that villagers set in ditches and channels along the Wúsōng River to catch crabs and fish. This name has evolved into a nickname for Shanghai—Hù 沪—which is still in use today (and can be seen, for example on the license plates of the city's cars). The Wúsōng River originally had two branches that drained into the sea. One branch was called Xiàhǎipǔ 下海浦 'lower river mouth,' the other branch was called Shànghǎipǔ 上海浦 'upper river mouth.' A small port town evolved at the upper Shànghǎipǔ, where government offices taxed and managed the river traffic.

Later, as the Yangtze Delta continued to expand eastward, the Wúsōng River and its branches were blocked and redirected by the continuously increasing sediment and ultimately settled into their present course by which the Wúsōng now drains into the Huángpǔ River 黄浦江 on the latter's northeastern flow into the Yangtze and the sea. But the port town that had grown on the banks of the Shànghǎipǔ managed to stay astride the shifting waters and continued to serve as a harbor and gateway to the sea. Its position was enhanced by waterworks projects in the Míng Dynasty (1368-1644) that expanded the region's canal system eastward and enhanced the drainage and arability of the surrounding land. The waterborne commerce there became active enough by the middle of the Míng Dynasty to attract the unwanted attention of Japanese pirates, who harassed and plundered the port and its trade, forcing the

Míng government to build a wall around Shanghai in the mid-sixteenth century.

This was the small port town that attracted the British in the nineteenth century and whose environs they demanded to have access to in the Treaty of Nanking that was forced on the Qīng Dynasty (1644-1911) in 1842. The British were soon joined by the Americans and the French in administering a set of "concessions," which were essentially colonial plots established on land to the north and west of the walled Chinese town of Shanghai that could be governed through the provisions of extra-territoriality. The foreign powers came to control Shanghai's maritime customs activity and navigation into and up the Yangtze River. They built banks, trading companies, and factories, and developed Shanghai into the center of a trade network that reached to Hong Kong, Japan, Southeast Asia, India, Europe, the United States, and Australia.

The old port town and the concessions evolved into a grand city of international trade, a crossroads of world cultures, and a seething den of vice-fueled decadence. The city's population at least doubled from about five-hundred thousand in the mid-nineteenth century to around one million by the start of the twentieth. This population had tripled by the 1930's, and then continued to grow through the turmoil of the Sino-Japanese war, the Chinese civil war, and the Cultural Revolution to reach nearly fifteen million in the 1990s, and over eighteen million today.

The dialect that was spoken in the old walled city and its environs prior to the arrival of the foreign powers was fairly typical of the Wú dialects in the region. It had, for instance, a close affinity with the dialect of nearby Sūzhōu. As the population grew, the language of the old walled city was buffeted by the patois of Chinese speakers from near and far, and to a lesser extent by the western tongues in their midst. Their dialect adapted and accommodated to the many outside influences, evolving along with the city as Shanghai grew beyond the confines of the old port town. The result is a dialect that is perhaps even more typical of Wú dialects in general, but one which has followed to the extreme many of the evolutionary tendencies and transformational inclinations common to those dialects.

The affinities with Sūzhōu and other Wú dialects are still strong in the city's speech, while at the same time the dialect and its speakers have collectively long held an air of cosmopolitan modernity. Thus modern Shanghainese serves as a prestigious lingua franca among many Wú speakers in the neighboring provinces of Zhèjiāng and Jiāngsū and the terms Wú and Shanghainese are synonomous in the minds of many, whether they speak the dialect or not.

Useful histories of Shanghai include: *Shanghai: the Rise and Fall of a Decadent City* by Stella Dong (New York: HarperCollins, 2000); *Shanghai: Crucible of Modern China* by Betty Peh-T'i Wei (New York: Oxford University Press, 1987); and *In Search of Old Shanghai* by Pan Ling (Hong Kong: Joing Publishing Co., 1982).

Chinese pronunciation is most commonly described syllable by syllable, rather than letter by letter. This approach works well with Shanghainese also. Like Mandarin, the Shanghainese syllable is composed of an *initial*, a consonant, if any, that is pronounced at the start, and a *final*, the vowels of the syllable and any consonants that may follow at the end. Shanghainese pronunciation also has *tones*—different pitches or intonations pronounced across whole syllables or words that can affect meaning. Below we provide descriptions of the basics regarding the initials, consonants, finals, vowels, and tones in Shanghainese.

Initials and Consonants

Initials are the consonants that begin a syllable. Many Shanghainese initial consonants are pronounced similar to how they are pronounced in English and usually are similar to the way they are pronounced in Mandarin *pīnyīn* as well. Shanghainese initial consonants that are pronounced similar to English are:

> **b, ch, d, f, g, h, j, k, l, m, n, p,**
> **s, sh, t, v, z**

Shanghainese initial consonants that are pronounced similar to Mandarin *pīnyīn* include:

> **b, d, f, g, h, j, k, l, m, n, p, s, t, w, y**

Note that Shanghainese **ch**, **sh**, and **z** are pronounced more closely to how they sound in English and differ somewhat from the Mandarin *pīnyīn*. Shanghainese **ch** and **sh** are similar to the *q* and *x* in Mandarin *pīnyīn*, respectively. The sound of *z* in Mandarin *pīnyīn* is **dz** in Shanghainese, which additionally has a more English-like **z**. Shanghainese **y** and **w** are like their Mandarin *pīnyīn* counterparts, and are pronounced more like pure vowels *i* and *u*, respectively, rather that the semi-vowels they represent in English. Shanghainese **h** is more like the English *h* and less guttural than it is in Mandarin

Quick Start Guide to Pronunciation

If you don't have the time to go carefully through all the description of Shanghainese consonants and vowels, the following is a thumbnail guide to the essentials. (Additionally, a handy guide to all the consonants and vowels in Shanghainese spelling is found in the "Quick Pronunciation Chart" at the end of the Phrasebook section.):

1. An apostrophe ' or ' before or after the first letter in a syllable indicates the syllable is pronounced with a low, breathy quality.

2. An ï with two dots above it is pronounced *zzz*.

3. Shanghainese **i** is pronounced like the *ee* in *see*, except before **q** where it is pronounced like the *i* in *ick*.

4. Shanghainese **e** and **eu** are pronounced like the *u* in *fun*, except in the combinations **ae** and **oe**, which represent single vowels.

5. A tilde ˜ means the vowel is pronounced with nasality, through the nose.

6. A final **q** indicates the syllable is pronounced short and ends quickly—it is "checked."

7. A falling accent ˋ means the word is pronounced with a falling tone and/or the *first* syllable is stressed.

8. A rising accent ´ means the word is pronounced with a rising accent and/or the *second* syllable is stressed.

pīnyīn. Shanghainese has a **v** pronounced like that in English, which is not found in Mandarin.

An apostrophe ' or ' with the initial—before or after the first letter—indicates that there is a *low pitched* breathiness that accompanies the pronunciation of the initial and continues into the final. It sounds like the *h* in *hah* pronounced in a very low voice. The initials that can have this breathy pronunciation are:

b', d', g', h', j', 'w, 'y

This breathiness is also usually pronounced in syllables beginning with **l, m, n, ng, v,** and **z,** as well as with the syllabic **m̃** and **ñg,** though we do not write the apostrophe with any of these.

There are just a few Shanghainese initial consonants not found in English and that also differ from Mandarin *pīnyīn*. They are:

dz, ng, ts, zy

Following is a brief description of each of these four initials (**SH** = Shanghainese; **M** = Mandarin):

SH	Pronunciation	M *pīnyīn*	Examples
dz	like the *ds* in *fads*	*z*	**dzòng** [dsowng] (*middle*)
ng	like the *ng* in *sing*	—	**ngú** [ngoo] (*hungry*)
ts	like the *ts* in *cats*	*c*	**tsáw** [tsaw] (*stir-fry*)
zy	like the *s* in *measure*	—	**zyiá** [jhee-ya] (*thank*)

Finals and Vowels

Finals are the remainder of a syllable after the initial consonants. They are composed of one or more vowels and can end in either a vowel or consonant.

Vowels that can be followed by other vowels
Shanghainese has three vowels that might be the only vowel in a syllable, or that can come before other vowels. They are:

> **i, u, ü**

The **i** and **u** are not pronounced like they usually are in English, which does not have an **ü** at all. But all three vowels are pronounced like their counterparts in Mandarin *pīnyīn*. We can describe them as follows (**SH** = Shanghainese; **M** = Mandarin):

SH	Pronunciation	M *pīnyīn*	Examples
i	like *ee* in *see*	*i*	**jí** [jee] (*how many*)
u	like *oo* in *mood*	*u*	**hú** [hoo] (*fire*)
ü	like German *ü* or French *u* (round your lips to say *oo* but then say *ee*)	*ü*	**jǘ** [jü] (*expensive*)

Vowels that are always last
There are several more vowels that are always last in an open syllable, though many of them may be preceeded by **i**, **u**, and **ü**. They are:

> **a, ae, aw, eu, ï, oe, uo/o**

Note that even though we write **ae, aw, eu, oe** and **uo** with two letters, each of them actually represents only one vowel sound. Shanghainese **o** and **uo** are pronounced the same; **o** is used after **b, f, m,** and **p**, while **uo** is used after other consonants. Below we describe how to pronounce each of these vowels (**SH** = Shanghainese; **M** = Mandarin):

SH	Pronunciation	M *pīnyīn*	Examples
a	like the *a* in *father* and *ah*	*a*	**má** [mah] (*buy*)
ae	like the *a* in *fad* and *at*	—	**láe** [lae] (*come*)
aw	like British *o* in *hot* or American *aw* in *law*	—	**háw** [haw] (*good*)
eu	like the *u* in *gun*, the *e* in *problem*, and the *o* in *some*	*e*	**d'éu** [dhuh] (*head*)
ï	like the *zz* in *fuzz*	*i* after *z, c, s*	**sḯ** [sszz] (*four*)
oe	like German *ö* in *schön* or French *eu* in *feu* (round your lips to say *oo* but then say the *e* in *end*)	—	**gòe** [gö] (*dry*)
uo/o	like the *u* in *put* and the *oo* in *foot*	—	**zuó** [zuoo] (*tea*) **mó** [muoo] (*horse*)

Finals with nasal endings

This set of finals includes nasal vowels and vowels followed by **n** or **ng**:

ã, ãw, en, in, ün, ong

These finals may be preceeded by **i**, **u**, and **ü**. The tilde ˜ over the vowel in Shanghainese **ã** and **ãw** means these vowels are pronounced partially through the nose, similar to the pronunciation of the French nasal vowel in *an* (year). The pronunciations of the vowels in all of these finals are somewhat different from the vowels discussed above. So we describe them individually here (**SH** = Shanghainese; **M** = Mandarin):

SH	Pronunciation	M *pīnyīn*	Examples
ã*	like the *o* in *long*, *ah* spoken through the nose: ah^n	—	**lá** [lah^n] (*cold*)
ãw*	like the *aw* in *awning* and *lawn*, spoken through the nose	—	**mãw** [mawh^n] (*busy*)

*Note: there is a trend among younger speakers in Shanghai to merge **ã** and **ãw**. Speakers who do this pronounce both vowels the same and do not distinguish them. Hence you need not struggle too hard to make the distinction between these two vowels if you cannot hear it or find them difficult to differentiate.

The remaining four of this set are pronounced similar to Mandarin *pīnyīn*, as noted below:

en	like the *un* in *fun* and *undone*	en	**dén** [dun] (*wait*)
in	like the *in* in *pink* and the *een* in *seen*	in	**nín** [neen] (*person*)
ün	like German *ü* or French *u* followed by *n*	ün	**j'ún** [dgü-n] (*skirt*)
ong	like *own*, but ending in *-ng*	ong	**fòng** [fowng] (*wind*)

Abrupt q ending
Shanghainese has a set of finals that end in a **q**, which represents a glottal stop. A glottal stop is pronounced by stopping the word deep in one's throat, as done by

English speakers in the middle of pronouncing 'uh-oh.'
A glottal stop brings an abrupt end to the syllable, like
pronouncing *hock* without fully enunciating—releasing
and aspirating—the *ck*. Syllables that end this way have
a short, abrupt quality and include:

aq, eq, iq, oq

These may be preceeded by **i**, **u**, and **ü**. This glottal stop
ending is not found in Mandarin *pīnyīn*; and the vowels
in these four finals are somewhat different from the
vowels in other finals. So we describe them individually
below (**SH** = Shanghainese; **M** = Mandarin):

SH	Pronunciation	M *pīnyīn*	Examples
aq*	like *awk* in *awkward*, but swallowing the *k*	—	**bāq** [baw^k] (*eight*)
eq*	like *uck* in *buck*, swallowing the *k*	—	**bēq** [buh^k] (*give*)
iq	like the *iq* in *liquid* and the *ick* in *pick*, swallowing the *k*	—	**chīq** [chi^k] (*eat*)
oq	like *olk* in *folkways*, with no *l* sound and swallowing the *k*	—	**bōq** [bow^k] (*north*)

*Note: there is a trend among younger speakers in Shanghai
to merge **eq** with **aq** (and **ueq** with **uaq**), **ioq** with **üeq**, and
sometimes **iaq** with **iq**. This means that some words have
competing common pronunciations, for example 'tangerine'
橘子 can be pronounced both **jüēq-dzǐ** and **jiōq-dzǐ**; 'moon'
月亮 can be pronounced **'yüeq-liã** or **'yoq-liã**; and 'foot' 脚
can be pronounced **jiāq** or **jīq**. The choice of pronunciation
depends on the individual speaker, and often their age.
Hence you need not struggle too hard to make the distinctions between these various pairs of finals if you cannot hear
them or find them difficult to differentiate.

Other syllables

Finally, there are two Shanghainese finals that have no
vowels at all, and one that ends in **r**. They are:

m̃, ñg, er

The tilde ˜ over the **m** and **n** here means these are pronounced as a complete syllable without a vowel, as described below. (The tilde is replaced by a tone mark
over **m** when **m** is the first syllable in a Shanghainese
word.) The pronunciation of Shanghainese **er** is similar
to the same syllable in Mandarin *pīnyīn*.

SH	Pronunciation	M *pīnyīn*	Examples
m̃ m̀ ḿ	like the *mm* in *hmm*	—	**m̀-ma** [mm-ma] (*mother*)
ñg	like the *ng* in *sung*	—	**ñǵ** [ng] (*five*)
er	like *are* and the *ar* in *far*	*er*	**'ér** [h-are] (*ear*)

Tones

Shanghainese tones are quite different from Mandarin
tones and are pronounced across whole words, whether
single or multisyllabic. Syllables connected by hyphens
form a single word, or a *tone envelope*, across which a
tone is pronounced. Thus a word in Shanghainese is
usually one or more syllables connected by a hyphen,
though sometimes the tone envelope may spread across
more than one word or between a word and grammatical particle that follows it. (Note: In the phrasebook section we connect separate words with hyphens when
they share one tone envelope where it is useful as an
aid to assist the reader in more accurate pronunciation,
but only where it will not lead to ambiguity or confu-
sion. Hyphens are avoided in cases where the scope of
the tone can be determined in context, such as before

the question particle **va** which is included in the tone envelope of the preceding word.)

In Shanghainese there are three basic tone contours—rising, falling, and rising-falling; two registers—high and low; and two tone types—abrupt and non-abrupt. The contours, registers, and types combine to make the following tones:

1) Rising: mid ↗ & low ↗
(have a rising tone mark ´ on the first syllable in one and two syllable words or a high tone mark ¯ in two syllable words)

2) Rising-falling ↗↘
(have a rising tone mark ´ or high tone mark ¯ on the first syllable in words of three or more syllables)

3) Falling ↘
(have a falling tone mark ` on the first syllable)

4) Abrupt: high →| & low ↗|
(have a high tone mark ¯ or no tone mark on first syllable)

5) Level: mid → & low →
(followed by a dot •)

The above quick description is sufficient to get started. For readers who want a more detailed picture, we describe each tone in more detail below:

1a) Rising (mid) ↗
On most one and two syllable words there is a slight rise across the whole word. These are marked with a rising tone mark:

dén ↗	等	*wait*
dí-ga ↗	商店	*store*

1b) Rising (low) ↗
The rising tone is pronounced with a lower pitch in words of one and two syllables with *voiced initials*,

i.e. those with an apostrophe ' or with **l**, **m**, **n**, **ng**, **v**, **z**, and **zy**. These are also marked with a rising tone mark:

nín ↗	人	*person*
d'ín-naw ↗	电脑	*computer*

2) Rising-falling ↗ ↘

All words with three or more syllables rise to a stress on the second syllable and all subsequent syllables go down after that. The tone begins slightly lower in words with voiced initials. This tone is marked with a rising tone mark in words of three or more syllables:

hú-tsuo-zae ↗↘	火车站	*train station*
zǎw-hae-nin ↗↘	上海人	*Shanghainese (person)*

3) Falling ↘

The only exception to #1 and #2 above is that all words with a falling accent (`) over the first syllable have a falling tone that spreads across the whole word (starting in the first syllable):

sì ↘	书	*book*
bìn-guoe ↘	宾馆	*hotel*
Dzòng-chieu-jiq ↘	中秋节	*Mid-Autumn Festival*

4a) Abrupt (high) →

Syllables ending in **q** (glottal stop) are pronounced short and quick and have little rise or fall. Those with the high tone mark (ˉ) are pronounced high and abruptly:

chiēq →|	吃	*eat*

Two syllable words beginning with the high abrupt syllable have the high rising contour (in which the first syllable is pronounced slightly lower):

kāq-chi ↗	客气	*polite*

Three syllable words beginning with the high abrupt syllable have the rising-falling contour (in which the first syllable is pronounced slightly lower):

jiāq-d'aq-tsuo ↗↘	脚踏车	*bicycle*

4b) Abrupt (low) ↗|

Abrupt syllables (those ending in **q**) with no tone mark (all of which have voiced initials) are pronounced with a low, but slightly rising abrupt tone:

b'aq ↗|	白	*white*
loq ↗|	绿	*green*

Words of two or more syllables beginning with the low abrupt tone usually have the low rising contour:

zeq-beng ↗	日本	*Japan*
voq-dzãw-di ↗	服装店	*clothing shop*

5a) Level (mid) →

Verbs followed by an object often lose their original contour and are pronounced with a mid-level tone, while the words that follow maintain their expected tone. Verbs in contexts where this tone is frequently or usually pronounced are followed by a dot (•):

kàe•tsuò 开车 (drive a car) is pronounced
   kàe→tsuò ↘

pāq•séu 拍手 (clap one's hands) is pronounced
   pāq→séu ↗

jí•shín 寄信 (mail a letter) is pronounced
   jí→shín ↗

5b) Level (lower) →

The level tone is pronounced slightly lower in verbs with voiced initials:

d'á•séu 洗手 (wash one's hands) is pronounced
   d'á→séu ↗

loq•'yǘ 下雨 (to rain) is pronounced *loq→'yǘ* ↗

Finally, note that grammatical particles (such as the **va** that forms questions and the sentence final **h'eq**) are unstressed—pronounced with no stress, and thus have no tone. They follow the tone contour pattern (are in the tone envelope) of the word that precedes them. For this reason, particles do not have a tone mark, even when they are written without a preceding hyphen as unconnected syllables:

G'eq-daq vú-j'in 'yéu mǎw-ba **va**?
这附近有网吧吗？
Is there an Internet café nearby?

BASIC GRAMMAR

The basic grammar of Shanghainese is in many ways rather simple and straightforward. For example, Shanghainese has no complicated verb tenses, verb agreement, or verb inflections. As in Standard Chinese (Mandarin) the most important elements of Shanghainese grammar are word order, particles, and prepositions. In fact, Shanghainese grammar is essentially similar to the grammar of Mandarin. The differences are largely lexical. Colloquial Shanghainese word order and sentence structures are generally the same as spoken Mandarin. So those who know Standard Chinese will often find that they need merely to find the right Shanghainese word or particle to put in the position in which it would be found in a corresponding Mandarin sentence. Yet there are subtle points of divergence and the Mandarin speaker is well advised to look out for them. Below we give a brief sketch of the essentials of Shanghainese grammar that will be of use both to those who have a background in Standard Chinese as well as to readers who are getting their first exposure to a Chinese language via Shanghainese. To assist the user of this volume, we focus on grammar and forms that will clarify usage and structures found in the phrasebook section.

Word Order

The basic Shanghainese sentence is generally subject-verb-object, just like English. In the following examples the verb is in bold, with the subject to the left and the object to the right:

> Ngú **fú** h'í-jin.
> 我付现金。
> *I (will)* **pay** *cash.*

> Āq-laq **zí** biàw-vãw.
> 我们住标准房间。
> *We (will)* **stay (in)** *a standard room.*

Yet, the object of the verb is frequently stated first in a sentence for emphasis and focus. This is done without any explicit marker and happens much more frequently in Shanghainese than in Mandarin.

> **H'ú-dzaw** dá-lae va?
> 护照带了吗？
> *Did you bring (your) passport?*

Often what comes first in a sentence can be seen to be the topic which one is asking about or commenting on.

> **Tsén-sae** laq sá-d'i-fāw má?
> 衬衫在哪儿买？
> *Where can I buy shirts?*

Also, sentences often leave the subject of a sentence, whether actor or object, unstated. Notice there is no counterpart to the bolded English in the following Shanghainese examples:

> 'Yéu kóng-vāw-gae va?
> 有空房间吗？
> *Do you have any vacant rooms?*

Adjectives

Adjectives are verbal in Shanghainese—they contain within them the sense of 'to be, is, are'—and they are used *without* any word that corresponds to the English 'to be'.

> Ngú **ngú** leq.
> 我饿了。
> *I am hungry.*

Shanghainese adjectives are usually modified by an adverb. In the below example the adverb is in bold and the adjective is underlined:

> G'eq-dzāq zǎw **tēq** <u>nüóe</u>.
> 这张床太软。
> *This bed is too <u>soft</u>.*

Time

In expressing time, the time *when* something happens is always stated at the beginning of a sentence, just before or after the subject.

> **Mén-dzaw** h'uae!
> 明天见!
> *See you **tomorrow**!*

However, when stating *how long* something took, takes, or will take (time duration), the time phrase comes at the end of the sentence after the verb. In the below example the time duration expression is in bold and the verb is underlined:

> Āq-laq <u>zí</u> **sí-niq**.
> 你们<u>住</u>四天。
> *We will <u>stay</u> **four nights**.*

Location

Where something happens or takes place is also always stated early in the sentence. Phrases indicating the place of an action are usually introduced by the preposition *laq*, (in, at, on) which corresponds to Mandarin *zài* 在 (in, at, on) and which—like all prepositions—comes before the verb.

> Ngú laq **g'eq-d'eu** h'uó•tsuò.
> 我在**这儿**下车。
> *I will get off (the bus) **here**.*

Note that similar to the Mandarin *zài* 在 (to be [in, at, on]), *laq* can also function as a verb.

> Shí-seu-gae **laq** g'eq-d'eu.
> 洗手间**在**这儿。
> *The restroom **is** here.*

Just as in Mandarin, it is quite common for prepositions to have one or more additional verbal functions in Shanghainese.

Questions

Questions in Shanghainese are formed for the most part with the final particle **va** or with question words such as **sá** (*what, which*). With either type of question form, and in contrast to English but similar to Mandarin, the word order of the sentence remains the same as the corresponding statement or answer. The final particle **va**, similar to the Mandarin particle *ma* 吗, is simply added at the end of a statement to turn it into a question, rather like a question mark.

> G'eq-daq vú-j'in 'yéu kà-ba **va**?
> 这附近有咖啡吧**吗**?
> *Is there a coffee shop nearby?*

In questions formed with questions words, the question word is simply placed in the sentence in the position where the answer will be—creating a sort of fill-in-the-blank structure.

Question: G'eq-bae hú-tsuo **jí-di-dzong** kàe?
这班火车**几点**开?
What time *does this train leave?*
Answer: G'eq-bae hú-tsuo **sàe-di-dzong** kàe.
这班火车**三点**开。
*This train leaves at **three**.*

(Note: The most common question words are listed in the "Thumbnail Guide to Basics" in the Phrasebook section.)

Questions can also be formed by providing a choice between affirmative and negative, in a verb-not-verb construction.

> 'Yí **chīq veq chīq**·jiéu.
> 他**喝不喝**酒?
> *Does he drink alcohol?*

Two Useful Particles: *leq* and *h'eq*

The Shanghainese particle **leq** is similar to Mandarin *le* 了 and used as a verb suffix or at the end of a sentence to indicate that an action has happened, is done, is complete, is accomplished, etc.

> Ngú chīq-gu-**leq**.
> 我吃过了。
> *I have eaten.*

> Bò-shi-d'ae 'yín-**leq**.
> 巴西队赢了。
> *The Brazilian team won.*

At the end of a sentence, **leq** can also indicate a new situation or a change—and thus can often be interpreted to mean *now* or *already*.

> Chí•fòng **leq**.
> 起风了。
> *It is windy now.*

> Dáw Láw-shi-men záe **leq** va?
> 到老西门站了吗?
> *Are we at the Lǎoxīmén stop now?*

The Shanghainese particle **h'eq** and the alternate **g'eq** are similar to the Mandarin particle *de* 的 that is used as a suffix to mark possessives and other modifiers of a following noun. Modifiers can simply be nouns:

> **ngú-h'eq** mín-pi
> 我的名片
> *my name card*

> **ná gòng-sï-g'eq** jìn-li
> 你们公司的经理
> *your company's manager*

Or they can be more complex adjective or verb phrases:

b'í-ni-di-h'eq lǘ-guoe
便宜一点的旅馆
inexpensive hotels

má•piáw-h'eq tsǎw-keu
买票的窗口
the window *that sells tickets*

The initial consonant in **h'eq** and **g'eq** is often dropped.

háw-chiq-di-**eq** váe-di
好吃点的饭店
good restaurant

āq-la-**eq**   我们的   *ours*
'yí-**eq**   他的 / 她的   *his / hers*

H'eq is also used at the end of sentences to emphasize a state or situation.

Màe d'í **h'eq**.
很甜的。
It's rather sweet.

G'eq-g'eq jiàw-guae yáw-jin **h'eq**!
这个很要紧的！
This is important!

Counting

Just as in Mandarin, there is no distinction between singular and plural in Shanghainese. All nouns have the same form for both. Number is determined in context. When counting, specific *measure words* that correspond to particular nouns are suffixed to numbers, between the number and the noun counted.

Ngú 'yéu **liǎ-d'iaw** j'ún-dzǐ.
我有**两条**裤子。
I have **two** skirts.

Ngú má **loq-dzã** piáw.
我买**六张**票。
I'll buy **six** tickets.

(Note: Further information on measure words, including a list of the most common and useful ones, is provided in the Phrasebook section.)

Ngáe and dí

Shanghainese **(yīq)-ngáe** and **(yīq)-dí** (*a little, a bit*) are similar to Mandarin (*yǐ*)*diǎn* (一)点. They can come before or after adjectives. If they follow adjectives they have a comparative sense—*a little (more), a bit (more)*.

Ngú 'yéu **di** h'óe-niq.
我**有点**发烧。
*I have **a bit of** a fever.*

G'eq-dzaq ngáe-seq d'áe-**yiq-ngae**.
这种颜色淡**一点**。
*This color is **a bit** lighter.*

Negatives

The plain negative is **veq** (*not, is/will not*) and is similar to Mandarin *bù* 不. It is used with verbs and adjectives.

Ngú **veq** chīq nioq.
我**不**吃肉。
*I **don't** eat meat.*

Veq laq.
不辣。
*It's **not** hot (spicy).*

The existential negative ***ḿ-meq*** is similar to Mandarin *méiyǒu* 没有 and means *not have, there is/are not*.

Ngú **ḿ-meq** liq-chi.
我**没有**力气。
*I **don't have** any energy.*

Ḿ-meq 'wáe-dzǐ.
没有位子.
There are no seats.

Ḿ-meq is also used with verbs to indicate an action did not happen.

Ngú **ḿ-meq** kóe.
我**没有**看。
*I **didn't** watch.*

Āq-laq **ḿ-meq** jí-gu-mi.
我门**没**见过面。
*We **have not** met before.*

The negative imperative is **viáw** (*do not*), which is similar to Mandarin *bié* 别 or *búyào* 不要.

Chín **viáw** jí tēq dóe.
请**别**剪太短。
*Please **don't** cut it too short.*

CHINESE CHARACTERS IN THIS BOOK

Shanghainese is a spoken language, not a written language. When Shanghainese people write, they write in Standard Chinese, which uses Mandarin vocabulary and grammar. The purely colloquial nature of Shanghainese and its various differences from Mandarin mean that there are many words in Shanghainese that are not found in Mandarin or Standard Chinese. Because Shanghainese is rarely written, there is no common conventional way to write the great majority of these exclusively Shanghainese words in Chinese characters. While appropriate and often etymologically correct characters can be identified to write such words, only a few expert linguists know them. Most speakers of Shanghainese do not know them and would not recognize the meaning and pronunciation of such characters on the printed or written page.

It is thus of no practical use to write Shanghainese with Chinese characters. And we do not do so in this volume. Instead we give Standard Mandarin Chinese glosses of the Shanghainese using Chinese characters. These glosses can be read by any literate Chinese speaker one may encounter in Shanghai and will allow them to understand the entries in the dictionary and phrasebook. More often than not the Chinese characters used to translate the Shanghainese words in this volume are the etymological characters for those words. This is the case in the following entries, for example:

lǔ-h'in 旅行 *v.* travel, take a journey
hotel *n.* jiéu-di 酒店; lǔ-guoe 旅馆

But in many cases the Chinese characters are merely translations for the colloquial Shanghainese expressions that have no conventional written form. In such cases the characters are simply a Mandarin gloss, as in the following:

meq-zǐ 东西 *n.* thing
we *prn.* āq-laq, āq-la 我们

Other times, Shanghainese has its own colloquial expressions, but also uses Mandarin equivalents as synonymous alternates, such as in the following, where the first entry parallels the Mandarin, but the additional entries are more colloquial Shanghainese words with the same meaning:

bus stop *n.* tsuò-zae 车站, záe-d'eu

meq-bu 抹布 *n.* wiping cloth, dish rag,
   Alt.: **kà-bu, kà-d'ae-bu**

niq-naw 热闹 *adj.* lively, buzzing with
   excitement, *Alt.*: **náw-mã, náw-niq**

There are other variations in the differences between Shanghainese and Mandarin. For example, sometimes Shanghainese words encompass more than one meaning in Mandarin. In those cases we give more than one Mandarin gloss in Chinese characters, as in:

be in/at/on *v.* laq 在, laq-hae, laq-laq,
   laq-lãw 在里头、在那儿

ladle *n.* sĭ-zoq, sĭ-b'iaw 舀子、瓢

móe-d'eu 包子、馒头 *n.* steamed bun
   (stuffed or unstuffed)

sà-du 劳累、疲惫 *adj.* exhausted,
worn-out

It is too complex a task for this volume to identify all the various types of correspondence between the Shanghainese words and the Mandarin glosses in Chinese characters for each individual entry. But the reader who knows Mandarin will begin to get a feel for them as he or she becomes more familiar with Shanghainese. Others should not worry too much about the Chinese characters and should concentrate on learning the pronunciation, vocabulary, and usage of Shanghainese as it is represented in the Romanization used in these pages.

BIBLIOGRAPHY OF SHANGHAINESE TEXTBOOKS AND GRAMMARS

This is a list of textbooks, dictionaries, and studies of Shanghainese that the author consulted in the compilation of the present volume. Published in English and Chinese within the past thirty years, these books may prove useful for readers interested in further exploring the contemporary dialect of the city of Shanghai.

Eccles, Lance. 1993. *Shanghai Dialect: An Introduction to Speaking the Contemporary Language.* Kensington, Maryland: Dunwoody Press.

Qián Nǎiróng 钱乃荣. 2003. *Shànghǎi yǔyán fāzhǎn shǐ* 上海语言发展史 [A history of the Shànghǎi dialect]. Shànghǎi: Shànghǎi rénmín chūbǎnshè 上海人民出版社.

_____. 1997. *Shànghǎihuà yǔfǎ* 上海话语法 [Grammar of Shanghainese]. Shànghǎi: Shànghǎi rénmín chūbǎnshè 上海人民出版社.

Qián Nǎiróng and Wáng Xiǎomíng 钱乃荣、王晓鸣. 2006. *Zhōng-Yīng duìzhào Shànghǎihuà 600 jù* 中英对照上海话600句 [600 Sentences in Shanghainese and English]. Shànghǎi: Hànyǔ dà cídiǎn chūbǎnshè 汉语大词典出版社.

Qián Nǎiróng, Xúbǎohuá, and Tāng Zhēnzhū 钱乃荣、许宝华、汤珍珠. 2003. *Shànghǎihuà dà cídiǎn* 上海话大词典 [Unabridged dictionary of the Shànghǎi dialect]. Shànghǎi: Shànghǎi císhū chūbǎnshè 上海辞书出版社.

Sherard, Michael. 1982. *A Lexical Survey of the Shanghai Dialect.* National Inter-University Research Institute of Asian & African Languages & Cultures, Project on Lexicological Analysis. *Computational Analysis of Asian & African Languages* (CAAAL), No. 20; CAAAL Monograph Series, No. 8. Tokyo.

Tāng Zhìxiáng 汤志祥. 2000. *Shíyòng Shànghǎihuà* 实用上海话 [Practical course in Shanghainese]. Shànghǎi: Shànghǎi jiàoyù chūbǎnshè 上海教育出版社.

⸻. 2000b. *Jīchǔ Shànghǎihuà* 基礎上海話 [Basic Shanghainese]. Hong Kong: Zhōnghuá shūjú 中華書局.

Xú Bǎohuá 许宝华, et al. 1988. *Shànghǎi shìqū fāngyán zhì* [Record of the Shanghai city dialect]. Shànghǎi: Shànghǎi jiàoyù chūbǎnshè 上海教育出版社.

Xú Lièjiǒng and Shào Jìngmǐn 徐烈炯、邵敬敏. 1998. *Shànghǎi fāngyán yǔfǎ yánjiū* 上海方言语法研究 [Research in Shanghainese Grammar]. Shànghǎi: Huádōng shīfàn dàxué chūbǎnshè 华东师范大学出版社.

Yè Pànyún 叶盼云. 1994. *Xué shuō Shànghǎihuà* 学说上海话 [Learn to speak Shanghainese]. Shànghǎi: Shànghǎi jiāotōng dàxué chūbǎnshè 上海交通大学出版社.

ABBREVIATIONS

adj.	*adjective*	形容词
adv.	*adverb*	副词
Alt.	*alternate Shanghainese form (as a synonym or alternate pronunciation)*	
attr.	*attributive*	定语
aux.	*auxiliary verb*	能愿动词
conj.	*conjunction*	连词
d.c.	*degree complement*	程度补语
interj.	*interjection*	感叹词
l.n.	*location noun*	方位词
m.w.	*measure word*	量词
n.	*noun*	名词
n.adj.	*noun-adjective compound*	主谓结构
n.m.	*number-measure compound*	数量词组
num.	*number word*	数词
p.c.	*potential complement*	可能补语
pfx.	*prefix*	前缀
ph.	*phrase*	短句
prep.	*preposition*	介词
prn.	*pronoun*	代词
ptl.	*particle*	语气助词
sfx.	*suffix*	后缀
t.n.	*time noun*	时间词
v.	*verb*	动词
v.c.	*verb-complement phrase*	动补结构
v.o.	*verb-object compound*	动宾结构

Note: In the dictionary sections, where the part of speech of the entry word is different from that of its translation, the part of speech of the translation is provided in parentheses. For example:

dizzy *adj.* d'éu•huèn 头晕 *(n.adj.)*
embroider *v.* shiáw-huo 绣花 *(v.o.)*
b'áw-chi 抱歉 *v.o.* sorry *(adj.)*

ENGLISH–SHANGHAINESE DICTIONARY

with Mandarin glosses in
Chinese Characters

A

abacus *n.* sóe-b'oe 算盘
ability *n.* bén-zǐ 本事
about *adv.* dzú-'yeu 左右, zǎw-h'uo, zǎw-shia 上下
  (sfx.)
above *l.n.* zǎw-d'eu 上头, zǎw-mi 上面, gàw-d'eu
accent *n.* chiǎ-d'iaw 腔调
accept *v.* jǐq-zeu 接受
account *n.* dzǎ-h'u 账户
accountant *n.* guáe-ji, kuáe-ji 会计
accurate *adj.* dzén 准, dzén-dzoq
acne *n.* chìn-tsen-lae 青春痘
activity *n.* h'ueq-d'ong 活动
actor *n.* yí-'yüoe 演员
actually *adv.* j'í-zeq 其实
acupuncture *n.* dzèn-jieu 针灸; *v.* dǎ•jìn-dzen 行针
  灸 *(v.o.)*
add *v.* tì 添
addiction *n.* ní-d'eu 瘾
adept *adj.* ná-seu 拿手
adjacent *adj.* tíq-j'in 贴近
adjust *v.* d'iáw 调
admonish *v.* shǔn 训
adopt *v.* lín-'yā 领养
adopted child *n.* 'yǎ-dzï 养子
advertisement *n.* guǎw-gaw 广告
advise *v.* dzǐ-jiaw 指教
advisor *n.* gú-ven 顾问
affected *adj.* dzú-dzoq 做作
affectionate *adj.* chìn-niq 亲热
afraid of *adj.* pó 怕 *(v.)*
Africa *l.n.* Fì-dzeu 非洲
after *adv., prep.* yì•h'éu 以后 *(t.n.)*
after all *adv.* dáw-di 到底, dáw-jieu
afternoon *t.n.* h'uó-boe-ti, h'uó-boe-niq, h'éu-boe-niq
  下午
again *adv.* *(in the future)* dzàe 再; *(in the past)* 'yéu
  又, 'yí
agate *n.* mó-naw 玛瑙
agile *adj.* lín-min 灵敏

agree on *(a time to meet)* *v.* yāq-haw 约好 *(v.c)*

air *n.* kòng-chi 空气

air dry *v.* lǎw 晾

air freshener *n.* chìn-shiā-ji 清香剂

air-conditioned car (or bus) *n.* kòng-d'iaw-tsuo 空调车

air-conditioned room *n.* kòng-d'iaw-vāw 空调房

air-conditioner *n.* kòng-d'iaw(-ji) 空调机

airmail letter *n.* h'ǎw-kong-shin 航空信

airplane *n.* fi-ji 飞机

airport *n.* fi-ji-zā 飞机场, kòng-gǎw

airport bus *n.* jì-zā-ba-sǐ 机场巴士

alfalfa greens *n.* tsáw-d'eu 苜蓿

alive *adj.* h'ueq 活 *(v.)*

all *adv.* záe, zyí-bu 全□

all along *adv. (consistently)* yīq-shiā 一向, yīq-jiaq, yīq-zeq, yīq-jin

alley *n.* lóng-d'ǎw 弄堂

allow *v.* niǎ 让, shú 许

almanac *n.* h'uǎw-liq 黄历

almost *adv.* jì-hu 几乎; ~ **didn't** *adv.* shí-shi-jiaw veq 差点儿不, m̀-meq 没; ~ **the same** *adj.* tsuò-veq-du, tsà-veq-du 差不多

along *prep. (in the same direction as)* zén 顺

already *adv.* yí-jin, 'yí-jin 已经

also *adv.* 'yá 也, 'yáe, dù

although *conj.* sòe-zoe 虽然

altogether *adv.* yīq-g'ong 一共, dzóng-g'ong 总共, g'óng-dzong, lóng-dzong

always *adv.* dzóng-guae, dzōq-guae 总是

amaranth *n.* mí-shi 苋菜

ambulance *n.* jiéu-h'u-tsuo 救护车, jiéu-min-tsuo

America *l.n.* Máe-goq 美国

American *n.* Máe-goq-nin 美国人

amiable *adj.* zóe-h'u 随和

ancestral hall *n.* zǐ-d'ǎw 祠堂

anchor *n.* máw 锚

and *conj.* tēq, dēq, tēq-dzǐ, dēq-dzǐ, gàw, gáw, bǎw 跟、和 *(prep.)*

angry *adj.* fāq•b'í-chi 发脾气, fāq•gāq, d'óng-chi 生气 *(v.o.)*

anise *n.* h'uáe-shiã 茴香

ankle *n.* jiãq-ku-gueq 踝骨

ankle bracelet *n.* jiãq-li 脚链

anklet socks *n.* maq-zoe 短袜

another *prn.* bĩq-h'eq 别的

another day *n.* gáe-niq 改天 *(v.o.)*

answer *v.* dãq 答, h'uáe-daq 回答; *n.* h'uáe-daq, dãq-foq 答复

ant *n.* mó-ni 蚂蚁

Antarctica *n.* Nóe-j'iq-dzeu 南极洲

antique store *n.* gú-'woe sãw-di 古玩商店

anxious to *adj.* bò-veq-deq 巴不得, bò-veq-dzaq-deq, bò-veq-nen-geu *(v.c.)*

apartment *n.* gòng-nü, gòng-'yü 公寓

appear *v. (show up)* tsēq•d'éu, tsēq•zã 出面 *(v.o.)*

appearance *n.* 'yã-dzï 样子

appetizer *n.* liã-tsae 凉菜, lã-b'en 冷盘

apple *n.* b'ín-gu 苹果

apple pie *n.* b'ín-gu-pa 苹果派

apply ointment *v.o.* tãq•'yaq-gaw 抹药

apprehensive *adj.* dàe-yeu 担忧

apprentice *n.* h'oq-d'u 学徒

approach *v.* káw 靠

approximately *adv.* d'á-yaq 大约, d'á-yaq-moq (-dzoq)

apricot *n.* h'ã-dzï 杏子

April *t.n.* sĩ-'yüeq 四月, sĩ-'yoq

apron *n.* 'yũ-j'ün 围裙, 'wáe-j'iong, váe-dae

architect *n.* jí-dzoq-sï 建筑师

architecture *n.* jí-dzoq 建筑

are *v.* zï 是

argue *v.* tsáw-shiã-mo, zyín-shiã-mo 吵架

arm *n.* bí-bo, séu-bi-bo 胳膊、手臂

armchair *n.* kàw-seu-yi 靠手椅

armpit *n.* gēq-dzï-wu, gēq-leq-dzoq 腋窝

arrive at *v.* dáw 到

arrogant *adj.* biàw-jin, jiàw-ngaw 骄傲, kuàe, láw-kuae 傲慢

artemesia *(fragrant herb used in moxibustion)* *n.* ngáe-b'ong 艾

ascend *v.* zãw-chi 上去

ash *n.* huàe 灰

ashes of the dead *n.* guēq-huae 骨灰

Asia *l.n.* Yá-dzeu 亚洲

ask *v.* mén 问

ask for *v. (seek)* táw 讨; *(entreat)* yằ 求

asking price *n.* táw•gá 要价

asparagus *n.* lú-sen 芦笋

aspic *n.* nioq-dong 肉冻

aspirin *n.* à-sǐ-pi-lin 阿斯匹林

assemble *v. (put together)* dzằw 装; *(come together in a group)* dzōq 聚集

assistant *n.* bằw-seu 帮手, tí-seu

assorted cold appetizers *n.* pìn-b'en 拼盘

aster greens *n.* mó-lae-d'eu 马兰头

astringent *(taste) adj.* sēq 涩

astute *adj.* jìn 精, jìn-min 精明, jìn-guaq

at *prep.* laq 在

at least *adv.* dzǐ-saw 至少, chí-mo 起码

at that time *adv.* dằw-zǐ(-h'eu) 当时 *(t.n.)*

athlete *n.* 'yǔn-d'ong-'yüoe 运动员

athlete's foot *n.* jiāq-shi 脚癣, jiāq-chi, shiằ-gāw-jiaq

athletic field *n.* 'yǔn-d'ong-zā, 'yóng-d'ong-zā 运动场

athletic shoes *n.* j'iéu-h'a 球鞋

ATM *n.* d'í-kuae-ji 提款机, chǔ-kuoe-ji

ATM card *n.* zǐ-ka 磁卡

attendant *n.* voq-h'u-'yüoe 服务员

attentive *adj.* 'yóng-shin 用心

attentive to detail *adj.* dzǐ-shi 仔细, bó-shi

audit account *v.o.* zuó•dzǎ 查账

auditorium *n.* lí-d'āw 礼堂

August *t.n.* bāq-'yüeq 八月, bāq-'yoq

aunt *n. (father's elder sister)* gù-mu-aq-jia 姑母阿姐; *(father's sister)* niằ-niā 姑母; *(father's younger sister)* gù-ma 姑妈; *(mother's sister)* 'yí-ma, à-'yi 姨妈; *(wife of father's elder brother)* bāq-m̃, bāq-mu 伯母; *(wife of father's younger brother)* sén-sen, sén-niā 婶母; *(wife of mother's brother)* j'iéu-ma 舅母; *(capitalized form of address)* À-'yi 阿姨

Australia *l.n.* Áw-d'a-li-ya 澳大利亚

Australian *n.* Áw-d'a-li-ya-nin 澳大利亚人

authentic *adj.* d'áw-d'i 地道

automatic transmission *n.* zǐ-d'ong-dāw 自动排挡

automobile *n.* chí-tsuo 汽车
autumn *n.* chièu-ti 秋天
awkward *(situation)* *adj.* gàe-ga 尴尬
awl *n.* dzi̇̀-dzoe 锥子
awning *n.* dín-b'ā 天棚
axe *n.* fú-deu 斧头
azalea *n.* d'ú-jüoe-huo 杜鹃花

B

bachelor *n.* dàe-sen-hoe 单身汉, guǎw-guen 光棍
back *n.* h'éu-d'eu 后头, h'éu-mi
back door *n.* h'éu-men 后门
backbone *n.* báe-jiq-gueq 背脊骨, jīq-dzoe-gueq 脊椎骨
backpack *n.* báe-baw 背包
backstage *n.* h'éu-d'ae 后台
bacon *n.* b'áe-gen 培根
bad *adj.* h'uá 坏
bad weather *n.* h'uá-ti-chi 坏天气
badminton *n.* 'yǔ-maw-j'ieu 羽毛球
bag *n.* bàw 包
baggage check *n.* h'ǎ-li-piaw 行李票
baguette *n.* zǎ-guen 长棍
bakery *n.* mí-baw-vāw 面包房
balcony *n.* 'yǎ-d'ae 阳台
bald head *n.* guǎw-lāw-d'eu, h'ú-zāw-d'eu 光头
ball field *n.* j'iéu-zā 球场
ball game *n.* j'iéu-sae 球赛
ballet *n.* bà-lae-'wu 芭蕾舞
balloon *n.* chí-j'ieu 气球
bamboo *n.* dzōq-d'eu 竹子
bamboo mat *n.* dzōq-zyiq 竹席
bamboo shoot *n.* sén 笋, dzōq-sen 竹笋
bamboo strip *n.* dzōq-b'ae 竹片
banana *n.* shià-jiaw 香蕉
bandage *n.* bǎw-da 绑带
bandit *n.* j'iǎ-d'aw 强盗
bangs *n.* liéu-hae 刘海, zyí-liéu-hae
bank *n.* nín-h'āw 银行
bank account *n.* h'ú-d'eu 户头
bankrupt *v.* dáw-bi 倒闭

bar *n.* bà 吧, jiéu-ba 酒吧
bar counter *n.* bà-d'ae 吧台
barbecue *n.* sàw-kaw 烧烤
barbershop *n.* lí-faq-di 理发店
barefoot *adj., adv.* tsāq•jiāq, guǎw•jiāq 赤脚 *(v.o.)*
bargain *v.* táw•gá•h'uáe-ga 讨价还价 *(v.o.)*
bark *(of a tree)* *n.* zǐ-b'i 树皮
barley *n.* d'á-maq 大麦
base price *n.* dí-bae-ga, chí-bae-ga 基价、最底价
baseball *n.* b'ǎw-j'ieu 棒球
baseball cap *n.* b'ǎw-j'ieu-maw 棒球帽
basin *n.* b'én-dzǐ 盆子
basket *n.* láe(-d'eu) 篮子
basketball *n.* láe-j'ieu 篮球
bat *n.* *(animal)* bi-foq 蝙蝠; *(club)* b'ǎw-d'eu 棍子
bath towel *n.* 'yoq-jin 浴巾
bathe *v.* d'á•'yoq 洗澡 *(v.o.)*
bathroom *n.* d'á-'yoq-gae, 'yoq-gae 洗澡间
bathtub *n.* 'yoq-kǎw 浴缸
battery *n.* d'í-zǐ 电池
be *v.* zǐ 是
be in/at/on *v.* laq 在, laq-hae, laq-laq, laq-lāw 在里头、在那儿
bead *n.* dzǐ-dzǐ 珠珠
bean *n.* d'éu 豆
bean curd *n.* d'éu-h'u, d'éu-vu 豆腐
bean sprouts *n.* d'éu-nga 豆芽
bean thread vermicelli *n.* shì-fen 粉丝
bear *n.* h'ióng 熊
bear a child *v.o.* 'yǎ•shiáw-noe 生小孩
beard *n.* h'ú-su 胡须, ngá-su, h'ú-dzǐ
beast *n.* tsōq-sā 畜生
beautiful *adj.* piáw-liǎ 漂亮
beauty parlor *n.* máe-'yong-'yüoe 美容院
bed *n.* zǎw 床
bedbug *n.* tséu-zong 臭虫
bedroom *n.* ngú-seq 卧室
bedsheet *n.* zǎw-dae 床单, b'í-dae 被单
bee *n.* miq-fong 蜜蜂
beef *n.* niéu-nioq 牛肉
beef jerky *n.* niéu-nioq-goe 牛肉干

beer *n.* b'í-jieu 啤酒

beetle *n.* jiāq-koq-zong 甲壳虫

before *adv., adj. (in the past)* yì•zyí 以前 *(t.n.)*

beg *v.* yǎ 求

beggar *n.* chīq-gae 乞丐, gáw-huo-dzï 叫花子

begin *v.* kàe-sï 开始

beginning *n.* kàe-sï 开始, kàe-d'eu 开头

behave *v.* dzú•nín 做人 *(v.o.)*

behind *prep., adv. adj.* h'éu-d'eu 后头, h'éu-mi 后面, h'éu-di(-d'eu) *(l.n.)*

beige *adj.* mí-h'uāw 米黄 *(attr.)*; *n.* mí-seq 米色

Beijing *l.n.* Bōq-jin 北京

Beijing opera *n.* jìn-shi 京剧

believe *v.* shiǎ-shin 相信

bell *n.* dzòng 钟

bell-bottom pants *n.* lá-ba-ku 喇叭裤

bellows *n.* fòng-shiā 风箱

belly *n.* d'ú-b'i 肚子

bellyache *n.* d'ú-b'i•tóng, d'ú-li•tóng 肚子疼 *(n.adj.)*

belly button ring *n.* zyí-g'uae 脐环

below *adv., prep.* h'uó-d'eu 下头, h'uó-mi 上面, h'uó-di(-d'eu) *(l.n.)*

belt *n.* yàw-da 腰带, kú-yaw-da 裤腰带

bench *n.* báe-den 板凳

bend *v.* wàe 弯

best man *n.* (nóe-)bìn-shiā 男傧相

bet *v.* h'uǎ•sǐ-'yin 打赌 *(v.o.)*

biased *adj.* pì-shin 偏心

bib *n.* 'yǔ-d'ae-d'ae, tsuò-shiong-d'ae 围嘴

bicycle *n.* jiāq-d'aq-tsuo 脚踏车

big *adj.* d'ú 大

big dipper *n.* bōq-deu-shin 北斗星

bikini *n.* bí-ji-ni 比基尼

bind *v.* bǎ 绑

bird *n.* niáw, diáw 鸟

birth control *n.* b'í-'yün 避孕

birthday *n.* sǎ-niq 生日; **celebrate a ~** dzú•sǎ-niq 庆祝生日

bite *v.* ngáw 咬

bitter *adj.* kú 苦

black *adj.* hēq 黑; *n.* hēq-seq 黑色

black tea *n.* h'óng-zuo 红茶
blackboard *n.* hēq-bae 黑板
blackmail *v.* dzuó•nín 敲诈
bladder *n.* b'ăw-guāw 膀胱, sǐ-paw
blame *v.* guá 怪
bland *(lacking flavor) adj.* d'áe 淡
blanket *n.* tàe-dzǐ 毯子
blind *adj.* hāq-ngae 瞎眼 *(v.o.)*
blink *v.* gāq, sāq 眨
blister *n.* páw 泡, sǐ-paw 水泡
blocks *(toy) n.* jīq-moq 积木
blood *n.* shūēq, shiōq 血
blood pressure *n.* shūēq-aq, shiōq-aq 血压
blood vessel *n.* shūēq-guoe, shiōq-guoe 血管
blow *v.* tsǐ 吹
blow one's nose *v.o.* hén b'iq-ti 擤鼻涕
blow-dry hair *v.o.* tsǐ d'éu-faq 吹头发
blue *adj.* láe 蓝; *n.* láe-seq 蓝色
blunt *adj.* d'én 钝
board *(~ a flight) v.* dèn•jì 登机 *(v.o.)*
boat *n.* zóe 船
body *n.* sèn-ti 身体
body hair *(on people) n.* h'óe-maw 汗毛
bodyguard *n.* báw-biaw 保镖, jín-'wae-'yüoe 警卫员
boil *v. (transitive)* sàw 煮, *(intransitive)* guén 滚
boil over *v.* pù 沸溢
boiled dumpling *n.* sǐ-jiaw 水饺
boiled water *n.* kàe-sǐ 开水
bold *adj.* dáe•d'ú 胆大
bone *n.* guēq-d'eu 骨头
bonus *(money) n.* jiǎ-jin 奖金
book *n.* sǐ 书
bookcase *n.* sǐ-zǐ 书橱
bookkeeper *n.* guáe-ji, kuáe-ji 会计
bookmark *n.* sǐ-chi 书签
bookstore *n.* sǐ-di 书店
boss *n.* láw-bae 老板
bottle *n.* b'ín(-dzǐ) 瓶子
bottom *l.n.* dí-h'uo(-d'eu) 底下
boulevard *n.* d'á-d'aw 大道
bow knot *n.* h'ú-d'iq-jiq 蝴蝶结

bowl *n.* wóe 碗

bowling *n.* báw-lin-j'ieu 保龄球

box *n.* h'aq-dzï 盒子

boxing *n.* b'oq-keq-shiong 拳击

bra *n.* ná-dzaw, vén-shiong 胸罩

bracelet *n.* séu-zoq 手镯, zoq-d'eu

brag *v.* tsï•niéu-b'i, tsï•niéu-sae 吹牛 *(v.o.)*

braid *n.* b'í-dzï 辫子

braid one's hair *v.o.* bāq•b'í-dzï 编辫子

brain *n.* náw-dzï 脑子, náw-d'ae 脑袋, náw-jin, d'éu-naw-dzï

braise *v.* mèn 焖

branch *n.* zï̆-gã-dzï 树枝

branch road *n.* tsuò-lu 岔路

brand *n.* b'á-dzï 牌子; **name ~** *n.* mín-b'a 名牌

Brazil *l.n.* Bò-shi 巴西

bread *n.* mí-baw 面包

break off *v.* áw-d'oe 拗断

break the rules *v.o.* váe-guae 犯规

breakfast *n.* dzáw-vae, dzáw-di 早饭

breast *(of a woman)* *n.* ná, ná-na 乳房

breastfeed *v.* yǔ•ná 喂奶 *(v.o.)*

breathless *adj.* hẵ 气喘喘

brew tea *v.o.* chí•zuó 沏茶, páw•zuó

brew wine *v.o.* tsú•jiéu 酿酒

bribe *v.* dǎ-di 打点、 贿赂

brick *n.* dzòe-d'eu 砖头, loq-dzoe

bride *n.* shìn-niã̌(-dzï) 新娘

bridesmaid *n.* (nǔ-)bìn-shiã 女傧相

bridge *n.* j'iáw 桥; *(card game)* j'iáw-b'a 桥牌

bright *adj.* *(of light)* liǎ 亮; *(of colors)* shí 显

Britain *l.n.* Yìn-goq 英国

Briton *n.* Yìn-goq-nin 英国人

broad *adj.* kuòe-kueq 宽阔

broad bean *n.* h'óe-d'eu, zóe-d'eu 蚕豆

broadband internet *n.* kuòe-da-mãw 宽带网

broadcast *v., n.* guǎw-bu 广播

broadcasting station *n.* guǎw-bu-d'i-d'ae 广播电台

broken *adj.* h'uá 坏

brooch *n.* biq-dzen 别针

broom *n.* sáw-dzeu 扫帚

broth *n.* chìn-(sǐ-)tāw 清汤

brother *n. (elder)* gù-gu, āq-gu 哥哥; *(younger)* d'í-d'i, āq-d'i 弟弟

brother-in-law *n. (husband's elder brother)* d'á-baq, d'ú-baq 大伯子; *(husband's younger brother)* shiáw-soq 小叔子; *(wife's older brother)* d'á-j'ieu-dzǐ 大舅子; *(wife's younger brother)* shiáw-j'ieu-dzǐ 小舅子; *(elder sister's husband)* jiá-fu 姐夫; *(younger sister's husband)* máe-fu 妹夫

brothers *(elder and younger) n.* shiòng-d'i 兄弟

brown *adj., n.* kà-fi-seq 咖啡色

bruise *n.* wù-chin-kuae 血晕

brush *n.* báe-seq 板刷; *v.* sēq 刷

bubble *n.* pàw-paw 泡儿

bucket *n.* sǐ-d'ong 水桶

buckwheat noodles *n.* j'iáw-maq-mi 荞麦面

Buddha *n.* zǐ-lae-veq 如来佛, veq 佛

Buddhism *n.* veq-jiaw 佛教

Buddhist monk *n.* h'ú-zāw 和尚

Buddhist nun *n.* ní-gu 尼姑

Buddhist nunnery *n.* ní-gu-oe 尼姑庵, òe-d'ǎw

buffalo *n.* niéu 牛; **water ~** *n.* sǐ-nieu 水牛

buffet *n.* zǐ-zu-tsoe 自助餐

bug *n.* zóng-dzǐ 虫子

building *n.* léu-vāw 楼房

bulging *adj.* gú 鼓

bull *n.* h'ióng-nieu 公牛

bump into *v.* b'ǎ 碰

bun *(steamed) n.* móe-d'eu 包子、馒头

bunjee jumping *n.* bèn•j'iq 蹦极

burlap *n.* mó-bu, h'uó-bu 麻布

burnt *adj.* jiàw 焦

burp *n.* g'áe 嗝儿; *v.* dǎ•g'áe 打嗝儿 *(v.o.)*

burst *v.* guǎ-kae 胀大裂开 *(v.c.)*

bury *v.* má 埋; **~ the dead** òe-dzāw 安葬, loq•dzāw

bus *n.* chí-tsuo, gòng-g'ong-chi-tsuo 公共汽车

bus stop *n.* tsuò-zae 车站, záe-d'eu

bus ticket *n.* tsuò-piaw 车票

business *n. (matters, affairs)* zǐ-ti 事情; *(commercial)* sǎ-yi 生意

business trip *n.* tsēq•tsà 出差 *(v.o.)*

businessman *n.* sầw-nin 商人, sà-yi-nin 生意人
busy *adj.* mấw 忙
but *conj.* dáe-zĭ 但是
butter *n.* b'aq-teq(-'yeu) 黄油
butterfly *n.* h'ú-d'iq 蝴蝶
buttocks *n.* pì-gu(-d'eu) 屁股
button *n.* niéu-dzĭ 纽扣
buy *v.* má 买
buyer *n.* tsáe-geu-'yüoe 采购员, má-dzĭ 买主
by *(passive marker) prep.* bēq, bēq-laq 被

C

cabbage *n.* b'aq-tsae 白菜
cabinet *n.* zĭ 橱
cactus *n.* shì-nin-dzãw 仙人掌
cadre *n.* góe-b'u 干部
cafeteria *n.* zeq-d'ãw 食堂
cake *n.* gàw 糕; *(Western style)* d'áe-gaw 蛋糕
calendar *n. (daily)* zeq-liq 日历; *(monthly)* 'yüeq-liq, 'yoq-liq 月历
call *(~ out; ~ after) v.* jiáw 叫
calm *(unruffled) adj.* dōq-tae 笃坦
camera *n.* dzáw-shiã-ji 相机
can *aux. (able to)* nén-geu 能够; *(know how to)* wáe, h'uáe 会, wáe-deq, h'uáe-deq; *(permissible)* kú-yi 可以, háw 好; *n.* guóe-d'eu 罐头
Canada *l.n.* Gà-na-da 加拿大
Canadian *n.* Gà-na-da-nin 加拿大人
cancer *n.* ngáe 癌
candid *adj.* zeq-sãw 直爽
candle *n.* dzōq, 'yấ-laq-dzoq 蜡烛
candlestick *n.* dzōq-d'ae 烛台
candy *n.* d'ấw 糖
candy shop *n.* d'ấw-gu-di 糖果店
canola *n.* 'yéu-tsae 油菜
Canton *l.n.* Guấw-dzeu 广州
Cantonese *(language) n.* Guấw-dzeu-h'ae-h'uo 广州话
capable *adj.* láe-zĭ, láe-sae 能干
capital *(sum invested) n.* bén-d'i 本钱
cappuccino *n.* ká-bu-j'i-nuo 卡布其诺

car *n.* tsuò-dzï 车子, chí-tsuo 汽车

card *n.* ká-pi 卡片; **game ~** b'á 牌; **name ~** mín-pi 名片

cardboard box *n.* dzï-bae-shiã 纸箱

care for *v.* dzàw-gu 照顾

careful *adj.* dǎw-shin 小心

careless *adj.* tsù-shin 粗心

carp *n.* lí-ñg 鲤鱼

carpenter *n.* moq-zyiã 木匠

carpenter's plane *n.* b'áw 刨

carpet *n.* d'í-tae 地毯

carrot *n.* h'ú-law-b'oq 胡萝卜

carry *v. (in the hand)* lìn 拎; *(on one's back)* d'ú 背负; *(on the shoulder)* gǎw 扛, ǎw; *(together with someone)* d'áe 抬

cart *n.* tsuò-dzï 车子, *(handcart)* séu-tae-tsuo 手推车

cartoon *n.* ká-tong 卡通

cash *n.* kàe-shü, h'í-tsaw, h'í-jin 现金

cashier *n.* tsēq-naq-'yüoe 出纳员

cashmere sweater *n.* 'yǎ-niong-sae 羊绒衫

cast *v.* zaq 掷

casual *adj.* zóe-b'i 随便

cat *n.* máw 猫, máw-mi

catch *v. (capture)* dzōq 捉; *(receive something thrown)* jīq 接

catch a chill *v.o.* tsï•fòng 着凉

catch cold *v.o.* sǎ•fòng 感冒

catch on fire *v.o.* hú-zaq 着火

caterpillar *n.* máw-maw-zong 毛毛虫

cathedral *n.* jiáw-d'āw 教堂, lí-ba-d'āw

Catholicism *n.* tì-dzï-jiaw 天主教

catty *(Chinese unit of weight) n.* jìn 斤

cauliflower *n.* huò-tsae 花椰菜

cause *n.* nüóe-yin 原因

cave *n.* sàe-d'ong 山洞

cedar tree *n.* sàe-zï 杉树

ceiling *n.* tì-huo-pae 天花板, b'ín-din

celebrate *v.* chín-dzoq 庆祝

celery *n.* j'ín-tsae 芹菜

cell phone *n.* séu-ji 手机

cement *n.* sï-ni 水泥, sï-men-tin, 'yǎ-huae

cent *n.* fèn 分, fèn-d'eu

center *l.n.* dǎw-dzong 中间

centipede *n.* 'wú-gong 蜈蚣

central air-conditioning *n.* dzòng-yǎ-kong-d'iaw 中央
空调

century *n.* sǐ-ji 世纪

certain *prn.* méu 某

certainly *adv.* yīq-d'in 一定, dzén-d'in, báe

chair *n.* yǔ-dzǐ, yí-dzǐ 椅子

chairman of the board *n.* dóng-zǐ-dzǎ 董事长

chalk *(for writing)* *n.* fén-biq 粉笔

change *n.* bí-huo 变化; *(from money paid)* dzáw-d'eu
零钱; *v. (exchange)* h'uóe 换; *(transform)* bí 变

chant Buddhist scriptures *v.o.* ní•jìn 念经

chaotic *adj.* lóe 乱

chapped *adj.* tsèn 皱

charcoal *n.* moq-tae 木炭

charge *v.* tsòng 充; ~ **a battery** tsòng-di ~电

chat *v.* d'áe 谈; *(informal conversation)* *v.* gǎw-dzǎ
聊天; *n.* gǎw•h'áe-h'uo 讲话 *(v.o.)*

cheap *adj.* b'í-ni 便宜, b'í-niq, j'iǎ

check *n.* dzǐ-piaw 支票

cheers! *(drinking toast)* *interj.* gòe•bàe! 干杯！

cheese *n.* chì-sǐ, ná-loq 奶酪

chef *n.* zǐ-sǐ 厨师

cheongsam *(Chinese dress)* *n.* j'í-b'aw 旗袍

cherish *adj.* shìn-tong 心疼, nioq-tong

cherry *n.* ǎ-d'aw, yìn-d'aw 樱桃

chess *(Chinese style)* *n.* zyiǎ-j'í 象棋

chest *n.* shiòng 胸, shiòng-pu

chestnut *n.* liq-dzǐ 栗子

chew *v.* zyiaq 嚼

chick *n.* shiáw-ji 小鸡

chicken *n.* jì 鸡; ~ **breast** jì-shiong 鸡胸; ~ **feather** jì-
maw 鸡毛; ~ **feet** jì-jiaq-dzaw 鸡爪; ~ **gizzard** jì-
dzen 鸡胗; ~ **heart** jì-shin 鸡心; ~ **leg** jì-tae 鸡腿; ~
meat jì-nioq 鸡肉; ~ **wing** jì-bǎw 鸡翅

child *n.* nóe, shiáw-noe, shiáw-nin 小孩

child-care worker *n.* báw-'yüeq-'yüoe 保育员

children's wear *n.* shiáw-noe-yi-zǎw, d'óng-dzǎw 童装

chili oil *n.* laq-'yeu 辣油

chili pepper *n.* laq-jiaw 辣椒

chills *n.* fāq•j'ín 发寒颤 *(v.o.)*

chin *n.* h'uó-b'oq, h'uó-b'o 下巴

China *l.n.* Dzòng-goq 中国

china *n.* zǐ-chi 瓷器

china shop *n.* zǐ-chi-di 瓷器店

Chinese *(person) n.* Dzòng-goq-nin 中国人

Chinese chives *n.* jiéu-tsae 韭菜

Chinese cruller *n.* 'yeu-d'iaw 油条

Chinese medicine shop *n.* dzòng-'yaq-di 中药店

Chinese New Year's *n.* tsèn-jiq 春节

Chinese New Year's Eve *n.* zǐ-zyiq 除夕

chip *v.* ngaq(-deq) 弄个缺口

chisel *n.* zoq-d'eu, zoq-dzǐ 凿子

chocolate *n.* chiàw-keq-liq 巧克力

choke *v.* yīq, dǎ•yīq 噎

choose *v.* shí 选, gáe, d'áw

chop *v.* dzàe 剁; ~ **meat** dzáe•nioq 剁肉 *(v.o.)*

chopsticks *n.* kuáe, kuáe-dzǐ 筷子

chowder *n.* nióng-tāw 浓汤

Christ *n.* jì-doq 基督

Christianity *(Protestantism) n.* jì-doq-jiaw 基督教

chrysanthemum *n.* jiōq-huo, jüēq-huo 菊花

church *n.* jiáw-d'āw 教堂, lí-ba-d'āw

cicada *n.* dzǐ-liaw 蝉

cigar *n.* shīq-ga-yi 雪茄烟

cigarette *n.* shiǎ-yi 香烟

cilantro *n.* shiǎ-tsae 香菜

circle *v., n.* chüòe 圈

circumstances *n.* sǐ-d'eu 情势

city *n.* zén 城, zén-zǐ 城市

clam *n.* gēq-li 蛤蜊

clap *v.* pāq 拍; ~ **one's hands** pāq•séu 拍手

classmate *n.* d'óng-h'oq 同学

classroom *n.* jiáw-seq 教室, kú-d'āw(-gae)

clause *(like in a contract) n.* d'iáw-ven 条文

clean *adj.* chìn-sǎw, gòe-zin 干净

clean up *v.* dǎ-saw 打扫

clear *adj.* chìn 清

clear weather *n.* zín-ti 晴天

cleated shoes *n.* dìn-h'a 钉鞋

client *n.* h'ú-d'eu 户头

clip *n.* g'aq-d'eu 夹子

cloak *n.* pì-fong 披风, dèu-b'ong 斗篷

clock *n.* dzòng 钟

clog *v.* gǎ 梗, zaq 阻塞

clogged *adj* sēq 塞

close *v.* guàe 关

close a deal *v.o.* zén-jiaw 成交

close shop *(~ for the day) v.o.* dǎ•'yǎ 打烊

closet *n.* yì-zǐ 衣橱

closing price *(at an exchange) n.* sèu-b'oe 收盘

cloth *n.* bú 布

clothes hanger *n.* yì-zāw-ga 衣架

clothing *n.* yì-zāw 衣裳

clothing shop *n.* voq-dzāw-di 服装店

cloud *n.* 'yǔn, 'yóng 云

cloudy weather *n.* yìn-ti 阴天

club *n.* j'ǔ-loq-b'u 俱乐部

coach *n.* d'á-ba 大巴

coal *n.* máe 煤

coarse *adj.* tsù 粗, máw-tsaw 粗糙、毛糙

coaster *(for teacups) n.* zuó-d'i 茶垫

coat *n.* zǎw-dzāw 上衣, ngá-taw 外套

coat rack *n.* yì-zāw-ga 衣架

cockroach *n.* dzǎw-lāw 蟑螂

cocoon *n.* jí-dzǐ 茧子, jí 茧; **spin a ~** jīq-ji 结茧

coffee *n.* kà-fi 咖啡

coffee shop *n.* kà-ba 咖啡吧

coffin *n.* guòe-zae 棺材

cohabit *v.* d'óng-jü 同居

coincidentally *adv.* zyí-chiaw 恰巧, b'ǎ-chiaw 碰巧
  (v.o.)

cold *adj.* lǎ 冷

collaborator *n.* pāq-dāw 合作伙伴

collar *n.* lín-d'eu 领子

collect payment *v.o.* sèu•dzǎ 收账

college *n.* d'á-h'oq 大学

collide *v.* zǎw 撞, káe

color *n.* ngáe-seq 颜色, sēq 色

comb *n.* moq-sǐ 梳子; *v.* **~ one's hair** sǐ•d'éu 梳头 *(v.o.)*

combine *v.* bǎ-long-lae 合起来 *(v.c.)*

come *v.* láe 来

come in *v.* jín 进, jín-lae 进来
comet *n.* h'uáe-shin 彗星, sáw-tseu-shin 扫帚星
comfortable *adj.* shiá-yi 舒服; **agreeably ~** sēq-yi 适意
comfortably off *adj.* kuòe-sǐ 宽舒, kuòe-'yü 宽余
comic opera *n.* h'uaq-ji-shi 滑稽戏
commerce *n.* sǎw-niq 商业
common *adj.* pú-tong 普通
company *n.* gòng-sǐ 公司
comparatively *adv.* bí-jiaw 比较
compare *v.* bí 比, bí-dzǐ *(prep.)*
compass *(for math and drafting)* *n.* 'yüóe-guae 圆规
compete *v.* bí-sae 比赛
competition *n.* bí-sae 比赛
complacent *adj.* wù-shin 得意
complain *v.* má-yüoe 埋怨
comply with *v.* yì 依
computer *n.* d'í-naw 电脑
concave *adj.* àw 凹
conceal *(~ facts)* *v.* móe 瞒, yín-moe 隐瞒
concentrated *adj.* nióng 浓
concrete *n.* sàe-h'u-tu 混凝土
conditioner *n.* h'ú-faq-su 护发素
condolences *n.* jīq-ae-zen-bi 节哀顺变 *(ph.)*
condom *n.* táw-dzǐ 套子, b'í-'yün-taw 避孕套
condominium *n.* sǎw-pin-vǎw 商品房
congratulate *v.* dzōq-h'u 祝贺
congratulations! *interj.* gòng-shi! 恭喜!
connect *v.* jīq 接
conscientious *adj.* j'ín-kua 勤快
considerable *adj.* shiǎ-dǎ 相当, jiàw-guae *(adv.)*; ~
  amount jiàw-guae 相当多
consulate *n.* lín-zǐ-guoe 领事馆
consultant *n.* gú-ven 顾问
contact lens *n.* yín-h'in-ngae-jin 隐形眼镜
contain *v.* bàw-h'oe 包涵
content *adj.* sǎw-shin 爽心
convenience store *n.* b'í-li-di 便利店
convenient *adj.* fǎw-b'i 方便, b'í-dǎw
convent *n.* shièu-d'aw-'yüoe 修道院
convert *v.* d'áe-h'uoe 兑换
cook *(~ a meal)* *v.* sàw•váe 做饭 *(v.o.)*

cook noodles *v.o.* h'uó•mí 下面

cooked *adj.* zoq 熟

cookie *n.* bín-goe 饼干

cool *adj.* liǎ-sǎw, fòng-liã 凉快

copper *n.* d'óng 铜

coquettish behavior *n.* fãq•diá(-jin) 撒娇 *(v.o.)*

cord *n.* shí 线

corn *n.* dzèn-dzǐ-mi 玉米

corner *n.* gōq-loq(-d'eu) 角落

correct *adj.* dáe 对, dzén-chüeq, dzén-chioq 正确

correction fluid *n.* shièu-dzen-'yiq 修正液

cosmetics *n.* dzǐ-fen 脂粉

cost of building *n.* záw-ga 造价

cotton *n.* mí-huo 棉花; ~ **cloth** mí-bu 棉布; ~ **gauze** mó-suo (全棉的)麻纱

cough *v.* kēq-seu 咳嗽

country *n.* gōq-jia 国家, gōq-d'u

countryside *n.* nóng-tsen 农村, shià-h'uo 乡下

court *v.* d'áe•lí-ae 谈恋爱, d'áe•b'ǎ-'yeu, d'áe-kaw-d'in *(v.o.)*

cousin *n.* *(elder female, with a different surname)* biáw-(aq-)jia 表姐; *(elder female, with the same surname)* d'ǎw-aq-jia 堂姐; *(elder male, with a different surname)* biáw-shiong, biáw-(aq-)gu 表兄; *(elder male, with the same surname)* d'ǎw-shiong, d'ǎw-aq-gu 堂兄; *(younger female, with a different surname)* biáw-(aq-)mae 表妹; *(younger female, with the same surname)* d'ǎw-mae 堂妹; *(younger male, with a different surname)* biáw-(aq-)d'i 表弟; *(younger male, with the same surname)* d'ǎw-d'i 堂弟; *(female, with a different surname)* biáw-ji-mae 表姐妹; *(male, with a different surname)* biáw-shiong-d'i 表兄弟; *(male, with the same surname)* *n.* d'ǎw-shiong-d'i 堂兄弟

cover *v.* ēq 覆盖, dzuò 遮, dzáw 罩; *n.* gáe-d'eu 盖子; táw-dzǐ 套子

cow *n.* niéu 牛, tsǐ-nieu 母牛

cowardly *adj.* dáe•shiáw, sōq 胆小

crab *n.* há, b'ǎw-ha 螃蟹

crack *n.* liq-vong 裂缝, tsāq-tsaq, huāq-huaq; *v.* tsāq, kàe•tsāq, huāq•kàe 裂

cracker *n.* kēq-liq-ka 克力架

craftsman *n.* séu-ni-nin 手艺人

craftsmanship *n.* séu-ni 手艺

cramp a muscle *v.o.* tsèu•jìn 抽筋

crawl *v.* b'áe 爬

crayfish *n.* shiáw-long-huo 小龙虾

crayon *n.* laq-biq 蜡笔

crazy *adj.* fāq•fòng, fāq•tsǐ 发疯 *(v.o.)*

creek *n.* bǎ, h'ú-bā 小河

creepy *adj.* nioq-mo 肉麻

crescent moon *n.* 'yūeq-nga-nga 月牙

cricket *n.* záe-jiq 蟋蟀

criminal *n.* váe-nin 犯人

crisp *adj.* tsóe 脆

criticize *v.* pì-b'in 批评

crooked *adj.* huà, wàe 歪, chiá 斜

cross *v.* gú 过, tsòe-gu 穿过

crosswalk *n.* h'uǎ-d'aw-shi 人行横道

crow *n.* láw-h'uo, wù-ya 乌鸦

cruel *adj.* hén 狠

crumb *n.* liq-shiq 碎屑

cry *v.* kōq 哭

cucumber *n.* h'uǎw-guo 黄瓜

cuff *n.* zyiéu-keu 袖口

culture *n.* vén-huo 文化

cumin *n.* dzǐ-zoe 孜然

cup *n.* bàe-dzǐ 杯子

cure *v.* yì•máw-b'in 治病 *(v.o.)*

curriculum *n.* kú-zen 课程

curry *n.* gà-li 咖喱

curtain *n.* lí-dzǐ 帘子

curved *adj.* chūěq, chiōq 曲

cushion *n.* d'í-dzǐ 垫子

custodian *n.* chìn-jiq-gong 清洁工

customer *n.* kāq-h'u 客户, gú-kaq 顾客

cut *v.* (~ *with a knife*) chīq 切, (~ *with scissors*) jí 剪;
~ **apart** gēq, guēq 割; ~ **cloth**. záe 裁 *(v.o.)*; ~ **hair**
lí•fāq, tí•d'éu(-faq), jí•d'éu-faq 理发 *(v.o.)*; ~ **wages**
shīaq•gòng-d'i, gáe•gòng-d'i 减工资 *(v.o.)*

cutting board *n.* dzèn-den(-bae) 砧板

D

dam *n.* h'ú-bo 河坝, d'í-bo 坝

damp *adj.* sēq, sāq 湿

dance *n.* 'wú(-d'aw) 舞蹈; *v.* tiáw•'wú 跳舞 *(v.o.)*

dangerous *adj.* 'wáe-shi 危险

Daoism *n.* d'áw-jiaw 道教

Daoist *n.* d'áw-zǐ 道士

dare to *aux.* góe 敢

dark *adj. (little light)* óe 暗; *(of color)* sèn 深

date *n. (day)* niq-d'eu-niq-jiaq 日期; *(fruit)* dzáw-dzǐ
枣子

daughter *n.* nǔ-er 女儿, nǔ-shiaw-noe, nóe-ñg

daughter-in-law *n.* shìn-vu 媳妇

day *n.* niq, tì 天 *(n., m.w.)*; ~ **of the month** *(date) n.*
h'aw 号 *(m.w.)*

daybreak *n.* chìn-dzaw(-zen) 清晨

daylight *n.adj.* tì•liǎ 天亮

daylily flower *(dried to use as a vegetable) n.* jìn-
dzen(-tsae) 金针

days *n.* niq-jiaq 日子

daytime *n.* niq-li-d'eu, niq-li(-shiā), b'aq-ti 白天

dead *adj.* ḿ-meq-leq, gú-leq 死了 *(v.)*

deaf *adj.* lóng-b'ǎ 耳聋 *(v.)*

deceive *v.* chì 欺

December *t.n.* zeq-ni-'yüeq 十二月, zeq-ni-'yoq

declare *(dutiable goods) v.* sèn-baw 申报

decorate *v.* dzǎw-h'uāw 装潢

deep *adj.* sèn 深

defecate *v.* d'á-b'i 大便, tsāq•wú, zá•wú *(v.o.)*

definitely *adv.* chüēq-zeq, chiōq-zeq 确实

deflated *adj.* pīq 瘪

degree *(unit of measure or scale) n.* d'ú 度 *(m.w.)*

dejected *adj.* àw-sāw 懊丧, óng-dzong

delay *v.* ngá, d'á 拖延

delicious *adj.* háw-chiq 好吃

delinquent in payment *v.o.* tù•dzǎ 拖账

dense *adj.* mǎ, miq 密

dented *adj.* àw 凹

deny *v.* lá 抵赖

depart *v.* lí-kae 离开

deposit *n.* zén-kuoe 存款; ~ **book** *n.* zén-dzeq 存折;
   v. (~ money) zén tsáw-piaw 存钱 *(v.o.)*

descend *v.* h'uó-chi 下去

desk *n.* sǐ-dzoq 书桌, shiá-zǐ-d'ae

detergent *(liquid) n.* shí-jiq-jin 洗洁精

detest *v.* táw-yi 讨厌

development zone *n.* kàe-faq-chü 开发区

dew *n.* lú-sï 露水; loq•lú-sï 下露 *(v.o.)*

diagonal *adj.* h'iá-du-li 斜的 *(n.)*

diagonally opposite *adj.* zyiá-dae-mi 斜对面, chiá-
   dae-gu, h'uǎ-zaq-goq *(l.n.)*

dialect *n.* fǎw-'yi 方言

diaper *n.* sǐ-bu 尿布

diarrhea *n.* d'ú-li-za, d'ú-b'i-za 拉肚子 *(ph.)*

dice *n.* d'éu-dzï 色子; **roll** ~ *v.* zaq•d'éu-dzï 掷色子

dictate *v.* tìn-shia 听写, kéu-zeu 口授

dictation *n.* tìn-shia 听写

did not *aux.* m̌-meq 没有 *(adv.)*

die *v.* shí 死

differ *v.* tàe-bae, tàe-wae 相差

different *adj.* veq-yiq-'yǎ 不一样

different one *n.* bǐq-h'eq 别的

difficult *adj.* náe 难

dig *v.* wāq 挖

digital camera *n.* sú-mo-shiǎ-ji 数码相机

digital clock *n.* sú-zǐ-dzong 数字钟

dignified *adj.* tí-mi 体面

dignity *("face") n.* zyín-mi 情面

diluted *adj.* d'áe 淡

dim sum *(traditional Chinese food) n.* dí-shin 点心

dimple *n.* jiéu-yiq, jiéu-wu 酒窝

dining hall *n.* tsóe-tin 餐厅

dinner *n.* 'yá-vae 晚饭

diploma *n.* vén-b'in 文凭, bǐq-niq-dzen-sï 毕业证书

direction *n.* fǎw-shiǎ 方向

director *n.* dzǐ-zen 主任

dirty *adj.* ōq-tsoq, laq-taq 肮脏

disco *n.* d'iq-ku 迪斯科舞

discontinue *v.* d'óe-dǎw 断档 *(v.o.)*

discothèque *n.* d'iq-tin 迪斯科舞厅

discount *n.* dzēq(-d'eu) 折扣

discuss *v.* táw-len 讨论, sǎw-liǎ 商量

disease *n.* b'ín 病, máw-b'in

dishwasher *n.* d'á-woe-ji 洗碗机

dislike *v.* h'í 嫌, h'í-bi, yì-dzǐ

dispatch *v.* dzǐ-pa 派

display window *n.* zǐ-tsǎw 橱窗

disposable *n.* yīq-tsǐ-shin 一次性

disposition *n.* shín-dzǐ 性格, b'í-chi 脾气

dissatisfied *adj.* veq-tsen-shin 不满意

disturb *v.* dǎ-zaw 打搅

ditch *n.* sǐ-geu 水沟

divination *n.* dzóe-boq 占卜

division chief *n.* kù-dzã 科长

divorce *v.* lí-huen 离婚 *(v.o.)*

dizzy *adj.* d'éu•huèn 头晕 *(n.adj.)*

do *v.* nòng 弄, g'áw 搞

do not have *adv.* m̀-meq 没有

doctor *n.* yì-sã 医生

dog *n.* géu 狗

doll *n.* 'yǎ-wa-wa 洋娃娃, 'yǎ-noe-noe

dollar (U.S.) *n.* máe-'yüoe 美元, máe-jin 美金

don't *aux.* veq-yaw 不要, viáw 别 *(adv.)*

door *n.* mén 门

door-god *n.* mén-zen(-b'u-saq) 门神

dormitory *n.* sōq-suo, sōq-sae 宿舍

dot *n.* dí(-dzǐ) 点儿

dove *n.* gēq-dzǐ 鸽子

down *adv.* mǎw-h'uo, 'wǎw-h'uo 往下

down coat *n.* 'yǔ-niong-sae 羽绒衫

down payment *n.* d'ín-jin 定金, d'ín-h'iǎ

downstairs *n.* léu-h'uo-d'eu 楼下

dowry *n.* gá-dzãw 嫁妆, b'áe-ga

drag *v.* tà 拖

dragonfly *n.* shìn-d'in, chìn-d'in 蜻蜓

drawer *n.* tsèu-d'eu, tsèu-ti 抽屉

drenched by the rain *v.o.* lín•'yǔ 淋雨, dōq•'yǔ

dress *n.* j'ǔn-dzǐ, j'ióng-dzǐ 裙子, zǎ-j'ün 长裙, lí-sae-j'ün 连衣裙; *v.* tsòe•i-zǎw 穿衣服, dzãq•i-zãw

dress up *v.* dǎ-bae 打扮

dressing table *n.* sù-dzãw-d'ae 梳妆台

drill *n.* dzòe-dzǐ 钻; *v.* dzòe 钻

drink *n.* yín-liaw 饮料; *v.* chīq 喝; ~ **tea** chīq•zuó 喝
茶; ~ **wine** *(or spirits)* chīq•láw-jieu 喝酒
drip *v.* lín 淋, dōq 滴
drip-dry *v.* liq 滴干、漏干 *(v.c.)*
drive *(~ a car)* *v.* kàe•tsuò 开车 *(v.o.)*
driver *n.* sǐ-ji 司机
drizzle *n.* máw-maw-'yü 毛毛雨
drop *v.* loq-teq 掉
drown *v.* zén-saq 淹死 *(v.c.)*
drugstore *n.* 'yaq-di 药店
dry *adj.* gòe 干, gòe-saw 干燥
duck *n.* āq, āq-dzǐ 鸭子; ~ **egg** āq-d'ae 鸭子蛋; ~
gizzard āq-dzen 鸭子胗; ~ **wing** āq-bãw 鸭子翅
dulcimer *n.* 'yiǎ-j'in 扬琴
dumb *adj.* g'ǎw 戆
dumpling *(steamed or boiled)* *n.* jiàw-dzǐ, jiáw-dzǐ 饺
子
durable *adj.* jìn-'yong 经用, jīq-zeq 结实
dusk *n.* 'yá-kua-d'eu, h'uǎw-huen-d'eu 黄昏
dust *n.* huàe-zen 灰尘, b'óng-zen
duster *n.* dóe-dzeu 掸子
dustpan *n.* fén-ji, fèn-ji, bèn-ji 簸箕
dye *v.* ní 染
dyke *n.* h'ú-bo 河坝, d'í-bo 堤坝
dysentery *n.* lí-zyiq 痢疾

E

each *prn.* gōq 各, gōq-g'eq 各个
eagle *n.* láw-yin 老鹰
ear *n.* ní-du, 'ér-du 耳朵
early *adj.* dzáw 早; ~ **morning** dzáw-zen(-d'eu),
dzáw-lãw(-shiã) 早晨 *(t.n.)*
earmuff *n.* ní-du-taw 耳朵套
earn money *v.o.* záe•tsàw-piaw, záe•d'óng-d'i 赚钱
earphone *n.* 'ér-ji 耳机
earring *n.* 'ér-g'uae, ní-du-g'uae 耳环
earthworm *n.* chüēq-zoe, chiōq-zoe, bīq-shi, chiéu-
h'in 蚯蚓
east *l.n.* dòng 东, dòng-mi, dòng-d'eu 东边
easy *adj., adv.* 'yóng-yi 容易, b'í-dãw, háw 好

eat *v.* chīq 吃; ~ **a meal** chīq•váe 吃饭; ~ **vegetarian** chīq•sú 吃素 *(v.o.)*

eclipse *n. (of the moon)* 'yüeq-zeq, 'yoq-zeq 月食; *(of the sun)* zeq-zeq 日食

economical *adj.* zeq-h'uae 实惠

economy *n.* jìn-ji 经济

edamame *n.* máw-d'eu 毛豆

edge *l.n.* bì-bi(-d'eu), 'yí-'yi-d'eu 沿儿, bì-lāw 边上

edible *adj.* háw-chiq 好吃、可以吃

eel *n.* móe, máe-ñg 鳗鱼; **ricefield** ~ h'uǎw-zoe 鳝鱼

efficacious *adj.* lín 灵, lín-guāw 灵光

egg *(chicken) n.* jì-d'ae 鸡蛋

eggplant *n.* g'á-dzǐ 茄子, loq-su

eight *num.* bāq 八

eighteen *num.* zeq-baq 十八

eighty *num.* bāq-seq 八十

elastic *n.* kuòe-jin-da 松紧带

elbow *n.* bí-tsā-dzǐ 臂肘

elder *n.* dzǎ-bae 长辈

electric *adj., n.* d'í 电 *(n.)*; ~ **blanket** d'í-niq-tae 电热毯; ~ **cord** d'í-shi 电线; ~ **fan** d'í-fong-soe 电风扇; ~ **kettle** d'í-niq-h'u 电热壶; ~ **light** d'í-den 电灯; ~ **meter** d'í-biaw 电表; ~ **tram** d'í-tsuo 电车

electricity *n.* d'í 电

elementary school *n.* shiáw-h'oq 小学

elephant *n.* zyiǎ 象

elevated roadway *n.* gàw-ga 高架

elevator *n.* d'í-ti 电梯

eleven *num.* zeq-yiq 十一

e-mail *n.* yì-mae-er 电子邮件

embarrassed *adj.* náe-'wae-zyin 难为情; veq-haw-yi-sǐ 不好意思

embezzle *v.* kēq-keu 克扣

embroider *v.* shiéu-huo 绣花 *(v.o.)*

emergency *n.* jín-jiq-h'eq zǐ-ti 紧急的事情, jīq-zǐ 急事

emergency room *n.* jīq-dzen 急诊

empty *adj.* kòng 空

end *n.* jīq-vi 结尾; *v.* jīq-soq 结束; ~ **of the month** 'yüeq-di, 'yoq-di 月底 *(t.n.)* ; ~ **of the year** ní-jiaq-bi, ní-'ya-jiaq-bi, ní-di 年底 *(t.n.)*

engaged *(~ to marry) adj.* dín•huèn 订婚, páe-chin *(v.o.)*

engineer *n.* gòng-zen-sï 工程师

English *n.* Yìn-nü, Yìn-ven 英语、英文

enough *adj.* dzōq-geu 足够, géu-zï, gèu-zï

enter *v.* jín 进

entertainment *n.* nǜ-loq, 'yǘ-loq 娱乐

enthusiastic *adj.* (warmhearted) niq-shin 热心; (excited) chí-jin 起劲

entire *adj.* zyí 全

envelope *n.* shín-koq, shín-fong 信封

erase *v.* kà 擦

eraser *n.* zyiǎ-b'i 橡皮

erect *v.* dāq 搭

escape *v.* d'áw 逃

especially *adv.* d'eq-b'iq 特别

estimate *v.* gú-ji 估计

Ethernet cable *n.* mǎw-shi 网线

Europe *n.* Èu-dzeu 欧洲

even (straight and neat) *adj.* zyí 齐

even including *prep.* lí 连, lí-deq

even more *adv.* gén-ga 更加, gà-ni

even out *v.* là•b'ín 扯平 (v.c.)

evening *t.n.* 'yá, 'yá-li, 'yá-d'eu, 'yá-daw 晚上

every *adj.* màe, máe 每 (num.); ~ **day** niq-niq 日日, tì-ti 天天, màe-niq 每天 (adv.)

everyone *prn.* d'á-ga 大家

exaggerate *v.* kuà-dzā 夸张

examination paper *n.* káw-jüoe 考卷

examine *v.* zuó 查

example *n., adv.* bí-fǎw, pí-zï 比方

except *prep.* zǐ-leq, zǐ-teq, zǐ-tseq 除了

exchange *v.* d'iáw 调换, d'áe-h'uoe 兑换

exchange rate *n.* d'áe-h'uoe-liq 兑换率

excuse *n.* jiá-keu, yìn-d'eu, tàe-d'eu 借口

exercise *v.* dóe-li sèn-ti 锻炼身体 (v.o.); *n., v.* 'yǘn-d'ong 运动

exercise book *n.* lí-zyiq-b'u 练习本

exercise room *n.* j'í-sen-vǎw 健身房

exhausted *adj.* sà-du 疲惫

expect *v.* j'í-j'ieu 期盼

expenditure *n.* dzǐ-tseq 支出, tsēq-dzā 出账

expenses *n.* kàe-shiaw 开销

expensive *adj.* jŭ 贵
experienced *adj.* láw-jü, jŭ•láw(-lae) 经验丰富
expert *n.* d'aq-nin 高手, h'ǎw-ga, h'ǎw-jia 行家,
  náe-h'āw 内行
explode *v.* báw 爆
Expo *(World's fair)* *n.* sǐ-boq-h'uae 世博会
expose *v.* tsāq-tsoe 拆穿
express *adj.* d'eq-kua 特快
express delivery *n.* d'eq-kua dzòe-d'i 特快专递
express mail *n.* kuá-d'i 快递, kuá-j'i
expressly *adv.* dzòe-men 专门
extort *v.* dzuó•nín 敲诈
extraordinarily *adv.* fi-zā(-dzǐ) 非常, hāq, lae-deq
  (-g'eq)
extraordinary *adj.* d'eq-b'iq 特别, fi-zā(-g'eq) 非常
  (的), veq zyín-zā 不寻常
extremely *adv.* ōq 非常; j'iq 极了 *(d.c.)*, sāq 煞,
  sāq-deq, téu 透, tsēq•jìn 到极点
eye *n.* ngáe-jin 眼睛
eyeball *n.* ngáe-wu-dzǐ 眼珠
eyebrow *n.* mí-maw 眉毛
eyeglasses *n.* ngáe-jin 眼镜
eyelash *n.* ngáe-ji-maw 睫毛
eyelid *n.* ngáe-b'i 眼皮

F

facade *n.* mén-mi 门面
face *n.* mí-kong 脸
factory *n.* tsǎ 厂, tsǎ-ga 工厂
factory director/manager *n.* tsǎ-zā 厂长
factory floor manager *n.* tsuò-gae dzǐ-zen 车间主任
fair *(at a temple)* *n.* miáw-h'uae 庙会
fake *adj.* gá, jiá 假
fake goods *n.* gá-d'eu, d'á-ka 假货
fall down *v.* dáw 倒, g'uáe-gaw, dīq-gaw 摔跤、跌跤
  (v.c.)
false *adj.* gá 假
familiar *adj.* zoq 熟, mí•zoq 面熟
family *n.* gà 家
family members *n.* jià-zoq 家属

famous *adj.* 'yéu-min 有名

fan *n.* sóe-dzï, sòe-dzï 扇子; *v.* sòe 扇

far *adj.* 'yüóe 远

farmer *n.* nóng-min 农民

farmland *n.* d'í 田

farsighted *adj.* 'yüóe-zï 远视

farsightedness *n.* 'yüóe-zï-ngae 远视眼

fashionable *adj.* zï-maw, zï-shin 时髦; *(in fashion)* h'ǎ 风行 *(v.)*

fast *adj.* kuá 快

fast food *n.* kuá-tsoe 快餐

fast food restaurant *n.* kuá-tsoe váe-di 快餐饭店

fat *adj.* *(of people)* dzǎw, pǎw 胖; *(of pigs and other animals)* dzǎw 肥

fate *n.* mín 命

father *n.* bà-ba, dià-dia, láw-ba 爸爸

father-in-law *n.* *(husband's father)* gòng-gong, āq-gong 公公; *(wife's father)* ngoq-vu 岳父, zǎ-nin

fatty meat *n.* 'yéu-nioq 肥肉

faucet *n.* sï-long-d'eu 水龙头

fax *n.* d'í-zoe 传真, fà-kaq-sï; *v.* fāq•d'í-zoe 发传真 *(v.c.)*

fear *v.* pó 怕

feather *n.* máw 毛

February *t.n.* liǎ-'yüeq 二月, liǎ-'yoq

feces *n.* wú 粪

feel *v.* gōq-zaq 觉得

feel bad *ph.* náe-gu 难过 *(adj.)*

feel ill *ph.* veq-seq-yi 不舒服 *(adj.)*

feel like *(~ doing something)* *ph.* shiǎ 想 *(aux.)*

felt hat *n.* ní-maw 呢帽

feng-shui geomancy *n.* fòng-sï 风水

ferry(boat) *n.* bá-d'u-zoe 渡船

ferry crossing *n.* bá-d'u-keu 渡口

fever *n.* h'óe-niq, gàw-saw 高烧

few *adj.* sáw 少

fifteen *num.* zeq-ñg 十五

fifty *num.* ñg-seq 五十

file *(metal)* *n.* tsú-daw 锉刀

fill in *v.* d'í 填

filling *(in food)* *n.* niǎ 馅儿

finally *adv.* dzòng-'yü 终于, dzóng, 'yü

finance *n.* jìn-'yong 金融, záe-dzen 财政

financial division *n.* záe-wu-ku 财务科

fine *(detailed, not coarse) adj.* shí 细; *(impose a fine) v., n.* vaq-d'ong-d'i 罚款 *(v.o.)*

finger *n.* séu-jiq-d'eu, séu-dzǐ-d'eu 手指头

fingernail *n.* séu-jiq-kaq, séu-dzǐ-kaq 手指甲; ~ **polish** jīq-kaq-'yeu 指甲油; ~ **clipper** dzǐ-kaq-j'i, g'aq-dzǐ-j'i 指甲刀

fingerprint *n. (on a surface)* jīq-d'eu-yin 指印; *(on the finger)* lú, vén-lu 指纹

firecracker *n.* pàw-zā, bì-paw 鞭炮

firefly *n.* 'yín-hu-zong 萤火虫

firepot *n.* hú-gu 火锅

first *adv.* shì 先; *n.* d'í-yiq 第一

fish *n.* ńǵ 鱼; *v.* diáw•ńg 钓鱼 *(v.o.)*; ~ **air bladder** ńǵ-paw-paw 鱼鳔; ~ **ball** ńǵ-'yüoe 鱼丸子; ~ **bone** ńǵ-gueq-d'eu 鱼刺; ~ **eggs** ńǵ-dzǐ 鱼卵; ~ **fin** ńǵ-tsǐ 鱼翅; ~ **meat** ńǵ-nioq 鱼肉; ~ **scales** ńǵ-lin-b'ae 鱼鳞

fisherman *n.* dzōq•ńg-g'eq 渔夫

five *num.* ńǵ 五

flaky *adj.* sù 酥

flannel *n.* fāq-lae-niong 绒布

flashlight *n.* séu-d'i-d'ong, d'í-d'ong 手电筒

flat *adj.* bí 扁

flavor *n.* dzǐ-mi 滋味, chīq-keu, mí(-d'aw) 味道

flea *n.* dzáw-seq, tiáw-seq, tiáw-dzaw 跳蚤

flight *n.* fì-h'in 飞行

flight number *n.* bàe-d'eu 班次

flip-flops *n.* tù-h'a 拖鞋

float *v.* véu, vú 浮

flood *n.* h'óng-sǐ 洪水; *v.* fāq•d'ú-sǐ 发大水 *(v.o.)*

floor *n.* d'í-lāw-shiā, d'í-gaw-d'eu 地上; *(level, story)* zén-leu 层楼; *(flooring)* d'í-bae 地板

florist *n.* huò-di 花店

flounder *n.* báe-ńg, niaq-taq-ńg 比目鱼

flour *n.* mí-fen 面粉

flower *n.* huò 花; ~ **bud** nú-d'eu 花蕾

flowerpot *n.* huò-b'en 花盆

flu *n.* liéu-h'in-shin góe-maw 流行性感冒

fly *n. (insect)* tsǎw-yin 苍蝇; *v.* fì 飞

foam *n.* mó 沫子

fog *n.* 'wú 雾, mí-'wu; ~ **up** chí•'wú 起雾

fold *v.* d'eq, d'iq 叠

folk song *n.* mín-gu 民歌

follow *v.* zóe 随, zóe-leq

follow along *v.* 'yí 沿, 'yí-leq, 'yí-dzï 沿着 *(prep.)*

follower of a religion *n.* jìn-jiaw-dzae 教徒

food *n.* zeq-pin 食品; *(non staple)* tsáe 菜

foot *n.* jiāq 脚

for *prep.* *(on behalf of)* d'áe 代; *(~ the sake of)* 'wáe 为, 'wáe-leq 为了, 'wáe-dzï

force *v.* jiǎ-paq 强迫

forefinger *n.* zeq-dzï 食指

forehead *n.* ngaq-goq-d'eu 额头

foreigner *n.* ngá-goq-nin 外国人, 'yǎ-nin 洋人

foreman *n.* gòng-d'eu 工头

forest *n.* sèn-lin 森林

forever *adv.* yóng-'yüoe 永远

forget *v.* mǎw-ji 忘记

formal *adj.* dzén-seq 正式

formerly *adv.* zóng-zyi 从前, gú-chi 过去 *(t.n.)*; *(originally)* nüóe-lae 原来

formidable *adj.* lí-h'ae 厉害

fortunately *adv.* h'ín-kuae 幸亏, chǔ-deq, kuàe-deq

fortune *n.* *(blessing)* fōq-chi, fōq-ven 福气; *(luck)* 'yǔn-chi, 'yóng-chi 运气, 'yǔn-d'aw

fortune-teller *n.* sóe-min-shi-sǎ 算命先生

fortune-telling *n.* sóe-min 算命 *(v.o.)*

forty *num.* sǐ-seq 四十

four *num.* sǐ 四

fourteen *num.* zeq-sï 十四

fox *n.* h'ú-li 狐狸

fragile *adj.* tsóe 脆

fragrant *adj.* shiǎ 香

France *l.n.* Fāq-goq 法国

free *adj.* zǐ-'yeu 自由

free market *n.* zǐ-'yeu-zï-zǎ 自由市场

freeze *v.* jīq•bìn 结冰 *(v.o.)*

French *(language)* *n.* Fāq-nü 法语; *(people)* Fāq-goq-nin 法国人

French fries *n.* sú-d'iaw 薯条

frequently *adv.* zǎ-zā 常常, zǎ-dzāw

fresh *adj.* shìn-shi 新鲜; ~ **and delicious** shì 鲜

freshwater clam *n.* b'ǎ 蚌, h'ú-b'ā 河蚌

Friday *t.n.* lí-ba-ñg 礼拜五

fried *adj.* jì-h'eq 煎的; *(stir-fried)* tsáw-h'eq 炒的, *(deep-fried)* dzuó-h'eq 炸的

fried egg *n.* h'ú-baw-d'ae 荷包蛋

fried noodles *n.* tsáw-mi 炒面

friend *n.* b'ǎ-'yeu 朋友

friendship *n.* jiàw-zyin 交情

frighten *v.* hāq 吓

frog *n.* chìn-wo 青蛙, d'í-ji

from *prep.* zóng 从; *(separated by distance)* lí 离

front *l.n.* zyí-d'eu 前头, zyí-mi 前面

frost *n.* sǎw 霜; *v. (have frost)* loq•sǎw 下霜 *(v.o.)*

froth *n.* mó 沫子

frugal *adj.* sǎ 省

fruit *n.* sǐ-gu 水果

fry *(~ in shallow oil)* *v.* jì 煎

frying pan *n.* b'ín-di-gu 平底锅

full *adj.* móe 满, dzōq; *(after a meal—satiated)* báw 饱

funeral *n.* tsēq•bìn 出殡, tsēq•sǎw *(v.o.)*

funeral home *n.* bin-ni-guoe 殡仪馆

funnel *n.* léu-deu 漏斗

funny *adj.* h'uaq-ji 滑稽, shüēq, shiōq, fāq•shüēq, fāq•shiōq

fur *n.* máw 毛

furniture *n.* gà-jü, jià-jü 家具

future *n.* jiǎ-lae 将来

G

gallbladder *n.* dáe 胆

galoshes *n.* tàw-h'a, táw-h'a 套鞋、雨鞋

gamble *(for money)* *v.* dú•d'óng-d'i 赌钱 *(v.o.)*

garbage *n.* lá-shi, leq-seq 垃圾

garlic *n.* d'á-soe 大蒜

gas *n.* máe-chi 煤气, gáe-sï

gasoline *n.* chí-'yeu 汽油, g'áe-zï-lin

gate *n.* mén 门

gather together *v.* tséu 凑

genealogy *n.* jià-pu 家谱

general store *n.* zaq-hu-di 杂货店

generous *adj.* d'ú-fāw 大方, d'ú-pa

genitals *n.* h'uó-sen 阴部

genuine *adj.* dzén-dzong 正宗; **~ product** zén-ka ~货物

geomancy *n.* fòng-sǐ 风水

German *(language) n.* Dēq-nü 德语; *(person)* Dēq-goq-nin 德国人

Germany *l.n.* Dēq-goq 德国

get off *v.* h'uó, loq 下

get on/into *v.* zǎw 上

get out of *v.* h'uó, loq 下

get up *v.* chí-lai 起来

ghost *n.* jǔ, guáe 鬼

gill *n.* ñg-geq-sae, gēq-sae 鳃

ginger *n.* jiǎ, sǎ-jiǎ 姜

girl *n.* wò-d'eu 丫头, gù-niang 姑娘

give *v.* bēq 给; **~ gifts** sóng•lí 送礼, sóng•nín-zyin 送人情

give birth to *v.* 'yǎ 生

glass *n.* bù-li 玻璃; *(for drinking)* bù-li-bae 玻璃杯

glass window bù-li-tsǎw 玻璃窗

glasses *(eyewear) n.* ngáe-jin 眼镜

gloves *n.* séu-taw 手套

glue *n.* gàw-sǐ 胶水

glutinous rice *n.* nú-mi 糯米

gluttonous *adj.* záe-law 嘴馋

gnaw on *v.* kén 啃, ngà, ngá

go *v.* chí 去; **~ down** loq-chi 下去; **go!** *interj.* gà•'yéu! 加油!

go dutch *ph.* àe-ae-dzǐ AA制 *(n.)*

go on the market *v.o.* mí•zǐ 面市

go on-line *(on the Internet) v.o.* zǎw•mǎw 上网

go out of business *v.o.* shīq•niq 歇业, guàe•dí 关店

goat *n.* 'yǎ 羊; sàe-'yǎ 山羊

God *n. (Catholic)* tì-dzǐ 天主; *(Protestant)* zǎw-di 上帝

god of wealth *n.* záe-zen(-b'u-saq) 财神

goggles *n.* bǎw-fong-jin, vǎw-fong-jin 风镜

gold *n. (metal)* jìn-dzǐ 金子; *(color)* jìn-h'uǎw 金黄

goldfish *n.* jìn-ñg 金鱼

golf *n.* gàw-'er-fu-j'ieu 高尔夫球

gong *n.* lú 锣

good *adj.* háw 好

good morning! *interj.* nóng záw! 你早！

good-bye! *interj.* dzáe-h'uae! 再见！

good-looking *adj.* háw-koe 好看

goose *n.* ngú 鹅

grab *v.* dzuò 抓, wò

grade *n. (achievement)* fèn-su 分数; *(quality)* pín-'wae 品位

graduate *v.* bīq-niq 毕业 *(v.o.)*

grain *n.* gōq 谷

granddaughter *n. (daughter's daughter)* ngá-sã-noe 外孙女; *(son's daughter)* sèn-nü 孙女, sèn-noe(-ñg)

grandfather *n. (maternal)* ngá-dzu-vu, ngá-gong 外祖父; *(paternal)* dzú-vu 祖父, 'yá-'ya, láw-dia

grandmother *n. (maternal)* ngá-dzu-mu, ngá-b'u 外祖母; *(paternal)* dzú-mu 祖母, ñg̀-na, āq-na

grandson *n. (daughter's son)* ngá-sã 外孙; *(son's son)* sèn-dzǐ 孙子

granulated sugar *n.* suò-d'ãw 砂糖

grape *n.* b'eq-d'aw, b'u-d'aw 葡萄

grasp *v.* niaq 握、持

grass *n.* chìn-tsaw 青草

grasshopper *n.* gēq-mã 蚱蜢

grater *n.* b'áw 刨

grave *n.* vén 坟, vén-mo, vén-mu 坟墓

gravel *n.* zaq-dzǐ 碎石头

gray *adj.* huàe 灰; *n.* huàe-seq 灰色

greasy *adj.* 'yéu-dzǐ-gaq-ni 油滋滋

green *adj.* loq 绿; *n.* loq-seq 绿色

green vegetables *n.* chìn-tsae 青菜

greenery *n.* loq-d'i 绿地

greenhouse *n.* nóe-vãw 温室

grime *(as on skin) n.* kén, láw-ken 积垢

grind *v.* mó, mú 磨, nì, ní 研

groom *n.* shìn-lãw 新郎, shìn-lãw-guoe, shìn-guoe-nin

ground *n.* d'í-'yã 地

group *n.* pì, pēq 批 *(m.w.)*

Guanyin *(a Bodhisattva) n.* guòe-yin-b'u-saq 观音菩萨

guarantee *v.* báw-dzen 保证

guess *v.* tsòe, ní 猜

guest *n.* kāq-nin 客人, nín-kaq
guest room *n.* kēq-vãw 客房
guesthouse *n.* bìn-guoe 宾馆
gums *(in the mouth)* *n.* ngá-nin 牙龈, ngá-nioq
gym *n.* tí-'yũeq-zã, tí-'yoq-zã 体育场
gymnastics *n.* tí-tsaw 体操

H

hailstone *n.* bìn-b'aw 冰雹
hair *(on the head)* *n.* d'éu-faq 头发
hair dryer *n.* tsĭ-fong-ji 吹风机
haircut *n.* tí•d'éu-faq 理发 *(v.o.)*
hairpin *n.* g'aq-tsuo 发夹; dzóe, d'éu-faq-dzoe 簪子
half *num.* bóe 半
ham *n.* hú-tae 火腿
hamburger *n.* hóe-baw-baw 汉堡包
hammer *n.* lắw-d'eu 锤子
hammock *n.* diáw-zãw 吊床
hand *n.* séu 手
handicraft *n.* gòng-ni 工艺
handkerchief *n.* jüóe-d'eu 手帕
handle *n.* bò-seu, bó-seu 把手, bín 柄
handouts *(instructional)* *n.* gắw-ni 讲义
handprint *n.* séu-ven 手纹
hang *v.* diáw 吊
happy *adj.* kuá-loq 快乐, kàe-shin 开心, gàw-shin 高兴, kuá-h'ueq 快活
hard *adj.* *(difficult)* náe 难; *(not soft)* ngắ 硬
hat *n.* máw-dzĭ 帽子; ~ **brim** máw-'yi 帽檐
hate *v.* h'én 恨
have *v.* 'yéu 有
hawk *n.* láw-yin 老鹰
he *prn.* 'yí 他
head *n.* d'éu 头, náw-d'ae 脑袋
headache *n.* d'éu•tóng 头痛 *(v.o.)*
headband *n.* d'éu-gu 头箍
head-hunter *n.* laq-d'eu 猎头
health *n.* sèn-ti 身体
healthy *adj.* j'í-kã 健康
hear *v.* tìn-ji 听见 *(v.c.)*

heart *n.* shìn 心, shìn-zã 心脏

heat *n.* niq-chi 热气, nóe-chi 暖气

heat rash *n.* b'áe-dzǐ 痱子

heavy *adj.* zóng 重

heel *n.* jiāq-h'eu-gen 脚跟

helicopter *n.* zeq-sen-fi-ji 直升机

hello! *interj.* nóng háw! 你好！

help *v.* bǎw, shiǎ-bāw 帮助

hemp *n.* mó 麻

hen *n.* tsǐ-ji 母鸡

her *prn.* 'yí 她

here *adv.* g'eq-d'eu, g'eq-daq-kuae, g'eq-daq(-li), d'iq-daq, d'eq-daq(-li) 这儿 *(prn.)*

hi! *interj.* nóng háw! 你好！

hide *(~ oneself)* *v.* b'óe, yà 躲

high *adj.* gàw 高

high-heel shoes *n.* gàw-gen-h'a 高跟鞋

high-speed rail *n.* gàw-tiq 高铁, d'óng-tsuo 动车

hill *n.* shiáw-sae 小山

him *prn.* 'yí 他

hinder *v.* vǎw-h'ae 妨碍; ngáe-zǐ 碍事

hit *v.* dǎ 打

hive *n.* fòng-ku 蜂窝

hold *v. (in the hand)* nàw, nàe, nuò, nuó 拿; *(with both hands)* póng, hóng 捧

hole *n.* d'óng-d'ong-ngae 洞

home *n.* ōq-li, ōq-li-shiā 家里

home cooking *n.* jià-zã-vae 家常饭

home theater *n.* jià-d'in-yin-'yüoe 家庭影院

homeland *n.* jià-shiā 家乡

homework *n.* gòng-ku 功课

honey *n.* miq-d'ãw 蜂蜜

Hong Kong *l.n.* Shiǎ-gã 香港

Hong Kong dollar *n.* gǎ-b'i 港币

hope *v.* shì-h'uãw 希望

horizontal *adj.* h'uǎ-li-shiā 横的 *(n.)*

horse *n.* mó 马

hospital *n.* yì-'yüoe 医院

host *n.* dzǐ-nin-ga 主人

hostel *n.* dzàw-d'ae-su 招待所; sōq-suo, sōq-sae 宿舍

hot *adj.* *(temperature)* niq 热; *(to the touch)* tǎ 烫; *(spicy)* sòe-laq 酸辣

hot dog *n.* niq-geu 热狗

hotel *n.* jiéu-di 酒店, lǘ-guoe 旅馆

hotpot *n.* hú-gu 火锅

hour *n.* dzòng-d'eu 钟头 *(n., m.w.)*

hourly labor *n.* dzòng-di-gong 钟点工

house *n.* vǎw-dzǐ 房子

house lizard *n.* bīq-hu 壁虎

housekeeper *n.* báw-mu 保姆

how *adv.* ná-nen 怎么, ná-nen-ga 怎么样

how long *ph.* dù-saw zén-guāw, jí-zǐ 多少时间 *(prn.)*

how many *ph.* jí 几, dù-saw 多少, jí-huo *(num.)*

how much *(does it cost)* *ph.* jí-d'i 多少钱 *(n.m.)*

however *conj.* bēq-gu, bīq-gu 不过; *adv.* chüēq 却

hug *v.* g'eq 搿

humble *adj.* chì-shü 谦虚

humid *adj.* záw-seq 潮湿

hundred *num.* bāq 百

hungry *adj.* ngú 饿, d'ú-b'i-ngu 肚子饿

hurry *(urge to hasten)* *v.* tsòe 催

hurry up *(~ and do something)* *v.* kuá-di 快点 *(adv.)*

husband *n.* zǎ-fu 丈夫, láw-gong

I

I *prn.* ngú, 'wú 我

ice *n.* bìn 冰

ice cream *n.* bìn-j'i-lin 冰淇淋

iced *adj.* bìn 冰; **~ tea** bìn-h'ong-zuo 冰红茶

icicle *n.* lín-d'ǎw 冰柱

idiotic *adj.* tsǐ 痴

idle *adj.* h'áe 闲

idol *n.* zén-zyiǎ 神像

if *conj.* lú-gu, zǐ-gu 如果, yáw-zǐ 要是

illness *n.* b'ín 病, máw-b'in

immediately *adv.* mà-zǎ, mó-zǎ 马上, jiq-keq, zóe-jiq, shīq-shiq

impatient *adj.* shìn•jīq 心急, shín•jīq 性急

important *adj.* yáw-jin 要紧

in *prep.* laq 在; **~ the corner** gōq-lǎw 角上, gōq-goq-

lāw-shiǎ *(l.n.)*; ~ **the end** *adv.* dzóe•h'eu 最后, (zaq-)
meq-jiaq, āq-meq, laq-meq; ~ **the future** záw-h'eu
往后 *(t.n.)*

incense *n.* shiǎ 香

incense burner *n.* shiǎ-lu 香炉

incense stick *n.* b'ǎw-shiǎ 棒香

include *v.* bàw-gua 包括; bàw-h'oe 包涵

indeed *adv.* dīq-chüeq, dīq-chioq 的确

indifferent *adj.* lǎ-d'ae 冷淡

indigestion *n.* jīq•zeq 积食, dén•zeq *(v.o.)*; veq-shiaw-
huo 消化不良 *(ph.)*

inexpensive *adj.* b'í-ni 便宜, b'í-niq

infant *n.* yìn-'er 婴儿, shiáw-shiaw-noe, shiáw-maw-
d'eu

infect *v.* zóe-zoe 传染

inferior *adj.* tàe-wae 差

inferior goods *n.* tsǐ-hu, tsǐ-pin 次货, 次品

inflexible *adj.* ngáe-bae 呆板

ingredients *n.* dzōq-liaw 作料

inhale *v.* shīq, hù 吸

inherent *adj.* tì-sā 天生

injection *n.* dzèn-d'eu 针; **get an** ~ dǎ•dzèn 打针 *(v.o.)*

ink *n.* meq-sǐ 墨水

inkstick *n.* meq 墨

inkstone *n.* ní-d'ae 砚台

in-laws *n. (husband's parents)* gòng-b'u 公婆; *(wife's
parents)* ngoq-vu-ngoq-mu 岳父岳母

inn *n.* lǔ-guoe 旅馆

innate *adj.* tì-sā 天生

insect *n.* zóng-dzǐ 虫子

insert *v.* tsāq 插

inside *l.n.* lí-d'eu 里头, lí-shiǎ(-d'eu)

insole *n.* h'á-d'i 鞋垫

inspector *n.* jí-ni-'yüoe 检验员, jí-hu-'yüoe 检货员

install *v.* dzǎw 装

intentionally *adv.* d'iq-'wae, d'eq-'wae 故意

interest *(on investment)* *n.* lí-shiq 利息, lí-d'i 利钱

interest rate *n.* lí-liq 利率; *(daily)* tsāq-shiq 拆息

interesting *adj.* 'yéu•yì-sǐ 有意思

intermediary *n.* dzòng-jia 中介

internet *n.* mǎw-loq 网络; ~ **café** mǎw-ba 网吧; ~

marriage mǎw-huen 网婚

interrupt *(in a conversation)* v. tsāq•dzí, dāq•dzí 插嘴 *(v.o.)*

intestines n. d'ú-zǎ 肠子

intravenous drip n. diáw•'yí-sǐ 输液 *(v.o.)*

introduce v. jiá-zaw 介绍, jí 荐

inventory v. b'óe•hú 盘货 *(v.o.)*

invitation n. chín-tiq 请帖

invite v. chín 请

invoice n. fāq-piaw 发票

iron n. *(the element)* tīq 铁; *(for pressing fabric)* yóng-deu, 'yǔn-deu 熨斗; v. ~ **clothing** tǎ•yì- zǎ 熨衣服 *(v.o.)*

irritable *adj.* jīq-tsaw, jīq-dzaw 急躁, b'áw-tsaw, b'áw-dzaw 暴躁

is v. zí 是

Islam n. h'uáe-jiaw 回教

it *pron. See* that, this, he, she

Italian n. *(language)* Yí-d'a-li-nü 意大利语; *(person)* Yí-d'a-li-nin 意大利人

Italy *l.n.* Yí-d'a-li 意大利

itchy *adj.* 'yǎ 痒

J

jab v. tsōq, zoq 戳

jack *(lifting device)* n. chì-jin-din 千斤顶, āq-veq-saq

jacket n. j'iá-keq(-sae) 夹克, ngá-taw 外套

jade n. nioq 玉

jadeite n. fì-tsoe 翡翠

jail n. láw-gae 监狱

January *t.n.* yīq-'yüeq 一月, yīq-'yoq

Japan *l.n.* Zeq-ben 日本

Japanese *(language)* n. Zeq-nü 日语; *(person)* Zeq-ben-nin 日本人

Japanese yen n. zeq-'yüoe 日元

jasmine n. meq-li-huo 茉莉花

jealous of v. dú-j'i 忌妒

jeans n. niéu-dzae-ku 牛仔裤

jeep n. jīq-pu-tsuo 吉普车

jello n. jü-li 果子冻

jellyfish *n.* háe-zeq 海蜇, b'aq-b'i-dzǐ

Jesus *n.* yà-su 耶稣

jewelry *n.* séu-seq 首饰

jewelry store *n.* dzǐ-baw-di 珠宝店

job *n.* sǎ-h'ueq 工作

joint *(in limbs and fingers) n.* guàe-jiq 关节, g'aq-jiq(-gueq-loq)

joke *v.* kàe•'wóe-shiaw 开玩笑, dǎ•b'ǎ *(v.o.)*

journalist *n.* jí-dzae 记者

Judaism *n.* 'yéu-ta-jiaw 犹太教

jujube *n.* dzáw-dzǐ 枣子

July *t.n.* chiēq-'yūeq 七月, chīq-'yoq

jump *v.* tiáw 跳

June *t.n.* loq-'yūeq 六月, loq-'yoq

just *adv.* gǎw(-gǎw) 刚刚

just right *adj.* dzén-haw 正好

K

karaoke *n.* ká-la-wo-kae 卡拉OK, kàe-gu; ~ **bar** tsǎw-kae-su 唱K所

katydid *n.* jiáw-gu-gu 蝈蝈

kernel *n.* h'ueq 核儿

kettle *n.* diáw-dzǐ 吊子

key *n.* 'yaq-zǐ 钥匙; ~ **card** *(for a hotel room)* vǎw-ka 房卡

kick *v.* tǐq 踢

kidney *n.* yàw-dzǐ 肾

kilogram *n.* gòng-jin 公斤

kind *n.* dzóng 种 *(n., m.w.)*; *adj.* h'ú-chi 和气

kindergarten *n.* yéu-'er-'yūoe 幼儿园, yéu-zǐ-'yūoe 幼稚园

kiosk *n.* d'ín 亭

kiss *v.* dǎ•kàe-sǐ, shiǎ•mí-kong, shiǎ•dzǐ-bo 接吻 *(v.o.)*; *n.* kàe-sǐ

kitchen *n.* zǐ-vǎw(-gae) 厨房

kiwi *(fruit) n.* mí-h'eu-d'aw 猕猴桃

knead *v.* nioq 揉

knee *n.* jiāq-moe-deu 膝盖

knock *v.* kàw 敲

know *v. (~ a fact)* shiáw-deq 晓得、知道; *(recognize)*

nín 认, nín-deq 认得

Korea *l.n.* H'óe-goq 韩国

Korean *n. (language)* H'óe-nü 韩语; *(person)* H'óe-goq-nin 韩国人

kowtow *v.* kēq•d'éu 磕头 *(v.o.)*

kungfu *n.* gòng-fu 功夫; **Chinese** ~ dzòng-goq gòng-fu 中国~

Kunqu opera *n.* kuèn-chüeq, kuèn-chioq 昆曲

L

label *n.* b'á-dzǐ 牌子

laborer *n.* lín-gong 零工, nín-gong 人工, gòng-nin 工人

laborious *adj.* shìn-ku 辛苦

lace *n.* láe-sǐ 蕾丝

lack *v.* chüēq, chiōq 缺

ladle *n.* sǐ-zoq, sǐ-b'iaw 舀子、瓢

ladle out *v.* 'yáw 舀

lake *n.* h'ú 湖, h'ú-paq 湖泊

lame *adj.* chiàw-jiaq 跛足、瘸 *(v.o.)*

lamp *n.* dèn 灯

lampshade *n.* dèn-dzaw 灯罩

land *n.* d'í-b'i 土地

landlord *n.* vǎw-dong 房东

lantern *(usually decorative)* *n.* dèn-long 灯笼

laptop computer *n.* bén-ben 笔记本电脑

large *adj.* d'ú 大

last *adj. (final)* dzóe•h'éu 最后, (zaq-)meq-jiaq, āq-meq, laq-meq; *(previous)* zǎw-yiq-g'eq 上一个; ~ **month** zǎw-g'eq-'yüeq 上个月 *(t.n.)*; ~ **week** zǎw-li-ba 上礼拜 *(t.n.)*; ~ **year** chǘ-ni(-dzǐ) 去年, j'iéu-ni(-dzǐ) *(t.n.)*

latch *n.* tsāq-shiaw, shiàw-dzǐ 插销

late *adj.* áe 晚

later on *t.n.* h'éu-lae 后来, h'éu-d'eu-lae, h'éu-seu-lae

Latin America *n.* Là-din Máe-dzeu 拉丁美洲

laugh *v.* shiáw 笑

laundry *n. (room or shop)* shí-yi-di 洗衣店, shí-yi-vāw 洗衣房; *(clothes)* yáw shí-h'eq yì-zāw 要洗的衣裳

laundry soap *n.* b'í-zaw-fen, d'á-yi-zāw-fen 洗衣粉

law *n.* liq-faq 法律

lax *adj.* sáe-song 松弛、松散

lazy *adj.* láe 懒, láe-du 懒惰, láe-poq

lead *n.* kàe 铅

leaf *n.* 'yiq-dzï 叶子

lean *(not fat, thin) adj.* séu 瘦; ~ **meat** jìn-nioq 精肉, séu-nioq 瘦肉

lean against *v.* g'áe 斜靠

leather belt *n.* b'í-da 皮带

leather shoes *n.* b'í-h'a 皮鞋

leave *v.* dzéu 走

left *adj.* dzú 左

left hand *n.* dzú-seu 左手, jí-seu

left over *adj.* zǎ 剩 *(v.)*

left side *n.* dzú-mi 左边

leg *n.* jiāq-pāw 腿

legitimate *adj.* dzéndǎw, h'eq-faq 合法

legitimate goods *n.* h'ǎw-hu 行货

leisure *n.* kòng-h'ae 空闲, h'ae-kong 闲空

leisure clothing *n.* shièu-h'ae-dzāw 休闲装

lemonade *n.* nín-mong-sï 柠檬水

letter *n.* shín 信

lettuce *n.* sǎ-tsae 生菜

level *adj.* b'ín 平

license *(obtained upon payment of tax, duty, etc.) n.* dzàw-h'uae 照会

lick *v.* tí 舔

lid *n.* gáe-d'eu 盖子

lie down *v.* tǎw 躺

lift *(~ a cover) v.* shīq 掀

light *n.* guǎw-shi 光线, liǎ-guǎw; *adj. (not heavy)* chìn 轻; *(not dark—of color)* d'áe 淡

light rail *n.* chìn-guae 轻轨

lightning *n.* sóe-d'i 闪电, hōq-shi *(v.o.)*

like *v.* huòe-shi 喜欢

lily bulb *n.* bāq-h'eq 百合

line *n. (subway)* shí 线; *(queue)* d'áe 队

line up *v.* b'á-d'ae 排队

lining *(in clothing) n.* gāq-li 里子

lion *n.* sǐ-dzï 狮子

lip *n.* dzǐ-zen(-b'i) 嘴唇

lipstick *n.* dzǐ-zen-gaw 唇膏

liquid crystal display *(LCD) n.* 'yiq-jin-b'in 液晶屏

liquid medicine *n.* 'yaq-sï 药水

liquor *n.* jiéu 酒

list *n.* chìn-dae 清单

listen *v.* tìn 听

literate *adj.* sēq•zï 识字 *(v.o.)*

little *adj.* shiáw 小

little bit *n.* dí, ngáe 点 *(m.w.)*

live *(to be alive) v.* h'ueq 活

live at *v.* zï 住

lively *adj. (buzzing with excitement)* náw-mã, niq-naw, náw-niq 热闹; *(quick-witted)* h'ueq-fae 活泼、伶俐; *(vivacious)* h'ueq-paq 活泼

liver *n.* gòe 肝

living room *n.* kēq-tin 客厅

lizard *n.* sï-jiaq-zuo 蜥蜴

load *v.* dzǎw 装

lobster *n.* lóng-huo 龙虾

lock *n., v.* sú 锁

loft *n.* gōq-leu 阁楼

long *adj.* zǎ 长

long-distance call *n.* zǎ-d'u-d'i-h'uo 长途电话

loofah gourd *n.* sï-guo 丝瓜

loofah sponge *n.* sï-guo-jin 丝瓜筋

look *v.* kóe 看

look for *v.* zyín 寻找

loose *adj. (not tight)* sòng 松; *(scattered)* sáe 散

loquat *n.* b'iq-b'oq 枇杷

lose *v. (not win)* sï 输; *(misplace something)* loq-teq 丢失

lose capital *v.o.* zeq•bén, kuàe•bén 亏本, 折本

lotion *n.* h'ú-seu-sãw 护手霜

lotus flower *n.* h'ú-huo 荷花

lotus root *n.* ngéu 藕

lotus seed *n.* lí-shin 莲子

louse *n.* sēq-dzï 虱子, láw-b'aq-seq

love *n., v.* áe 爱

lover *n.* zyín-nin 情人

low *adj.* dì 低

luck *n.* 'yũn-chi, 'yóng-chi, 'yũn-d'aw 运气

luggage *n.* h'ǎ-li 行李

lunch *n.* dzòng-vae 午饭

lungs *n.* fî 肺
luxurious *adj.* h'áw-h'uo 豪华
lychee *n.* liq-dzǐ 荔枝, mó-liq-dzǐ

M

macaroni *n.* tòng-shin-fen 通心粉
mackerel *n.* mó-gaw-ñg 鲅鱼
maggot *n.* chì 蛆
magic *n.* bí•shí-faq 变魔术 *(v.o.)*
maglev train *(magnetic levitation train)* *n.* zǐ-veu-
   tsuo 磁浮车
magnet *n.* shīq-tiq-zaq 磁石
magnolia *n.* nioq-lae-huo, nüeq-lae-huo 玉兰花
magpie *n.* shí-chiaq 喜鹊
mahjongg *n.* mó-jiā 麻将; ~ **tile** mó-jiā-b'a 麻将牌
mail *v.* jí 寄; ~ **a letter** jí•shín 寄信; ~ **a package**
   jí•bàw-gu 寄包裹; *n. (letter)* shín 信, shín-j'i 信件;
   (package) bàw-gu 包裹; **ordinary** ~ b'ín-shin 平信;
   express ~ kuá-d'i 快递, kuá-j'i
mailbox *n.* 'yéu-d'ong 邮筒, 'yéu-shiā 邮箱
make *v.* dzú 做
make friends *ph.* g'aq•b'ǎ-'yeu 交朋友 *(v.o.)*
make money *ph.* záe•tsàw-piaw, záe•d'óng-d'i 赚钱
   (v.o.)
makeup *n.* huó-dzāw-pin 化妆品
mall *n.* sǎw-zā 商场; b'ú-h'in-ga 步行街
malt sugar *n.* zyín-d'āw, maq-nga-d'āw 饴糖
man *n.* nóe-nin(-ga) 男人, nóe-g'eq 男的
manager *n.* jìn-li 经理
Mandarin *n.* Pú-tong-h'uo 普通话
mandarin duck *n.* yüòe-yā-diaw 鸳鸯
mango *n.* mǎw-gu 芒果
mansion *n.* d'á-h'uo, d'á-shia 大厦
mantis *n.* d'ǎw-lāw 螳螂
manual transmission *n.* séu-b'a-dāw 手排挡
manufacture *v.* tsēq-tsae 出产
many *adj.* dù 多, shǔ-du 许多
marble *n.* d'áe-dzǐ 弹子
March *t.n.* sàe-'yüeq 三月, sàe-'yoq
march *v.* 'yéu-h'in 游行

mark *n.* jì-nin 记号

marker *n.* mó-keq-biq 马克笔

market *n.* zí-zā 市场, sǎw-zā 商场

market conditions *n.* hǎw-zyin 行情

marketing division *n.* gòng-shiaw-ku 供销科

marriage *n.* huèn-yin 婚姻

marry *v. (of a man)* táw•láw-b'u 讨老婆, táw•shìn-h'u; *(of a woman)* gá•nóe-nin 嫁男人, tsēq•gá 出嫁; *(of both bride and groom)* jīq-huen 结婚 *(v.o.)*

mason *n.* ní-sǐ-gong 泥瓦工

massage *v.* òe-mo 按摩

master *(term of respect)* *n.* sǐ-vu 师傅

mat *(bamboo ~)* *n.* zyiq-dzǐ 席子

match *n.* zí-lae-hu 火柴

matchmaker *n.* máe-nin 媒人, jiá-zaw-nin 介绍人

matter *n.* zí-ti 事情

May *t.n.* ñǵ-'yüeq 五月, ñǵ-'yoq

maybe *adv.* 'yáe-shü 也许, dzōq-shin 可能

me *prn.* ngú, 'wú 我

meat *n.* nioq 肉

meat dish *n.* huèn-tsae 荤菜

meatball *n.* nioq-'yǜoe 肉圆

meddle in *v.* tsuó•yīq-jiaq, dāq-yiq-jiaq 插手 *(v.o.)*

medicated bandage *n.* gàw-'yaq 膏药

medicinal powder *n.* 'yaq-fen 药粉

medicine *n.* 'yaq 药

medium *adj.* dzòng 中

meet *v.* b'ǎ•d'éu 碰头, jí•mí 见面 *(v.o.)*

meeting *n.* wáe, h'uáe 会

melt *v.* 'yǎ 化; **the ice has ~ed** *ph* bìn•'yǎ-leq 冰化了

memorize *v.* b'áe 背

memory *n. (faculty)* jí-shin 记忆力; *(in a computer)* náe-zen 内存

menstrual period *n.* 'yüeq-jin, 'yoq-jin 月经

mental disorder *n.* zén-jin-b'in 神经病

menu *n.* tsáe-dae 菜单

merchant *n.* sǎw-nin 商人, sǎ-yi-nin 生意人

mercurochrome *n.* h'óng-'yaq-sǐ 红药水

merge *v.* bǎ-long-lae 合起来 *(v.c.)*

meteor *n.* liéu-shin 流星

microphone *n.* maq-keq-fong 麦克风

microwave oven *n.* ví-bu-lu 微波炉

middle *l.n.* dǎw-dzong, dǎw-dzong-h'uǎ-li 中间

middle school *n.* dzòng-h'oq 中学

middle-man *n.* dǎw-dzong-'yüoe, dzòng-nin 中间人

midnight *n.* bóe-'ya 半夜

midwife *n.* zú-tsae-zï 助产士

migrant laborer *n.* mín-gong 民工

milk *(of a cow) n.* niéu-na 牛奶

Milky Way *n.* nín-h'u, tì-h'u 银河

mind *n.* náw-dzï 脑子, náw-jin, d'éu-naw-dzï

mine *prn. (belonging to)* ngú-g'eq, ngú-eq 我的; *n.*
    (mineral deposit) kuǎw

minibus *n.* mí-baw-tsuo 面包车

minute *t.n.* fèn 分

mirror *n.* jín-dzï 镜子

miscarriage *n.* shiáw-tsae 流产

miserable *adj.* tóng-ku 痛苦, kú-naw 苦恼

Miss *n.* shiáw-jia 小姐

mistaken *adj.* tsù, tsuò 错

mister *n.* shì-sǎ 先生

mistress *n.* shiáw-law-b'u 小老婆、妾

mix *v.* d'iáw, b'óe 搅拌; ~ **in** tsàe 掺, shiǎ, jiǎ

mobile phone *n.* séu-ji 手机

modern *adj.* mó-deng 摩登

modest *adj.* chì-shü 谦虚; shü-shin 虚心

mold *n.* mó-dzï 模子

momentarily *adv.* áe-shiq, áe-shiq-di 一会儿

Monday *t.n.* lí-ba-yiq 礼拜一

money *n.* d'óng-d'i, 'yǎ-d'i 钱; **paper ~** tsáw-piaw 钞票

money order *n.* h'uáe-kuoe-dae 汇款单

monkey *n.* h'ueq-sen 猴子

month *n.* 'yüeq, 'yoq 月

mood *n.* zyín-zyü 情绪, shín-dzï 兴致

moon *n.* 'yüeq-liǎ, 'yoq-liǎ 月亮

moonlight *n.* 'yüeq-liǎ-guǎw, 'yoq-liǎ-guǎw 月光

mop *n.* tù-fen 拖把

more or less *ph.* tsà-veq-du 差不多

morning *t.n.* dzáw-lǎw, zǎw-boe-niq, zǎw-dzeu 早上

mortgage *n.* vǎw-d'ae 房贷

mosquito *n.* mén-zong 蚊子

mosquito net *n.* mén-dzǎ, dzǎ-dzï 蚊帐

mosquito-repellent incense *n.* mén-zong-shiă 蚊香; *(electric)* d'í-men-shiă 电蚊香

most *adv.* dzóe 最, dín 顶

moth *n.* pōq-den-zong 灯蛾

mother *n.* m̀-ma, mà-ma, láw-ma 妈妈

mother-in-law *n. (husband's mother)* b'ú-b'u 婆婆, āq-b'u; *(wife's mother)* ngoq-mu 岳母, ză-m̃(-niă) 丈母娘

motor *n.* mó-d'a 马达

motorcycle *n.* mó-toq-tsuo 摩托车

mountain *n.* sàe 山

mouse *n.* láw-zong, láw-tsï 老鼠

mousse *n.* mó-sï 慕司、摩丝

moustache *n.* h'ú-su 胡须, ngá-su, h'ú-dzï

mouth *n.* dzḯ, dzḯ-bo 嘴

move *v.* d'óng 动; *(carry, transport)* bòe 搬; *(~ to a new home)* bòe•(nín-)gà, bòe•jià 搬家

movie *n.* d'í-yin 电影; ~ **star** d'í-yin-min-shin 电影明星; ~ **theater** d'í-yin-'yüoe 电影院; ~ **ticket** d'í-yin-piaw 电影票

moxibustion *(in Chinese medicine) n.* dzèn-jieu 针灸

Mrs. *n.* tà-ta 太太

Ms. *n.* nű́-zï 女士

MSG *n.* ví-dzï-su, mí-dzï-su 味精

mud *n.* láe-wu-ni, ná-ni, ní-d'eu 泥巴、泥土

muddy *adj.* h'uén 浑浊

muffle *v.* wù 捂

muffler *n.* 'yű́-jin 围巾

muggy *adj.* mèn-niq 闷热

mulberry leaf *n.* sằ-'yiq 桑叶

mung bean *n.* loq-d'eu 绿豆

muscle *n.* jì-nioq 肌肉

museum *n.* bōq-veq-guoe 博物馆

mushroom *n.* mó-gu 蘑菇; **shiitake** ~ shiằ-gu 香菇

must *adv.* bīq-shü 必须

mustard *n.* g'á-meq 芥末

mustard greens *n.* kà-tsae 芥菜

mute person *n.* wó-dzï 哑巴

mutton *n.* 'yằ-nioq 羊肉

my *adj.* ngú-g'eq, ngú-eq 我的 *(prn.)*

myna bird *n.* bāq-gu 八哥

N

nail *n. (metal)* dìn, 'yǎ-din 钉子; *(fingernail)* jīq-kaq, g'aq-dzǐ, dzǐ-kaq 指甲
nail clipper *n.* dzǐ-kaq-j'i, g'aq-dzǐ-j'i 指甲刀
nail polish *n.* jīq-kaq-'yeu 指甲油
naked *adj.* tsāq-gueq-loq 裸体、赤裸裸
name *n.* mín-zï 名字
name card *n.* mín-pi 名片
nap *n.* kēq-tsong 瞌睡
napkin *n.* tsòe-jin 餐巾; *paper ~* tsòe-jin-dzï 餐巾纸
narrow *adj.* h'aq 窄
nation *n.* gōq-jia 国家, gōq-d'u
native *n.* bén-di-nin 本地人
naughty *adj.* b'í 皮, d'iáw-b'i 调皮, 'wóe-b'i 顽皮, lá-b'i
nauseous *adj.* ōq-shin 恶心; dǎ•ōq-shin 恶心 *(v.o)*
navel *n.* d'ú-b'i-ngae, d'ú-zyi 肚脐
near *adj.* j'ín 近
nearby *adj., adv..* vú-j'in 附近, b'ǎw-b'i-hae-d'eu *(l.n.)*
nearsighted *adj.* j'ín-zï 近视
nearsightedness *n.* j'ín-zï-ngae 近视眼
neat *adj.* dzén-zyi 整齐
neck *n.* d'éu-jin 脖子
necklace *n.* h'ǎw-li 项链, lí-d'iaw
need *adv.* shǜ-yaw 需要
needle *n.* dzèn 针
neighbor *n.* lín-jü 邻居, lín-suo, gāq-biq(-d'eu) 隔壁
nephew *n. (brother's son)* zeq-dzï 侄子, āq-zeq; *(sister's son)* ngá-sã 外甥
nest *n.* kù 窝; *bird's ~* diáw-ku, niáw-ku 鸟窝
new *adj.* shìn 新
news *n.* shìn-ven 新闻
newspaper *n.* báw-dzï 报纸
newsstand *n.* sǐ-baw-d'in 书报亭
next *adj.* h'uó-yiq-g'eq 下一个; *~ month* h'uó-g'eq-'yüeq 下个月 *(t.n.)*; *~ time* h'uó-dzoe 下次 *(t.n.)*; *~ week* h'uó-li-ba 下礼拜 *(t.n.)*; *~ year* mín-ni(-dzï), kàe-ni(-dzï) 明年 *(t.n.)*
niece *n. (brother's daughter)* zeq-noe(-ñg) 侄女; *(sister's daughter)* ngá-sã-noe 外甥女

night *(nighttime) t.n.* 'yá-li(-shiǎ), 'yá-d'eu-di, tì•hēq 夜里

night market *n.* 'yá-zǐ-mi 夜市

night school *n.* 'yá-h'iaw 夜校

nightfall *n.* zyí-'ya-kua, b'ǎw-'wae-zen-guāw 傍晚

nightgown *n.* kuén-j'iong 睡衣

nimble *adj. (quick-witted)* lín-h'ueq 灵活; *(agile)* lín-chiaw 灵巧

nine *num.* jiéu 九

nineteen *num.* zeq-jieu 十九

ninety *num.* jiéu-seq 九十

nipple *n.* ná-na-d'eu, ná-d'eu 乳头

no *adv.* veq 不

nod *(~ one's head) v.* dí•d'éu 点头 *(v.o.)*

noisy *adj.* tsáw 吵

non-stick pan *n.* veq-dzae-gu, veq-tiq-gu 不粘锅

non-stop *adj.* zeq-kua 直快

noodles *(of wheat) n.* mí 面, mí-d'iaw 面条

noon *t.n.* dzòng-'wu 中午, dzòng-lǎ(-shiǎ), niq-dzong-shin(-li)

normal *adj.* dzén-zǎ 正常

north *l.n.* bōq 北, bōq-mi 北边

nose *n.* b'iq-d'eu, b'eq-d'eu 鼻子

nostril *n.* b'eq-d'eu-kong, b'iq-kong 鼻孔

not *adv.* veq 不

not have *v.* ḿ-meq 没有

note *n.* b'í-d'iaw 便条

notebook *n.* b'ú-dzǐ, bǐq-ji-b'u 本子、笔记本

notes *n.* bīq-ji 笔记

noveau riche *n.* b'áw-faq-h'u 暴发户

November *t.n.* zeq-yiq-'yüeq 十一月, zeq-yiq-'yoq

now *adv.* h'í-zae 现在, náe, g'eq-shiq 这会儿, gēq-shiq, d'iq-shiq, d'eq-shiq *(t.n.)*

numb *(from the cold) adj.* moq-g'oq 麻木(因冷所致)

number *n.* h'áw 号; sú-moq 数目

nurse *n.* h'ú-zǐ 护士

nursery *n.* tōq-'er-su 托儿所

nylon *n.* ní-long 尼龙

O

obey *v.* voq-tiq 服从

obscene *adj.* h'uó-dzoq, ōq-h'in 下流

obstruct *v.* ngáe 碍, gǎ 梗, zaq 阻塞

obvious *adj.* mín-shi 明显

obviously *adv.* mín-min(-jiaw), mín-min-dzï 明明

ocean *n.* háe 海

o'clock *adv.* dí-dzong 点钟 *(m.w.)*

October *t.n.* zeq-'yüeq 十月, zeq-'yoq

odd jobs *n.* lín-sae 零工

of *prep.* g'eq 的 *(ptl.)*; g'eq 个 *(m.w.)*

of course *adv.* tǎw-zoe 当然, zǐ-zoe

office *n.* báe-gong-seq 办公室

office building *n.* shiá-zǐ-leu 办公楼

often *adv.* zǎ-zā 常常, zǎ-dzāw

oil *n.* 'yéu 油

ointment *n.* 'yaq-gaw 药膏

old *adj.* *(not new)* j'iéu 旧; *(not young)* láw 老; ~ **stock** *n.* zén-hu 陈货

old-fashioned *adj.* láw-chi 老气

olive *n.* gáe-lae 橄榄

on *prep.* laq 在; *(locative suffix)* *sfx.* lǎw 上, lǎw-shiā; ~ **the bed** *ph.* zǎw-lāw(-shiā) 床上

on-duty personnel *n.* zeq-j'in-'yüoe 值勤员

on-line *adj.* mǎw-lǎw 网上 *(l.n.)*

once *adv.* yīq-tsï 一次, yīq-shiá 一下 *(n.m.)*

one *num.* yīq 一

one month old *(of babies)* *ph.* móe-'yüeq, móe-'yoq 满月 *(v.o.)*

one or two *ph.*, *num.* gú•bó 个把

one-day tour *n.* yīq-zeq-'yeu 一日游

one-piece dress *n.* lí-sae-j'ün, lí-sae-j'iong 连衣裙

oneself *prn.* zǐ-ga 自己

one-story house *n.* b'ín-vāw 平房

one-way *(not round-trip)* *adj.* dàe-zen 单程

one-way street *n.* dàe-h'in-d'aw, dàe-h'āw-d'aw 单行道

onion *n.* 'yǎ-tsong-d'eu 洋葱

only *adv.* dzēq 只, j'ín-j'in 仅仅, dzèn-dzen 才

open *v.* kàe 开; ~ **for business** *ph.* 'yín-niq-dzong 营业中

opening price *n.* kàe•gá 开价; *(at an exchange)* kàe•b'óe 开盘

opera *n.* shí 戏

operate *(surgery) v.* kàe•dàw 开刀, d'óng•séu-zeq 动手术 *(v.o.)*

operate a partnership business *ph.* gēq-dzu-sā-yi 合伙做买卖

opposite *(side) l.n.* dáe-mi 对面, dàe-gu, dáe-mi-zyi; *adj.* ~ **corner** zaq-goq 对角

or *(used in questions) conj.* àe-zǐ, h'áe-zǐ, h'uáe-zǐ 还是

orange *adj.* jüēq-h'ong, jiōq-h'ong 橘红, jüēq-h'uǎw, jiōq-h'uǎw 橘黄 *(attr.)*; *n. (fruit)* d'í-zen 橙子; *(color)* jüēq-h'ong-seq, jiōq-h'ong-seq 橘红色

orange juice *n.* jüēq-dzǐ-sǐ 橘子水

orchid *n.* láe-huo 兰花

order *v.* (~ *food from a menu*) dí•tsáe 点菜; (~ *take-out food*) jiáw•ngá-ma 叫外卖; (~ *goods or merchandise*) dín•hú 订货 *(v.o.)*

ordinary *adj.* pú-tong 普通

organ *n. (musical instrument)* fòng-j'in 风琴; *(in the body)* náe-zǎ 内脏

Orient *(the East) l.n.* dòng-fāw 东方

originally *adv. (formerly)* nüóe-lae 原来; *(at first)* bén-lae, bén-sǎ 本来

oriole *n.* h'uǎw-yin 黄莺

osmanthus *n.* guáe-huo 桂花

other *prn.* bǐq-h'eq 别的; *(prefix used with measure word)* b'iq, b'eq 别

otherwise *adv.* veq-zoe-ga 不然的话

outdated goods *n.* zén-hu 陈货

outgoing *(and sophisticated) adj.* tsēq-tǎw 上桌面、见过世面

outpatient office *n.* mén-dzen 门诊

outside *l.n.* ngá-d'eu 外头, ngá-mi 外面, ngá-di-d'eu

oven *n.* káw-shiǎ 烤箱

overcoat *n.* d'á-yi 大衣

overseas trade *n.* ngá-maw 外贸

overspend *v.* 'yóng-kong 超支 *(v.c)*

owe *v.* kóng, chí 欠

owl *n.* máw-d'eu-yin 猫头鹰

ox *n.* niéu 牛

P

pack *v.* dzầw 装
package *n.* bàw-gu 包裹
pad *n.* d'í-dzï 垫子
padded account *n.* huò-dzã 假账
page *n.* 'yiq 页 *(m.w.)*
pain *n.* tóng 痛
painful *adj.* tóng 痛
painter *(of buildings)* *n.* 'yéu-chiq-gong 油漆工
pajamas *n.* kuén-yi(-kuen-ku) 睡衣（睡裤）
palm *(of hand)* *n.* séu-dzầw 手掌
pancake *n.* bín 饼
panda *n.* h'ióng-maw 熊猫
pant leg *n.* kù-jiaq, kú-jiaq, kú-d'ong 裤腿
panties *n.* sàe-goq-ku 三角裤
pants *n.* kù-dzï, kú-dzï 裤子
papaya *n.* moq-guo 木瓜
paper *n.* dzḯ-d'eu 纸
paperclip *n.* h'uáe-h'in-b'iq-dzen 回形针
paperweight *n.* dzén-dzï 镇纸
parade *n.* 'yéu-h'in 游行
paralysis *n.* tàe-huoe 瘫痪, fòng-tae
paranoia *n.* ní-shin-b'in 疑心病
parboil *v.* sāq 涮
parcel *n.* bàw-gu 包裹, 'yéu-baw 邮包
pardon me *interj.* dáe-veq-chi 对不起
parents *n.* 'yá-niã 父母
park *n.* gòng-'yüoe 公园; *v.* d'ín 停; ~ **a car** d'ín•tsuò 停车
parka *n.* pà-keq 派克
parrot *n.* ầ-gu 鹦鹉
participate in *v.* tsòe-ga 参加
partition *n.* lí-biq 里壁、夹墙
partner *n.* dāq-dāw 搭档
partnership business *n.* gēq-dzu-sã-yi 合伙买卖 *(ph.)*
party *n.* pà-dae 派对
pass *n.* pà-sï 出入证; *v.* jìn-gu 经过
passenger ship *n.* lén-zoe 轮船
passport *n.* h'ú-dzaw 护照
paste *n.* jiầ-h'u 浆糊; *v.* ~ **onto** tīq 贴

pastry snacks *n.* shiáw-chiq 小吃, dí-shin 点心

pat *v.* pāq 拍

patch *n.* bú-din 补丁; *v.* bú 补, dǎ•bú-din 打补丁

patience *n.* náe-shin 耐心

patient *n.* sǎ-b'in-nin 病人

pave *v.* pù 铺

pawn *v.* dǎw 当; **~ shop** dǎw-di ~铺

pay *v.* gàw, jiàw 交, fú 付; **~ the check** tín-dzā 付钱; **~ with a credit card** sēq•ká 刷卡

payee *n.* d'áe-d'eu 台头

pea *n.* wóe-d'eu 豌豆

peace *n.* h'ú-b'in 和平

peach *n.* *(fruit)* d'áw-dzǐ 桃子; *(color)* d'áw-h'ong 桃红

peacock *n.* kóng-chiaq 孔雀

peanut *n.* huò-sen 花生

peanut butter *n.* huò-sen-jiā 花生酱

peanut oil *n.* sèn-'yeu 花生油

pear *n.* sǎ-li 梨

pearl *n.* dzèn-dzǐ 珍珠

peasant *n.* nóng-min 农民

pebble *n.* zaq-dzǐ 碎石头

peddler *n.* shiáw-fae 小贩

pedestrian mall *n.* b'ú-h'in-ga 步行街

pedicab *n.* sàe-len-tsuo 三轮车; **~ driver** sàe-len-tsuo-fu ~夫

peel *n.* gú-b'i 果皮; *v.* *(with a knife)* shiāq 削, chì 扦; *(with fingers)* bōq 剥

peephole *(in a door)* *n.* máw-ngae 猫眼

pen *n.* bīq 笔, gǎw-biq 钢笔; **~ container** bīq-d'ong 笔筒

pencil *n.* kàe-biq 铅笔

peony *n.* méu-dae-huo, máw-dae-huo 牡丹花

pepper *n.* h'ú-jiaw 胡椒; **black ~** hēq-h'u-jiaw 黑胡椒; **white ~** b'aq-h'u-jiaw 百胡椒; **green ~** chìn-laq-jiaw 青椒

peppermint *n.* b'ú-hu 薄荷

perform *v.* *(in a play)* yí•shí 演戏, dzú•shí; *(in traditional opera)* tsǎw•shí 唱戏 *(v.o.)*

performance *n.* yí-tseq 演出

performer *n.* yí-'yüoe 演员

perhaps *adv.* 'yáe-shü 也许, dzōq-shin 可能

perm one's hair *v.o.* tǎw•d'éu-faq 烫头发
permit *v.* niǎ 让, shǘ 许
perseverance *n.* zǎ-shin 恒心
persimmon *n.* zǐ-dzǐ 柿子
person *n.* nín 人
persuade *v.* chüóe 劝
pester *v.* zóe 纠缠
petal *n.* huò-b'ae 花瓣
phlegm *n.* d'áe 痰
photo studio *n.* dzáw-shiǎ-guoe 照相馆
photogenic *adj.* zǎw•dzáw 上照
photograph *n.* dzáw-pi 照片; *v.* pāq•dzáw(-shiǎ) 拍照 *(v.o)*
physics *n.* veq-li 物理
physical education *n.* tí-'yüeq, tí-'yoq 体育
physique *n.* d'iáw-goe 身材
piano *n.* gǎw-j'in 钢琴
pick up *(with chopsticks)* *v.* jì 搛, jīq
picky *adj* diàw 刁
pier *n.* mó-d'eu 码头
pierce *n.* dǎ•d'óng 打洞
pig *n.* dzǐ-lu 猪
pigeon *n.* gēq-dzǐ 鸽子
pig's foot *n.* dzǐ-jiaq-dzaw 猪爪
pigsty *n.* dzǐ-lu-b'ǎ, dzǐ-chüoe 猪圈
pile up *v.* d'eq, d'iq 叠
pill *n.* 'yaq-pi 药片; 'wóe-'yaq, 药丸
pillar *n.* zǐ-dzǐ 柱子
pillow *n.* dzén-d'eu 枕头
pillowcase *n.* dzén-d'eu-taw 枕头套
pilot *n.* gá-sǐ-'yüoe, jiá-sǐ-'yüoe 驾驶员
pin *n.* dzèn 针
pinch *(and pull)* *v.* dīq 捏
pineapple *n.* bù-lu-miq 菠萝
ping-pong *n.* pìn-pǎ 乒乓; ~ **ball** pìn-pǎ-j'ieu 乒乓球
pink *adj.* fén-h'ong 粉红 *(attr)*; *n.* fén-h'ong-seq 粉红色
pitiable *adj.* kú-li 可怜
pitiful *adj.* kú-naw-dzǐ 可怜的样子
pity *v.* kú-li 可怜; *n.* kú-shiq-h'eq 可惜的
place *n.* d'í-fǎw 地方, zǎ-huo, h'ú-d'ǎw
place under *(as a pad or cushion)* *v.* d'í 垫
plan *v.* dzén-b'ae 准备

plane *(wood)* *v.* b'áw 刨; *n. See* airplane

plastic *n.* sōq-liaw 塑料

platform *(at a rail station)* *n.* 'yüeq-d'ae, 'yoq-d'ae 月台

platter *n.* b'óe(-dzï) 盘子

play *v. (games, ball, etc.)* dǎ 打; ~ **ball** dǎ•j'iéu 打球; ~ **cards** dǎ•b'á 打牌, déu•b'á, dǎ•pōq-keq; ~ **mahjongg** dǎ•mó-jiǎ, tsuò•mó-jiǎ(-b'a) 打麻将; ~ **chess** dzāq•j'í 下棋; *(have fun)* b'eq-shiǎ(-shiǎ), b'í 玩儿; *n.(in theater)* h'uó-j'iq 话剧

please *interj.* chín 请; *(I beg of you!)* bá-toq-nong! 拜托你！

pleat *(in clothing)* *n.* gáe 裥

pliers *n.* láw-hu-j'i 钳子

plow *n.* lí, lí-daw 犁; *v.* gèn•d'í 耕田, lí•d'í 犁田 *(v.o.)*

plug *n.* tsāq-d'eu 插头

plum *n.* lí-dzï 李子

plum blossom *n.* máe-huo 梅花

plump *adj.* záe 饱满

pneumonia *n.* fǐ-'yi 肺炎

pod *n.* jīq 荚, d'éu-jiq 豆荚

podium *n.* gǎw-d'ae 讲台

poke *v.* tsōq, zoq 戳

poker *(game)* *n.* pōq-keq-b'a 扑克牌

poker cards *n.* pōq-keq-b'a 扑克牌

police *n.* jín-tsaq 警察

police precinct office *n.* pá-tseq-su 派出所

police station *n.* jín-tsaq-j'üeq 警察局

polite *adj.* kāq-chi 客气

pomegranate *n.* zaq-lieu 石榴

pomelo *n.* vén-dae 柚子

pond *n.* zï-d'āw 池塘, h'ú-d'āw

poor *adj.* j'ióng 穷

popsicle *n.* b'ǎw-bin 冰棍儿

popular *adj.* niq-men 热门; chīq-shiǎ 受欢迎; liéu-h'in 流行; ~ **songs** liéu-h'in-gu-chüeq 流行歌曲

pork *n.* dzï-nioq 猪肉; ~ **belly meat** ñg-huo-nioq 五花肉; ~ **hock** d'í-pā 蹄膀; ~ **ribs** b'áe-gueq 排骨; ~ **skin** nioq-b'i 肉皮; ~ **tenderloin** lí-jiq 里脊; ~ **tripe** dú-dzï 猪肚

porridge *n.* dzōq 粥

porter *(who uses a shoulder pole)* n. tiàw-fu 挑夫

possibly *adv.* 'yáe-shü 也许, kú-nen 可能, dzōq-shin

post office n. 'yéu-j'üeq 邮局

postage stamp n. 'yéu-piaw 邮票

postcard n. mín-shin-pi 明信片

pot n. h'oq-dzǐ, gù-dzǐ 锅; ~ **cover** h'oq-gae, gù-gae 锅盖

pot stickers *(fried dumplings)* n. gù-tiq 锅贴

potato n. 'yǎ-sae-'yü 土豆

potherb mustard n. shīq-li-hong 雪里红

pounds sterling n. yìn-bāw 英镑

pour *v.* dáw 倒

pout one's lips *ph.* chiáw-dzǐ-bo 噘嘴 *(v.o.)*

powdered milk n. ná-fen 奶粉

practical *adj* zaq-zeq 踏实

practice *v.* lí 练

pregnant *adj.* h'uá•'yǔn 怀孕, h'uá•yóng, 'yéu-shi *(v.o.)*, d'ú-d'u-b'i *(n.)*

pregnant woman n. 'yǔn-vu 孕妇, yóng-vu, tsáe-vu 产妇

premature birth n. dzáw-tsae 早产

prepare to *v.* dzén-b'ae 准备

prescription n. fàw-dzǐ, 'yaq-fāw 药方

presentable *adj.* zyiǎ•'yǎ 像样

preserved egg n. b'í-d'ae 皮蛋

press *v.* chín 按

pretty *adj.* chǔ, háw-koe 好看

price n. gá-d'i 价钱, gá-'wae 价位; **asking ~** n. táw•gá 要价; **base ~** n. dí-bae-ga, chí-bae-ga 基价、最底价; **closing ~** *(at an exchange)* n. sèu-b'oe 收盘; **lowest ~** n. dzóe-di-ga 最低价, chí-bae-ga; **opening ~** n. kàe•gá 开价; *(at an exchange)* kàe•b'óe 开盘

price ceiling n. dín-ga 顶价

prick *v.* dzāq 扎

priest *(Catholic)* n. zén-vu 神父

principal n. *(school authority)* h'iáw-dzā 校长; *(original sum invested)* bén-d'i 本钱; *adj. (main)* dzǐ-yaw 主要 *(attr.)*

printed matter n. 'yín-seq-pin 印刷品

printer *(for a computer)* n. dǎ-yin-ji 打印机

private *adj.* sǐ-nin-g'eq, sǐ-zen-g'eq 私人的; *(privately owned)* sǐ-'yeu-g'eq 私有的

private room *n.* bàw-vãw 包房

probably *adv.* kóng-po 恐怕, d'á-gae 大概, kóng-vãw (-b'ãw), zǎ-po

problem *n.* mén-d'i 问题

produce *v.* tsēq-tsae 出产

profession *n.* h'ǎw-dãw 行当

profit *n.* záe-d'eu 利润

proper *(prim and upright) adj.* dòe-dzen 端正

protect *v.* báw-h'u 保护

Protestantism *n.* jì-doq-jiaw 基督教

protruding *adj.* d'eq 凸

provoke *v.* zá 惹, zá-hu 惹火, zá-nin 惹人

public relations manager *n.* gòng-guae jìn-li 公关经理

public transportation *n.* gòng-jiaw 公共交通

publicly *adv.* gòng-kae 公开 *(adj., v.)*

pudding *n.* bú-din 布丁

puffed rice *n.* tsáw-mi-huo 米花

pufferfish *n.* h'ú-d'en-ñg 河豚鱼

pull *v.* là 拉, bàe; ~ **a tendon or muscle** tsèu•jin 抽筋 *(v.o.)*; ~ **out** tsèu 抽; ~ **up** b'aq 拔

pulled-dough noodles *n.* là-mi 拉面

pulse *n.* maq 脉; **take the** ~ bó•maq 把脉, dāq•maq

pumpkin *(or similar yellow squash variety) n.* nóe-guo 南瓜, váe-guo

punch *v.* sòng 搡; ~ **a ticket** g'aq•piáw 剪票 *(v.o.)*

puppet *n.* moq-ngeu 木偶

puppet show *n.* moq-ngeu-shi 木偶戏

purchase *v.* má 买, tsáe-geu 采购, géu-ma 购买

purchase on credit *v.* suò-chi 赊欠

purple *adj.* dzǐ 紫; *n.* dzǐ-seq 紫色

purse *n.* bí-baw 皮包

push *v.* tàe 推

push down on *v.* āq 压

put *v.* bá 摆, fǎw 放

Q

quail *n.* òe-zen 鹌鹑

quality of character *n.* nín-pin 人品

quality of goods *n.* hú-seq 货色
quality product *n.* dzén-dzong-hu 正品
quarrel *v.* tsáw 吵, dzã, dzã•dzǐ 争吵 *(v.o.)*; *n., v.*
  tsáw-shiã-mo 吵架
quarter *n.* sǐ-fen-dzǐ-yiq 四分之一
question *n.* mén-d'i 问题
quickly *adv.* góe-jin 赶紧, h'áw-saw
quiet *adj.* òe-jin 安静, chìn-jin 清静
quilt *n.* b'í-d'eu 被子
quilt cover *n.* b'í-taw 被套
quite *adv.* màe 蛮, jiàw-guae, sãq, zyiá-chi, láw 很
quiz *n.* tsēq-ni 测验
quota *(of people)* *n.* ngaq-dzǐ 名额

R

rabbit *n.* tú-dzǐ, tù-dzǐ 兔子
race *(running)* *n., v.* sáe-b'aw 赛跑
rack *(in a store)* *n.* hú-ga 货架
radio *n.* sèu-yin-ji 收音机
radish *n.* láw-b'oq, lú-b'oq 萝卜
rag *n.* meq-bu 抹布, kà-bu, kà-d'ae-bu
railing *n.* láe-gae 栏杆
railway car *n.* tsuò-shiã 车厢
railway station *n.* hú-tsuo-zae 火车站
rain *n.* 'yǔ 雨; *v.* loq•'yǔ 下雨 *(v.o.)*
rainbow *n.* h'óng, héu 彩虹
raincoat *n.* 'yǔ-yi 雨衣
raindrop *n.* 'yǔ-di-dzǐ 雨点子
rained upon *v.* lín•'yǔ, dõq•'yǔ 淋雨 *(v.o.)*
rainwater *n.* tì-loq-sǐ 雨水
rainy weather *n.* loq-'yü-ti 下雨天
raise *v.* *(hold up)* jǔ, j'í 举; *(rear)* 'yǎ 养; **~ wages**
  gà•gòng-d'i 加工资
rake *n.* b'ó 耙子; *v.* b'ó 扒
rancid *adj.* hàw 哈喇; **~ odor** *n.* hàw-chi ~气味
rapeseed *n.* tsáe-dzǐ 菜籽
rare *adj.* shì 稀, shì-j'i 稀奇
rat *n.* láw-zong, láw-tsǐ 老鼠
rather *adv.* nín-ku 宁可, nín-ken
rationality *n.* d'áw-li 道理

raw *adj.* så 生

razor *n.* tí-daw 剃刀

razor clam *n.* tsèn-dzǐ 蛏子

read *v.* kóe 看, d'oq 读; ~ **a book** kóe•sǐ 看书

ready *adj.* háw 好, d'ín-dāw 停当

real *adj.* dzèn 真

really *adv.* zeq-zae 实在, dzèn-zǐ 真是

rear *l.n.* báe-h'eu(-d'eu) 背后

reason *n.* nüóe-yin 原因, lí-'yeu 理由

rebel *v.* záw-fae 造反

receipt *n.* sèu-d'iaw 收条, sèu-jü 收据, fāq-piaw 发票

receive *v.* jīq 接, jīq-daw 接到, sèu 收, sèu-daw 收到

recently *adv.* g'eq-d'oe-zen-guǎw, g'eq-chiǎ-(-li), diq-chiǎ-li 这段时间 *(prn.)*; dzóe•j'ín 最近, shìn-j'in 近来

recharge *v.* tsòng 充; ~ **a battery** tsòng-di 充电; ~ **minutes** *(in a mobile plan)* tsòng-zeq 充值

reciprocate *v.* h'uáe-baw 回报

recklessly (act ~) *(behave foolishly)* *v.* h'ú-diaw 胡闹、乱来

recline *v.* tǎw 躺

recognize *v.* nín 认, nín-deq 认得

reconcile (~an account) *v.* g'aq•b'ín 结好 (账) *(v.c.)*

record *v.* *(in writing)* jí-loq 记录; *(via audio)* loq-yin 录音 *(v.o.)*

record on account *v.* jí•dzǎ 记账, dzú•dzǎ *(v.o.)*

recorder *n.* loq-yin-ji 录音机

red *adj.* h'óng 红; *n.* h'óng-seq 红色

red bayberry *n.* 'yǎ-mae 杨梅

red beans *(small)* *n.* tsāq-d'eu 赤豆

reflect *v.* dzáw 照

refreshing *adj.* sǎw 爽, sǎw-kua 爽快

refrigerator *n.* bìn-shiǎ 冰箱

regardless *adv.* h'uǎ-sǐ 横竖

registered letter *n.* guó-h'aw-shin 挂号信

regret *v.* h'éu-huae 后悔; *n.* h'uáe-wǎw-shin 后悔心

regretful *adj.* àw-law 懊悔

reincarnate *v.* d'éu-tae 投胎 *(v.o.)*

relatives *n.* chìn-jüoe 亲戚; ~ **by marriage** chìn-ga 亲家

relaxed *adj.* chìn-song 轻松

reliable *adj.* wén-dāw 稳当, bó•wén

relieved *(at ease) adj.* fǎw•shin 放心 *(v.o.)*

relocated *(to allow for demolition) v.* tsāq-chi 拆迁

reluctant *(~ to do something) adj.* suó-veq-deq, veq-suó-deq 舍不得 *(v.c.)*

remain *v.* liéu 留

remainder *n.* lín-d'eu 零头

remarry *(of a widower) v.* zoq-h'i 续弦 *(v.o.)*

remember *v.* jí-teq 记得

remit money *v.o.* h'uáe-kuoe 汇款

remnants *n.* zǎ-hu 剩货

remote *adj.* pì-piq 偏僻

remove *(from a hook, etc.) v.* tóe 撏

Rénmínbì *(the Chinese currency) n.* zén-min-b'i 人民币

renovate *v.* dzǎw-shieu 装修

reply *n.* h'uáe-yin 回音

report card *n.* zén-jiq-dae 成绩单

reporter *n.* jí-dzae 记者

repudiate a debt *v.o.* lá•dzǎ 赖账

reputation *n.* mín-chi 名气

request *v., n.* yàw-j'ieu 要求; ~ **leave** chín•gá 请假

requite *v.* báw-daq 报答

research *v., n.* nì-jieu 研究

resemble *v.* zyiǎ 像

reserve *v.* dín 订, liéu 留

residence *n.* zǐ-zaq 住宅, zaq-d'i

restaurant *n.* jiéu-ga 酒家, váe-di 饭店, váe-guoe 饭馆, tsáe-guoe 菜馆

restroom *n.* shí-seu-gae 洗手间, 'wáe-sen-gae 卫生间

return *v. (come back)* h'uáe-lae, dzóe-lae 回来; *(go back)* h'uáe-(dzoe-)chi 回去; *(give back)* h'uáe 还; ~ **merchandise** táe•hú 退货

return customer *n.* h'uáe-d'eu-kaq 回头客

revenue *n.* sèu-zeq 收入, jín-dzā 进账; ~ **and expenditures** sèu•dzǐ 收支, sèu•fú

reverse *adj.* fáe 反; *v.* fáe-gu-lae 反过来, dáw-gu-lae 倒过来

review *v.* fōq-zyiq 复习; *n.* b'ín-len 评论

revolt *v.* záw-fae 造反; *n.* b'áw-loe 暴乱

rib *n.* leq-b'ǎ-gueq 肋骨

ribbon *n.* tsáe-da 彩带

ribbonfish *n.* dá-ñg 带鱼

rice *n. (cooked)* váe 饭, mí-vae 米饭; *(uncooked)* mí 米; *(plant)* d'áw 稻

rice paddy *n.* d'áw-d'i 稻田

rice porridge *n.* shì-vae 稀饭

rice-crust *(at the bottom of a pot of cooked rice) n.* váe-zǐ, h'oq-jiaw 锅巴

rice-flour balls *(usually stuffed) n.* yüóe-dzï 圆子, tǎw-d'oe 汤团

rich *adj.* 'yéu•tsáw-piaw 有钱

ride *v. (a bicycle, horse, etc.)* j'í 骑; *(a bus or train)* tsén (tsuò-dzï) 乘 (车)

ridicule *v.* jì-shiaw 讥笑

right *adj. (correct)* dáe 对; *(opposite of left)* 'yéu 右 *(attr.)*

right hand *n.* 'yéu-seu 右手

right side *n.* 'yéu-mi 右边

rigid *adj.* ngǎ-tin 硬挺

ring *(for the finger) n.* gá-dzï 戒指

ring finger *(third finger) n.* 'wú-min-dzï 无名指

rinse *(by swishing in a container) v.* d'áw 淘

rinse one's mouth *v.o.* gōq•dzǐ 漱口

ripe *adj.* zoq 熟

river *n.* h'ú 河, gǎw 江

riverbank *n.* h'ú-tae-bi, ngóe 河岸

road *n.* lú 路, gòng-lu 公路, mó-lu 马路

roam *v.* máe-'yeu 漫游

roast *v.* káw 烤

rob *v.* tèu•meq-zï 偷东西 *(v.o.)*

robber *n.* j'iǎ-d'aw 强盗

rock *n.* zaq-d'eu 石头

rock sugar *n.* bìn-d'āw 冰糖

rod *n.* b'ǎw-d'eu 棍子

role *n.* jiāq-seq 角色

roll *v.* guén 滚

roll up *v.* jüóe 卷

roof *n.* ōq-din 屋顶, vǎw-din

room *n.* vǎw-gae 房间, vǎw-dzï 屋子

rooster *n.* h'ióng-ji 公鸡

root *n.* gèn 根, zǐ-gen 树根

rope *n.* zén-dzï 绳子

rose *n.* zyiǎ-vi, zyiǎ-b'i 蔷薇, máe-guae 玫瑰

rotten *adj.* láe 烂

rouge *n.* yì-dzï 胭脂

rough *adj.* tsù 粗

round *adj.* 'yüóe 圆

round-trip *n., adj.* wǎw-fae 往返 *(v.)*

rub *v.* nioq 揉, tsùo, tsù 搓

rubber *n.* zyiǎ-gaw 橡胶

rude *adj.* tsù-lu 粗鲁

ruler *n.* tsāq 尺

rump *n.* pì-gu(-d'eu) 屁股

run *v.* b'áw 跑, bèn 奔

runny nose *n.* liéu•b'iq-ti 流鼻涕 *(v.o.)*

rush *v.* tsǎw 闯

Russia *l.n.* Ngú-goq 俄国

Russian *(language) n.* Ngú-nü 俄语; *(person)* Ngú-goq-nin 俄国人

ruthless *adj. (cruel)* d'oq 毒、残忍; *(tricky)* sāq-laq 狠毒

S

sack *n.* d'áe-d'ae 袋子

sad *adj.* sǎ•shìn 伤心

safe *adj.* òe-zyi 安全

safe and sound *ph., adj.* òe-yiq 安逸

safety pin *n.* b'iq-dzen 别针

sail *n.* váe 帆; *v.* h'ǎw-h'in 航行

sailboat *n.* váe-zoe, tsà-b'ong-zoe 帆船

salad *n.* sāq-la 色拉

sales *n.* shiàw-zeu 销售 *(attr.); (marketing division)* 'ín-shiaw-ku 营销科

sales assistant *n.* zéu-hu-'yüoe 售货员, dí-'yüoe 店员

saliva *n.* záe-tu(-sï) 口水

salmon *n.* sàe-men-ñg 三文鱼

salt *n.* 'yí 盐

salty *adj.* h'áe 咸

same *adj.* yīq-'yã 一样; ~ **day** dǎw-ti 当天 *(t.n.)*

sand *n.* h'uǎw-suo 沙子

sandals *n.* fòng-liǎ-h'a 凉鞋

sandwich *n.* sàe-min-zï 三明治

sardine *n.* suò-din-ñg 沙丁鱼

sashimi *n.* sà-ñg-pi 生鱼片, sà-shi-mi

satchel *n.* sǐ-baw 书包

satisfied *adj.* dzòng-yi, dzóng-yi, móe-yi 满意

Saturday *t.n.* lí-ba-loq 礼拜六

saucer *n.* d'iq-dzǐ 碟子

sauna *n.* sà-na 桑拿

sauna bathing *n.* d'á sà-na 洗桑拿 *(v.o.)*

sausage *n.* shiǎ-zǎ 香肠

save *(~ money)* *v.* shüēq, shiōq 蓄

savings *n.* zǐ-shüeq 储蓄

saw *n.* gáe-dzǐ, g'á-dzǐ 锯子; *v.* gá, g'á, sà 锯

say *v.* gǎw 讲

scab *n.* yì 疮痂

scaffold *n.* séu-jiaq-ga, jiāq-seu-ga 脚手架

scalding *adj.* tǎw 烫

scales *(for weighing)* *n.* tsén 秤; *(of a fish)* ñg-lin-b'ae 鱼鳞

scallion *n.* tsòng 葱

scalper *(black market reseller of theater tickets)* *n.* h'uǎw-nieu 黄牛

scar *n.* bò 疤

scarf *n.* 'yǔ-jin 围巾, d'éu-jin 头巾

scattered *adj.* sáe 散

scenery *n.* jín-dzǐ 风景

scenic *adj.* fòng-jin hàw-g'eq 风景好的

scenic area *n.* fòng-jin-chü 风景区

school *n.* h'oq-h'iaw 学校, h'oq-d'ǎw

scissors *n.* jí-daw 剪刀

scold *v.* mó 骂

scratch an itch *v.o.* dzàw•'yǎ 搔痒

screwdriver *n.* nì-zoq 螺丝刀

sea *n.* háe 海

sea cucumber *n.* háe-sen 海参

seafood *n.* háe-shi 海鲜

seal *v.* fòng 封; *n.* *(stamp)* d'ú-dzǎ 图章; *(closure)* fòng-d'iaw 封条; *(animal)* háe-baw 海豹

seat *n.* 'wáe-dzǐ 位子

seaweed *n.* háe-da 海带

second *(2nd)* *n., adj.* d'í-ni 第二

secret *n.* bí-miq, mí-miq 秘密

secretary *n.* mí-sǐ, mì-sǐ 秘书

secretly *adv.* tèu-b'oe(-dzǐ) 偷偷地

section chief *n.* dzú-dzǎ 组长, kù-dzǎ 科长

sedan *n.* shiáw-j'iaw-tsuo 小轿车

see *v.* kóe 看

seed *n.* dzǐ 子, dzóng-dzǐ 种子

seek *v.* zyín 寻找

seems *v.* háw-zyiǎ 好像, zyiǎ-saq *(adv.)*

select *v.* gáe, d'áw 挑选

selfish *adj* diàw 吝啬

sell *v.* má 卖; ~ **by the piece** lín-ma, diáw-tsen 零售

separate *v. (keep apart)* gāq 隔; *(move apart)* fèn-kae
  分开

September *t.n.* jiéu-'yüeq 九月, jiéu-'yoq

serious *adj.* nín-dzen 认真, dín-dzen

servant *n.* 'yóng-nin 佣人, pōq-nin 仆人

serve food *v.o.* zǎw•tsáe 上菜

service fee *n.* séu-zoq-fi 手续费

serving spoon *n.* tǎw-zoq 汤勺

sesame *n.* dzǐ-mo 芝麻

sesame oil *n.* mó-'yeu 麻油

sesame paste *n.* dzǐ-mo-jiǎ 芝麻酱

settle accounts *v.o.* g'aq•dzǎ 结账

settled in *adj.* òe-d'in, òe-sǎ 安定

seven *num.* chīq 七

seventeen *num.* zeq-chiq 十七

seventy *num.* chīq-seq 七十

sew *v.* h'ǎw 缝

shade *n.* yìn-d'eu-li 阴凉处

shady *adj.* yìn-liǎ 阴凉

shake *v.* 'yáw 摇; ~ **one's head** 'yiáw•d'éu 摇头

shaky *adj.* huǎw 晃

shallow *adj.* chí 浅

shampoo *n.* d'á-d'eu-gaw 洗发乳

Shanghai *l.n.* Zǎw-hae 上海

Shanghai opera *n.* h'ú-j'iq 沪剧

Shanghainese *n. (person)* Zǎw-hae-nin 上海人;
  (language) Zǎw-hae-h'ae-h'uo 上海话

share certificate *n.* gú-piaw 股票

shark *n.* suò-ñg 鲨鱼

sharp *adj. (~ edge)* kuá 快; *(~ point)* jì 尖

shattered *adj.* sáe 碎

shave *(~ a beard)* *v.* shièu•mí 刮脸 *(v.o.)*

shaved ice *n.* b'áw-bin 刨冰

shawl *n.* pì-ji 披肩

she *prn.* 'yí 她

sheep *n.* mí-'yã 绵羊

shell *n.* kõq-dzï 壳子

shift *v.* tóng, 'yí 移、挪

shiitake mushroom *n.* shiã-gu 香菇

shine *v.* dzáw 照

shirt *n.* tsén-sae 衬衫

shiver *n.* h'óe-j'in 寒噤; *v.* fãq•déu 发抖, déu 抖, j'ín 噤

shoddy *adj.* b'iq-jiaq 鳖脚

shoe *n.* h'á-dzï 鞋子

shoe polish *n.* b'í-h'a-'yeu 鞋油

shop *n.* sãw-di 商店, dí-ga; *v.* d'áw•mó-lu, ãq•mó-lu 逛街 *(v.o.)*; ~ **for food** má•tsáe 买菜

shop clerk *n.* dí-'yüoe 店员

shop counter *n.* j'ú-d'ae, g'uáe-d'ae 柜台

short *adj. (not long)* dóe 短; *(not tall)* dóe 短, á 矮

should *aux.* yìn-gae 应该

shoulder *n.* jì-bãw 肩膀, jì-gaq

shower *(bath)* *n.* lín-'yoq 淋浴; ~ **cap** 'yoq-maw 浴帽; ~ **curtain** 'yoq-li 浴帘; ~ **head** pèn-d'eu 喷头; ~ **stall** lín-'yoq-vãw 淋浴房, tsòng-lin-vãw

shrewd *adj.* jìn 精, jìn-min 精明, jìn-guaq

shrimp *n.* huò, hòe 虾; *(shelled)* huò-nin, hòe-nin 虾仁

shrink *(in size or value)* *v.* sõq 缩, sõq•sï 缩水

shriveled *adj.* bīq 瘪

shuttlecock *n. (badminton)* 'yŭ-maw-j'ieu 羽毛球; *(for kicking)* jí-dzï 毽子

sick *adj.* sã•máw-b'in, sã•b'ín 生病 *(v.o.)*

sick leave *n.* b'ín-ga 病假

side *l.n.* b'áw-b'i 旁边, bì-d'eu, b'áw-bi-d'eu

sight *n. (scenic)* jín-chü 景区, jín-di 景点; *(eyesight)* zï-liq 视力

sightseeing boat *n.* 'yéu-zoe 游船

sign *n.* dzàw-b'a 招牌; *v.* ~ **one's name** chí-zï 签字 *(v.o.)*

sign up *v.* báw•mín 报名 *(v.o.)*

silk *n.* sï 丝`, dzèn-sï 真丝; ~ **shop** zéu-bu-di 绸布店

silkworm *n.* zóe-baw-baw 蚕

silky *adj.* nú 柔软

silver *n.* nín-dzǐ 银子

SIM card *n.* *SIM ká* 卡, *séu-ji-ka* 手机卡

similar *adj.* zyiã 像

simplified character *n.* jí-ti-zǐ 简体字, shiáw-shia-zǐ

since *conj.* jì-zoe 既然

sincere *adj.* dzēq-zen 挚诚

sing *v.* tsǎw 唱; **~ in a chorus** h'eq-tsǎw 合~

sink *v.* zén 沉, meq 没; *n.* sǐ-zaw 水槽, sǐ-zǐ-dzǐ 水池子

sister *n. (elder)* jiá-jia 姐姐, āq-jia, āq-ji; *(younger)*
máe-mae 妹妹, āq-mae

sister-in-law *n. (elder brother's wife)* sáw-saw 嫂嫂,
āq-saw; *(younger brother's wife)* d'í-shin-vu 弟媳;
(wife's elder sister) d'á-'yi-dzǐ 大姨子; *(wife's
younger sister)* shiáw-'yi-dzǐ 小姨子; *(husband's
elder sister)* d'á-gu-dzǐ 大姑子; *(husband's younger
sister)* shiáw-gu-dzǐ 小姑子

sisters *(elder and younger)* *n.* jí-mae 姐妹

sit *v.* zú 坐

six *num.* loq 六

sixteen *num.* zeq-loq 十六

sixty *num.* loq-seq 六十

size *n.* h'áw 号 *(n., m.w.)*

skin *n.* b'í 皮

skip class *v.o.* chiáw•kú 逃课

skirt *n.* j'ǘn-dzǐ, j'ióng-dzǐ 裙子

skull *n.* d'éu-naw-koq 脑壳

skullcap *n.* guò-b'i-maw 瓜皮帽

sky *n.* tì 天

slanting *adj.* zyiá, chiá 斜

slap *v.* guāq 掴

sleep *v.* kuén, kuén•gáw, kuèn-gaw 睡觉

sleeve *n.* zyiéu-dzǐ(-guoe) 袖子

slice *v.* chīq 切

slide *n.* h'uaq-h'u-ti 滑梯; *v.* shiá 滑

slightly *adv.* sàw-'wae 稍微

slip *(~ and fall)* *v.* tǎw, dǎ•h'uaq-d'aq 滑跌

slippers *n.* tù-h'a 拖鞋

slippery *adj.* h'uaq 滑

slope *n.* pù 坡

sloppy *adj.* mà-hu 马虎

slotted spoon *n.* léu-zoq 漏勺

slow *adj.* máe 慢

slug *n.* 'yí-'yeu, sǐ-'yi-'yeu, b'iq-ti-zong 蛞蝓

small *adj.* shiáw 小

small bowl *n.* bēq-d'eu 钵儿

smart *adj.* tsòng-min 聪明

smell *v.* mén, 'wén 闻, tèn; *n.* mí(-d'aw) 味道

smile *v.* shiáw 笑; *n.* shiáw-'yong 笑容

smoke *v.* chīq 吃; ~ **cigarettes** chīq•shiǎ-yi 吸烟; *n.* yì 烟

smooth *adj.* guǎw-h'uaq 光滑

smoothly *adv.* zén-li 顺利

smug *adj.* wù-deu 得意(含贬义)

smuggled goods *n.* sǐ-hu 水货

snack *n.* lín-zeq 零食, shiáw-chiq 小吃

snail *n.* *(land dwelling)* gú-nieu 蜗牛; *(water dwelling)* lú-sï 螺蛳

snake *n.* zuó 蛇

snatch *v.* chiǎ 抢

sneeze *n.* pèn-ti 喷嚏; *v.* dǎ-pen-ti 打喷嚏 *(v.o)*

snore *v.* dǎ•huèn-d'u 打呼噜

snow *n.* shīq 雪; *v.* loq•shīq 下雪 *(v.o.)*

snow peas *n.* h'ú-lae-d'eu 荷兰豆

snowflake *n.* shīq-huo 雪花

soak *v.* páw 泡

soap *n.* b'í-zaw 肥皂, shiǎ-zaw 香皂

soccer *n.* dzōq-j'ieu 足球

soccer ball *n.* dzōq-j'ieu 足球

socks *n.* maq-dzǐ 袜子, maq 袜

soda *n.* *(bicarbinate of soda)* sù-dǎ-fen 苏打粉; *(drink)* chí-sï 汽水

soda water *n.* sù-dǎ-sï 苏打水

sofa *n.* suò-faq 沙发, suò-faq-yi

soft *adj.* nüóe 软

soft drink *n.* chí-sï 汽水

sole *n.* *(of the foot)* jiāq-dzāw 脚掌, jiāq-di(-bae); *(of a shoe)* h'á-di 鞋底

solid *adj.* *(hard and firm)* dzāq-ngǎ 坚硬; *(durable)* jīq-zeq 结实

some *(a few)* *prn.* jí-g'eq, jí-eq 几个 *(n.m.)*

somersault *n., v.* fàe•gèn-deu 翻跟斗 *(v.o.)*

sometimes *adv.* 'yéu-zen-guǎw, 'yéu-zǎ-zǐ 有时候

son *n.* ní-dzǐ, 'ér-dzǐ 儿子, nóe-shiaw-noe

song *n.* gù 歌

son-in-law *n.* nǔ-shi, nǔ-shü 女婿

soon *adv.* kuá 快要

sorry *interj.* dáe-veq-chi 对不起; *adj.* b'áw-chi 抱歉

soul *n.* h'uén-lin(-d'eu), lín-h'uen 灵魂

sound *n.* sèn-yin 声音, sǎ-chi

soup *n.* tǎw 汤, tǎw-sï

soup spoon *n.* d'iáw-gǎ 汤匙

sour *adj.* sòe 酸

south *l.n.* nóe 南, nóe-mi 南边

soy milk *n.* d'éu-jiǎ 豆浆

soy sauce *n.* jiǎ-'yeu 酱油

soybean *n.* h'uǎw-d'eu 黄豆

soybean product *n.* d'éu-dzǐ-pin 豆制品

spaghetti *n.* yí-mi 意大利面

Spain *l.n.* Shì-bae-nga 西班牙

Spaniard *n.* Shì-bae-nga-nin 西班牙人

Spanish *n.* *(language)* Shì-bae-nga-nü 西班牙语

spare *(from harsh treatment)* *v.* niáw 饶

sparrow *n.* mó-chiaq, mó-jiaq 麻雀

sparse *adj.* shì 稀

spatula *(for cooking)* *n.* h'oq-tsae, tsáe-daw 锅铲

speak *v.* gǎw 讲, gǎw•h'áe-h'uo 讲话

speaker *n.* lá-ba 喇叭

speciality shop *n.* dzòe-ma-di 专卖店

specialty dish *n.* d'éq-seq-tsae 特色菜

spices *n.* shiǎ-liaw 香料

spicy *adj.* laq 辣

spider *n.* dzǐ-dzǐ 蜘蛛, jīq-dzǐ

spiderweb *n.* jīq-dzǐ-lu-mǎw 蜘蛛网

spinach *n.* bù-tsae 菠菜

spine *n.* báe-jiq-gueq 背脊骨, jīq-dzoe-gueq 脊椎骨

spirit *n.* h'uén-lin(-d'eu), lín-h'uen 灵魂

splash *v.* záe 溅

split *v.* tsāq, kàe•tsāq, huāq•kàe 裂

spoiled *(of food)* *adj.* sèu 馊

sport *n.* tí-'yǖeq, tí-'yoq 体育, 'yǔn-d'ong 运动

spray *v.* pèn 喷

spread out *v.* tàe 摊

spring *n. (mechanical)* d'áe-h'uãw 弹簧; *(season)* tsèn-ti 春天

Spring Festival *(Chinese New Year) n.* tsèn-jiq 春节

spring roll *n.* tsèn-jǔoe 春卷

spurt *v.* pèn 喷

square *n., adj.* fãw 方

squat *v.* dèn 蹲

squeeze *v.* dzèn, g'aq 挤压; ~ **into** g'aq-jin 挤进

squid *n.* 'yéu-ñg 鱿鱼

squirrel *n.* sòng-tsǐ 松鼠

stable *adj.* òe-d'in, òe-sã 安定

stadium *n.* tí-'yüeq-zã 体育场

stage *n.* shí-d'ae 戏台

stairs *n.* h'ú-ti 楼梯

stale *adj.* sõq 不新鲜

stamp *v. (~ one's foot)* zaq 跺; *n. (postage)* 'yéu-piaw 邮票

stand *v.* liq 站、立

standard room *n.* biàw-vãw 标准房间

staple *n.* dín-sǐ-din 钉书钉

stapler *n.* dín-sǐ-ji 钉书机

star *n.* shìn 星, shìn-shin 星星; **shooting** ~ liéu-shin 流星

starch *n.* jià-h'u 浆糊; *v.* jià 浆

stare *v.* dìn 盯

start *v.* kàe-sǐ 开始

startle *v.* hãq-yiq-tiaw 吓一跳 *(v.o.)*

statement *(of accounting) n.* chìn-dae 清单

station *n.* záe 站

stationery *n.* shín-dzǐ 信纸

stationery shop *n.* vén-j'ü-di 文具店

stay at *v.* zǐ 住

steal *v.* tèu 偷, zeq-teu 偷窃; ~ **things** tèu•meq-zǐ 偷东西

steam *v. (in a steaming tray)* dzèn 蒸; *(in a pot)* dén 炖

steamer *(for food) n.* dzèn-long 蒸笼

step *n.* d'áe-ga, d'áe-jia, gà-'yi-zaq 台阶

step on *v.* d'aq 踏、踩

stepfather *n.* jí-dia, gú-vãw-'ya 后父

stepmother *n.* máe-niã 后母

stew *v.* dõq 熬

steward *n.* guóe-ga, guóe-jia 管家
stick on *v.* dēq, tīq 粘、贴
stiff *adj.* ngǎ-tin 硬挺
stifling *adj.* chì-men, chí-men 气闷
still *adv.* àe, h'áe, h'uáe 还
stilts *n.* gàw-chiaw 高跷
stimulating *adj.* dzāq•jín 刺激而有趣
stingy *adj.* shiáw-chi 小气, gàe-diaw; kèu 抠
stinky *adj.* tséu 臭
stir *v.* d'iáw, b'óe 搅拌
stir-fry *v.* tsáw 炒
stock certificate *n.* gú-piaw 股票
stock with goods *v.o.* jín•hú 进货
stockings *n.* zǎ-tong-maq 长袜
stomach *n.* 'wáe 胃
stone *n.* zaq-d'eu 石头
stool *n.* báe-den 板凳, dén-dzǐ 凳子, dén 凳
stop *v.* d'ín 停
store *n.* sǎw-di 商店, dí-ga
store away *v.* kǎw 藏
story *n.* gú-zǐ 故事
storytelling *(traditional)* *v.* sēq•sǐ 说书 *(v.o.)*
stove *n.* dzáw-d'eu 灶
stove-god *n.* dzáw-ga-b'u-saq 灶家菩萨
straight *adj.* *(correct or right side up)* dzén 正; *(not bent or crooked)* zeq 直; *adv.* *(directly)* dáe-zeq 直着; **go ~ ahead** bīq-zeq b'áw 一直走
straightforward *adj.* sǎw-chi 爽快
strain one's back *v.o.* b'iq•yàw, sén•yàw 闪腰、伤腰
straining spatula *n.* dzá-li 笊篱
strange *adj.* j'í-gua 奇怪, 'yéu-jin
stranger *n.* maq-sā-nin 陌生人
straw *(for drinking)* *n.* shīq-guoe 吸管
straw hat *n.* tsáw-maw 草帽
straw mat *n.* tsáo-zyiq 草席
stream *n.* bǎ, h'ú-bā 小河
street *n.* mó-lu 马路, gà 街, gà-d'aw 街道, gà-lu
street vendor *n.* tàe-fae 摊贩
street vendor's stand *n.* tàe-d'eu, d'í-tae 摊子
strength *(physical)* *n.* liq-chi 力气, chí-liq, liq-d'aw
strenuous *adj.* chīq-liq 吃力

strike *v.* dá́ 打

string *n.* zén-dzǐ 绳子, shí 线

string beans *n.* sǐ-ji-d'eu 四季豆

stroke *n.* *(disabling thrombosis in the brain)* dzóng•fòng 中风 *(v.o.)*; *(in writing of Chinese characters)* bīq-h'uaq 笔画; *v.* *(rub)* moq 摸

stroll *v.* d'ǎw 逛, sáe-b'u 散步

strong *adj.* j'iǎ 强, j'iǎ-dzǎw 强壮

stubborn *adj.* j'üeq 倔, j'üeq-j'iǎ 倔强, jiǎ, gǎ 犟, j'ioq-jiǎ, ngǎ-j'iǎ, g'én

student *n.* h'oq-sǎ 学生

studious *adj.* 'yóng-gong 用功

study *n.* *(room)* sǐ-vǎw 书房; *v.* d'oq 读, d'oq•sǐ 读书; ~ **in depth** nì-jieu 研究

stuffed nose *n.* óng-b'iq-d'eu, óng-b'eq-d'eu 齆鼻

stuffing *(in food)* *n.* niǎ 馅儿

stumble *v.* báe 绊

stupid *adj.* g'ǎw, b'én 笨

stutter *n.* gēq-dzǐ 口吃; *v.* jīq-bo 结巴

subsidize *v.* tīq-bu 补贴

substandard product *n.* dén-nga-pin 等外品

subway *n.* d'í-tiq 地铁

subway car *n.* tsuò-shiǎ 车厢

suck in *v.* shīq, hù 吸

suck on *v.* sōq 吮

suckle *v.* chīq•ná 吃奶 *(v.o.)*

sudden *adj.* b'áw 暴

suddenly *adv.* d'eq-zoe 突然

suffocating *adj.* chì-men, chí-men 气闷

sugar *n.* d'ǎw 糖

sugarcane *n.* gòe-dzuo 甘蔗

suit *n.* shì-dzǎw 西装

suitcase *n.* shiǎ-dzǐ 箱子, h'á-li-shiǎ 行李箱

suite *n.* táw-vǎw 套房

summer *t.n.* h'uó-ti, niq-ti 夏天

summer hat *n.* liǎ-maw 凉帽, fòng-liǎ-maw

summer vacation *n.* sǐ-ga, sǐ-jia 暑假

sun *n.* tá-'yǎ 太阳; *v.* suó 晒

Sunday *t.n.* lí-ba-niq 礼拜日

sundress *n.* diáw-da-j'ün 吊带裙

sunflower seed *n.* shiǎ-guo-dzǐ 葵花子

sunglasses *n.* tá-'yã-ngae-jin 太阳眼镜
sunken in *adj.* àw 凹
sunscreen *n.* vǎw-suo-sãw 防晒霜
sunshine *n.* niq-guãw 太阳光
sunstroke *n.* dzòng•sï 中暑, fãq•suò *(v.o.)*
supervisor *n.* zǎw-sï 上司, gàe-gong 监工
support *v.* tsǎ 掌
surface mail *n.* b'ín-shin 平信
surname *n.* shín 姓
suspect *v.* ní-shin 疑心、怀疑; *n.* h'í-ni-vae 嫌疑犯
suspend *(an activity temporarily) v.* záe-d'in 暂停
suspenders *n.* bàe-da 背带
swallow *n. (bird)* yí-dzï 燕子; *v.* tèn 吞
swear *v.* vaq•dzéu 发誓、赌咒 *(v.o.)*
sweat *n.* h'óe 汗; *v.* liéu•h'óe 流汗
sweater *n.* nióng-shi-sae 毛线衣
sweep *v.* sáw 扫
sweet *adj.* d'í 甜
sweet potato *n.* sàe-'yü 甘薯
swell up *v.* shín, hàe 肿
swelling *n.* kuáe 块, gẽq-daq 疙瘩
swim *v.* 'yéu-'yong 游泳, 'yéu•sï 游泳 *(v.o.)*
swimming area *(beach) n.* 'yoq-zǎ 浴场
swimming pool *n.* 'yéu-'yong-zï 游泳池
swindler *n.* pí-dzï 骗子
switch *n.* kàe-guae 开关
swollen *adj.* dzǎ 胀
syringe *n.* dzèn-d'eu 针

T

table *n.* d'áe-dzï 桌子
tablecloth *n.* d'áe-bu 桌布
tactful *adj.* sẽq-shiǎ 识相 *(v.o.)*
tai chi *n.* tá-j'iq-j'üoe 太极拳
tail *n.* ní-bo, mí-bo 尾巴
tailor *n.* záe-vong 裁缝
tailor shop *n.* záe-vong-di 裁缝店, zén-yi-di
take delivery *v.o.* d'í•hú 提货
take-out *(food) n.* ngá-ma 外卖
talk *v.* gǎw•h'áe-h'uo 讲话 *(v.o.)*

tall *adj. (high)* gàw 高; *(of people)* zǎ 高（长）

tangerine *n.* jūēq-dzǐ, jiōq-dzǐ 橘子

Taoism *n.* d'áw-jiaw 道教

Taoist *n.* d'áw-zǐ 道士

tardy *adj.* zǐ-daw 迟到 *(v.)*

taro *n.* 'yǔ-na 芋艿, 'yǔ-d'eu 芋头, 'yǔ-na-d'eu

tart *(egg custard)* *n.* d'áe-ta 蛋挞

tasteful *(aesthetically pleasing, cultured)* *adj.*
  'yéu•pín(-'wae) 有品位、格调高

tasty *adj.* háw-chiq 好吃

tattered *adj., n.* pá-la 破烂

taxi *n.* dīq-sǐ 的士, tsà-d'eu, tsēq-dzu-chi-tsuo 出租
  汽车

tea *n.* zuó 茶; ~ **leaf** zuó-'yiq 茶叶

teach *v.* jiáw 教

teacher *n.* làw-sǐ, láw-sǐ 老师

teacup *n.* zuó-bae 茶杯

team *n.* d'áe 队; **sports** ~ j'iéu-d'ae 球队

teapot *n.* zuó-h'u 茶壶

tear *v.* tsá 扯

tears *n.* ngáe-li(-sǐ) 眼泪

tease *v.* chì-vu 欺负

technical advisor *n.* j'í-zeq gú-ven 技术顾问

technical personnel *n.* j'í-zeq-(zen-)'yüoe 技术人员

telephone *n.* d'í-h'uo 电话

television *n.* d'í-zǐ(-ji) 电视机

tell *v.* gàw-su 告诉

temperment *n.* shín-dzǐ 性格, b'í-chi 脾气

temple *n.* miáw 庙, zǐ 寺

ten *num.* zeq 十

ten thousand *num.* váe 万

tenant *n.* vǎw-kaq 房客

tender *adj.* nén 嫩

tense *adj.* jín-dzǎ 紧张

tent *n.* dzǎw-b'ong 帐篷

teppanyaki *n.* tīq-bae-saw 铁板烧

termite *n.* b'aq-mo-ni 白蚁

test *n.* káw-sǐ 考试

text message *n.* dóe-shin(-shiq) 短信息

textbook *n.* kú-ben 课本

thank *v.* zyiá 谢, zyiá-zyia 谢谢

thank you! *interj.* zyiá-zyia-nong! 谢谢你！

that *prn.* yì-g'eq, yì-eq, àe-g'eq, àe-eq 那个; àe-, yì-, àe-mi 那 *(pfx.)*

theater *n.* j'iq-zǎ 剧场, j'īq-'yüoe 剧院

their(s) *prn.* 'yí-laq-g'eq, 'yí-la-eq 他们的

them *prn.* 'yí-laq, 'yí-la 他们

then *adv.* zyiéu, j'iéu 就

there *prn.* hàe-d'eu, àe-d'eu, àe-mi, yì-mi 那儿

there is *v.* 'yéu 有

there is not *v.* ḿ-meq 没有

thermometer *n.* wèn-d'u-ji 温度计

these *prn.* g'eq-ngae, g'eq-di, d'iq-ngae, d'eq-di 这些、这点

they *prn.* 'yí-laq, 'yí-la 他们

thick *adj. (not thin)* h'éu 厚, *(stout)* tsù 粗; *(viscous)* nín 稠; **the congee is ~** *ph.* dzōq nín 粥稠; **~ soup** nióng-tǎw 浓汤

thief *n.* zeq 贼, zeq-gueq-d'eu, shiáw-teu 小偷

thigh *n.* d'ú-jiaq-pǎw, d'ú-pǎw 大腿

thin *adj. (not fat)* séu 瘦; *(not thick)* b'oq 薄

thing *n.* meq-zǐ 东西

third *n. (in a sequence)* d'í-sae 第三; **one-~** (⅓) sàe-fen-dzǐ-yiq 三分之一

thirsty *adj.* dzǐ•gòe 口渴

thirteen *num.* zeq-sae 十三

thirty *num.* sàe-seq 三十

this *prn.* g'eq-g'eq, g'eq-h'eq, d'iq-g'eq, d'eq-eq 这个; g'eq-, d'iq-, d'eq- 这 *(pfx.)*

this year *t.n.* jìn-ni 今年

those *prn.* àe-ngae, ì-di 那些、那点

thousand *num.* chì 千

thread *n.* shí 线

three *num.* sàe 三

threshold *(doorstep)* *n.* mén-kae 门槛

throat *n.* h'ú-long, h'éu-long 喉咙

throw *v.* g'uáe, dōq 扔

throw into *v.* d'éu 投

thumb *n.* d'ú-ḿ-dzǐ, d'á-mu-dzǐ 大拇指

thumbtack *n.* d'ú-din 图钉, chín-din

thunder *n.* láe 雷; *v.* dǎ•láe 打雷, láe-shiǎ *(v.o.)*

thunderstorm *n.* láe-zen-'yü 雷阵雨

Thursday *t.n.* lí-ba-sï 礼拜四

Tibet *l.n.* Shì-zã 西藏

ticket *n.* piáw 票, piàw-dzï; **admission** ~ mén-piaw 门票; **bus** ~ tsuò-piaw 车票; **boat** ~ zóe-piaw 船票; ~ **seller** zéu-piaw-'yüoe 售票员, má-piaw-'yüoe

tide *n.* záw 朝, záw-sï 潮水

tidy up *v.* sèu-dzoq 收拾, lí 理

tie up *v.* b'oq 缚, jīq 结

tiger *n.* láw-hu 老虎

tight *adj.* jín 紧

tile *n.* zǐ-dzoe 瓷砖; ngó-pi 瓦片, ngó-b'ae

time *(when)* *n.* zén-guãw 时候、时间

timid *adj.* dáe•shiáw 胆小, sõq

tip *n.* shiáw-fi 小费

tiramisu *n.* d'í-la-mi-su 提拉米苏

tire *n.* tsuò-tae 车胎

tired *adj.* chīq-liq 吃力、累

tissue *(paper)* *n.* dzǐ-jin 纸巾

to *prep.* dáw 到

toad *n.* lá-geq-bo, lá-sï-geq, lá-ha-mo 癞蛤蟆

toast *(salute to health, happiness, etc.)* gòe•bàe 干杯 *(v.o., interj.)*; *(brown with heat)* hòng 烘

today *t.n.* jìn-dzaw(-dzï) 今天

toe *n.* jiāq-jiq-d'eu, jiāq-dzï-d'eu 脚趾

together *adv.* yīq-d'aw 一起

toilet *n.* *(room: water closet)* tsǐ-su(-gae) 厕所; *(commode)* mó-d'ong 马桶, tsèu-sï-mo-d'ong 抽水马桶

toilet paper *n.* tsàw-dzï 草纸, jüóe-d'ong-dzï 卷筒纸、手纸

tolerance *n.* liã-chi, chí-liã 气量

tomato *n.* fàe-g'a 西红柿

tomorrow *t.n.* mín-dzaw(-dzï), mén-dzaw(-dzï) 明天

tongs *n.* láw-hu-j'i 钳子

tongue *n.* zeq-d'eu 舌头

too *adv.* tēq, tēq-saq 太

tooth *n.* ngá-tsï, ngá-dzï 牙齿

toothbrush *n.* ngá-seq 牙刷

toothpaste *n.* ngá-gaw 牙膏

top *l.n.* zǎw-d'eu 上头, zǎw-mi 上面, gàw-d'eu

torso *n.* sèn-bae 躯干

tortoise *n.* wù-jü 乌龟

toss *v.* g'uáe, dōq 扔

tough *adj. (not tender)* láw 老; *(~ but pliable)* nín 韧

tour *v.* 'yéu 游, lǘ-'yeu 旅游

toward *prep.* dáe 对, záw 朝, mǎw, 'wǎw 往

towel *n.* máw-jin 毛巾

towel rack *n.* máw-jin-ga 毛巾架

town *n.* dzén 镇

toy *n.* b'eq-shiǎ-goe 玩具

track *n.* guáe-d'aw, guàe-d'aw 轨道

track and field *n.* d'í-jin 田径

trade *n. (buying and selling)* má-ma 买卖; *(profession)* h'ǎw-dǎw 行当

trademark *n.* sǎw-biaw 商标

traditional characters *(non-simplified)* *n.* váe-ti-zǐ 繁体字, d'ú-shia-zǐ

traffic (jam) *n.* sēq•tsuò 堵车 *(v.o)*

traffic light *n.* h'óng-loq-den 红绿灯

train *n.* hú-tsuo 火车

train station *n.* hú-tsuo-zae 火车站

transcribe *v.* tsàw 抄

transmit *v.* zóe 传

transportation *n.* jiàw-tong 交通

travel *v.* lǘ-h'in 旅行

traveller's check *n.* lǘ-h'in dzǐ-piaw 旅行支票

tray *n.* b'óe(-dzǐ) 盘子

treat *(~ someone to a meal, show, etc.)* *v.* chín•kāq 请客 *(v.o.)*

tree *n.* zǐ 树

tremble *v.* fāq•déu 发抖, déu 抖, j'ín 哆嗦

trial marriage *n.* sǐ-huen 试婚 *(v.o)*

tricycle pedicab *n.* sàe-len-tsuo 三轮车

trip *v.* báe 绊

tripod *n.* sàe-jiaq-ga 三脚架

troublesome *adj.* mó-vae 麻烦

truck *n.* ká-tsuo 卡车

true *adj.* dzèn 真

truly *adv.* dzèn-zǐ 真是

trunk *n.* shiǎ-dzǐ 箱子

trust *v.* shiǎ-shin 相信

try *v.* sǐ-sǐ-koe 试试看

T-shirt *n.* tì-shüeq-sae T恤衫

Tuesday *t.n.* lí-ba-ni 礼拜二, lí-ba-liã

tumor *n.* dzóng-lieu 肿瘤

tunnel *n.* zóe-d'aw 隧道

turn *(~ a corner)* *v.* dzóe-wae 转弯 *(v.o.)*

turtle *n.* jiãq-ñg 鳖, wù-jü 乌龟

tweezers *n.* niq-dzǐ-j'i 镊子

twelve *num.* zeq-ni 十二

twenty *num.* niáe, náe 二十 (廿)

twice *adv.* liǎ-tsǐ 两次 *(n.m.)*

twins *n.* sǎ-baw-tae 双胞胎

twist *v.* liq 捩

two *num.* liǎ 两, ní, 'ér 二

typhoon *n.* d'áe-fong 台风

U

ugly *adj.* náe-koe 难看

umbilical cord *n.* zyí-da 脐带

umbrella *n.* sáe, 'yǎ-sae 雨伞

uncle *n. (father's elder brother)* bāq-baq, bāq-vu 伯伯; *(father's younger brother)* sōq-soq, sōq-vu 叔叔; *(husband of father's sister)* gù-fu 姑父; *(husband of mother's sister)* 'yí-fu 姨夫; *(mother's brother)* j'iéu-j'ieu, niǎ-j'ieu 舅舅

uncomfortable *adj.* veq-sǐ-voq 不舒服, wēq, wēq-seq 烦闷

underground *n.* d'í-h'uo(-d'eu), d'í-di-h'uo 地下

undershirt *n.* h'óe-sae 汗衫

underside *l.n.* h'uó-d'eu 下头, h'uó-mi 下面, h'uó-di(-d'eu)

understand *v.* dóng 懂

underwear *n.* náe-yi 内衣

undress *v.* tēq•yì-zāw 脱衣裳 *(v.o.)*

unisex *adj.* dzòng-shin-seq-'yã 中性式样

university *n.* d'á-h'oq 大学

unless *prep.* zǐ-fi 除非

unlucky *adj.* dáw•máe 倒霉, huàe-chi 晦气

unobstructed *adj.* tòng 通

unpopular *adj.* lǎ-men 冷门

untie *v.* g'á 解开

UPC symbol *n.* d'iáw-h'in-mo 条形码

upset *adj.* àw-naw 懊恼
upset stomach *n.* fáe•'wáe 反胃 *(v.o)*
upstairs *n.* léu-lāw 楼上
urge *v.* chüóe 劝
urinate *v.* shiáw-b'i 小便, tsāq•sǐ, zá•sǐ *(v.o.)*
urine *n.* sǐ 尿水
us *prn.* āq-laq, āq-la 我们
USB drive *n.* ièu-b'oe U 盘
use *v.* 'yóng 用; *n.* 'yóng-d'eu 用处
usually *adv.* b'ín-zā 平常

V

vacant room *n.* kóng-vāw-gae 空房间
vacation *n.* gá, jiá 假; **take a ~** fǎw•jiá 放假
valley *n.* sàe-goq 山谷
valuable *adj.* zeq•d'óng-d'i 值钱
van *n.* mí-baw-tsuo 面包车
variation *n.* huò-'yā 花样, huò-d'eu
vase *n.* huò-b'in 花瓶
vasectomy *n.* jīq-dzaq 结扎 *(v.)*
Vaseline *n.* váe-zǐ-lin 凡士林
vegetable *n.* tsáe 菜, sù-tsae 蔬菜
vegetable dish *n.* sú-tsae 素菜
vegetable knife *n.* b'oq-daw, chīq-tsae-daw, tsáe-daw 菜刀
vegetable oil *n.* tsáe-'yeu 菜油
vegetable peeler *n.* guò-b'aw 瓜刨
vegetarian *n.* chīq-su-nin 吃素的人
vegetarian food *n.* sú-tsae 素菜, b'aq-zeq 素食
velvet *n.* nióng 绒
very *adv.* màe, jiàw-guae, sāq, zyiá-chi, láw 很
vest *n.* báe-shin 背心, mó-gaq
vexed *adj.* váe-naw 烦恼
video game *n.* d'í-naw-yeu-shi 电脑游戏, d'í-d'ong-yeu-shi 电动游戏
video gaming *v.* dǎ•'yéu-shi-ji 打游戏机
Vietnam *l.n.* 'Yüeq-noe 越南
Vietnamese *n.* *(language)* 'Yüeq-noe-h'ae-h'uo 越南话; *(people)* 'Yüeq-noe-nin 越南人
view *n.* fòng-guāw 风光

vigor *n.* jín-d'eu 劲头; zén-sï 精力

vigorous *(as a flame or plants) adj.* 'yǎw, 'wǎw 旺

village *n.* tsèn-dzǎ 村庄

vinegar *n.* tsú 醋

violin *n.* shiáw-d'i-j'in 小提琴, váe-ou-lin

visit *v.* kóe 看, kóe-mǎw 看望; ~ **a grave** zǎw•vén 上坟 扫墓 *(v.o.)*

vitamin *n.* ví-ta-min 维生素、维他命

voice *n.* sèn-yin 声音

volleyball *n.* b'á-j'ieu 排球

vulgar *adj.* tsù-su 粗俗

W

wages *n.* gòng-d'i, gòng-dzï 工资

waist *n* yàw 腰

wait *v.* dén 等, h'éu 侯

waiter/waitress *n.* voq-h'u-'yüoe 服务员

wake up *v., v.c.* shín 醒, gáw, gáw-dzoe-lae 醒来; ~ **someone** jiáw-gaw 叫醒

walk *v.* dzéu 走, b'áw 跑

wall *n.* zyiǎ-biq 墙壁, zyiǎ-d'eu

wallet *n.* b'í-gaq-dzï 皮夹子

walnut *n.* b'ú-d'aw 核桃

want *v.* yáw 要

want to *(~ do something) aux.* shiǎ 想

warm *adj.* nóe 暖, nóe-niq

wasabi *n.* g'á-meq 芥末

wash *v.* d'á 洗

washbasin *n.* mí-b'en 脸盆

washing machine *n.* d'á-yi-zǎw-ji, shí-yi-ji 洗衣机

wasp *n.* h'ú-fong 蚂蜂

waste *v.* lǎw-fi 浪费, dāq-teq 耽误

wasteful *adj.* lǎw-fi 浪费

watch *v. (look at)* kóe 看; *n. (timepiece)* séu-biaw 手表, biáw 表

water *n.* sḯ 水; *v.* jiàw 浇

water buffalo *n.* sḯ-nieu 水牛

water caltrop *n.* lín, lín-goq 菱角

water chestnut *n.* b'eq-zyi, b'iq-zyi 荸荠, d'í-liq

water shield *(a vegetable) n.* zén-tsae 莼菜

water spinach *n.* óng-tsae, òng-tsae 空心菜
waterfall *n.* b'oq-bu, b'áw-bu 瀑布
watermelon *n.* shì-guo 西瓜
wave *n.* lǎw-d'eu 波浪
wax paper *n.* laq-dzǐ 蜡纸
way *n.* b'áe-faq 办法, fāq-dzǐ 法子
we *prn.* āq-laq, āq-la 我们
weak *adj.* zaq 弱
wean *v.* d'óe•ná 断奶, gāq•ná *(v.o.)*
wear *v. (clothing)* tsòe 穿, dzāq; *(accessories)* dá 戴
weary *adj.* táe 疲乏
weather *n.* tì-chi 天气
wedding dress *n.* huèn-suo 婚纱
Wednesday *t.n.* lí-ba-sae 礼拜三
week *n.* lí-ba 礼拜
weekend *n.* dzèu-meq 周末
weep *v.* kōq 哭, liéu•ngáe-li 流眼泪, loq•ngáe-li
weight *n.* vén-liǎ 重量
weird *adj.* j'í-gua 奇怪, 'yéu-jin
welcome *v.* huòe-nin 欢迎
well *n.* jín 井
well-behaved *adj.* guà 乖
west *l.n.* shì 西, shì-mi, shì-d'eu 西边
Western food *n.* shì-tsoe 西餐
wet *adj.* sāq, sēq 湿
wet nurse *n.* ná-ma 奶妈
whale *n.* j'ín-ñg 鲸鱼
what *prn.* sá, sá-g'eq, sá-h'eq 什么
wheat *n.* shiáw-maq 小麦
wheat gluten *n.* mí-jin 面筋
wheel *n.* lén-b'oe 轮子
when *(what time) prn.* sá•zén-guǎw, jí-zǐ, sá-g'eq•zén-guǎw 什么时候、什么时间
where *(what place) adv.* h'á-li, h'á-li-daq, sá•d'í-fǎw 哪儿、什么地方 *(prn.)*
which *prn., adj.* h'á-li- 哪 *(prn., pfx.)*; ~ **one** h'á-li-(yiq-)g'eq, h'á-li-(yiq-)h'eq 哪个
whirlwind *n.* zyí-fong 旋风
whiskers *n.* h'ú-su 胡须, ngá-su, h'ú-dzǐ
whistle *n.* jiáw-bi, jiáw-dzǐ 哨子
whistling kettle *n.* zǐ-min-h'u 自鸣壶

white *adj.* b'aq 白; *(n.)* b'aq-seq 白色
who *(what person) prn.* sá-nin 谁
whole day *n.* dzén-niq, dzén-ti 整天
whole wheat bread *n.* zyí-maq-mi-baw 全麦面包
wholesale *n.* pì-faq 批发
whose *prn.* sá-nin-g'eq, sá-nin-h'eq 谁的
why *adv., conj.* 'wáe-sa, sá•gǎw-jieu 为什么、什么
　原因 *(prn.)*
wide *adj.* kuēq 宽
widow *n.* guá-vu 寡妇, gù-sǎ
wife *n.* chì-dzï 妻子, tà-ta 太太, láw-b'u 老婆; *(polite)*
　fù-nin 夫人
wig *n.* gá-faq 假发
wild goose *n.* d'á-'yi 大雁
will *aux.* yáw 要
win *v.* 'yín 赢
wind *n.* fòng 风
windbreaker *n.* fòng-yi 风衣
window *n.* tsǎw, tsǎw-men 窗子; *(ticket, teller's, etc.)*
　tsǎw-keu 窗口
window curtain *n.* tsǎw-li 窗帘
window screens *n* suò-tsǎw 纱窗
window shopping *n.* d'ǎw•mó-lu, āq•mó-lu 逛街 *(v.o)*
windowsill *n.* tsǎw-d'ae 窗台, tsǎw-b'oe
windy *adj.* chí•fòng, guāq•fòng 刮风, fāq•fòng *(v.o.)*
wine *n. (generic liquor)* jiéu 酒; *(made from grapes)*
　b'ú-d'aw-jieu 葡萄酒
wing *n.* jí-kaq, tsǐ-bǎw 翅膀
winter *n.* dòng-ti 冬天, lǎ-ti
winter melon *n.* dòng-guo 冬瓜
winter vacation *n.* h'óe-ga, h'óe-jia 寒假
wipe *v.* kà 揩、擦
wish *v.* shì-h'uǎw 希望
with *prep.* tēq, dēq, tēq-dzï, dēq-dzï, gàw, gáw, bǎw
　和、跟
witness *n.* dzén-nin 证人
wok *n.* h'oq-dzï, gù-dzï 锅
wolf *n.* lǎw 狼
woman *n.* nǔ-nin(-ga) 女人（家）, nǔ-g'eq 女的
wonton *n.* 'wén-d'en 馄饨
wood *n.* moq-d'eu 木头**

woodpecker *n.* dzōq-moq-niaw 啄木鸟
woodworker *n.* moq-gong 木工
wool serge *n.* b'iq-ji 哔叽
woolen fabric *n.* máw-hu 毛料
work *n.* sǎ-h'ueq 工作; *(at a job)* *v., n.* gòng-dzoq 工作
work unit *n.* dàe-'wae 单位
worker *n.* nín-gong 人工, gòng-nin 工人
workshop *n.* gòng-zǎ 工场, tsuò-gae 车间
world *n.* sǐ-ga 世界
worry *v.* dàe-shin 担心 *(v.o.)*
worship *v.* dzú•lí-ba 做礼拜 *(v.o)*; ~ **Buddha** bá•veq
拜佛
worth *adj., n.* zeq 值 *(v.)*
worthwhile *adj.* gēq-soe 合算, zeq-deq 值得
wrap *v.* bàw 包, gú 裹, dǎ-baw 打包
wrench *n.* bàe-d'eu, bàe-seu 扳手
wrist *n.* séu-wae 手腕
write *v.* shiá 写, shiá•zǐ 写字
writing brush *n.* máw-biq 毛笔, meq-biq
wrong *adj.* tsù, tsuò 错

Y

yawn *n.* huò-shi 哈欠; *v.o.* dǎ•huò-shi 打哈欠
year *n.* ní 年
yellow *adj.* h'uǎw 黄; *n.* h'uǎw-seq 黄色
yesterday *t.n.* zoq-niq, zuó-niq, zoq-ti, zuó-ti 昨天
yogurt *n.* sòe-na 酸奶
yolk *n.* d'áe-huāw 蛋黄
you *prn.* *(singular)* nóng 你; *(plural)* ná 你们
young *adj.* ní-chin 年轻, h'éu-sǎ
young lady *n.* shiáw-jia 小姐
younger generation *n.* shiáw-bae 晚辈
you're welcome! *interj.* viáw zyiá! 不谢!, viáw kāq-
chi! 别客气！
yours *prn.* *(singular)* nóng-g'eq, nóng-eq 你的;
(plural) ná-g'eq, ná-eq 你们的
yuppie *n., adj.* shiáw-dzǐ 小资

Z

zero *num.* lín 零
zip code *n.* 'yéu-dzen bì-mo 邮政编码
zipper *n.* là-li 拉练
zone *n.* chù 区
zoo *n.* d'óng-veq-'yüoe 动物园

SHANGHAINESE–ENGLISH DICTIONARY

with Mandarin glosses in Chinese Characters

A

á 矮 *adj.* short *(not tall)*

à 挨、轮着 *v.* take turns, one after the other

à-sǐ-pi-lin 阿斯匹林 *n.* aspirin

à-'yi 阿姨 *n.* Aunt *(form of address)*, Auntie

à-zaq 轮到 *v.* be one's turn

ǎ-d'aw 樱桃 *n.* cherry, *Alt.:* **yìn-d'aw**

ǎ-gu 鹦鹉 *n.* parrot

áe 晚 *adj.* late

áe 爱 *n., v.* love

áe-shiq(-shi) 一会儿 *adv.* in a short while, momentarily, *Alt.:* **áe-shiq-di, áe-yiq-shiq**

áe-shiq-h'uáe 待会儿见 *interj.* see you later!

àe 还 *adv.* still, *Alt.:* **h'áe, h'uáe**

àe 那 *prn.pfx.* that, *Alt.:* **yì, àe-mi**

àe-ae-dzï AA制 *n.* go dutch, share the cost equally *(as of a meal)*

àe-d'eu 那儿 *prn.* there, *Alt.:* **yì-mi, hàe-d'eu, àe-mi**

àe-g'eq 那个 *prn.* that, *Alt.:* **àe-eq, yì-g'eq, yì-eq**

àe-ngae 那些 *prn.* those, *Alt.:* **yì-di**

àe-zï 还是 *conj.* or *(used in questions)*; *adv.* had better, *Alt.:* **h'áe-zï, h'uáe-zï**

āq 阿 *ptl. (question infix that turns a sentence into a yes-no question)*; **āq-'yeu** 阿有 *adv.* is there?, do/does ... have ...?; **āq-zï** 阿是 *adv.* is ...?

āq 压 *v.* press upon, push down on

āq(-dzï) 鸭子 *n.* duck; ~ **-bāw** 鸭子翅 duck wing; ~ **-d'ae** 鸭子蛋 *n.* duck egg; ~ **-dzen** 鸭子胗 *n.* duck gizzard

āq-laq 我们 *prn.* us, we, *Alt.:* **āq-la**

áw 拗 *v.* bend and break

Áw-d'a-li-ya 澳大利亚 *n.* Australia

Áw-d'a-li-ya-nin 澳大利亚人 *n.* Australian

áw-d'oe 拗断 *v.* break off

áw-miaw 奥妙 *adj.* subtle, mysterious

àw 凹 *adj.* concave, dented, sunken

àw-law 懊悔 *adj.* remorseful, regretful

àw-naw 懊恼 *adj.* upset, annoyed

àw-sāw 懊丧 *adj.* despondent, dejected, *Alt.:* **óng-dzong**

B′

b'á 排 *m.w. for rows, Alt.*: **d'á**

b'á 牌 *n.* card *(game)*

b'á-d'ae 排队 *v.* line up, queue up, stand in line

b'á-dzï 牌子 *n.* tag, label, brand

b'á-j'ieu 排球 *n.* volleyball

b'ǎ 坛子 *n.* earthen jar

b'ǎ 蚌 *n.* freshwater clam, *Alt.*: **h'ú-b'ã**

b'ǎ 碰 *v.* bump into, bump together; ~ •**d'éu** 碰头 *v.o.* meet, get together

b'ǎ•bīq 碰壁 *v.o.* run into a wall, encounter difficulties, be rebuffed

b'ǎ-chiaw 碰巧 *adv.* coincidentally; *v.o.* happen by chance

b'ǎ-din 最高 *ph.* no price higher than

b'ǎ-(veq-)b'ã 经常 *adv.* inevitably, usually, *Alt.*: **d'óng-(veq-)d'ong** 动不动

b'ǎ-'yeu 朋友 *n.* friend

b'áe 爿 *m.w. for shops, stores, fields*

b'áe 爬 *v.* crawl

b'áe 背 *v.* memorize, recite from memory

b'áe-dzï 痱子 *n.* prickly heat, heat rash

b'áe-faq 办法 *n.* way, means, practical method

b'áe-gen 培根 *n.* bacon

b'áe-gueq 排骨 *n.* pork ribs

b'aq 白 *adj.* white

b'aq 拔 *v.* pull up, pull out, draw out

b'aq(-b'aq) 白白地 *adv.* for nothing, in vain

b'aq-kae-sï 白开水 *n.* plain boiled water

b'aq-mi-vae 米饭、白饭 *n.* plain cooked rice

b'aq-mo-ni 白蚁 *n.* termite

b'aq-seq 白色 *n.* white

b'aq-teq(-'yeu) 黄油 *n.* butter

b'aq-ti 白天 *n.* daytime, *Alt.*: **niq-li(-shiã), niq-li-d'eu**

b'aq-tsae 白菜 *n.* cabbage

b'aq-zeq 白吃 *n.* free meal

b'aq-zeq 素食 *n.* vegetarian food, *Alt.*: **sú-tsae**

b'áw 刨 *n.* carpenter's plane; grater

b'áw 跑 *v.* go, leave; walk; run *(usually in more abstract sense)*

b'áw-bu 瀑布 *n.* waterfall, *Alt.*: **b'oq-bu**

b'áw-bin 刨冰 *n.* shaved ice

b'áw-chi 抱歉 *v.o.* sorry *(adj.)*

b'áw-dzaw 暴躁，急躁 *adj.* irritable, *Alt.*: **jīq-dzaw, jīq-tsaw, b'áw-tsaw**

b'áw-faq-h'u 暴发户 *n.* noveau riche

b'áw-tsuo 跑车 *n.* sports car

b'ăw-b'i 旁边 *l.n.* side, beside, *Alt.*: **bì-d'eu, b'ăw-bi-d'eu**

b'ăw-b'i-hae-d'eu 附近 *l.n.* nearby, vicinity, *Alt.*: **vú-j'in**

b'ăw-bin 冰棍儿 *n.* popsicle, ice pop

b'ăw-d'eu 棍子 *n.* rod, club

b'ăw-guăw 膀胱 *n.* bladder, *Alt.*: **sì-paw**

b'ăw-j'ieu 棒球 *n.* baseball; **~ -maw** 棒球帽 *n.* baseball cap

b'ăw-shiã 棒香 *n.* incense sticks

b'ăw-'wae-zen-guăw 傍晚 *n.* nightfall, *Alt.*: **zyí-'ya-kua**

b'én 笨 *adj.* stupid, *Alt.*: **g'ăw**

b'én-dzï 盆子 *n.* basin

b'eq-d'aw 葡萄 *n.* grape, *Alt.*: **b'u-d'aw**

b'eq-d'eu-kong 鼻孔 *n.* nostril, *Alt.*: **b'iq-kong**

b'eq-shiã(-shiã) 玩儿 *v.* play, have fun, enjoy oneself, *Alt.*: **b'í**

b'eq-shiã-goe 玩具 *n.* toy

b'eq-zyi 荸荠 *n.* water chestnut, *Alt.*: **b'iq-zyi, d'í-liq**

b'í 皮 *n.* skin; *adj.* naughty, mischievous, *Alt.*: **'wóe-b'i** 顽皮, **lá-b'i**

b'í-chi 脾气 *n.* disposition, temperment, *Alt.*: **shín-dzï** 性格

b'í-d'ae 松花蛋 *n.* preserved egg

b'í-d'eu 被子 *n.* quilt

b'í-d'iaw 便条 *n.* note

b'í-da 皮带 *n.* leather belt

b'í-dae 被单 *n.* bedsheets, *Alt.*: **zăw-dae** 床单

b'í-dãw 容易 *adj.* easy, *Alt.*: **'yóng-yi**

b'í-dzï 辫子 *n.* braid, plait

b'í-gaq-dzï 皮夹子 *n.* wallet

b'í-h'a 皮鞋 *n.* leather shoes

b'í-h'a-'yeu 鞋油 *n.* shoe polish

b'í-jieu 啤酒 *n.* beer

b'í-li-di 便利店 *n.* convenience store

b'í-ni 便宜 *adj.* cheap, inexpensive, *Alt.*: **b'í-niq, j'iǎ**

b'í-taw 被套 *n.* quilt cover

b'í-vae 便饭 *n.* simple meal

b'í-'yün 避孕 *n.* birth control

b'í-'yün-taw 避孕套 *n.* condom

b'í-zaw 肥皂 *n.* soap, *Alt.*: **shiǎ-zaw** 香皂

b'í-zaw-fen 洗衣粉 *n.* laundry soap or detergent, *Alt.*:
     d'á-yi-zǎw-fen

b'ín 平 *adj.* level

b'ín 瓶 *m.w. for bottles of things*

b'ín 病 *n.* illness, disease, *Alt.*: **máw-b'in**

b'ín-di-gu 平底锅 *n.* frying pan

b'ín-dzǐ 瓶子 *n.* bottle

b'ín-fong 屏风 *n.* freestanding screen

b'ín-ga 病假 *n.* sick leave

b'ín-gu 苹果 *n.* apple; ~ **-pa** 苹果派 *n.* apple pie

b'ín-shin 平信 *n.* ordinary mail, surface mail

b'ín-vǎw 平房 *n.* one-story house

b'ín-vǎw(-gae) 病房 *n.* hospital room

b'ín-zǎ 平常 *adv.* usually, ordinarily

b'iq 别 *prn.pfx.* other *(prefix used with measure
     words)*, *Alt.*: **b'eq**

b'iq-b'oq 枇杷 *n.* loquat

b'iq-d'eu 鼻子 *n.* nose, *Alt.*: **b'eq-d'eu**

b'iq-dzen 别针 *n.* brooch; safety pin

b'iq-ji 哔叽 *n.* wool serge

b'iq-jiaq 蹩脚 *v.o.* injure or sprain one's leg or foot;
     adj. shoddy, lousy

b'iq•yàw 闪腰 *v.o.* strain or injure one's back, *Alt.*:
     sén•yàw 伤腰

b'íq-zǐ 别墅 *n.* detached house, villa

b'ó 耙子 *n.* rake; 扒 *v.* rake

b'ó-fen 赚(额外的)钱 *n.* earnings made on the side

b'óe 盘 *m.w. for plates of things*

b'óe 躲 *v.* hide *(oneself)*, *Alt.*: **yà**

b'óe 搅拌 *v.* stir, mix, *Alt.*: **d'iáw**

b'óe(-dzǐ) 盘子 *n.* platter, tray

b'óe•hú 盘货 *v.o.* take inventory

b'óng-haw-tsae 茼蒿 *n.* chrysanthemum greens *(a
     type of leafy vegetable)*

b'oq 薄 *adj.* thin *(not thick)*

b'oq 趴 *v.* lie prone

b'oq 缚 *v.* tie up, bind

b'oq-bu 瀑布 *n.* waterfall, *Alt.:* **b'áw-bu**

b'oq-daw 菜刀 *n.* vegetable knife, *Alt.:* **chīq-tsae-daw, tsáe-daw**

b'oq-keq-shiong 拳击 *n.* boxing

b'ú 部 *m.w. for cars, vehicles*

b'ú-b'u 婆婆 *n.* mother-in-law *(husband's mother)*, *Alt.:* **āq-b'u**

b'ú-d'aw 核桃 *n.* walnut

b'ú-d'aw-jieu 葡萄酒 *n.* wine *(made from grapes)*

b'ú-dzï 本子 *n.* notebook, *Alt.:* **bīq-ji-b'u** 笔记本

b'ú-h'in-ga 步行街 *n.* pedestrian mall

b'ú-hu 薄荷 *n.* peppermint

B

bá 摆 *v.* put, place, *Alt.:* **fǎw** 放

bá-d'u-keu 渡口 *n.* ferry crossing, ford

bá-d'u-zoe 渡船 *n.* ferryboat

bá•ní 拜年 *v.o.* pay a New Year's visit

bá-toq 拜托 *v.* request, beg of

bá•veq 拜佛 *v.o.* worship Buddha

bà 吧 *n.* bar, café

bà-ba 爸爸 *n.* father, *Alt.:* **dià-dia** 爹爹, **láw-ba**

bà-d'ae 吧台 *n.* bar counter

bà-lae-'wu 芭蕾舞 *n.* ballet

bǎ 小河 *n.* creek, stream, *Alt.:* **h'ú-bǎ**

bǎ 绑 *v.* bind, tie up

bǎ-long-lae 合起来 *v.c.* join, merge, combine *(v.)*

báe 页 *m.w. for pages, Alt.:* **'yiq**

báe 绊 *v.* stumble, trip

báe-baw 背包 *n.* knapsack, backpack

báe-d'i 背垫 *n.* back cushion, *Alt.:* **g'áe-sen**

báe-den 板凳 *n.* bench, stool

báe-gong-seq 办公室 *n.* office

báe-h'eu(-d'eu) 背后 *l.n.* rear, the back

báe-jiq-gueq, 背脊骨 *n.* backbone, spine, *Alt.:* **jīq-dzoe-gueq** 脊椎骨

báe-ñg 比目鱼 *n.* flounder, *Alt.:* **niaq-taq-ñg**

báe-seq 板刷 *n.* brush

báe-shin 背心 *n.* vest, *Alt.*: **mó-gaq** 马甲

bàe 杯 *m.w. for cups of things*

bàe 班 *m.w. for flights, trains, etc.*

bàe-d'eu 班次 *n.* flight or train number

bàe-da 背带 *n.* suspenders

bàe-dzï 杯子 *n.* cup, mug, glass

bàe•gá 扳价 *n.* lowest acceptable price

bàe-d'eu 扳手 *n.* wrench, spanner, *Alt.*: **bàe-seu**

bāq 八 *num.* eight

bāq 百 *num.* hundred

bāq 编 *v.* braid, plait; ~•**b'í-dzï** 编辫子 braid one's hair

bāq 擘 *v.* tear open, pull apart

bāq-baq 伯伯 *n.* uncle *(father's elder brother)*, *Alt.*: **bāq-vu**

bāq-gu 八哥 *n.* myna bird

bāq-h'eq 百合 *n.* lily bulbs

bāq-m̃ 伯母 *n.* aunt *(wife of father's elder brother)*, *Alt.*: **bāq-mu**

bāq-seq 八十 *num.* eighty

bāq-'yiq 百页 *n.* layered sheets of dried bean curd

bāq-'yüeq 八月 *t.n.* August, *Alt.*: **bāq-'yoq**

báw 饱 *adj.* full *(after a meal)*, satiated

báw 爆 *v.* explode

báw-bae(-noe) 宝贝 *n.* treasured child

báw-biaw 保镖 *n.* bodyguard, *Alt.*: **jín-'wae-'yüoe** 警卫员

báw-d'ing 保证 *adv.* for sure, absolutely, *Alt.*: **báw-shi**

báw-daq 报答 *v.* requite, repay

báw-dzen 保证 *v.* guarantee

báw-dzï 报纸 *n.* newspaper

báw-h'u 保护 *v.* protect

báw-lin-j'ieu 保龄球 *n.* bowling

báw•mín 报名 *v.o.* sign up *(v.)*

báw-mu 保姆 *n.* housekeeper

báw-'yüeq-'yüoe 保育员 *n.* child-care worker

bàw 包 *v.* wrap; *n.* bag, purse, bundle, package; *m.w. for packages of things*

bàw-gu 包裹 *n.* package, parcel

bàw-gua 包括 *v.* include

bàw-h'oe 包涵 *v.* contain, include

bàw-vãw 包房 *n.* private room

bãw 磅 *m.w.* pounds

bãw-da 绑带 *n.* bandage

bãw-fong-jin 风镜 *n.* goggles, *Alt.*: **vãw-fong-jin**

bãw 和、跟 *prep.* with; and *(conj.)*, *Alt.*: **gàw, gáw, tēq, tēq-dzï, dēq, dēq-dzï**

bãw 帮 *v.* help

bãw-seu 帮手 *n.* assistant, *Alt.*: **tí-seu**

bén 本 *m.w.* for books

bén-ben 笔记本电脑 *n.* notebook computer

bén-d'i 本钱 *n.* capital, principal *(original sum invested)*

bén-di-nin 本地人 *n.* native, a local

bén-lae 本来 *adv.* originally, *Alt.*: **nüóe-lae** 原来 **bén-sã**

bén-zï 本事 *n.* skill, ability

bèn 奔 *v.* run

bēq 被 *prep.* for, to, by *(passive marker)*, *Alt.*: **bēq-laq**

bēq 给 *v.* give

bēq-d'eu 钵儿 *n.* small bowl

bēq-fãw 不妨 *adv.* might as well, can't hurt to, *Alt.*: **veq-fãw**

bēq-gu 不过 *conj.* but, however, *Alt.*: **bïq-gu**

bí•扁 *adj.* flat

bí 遍 *m.w.* for something done from start to finish, whole way through

bí 变 *v.* change, transform

bí 比 *v., prep.* compared to, *Alt.*: **bí-dzï**

bí-baw 皮包 *n.* purse

bí-bo 胳膊 *n.* arm, *Alt.*: **séu-bi-bo** 手臂

bí-d'eu 扁豆 *n.* green beans

bí-fãw 比方 *n.* example; *adv.* for example, *Alt.*: **pí-zï** 譬如

bí-huo 变化 *n.* change

bí-ji-ni 比基尼 *n.* bikini

bí-jiaw 比较 *adv.* comparatively

bí-miq 秘密 *n.* secret, *Alt.*: **mí-miq**

bí•ngáe-jin 闭眼 *v.o.* close one's eyes

bí•shí-faq 变魔术 *v.o.* perform magic; *n.* magic performance

bí-sae 比赛 *n.* competition; *v.* compete

bí-tsã-dzï 臂肘 *n.* elbow

bì-bi(-d'eu) 边上 *l.n.* edge, rim, side, *Alt.*: **'yí-'yi-d'eu** 沿儿, **bì-lãw**

bì-foq 蝙蝠 *n.* bat *(the animal)*

biáw+*(sibling relation)* 表+ *pfx.* cousin *(with a different surname)*; ~ **(aq-)d'i** 表弟 younger male cousin; ~ **(aq-)jia** 表姐 elder female cousin; ~ **(aq-)mae** 表妹 younger female cousin; ~ **ji-mae** 表姐妹 female cousins; ~ **shiong** 表兄 elder male cousin, *Alt.*: ~ **(aq-)gu**; ~ **shiong-d'i** 表兄弟 male cousins

biàw-jin 傲慢 *adj.* arrogant, haughty, conceited

biàw-vãw 标准房间 *n.* standard room

biàw-dzï 标致 *adj.* lovely, attractive

bín 柄 *n.* handle, shank, shaft

bín 饼 *n.* pancake, crepe

bín-goe 饼干 *n.* cookie, cracker

bìn 冰 *n., adj.* ice

bìn-b'aw 冰雹 *n.* hailstone

bìn-d'ãw 冰糖 *n.* rock sugar, sugar crystals

bìn-guoe 宾馆 *n.* guesthouse

bìn-h'ong-zuo 冰红茶 *n.* iced tea

bìn-j'i-lin 冰淇淋 *n.* ice cream

bìn-ni-guoe 殡仪馆 *n.* funeral home

bìn-shiã 傧相 *n.* best man; bridesmaid

bìn-shiã 冰箱 *n.* refrigerator, ice box

bīq 瘪 *adj.* shriveled, deflated

bīq 笔 *n.* pen, pencil, writing brush; *m.w. for sum of money*

bīq-d'ong 笔筒 *n.* pen container

bīq-h'eq 别的 *prn.* another, other, different one

bīq-h'uaq 笔画 *n.* strokes of Chinese characters

bīq-hu 壁虎 *n.* house lizard

bīq-ji 笔记 *n.* notes

bīq-niq 毕业 *v.o.* graduate *(v.)*

bīq-niq-dzen-sï 毕业证书 *n.* diploma

bīq-shü 必须 *adv.* must

bīq-zeq 一直 *adj.* straight *(ahead)*

bó 把 *m.w. for knives, tools (that are held in the hand)*

bó•maq 把脉 *v.o.* take the pulse, *Alt*: **dāq•maq**

bò 疤 *n.* scar

bò-deu 栲栳(小的) *n.* bamboo or wicker basket
  (small), Alt.: **sàe-bo**

bò-jiq 勤俭 *adj.* hardworking and thrifty, *Alt.:* **j'ín-j'i**

bò-jiq 巴结 *v.* play up to, fawn on

bò-mãw 盼望 *v.* long for, look forward to

bò-seu 把手 *n.* handle, grip, knob, *Alt.:* **bó-seu**

bò-veq-deq 巴不得 *v.c.* anxious to, *Alt.:* **bò-veq-dzaq-
  deq, bò-veq-nen-geu**

Bò-shi 巴西 *n.* Brazil

bóe 半 *num.* half

bóe-niq 半天 *n.* half a day, a long time, *Alt.:* **bóe-ti**

bóe-'ya 半夜 *n.* midnight, middle of the night

bòe 搬 *v.* move *(something)*

bòe•(nín-)gà 搬家 *v.* move *(to a new home), Alt.:*
  bòe•jià

bōq 剥 *v.* peel *(with fingers)*

Bōq-jin 北京 *n.* Běijīng

bōq-veq-guoe 博物馆 *n.* museum

bōq 北 *l.n.* north, north side, *Alt:* **bōq-mi** 北边

bōq-deu-shin 北斗星 *n.* big dipper

bōq•min 拼命 *v.o.* go all out in intense effort, risk
  one's life

bú 布 *n.* cloth

bú 补 *v.* patch

bú-din 补丁 *n.* patch

bú-din 布丁 *n.* pudding

bù-li 玻璃 *n.* glass; ~ **-bae** 玻璃杯 glass *(for drinking)*;
  ~ **-tsãw** 玻璃窗 glass window

bù-lu-miq 菠萝 *n.* pineapple

bù-tsae 菠菜 *n.* spinach

CH

chí 浅 *adj.* shallow

chí 欠(债) *v.* be in debt, owe money, *Alt.:* **kóng•d'óng-
  d'i**

chí 去 *v.* go

chí-d'eu 开头 *v.* begin, start

chí•fòng 刮风 *v.o.* wind blows; windy *(adj.), Alt.:*
  guāq•fòng, fāq•fòng

chí-j'ieu 气球 *n.* balloon

chí-jin 起劲 *adj.* enthusiastic, energetic
chí-lai 起来 *v.* get up
chí-liã 气量 *n.* tolerance, *Alt.*: **liã́-chi**
chí-mo 起码 *adv.* at least
chí-seq 气色 *n.* vitality of one's complexion
chí-sï 汽水 *n.* soft drink, soda pop
chí-tsuo 汽车 *n.* automobile, car
chí•'wú 起雾 *v.o.* fog up, fog arises
chí-'yeu 汽油 *n.* gasoline, *Alt.*: **g'áe-zï-lin**
chí-zï 签字 *v.o.* sign one's name
chí•zuó 沏茶 *v.o.* brew tea, *Alt.*: **páw•zuó**
chì 蛆 *n.* maggot
chì 千 *num.* thousand
chì 欺 *v.* deceive, cheat
chì-dzï, 妻子 *n.* wife, *Alt.*: **tà-ta** 太太, **láw-b'u** 老婆
chì-ji 惦记、挂念 *v.* worry about, be concerned for
chì-jin-din 千斤顶 *n.* jack *(lifting device)*, *Alt.*: **āq-veq-saq**
chì-men 气闷 *adj.* stifling, suffocating, *Alt.*: **chí-men**
chì-mi 气味怪、难闻 *adj.* smelly, malodorous, *Alt.*: **chí-tsï**
chì-shü 谦虚 *adj.* humble, modest
chì-sï *n.* cheese, *Alt.*: **ná-loq** 奶酪
chì-vu 欺负 *v.* tease, pick on, take advantage of
chì-'yün 均匀 *adj.* even, well-distributed
chiá 歪 *adj.* crooked, askew, *Alt.*: **wàe, huà**
chiá 斜 *adj.* slanting, oblique, *Alt.*: **zyiá**
chiá-dae-gu 斜对面 *l.n.* diagonally opposite *(adj.)*, *Alt.*: **zyiá-dae-mi, h'uã́-zaq-goq**
chiã́ 抢 *v.* snatch, rob, grab
chiã̀-d'iaw 腔调 *n.* accent, sound of one's voice
chiáw 翘 *v.* stick up, bend upwards, warp
chiáw-dzï-bo 噘嘴 *v.o.* pout one's lips
chiáw•kú 逃课 *v.o.* skip class
chíaw-men 窍门 *n.* key to a problem, trick to success
chiàw-jiaq 跛足、瘸 *v.o.* lame *(adj.)*
chiàw-keq-liq 巧克力 *n.* chocolate
chièu-law-hu 秋老虎 *n.* hot autumn weather
chièu-ti 秋天 *n.* autumn, fall
chín 请 *v.* invite; *interj.* please
chín 按 *v.* press

chín•gá 请假 *v.o.* request leave

chín•kāq 请客 *v.o.* treat *(someone to a meal, show, etc.)*

chín-dzoq 庆祝 *v.* celebrate

chín-tiq 请帖 *n.* invitation

chìn 清 *adj.* clear

chìn 青 *adj.* greenish-blue, bluish-green, nature's greens and blues

chìn 轻 *adj.* light *(not heavy)*

chìn-(sǐ-)tāw 清汤 *n.* broth

chìn-dae 清单 *n.* account statement; detailed list

chìn-dzaw(-zen) 清晨 *n.* daybreak

chìn-ga 亲家 *n.* relatives by marriage

chìn-guae 轻轨 *n.* light rail transit, LRT

chìn-jiq-gong 清洁工 *n.* custodian, street cleaner

chìn-jüoe 亲戚 *n.* relatives

chìn-niq 亲热 *adj.* affectionate, intimate, warm

chìn-sǎw 清爽 *adj.* clean, clear, fresh

chìn-shiǎ-ji 清香剂 *n.* air freshener

chìn-song 轻松 *adj.* relaxed

chìn-tsae 青菜 *n.* green vegetables

chìn-tsaw 青草 *n.* green grass

chìn-tsen-lae 青春痘 *n.* acne

chìn-wo 青蛙 *n.* frog, *Alt.*: **d'í-ji** 田鸡

chīq 七 *num.* seven

chīq 吃、喝 *v.* eat; drink; smoke; ~ **•váe** 吃饭 eat a meal; ~ **•zuó** 喝茶 drink tea; ~ **•láw-jieu** 喝酒 drink wine or spirits

chīq 切 *v.* slice, cut

chīq•chǔ 吃亏 *v.* suffer loss, lose out, *Alt.*: **chīq•kuàe**

chīq-gae 乞丐 *n.* beggar, *Alt.*: **gáw-huo-dzǐ** 叫花子

chīq-j'ioq 饭局 *n.* dinner engagement

chīq-jin 吃劲 *adj.* require effort, a strain

chīq-keu *n.* flavor, taste, *Alt.*: **dzǐ-mi** 滋味

chīq-liq 累 *adj.* tired, weary; strenuous

chīq•ná 吃奶 *v.o.* suckle *(v.)*

chīq-seq 七十 *num.* seventy

chīq•shí-jieu 吃喜酒 *v.o.* attend a wedding banquet

chīq-shiǎ 吃香、受欢迎 *adj.* popular

chīq•shiǎ-yi 吸烟 *v.o.* smoke cigarettes

chīq•sú 吃素 *v.o.* eat only vegetarian food

chīq-su-nin 吃素的人 *n.* vegetarian

chīq-veq-dzen 确不准 *v.c.* cannot be sure

chīq-veq-kae 吃不开 *v.c.* unpopular *(adj.)*

chīq-veq-shiaw 吃不消 *v.c.* unable to stand, cannot bear, *Alt.*: **h'ǎw-veq-loq**

chīq-'yüeq 七月 *t.n.* July, *Alt.*: **chīq-'yoq**

chǔ 美、好看 *adj.* pretty

chǔ-ni(-dzǐ) 去年 *t.n.* last year, *Alt.*: **j'iéu-ni(-dzǐ)**

chǔ 区 *n.* zone

chüēq 曲 *adj.* curved, angled, crooked, *Alt.*: **chiōq**

chüēq 却 *adv.* however

chüēq 缺 *v.* lack, be short of, *Alt.*: **chiōq**

chüēq-zeq 确实 *adv.* assuredly, definitely, *Alt.*: **chiōq-zeq**

chüēq-zoe 蚯蚓 *n.* earthworm, *Alt.*: **chiōq-zoe, chiéu-h'in, bīq-shi**

chüóe 劝 *v.* urge, persuade, exhort

chüòe 圈 *n.* circle; *v.*encircle, draw a circle

D'

d'á 洗 *v.* wash; ~ •séu 洗手 wash one's hands; ~ •d'éu (-faq) 洗头(发) wash hair; ~ •ì-zā 洗衣服 wash clothing; ~ sǎ-na 洗桑拿 take a sauna bath

d'á-b'i 大便 *v.o.* defecate, *Alt.*: **tsāq•wú, zá•wú**

d'á-ba 大巴 *n.* large bus, coach

d'á-baq 大伯子 *n.* brother-in-law *(husband's elder brother)*, *Alt.*: **d'ú-baq**

d'á-d'aw 大道 *n.* boulevard

d'á-d'eu-gaw 洗发乳 *n.* shampoo

d'á-ga 大家 *prn.* everyone

d'á-gae 大概 *adv.* probably

d'á-gu-dzǐ 大姑子 *n.* sister-in-law *(husband's older sister)*

d'á-h'oq 大学 *n.* college, university

d'á-h'uo 大厦 *n.* mansion, tall building, *Alt.*: **d'á-shia**

d'á-j'ieu-dzǐ 大舅子 *n.* brother-in-law *(wife's older brother)*

d'á-maq 大麦 *n.* barley

d'á-shin-hu *n.* imitation goods, pirated products, *Alt.*: **máw-b'a-hu** 冒牌货

d'á-soe 大蒜 *n.* garlic

d'á-woe-ji 洗碗机 *n.* dishwasher

d'á-'yi 大雁 *n.* wild goose

d'á-'yi-dzï 大姨子 *n.* sister-in-law *(wife's elder sister)*

d'á•'yoq 洗澡 *v.o.* bathe, take a bath

d'á-'yoq-gae 洗澡间 *n.* bathroom, *Alt.:* **'yoq-gae**

d'á-yaq 大约 *adv.* approximately, *Alt.:* **d'á-yaq-moq (-dzoq)**

d'á-yi 大衣 *n.* overcoat

d'áe 抬 *v.* carry *(something heavy together with someone)*

d'áe 淡 *adj.* diluted, thin, weak; insipid, bland, tasteless, not salted; light *(color)*

d'áe 痰 *n.* phlegm

d'áe 队 *n.* team; line, queue

d'áe 代 *prep.* for, on behalf of

d'áe 谈 *v.* talk, chat

d'áe-bu 桌布 *n.* tablecloth

d'áe-d'ae 袋子 *n.* bag, sack

d'áe-d'eu 台头 *n.* payee, recipient *(of a check)*

d'áe-den 台灯 *n.* table lamp

d'áe-dzï 弹子 *n.* marbles

d'áe-dzï 桌子 *n.* table

d'áe-fong 台风 *n.* typhoon

d'áe-ga 台阶 *n.* steps, *Alt.:* **d'áe-jia, gà-'yi-zaq**

d'áe-gaw 蛋糕 *n.* cake *(Western style)*

d'áe-h'uãw 弹簧 *n.* spring *(mechanical)*

d'áe-h'uoe 兑换 *v.* exchange, change, convert, *Alt.:* **d'iáw** 调换

d'áe-h'uoe-liq 兑换率 *n.* exchange rate

d'áe•lí-ae 谈恋爱 *v.o.* court, woo, *Alt.:* **d'áe•b'ã́-'yeu, d'áe-kaw-d'in**

d'áe-ta 蛋挞 *n.* egg custard tart

d'aq 踏、踩 *v.* step on

d'aq-nin 高手 *n.* ace, expert

d'áw 稻 *n.* rice plant

d'áw 逃 *v.* escape, flee

d'áw 淘 *v.* rinse *(by swishing in a container)*

d'áw-d'i 地道 *adj.* authentic, typical

d'áw-d'i 稻田 *n.* rice paddy

d'áw-dzï 桃子 *n.* peach *(fruit)*

d'áw-h'ong-seq 桃红色 *n.* peach *(color)*

d'áw-jiaw 道教 *n.* Daoism, Taoism

d'áw-li 道理 *n.* rationality, explanation

d'áw-zï 道士 *n.* Daoist, Taoist

d'ǎw 糖 *n.* sugar, candy

d'ǎw 逛 *v.* stroll, ramble about

d'ǎw+(sibling relation) 堂+ *pfx.* cousin (with the same surname); ~ **aq-jia** 堂姐 elder female cousin; ~ **d'i** 堂弟 younger male cousin; ~ **mae** 堂妹 younger female cousin; ~ **shiong** 堂兄 elder male cousin, *Alt.*: ~ **aq-gu**; ~ **shiong-d'i** 堂兄弟 male cousins

d'ǎw-gu-di 糖果店 *n.* candy shop

d'ǎw-lǎw 螳螂 *n.* mantis

d'ǎw•mó-lu 逛街 *v.o.* window shopping (n.), *Alt.*: **āq•mó-lu**

d'én 钝 *adj.* blunt, dull

d'én 腾 *v.* clear a space, make room or time for

d'eq 凸 *adj.* protruding, convex; *v.* protrude

d'eq 这 *prn. pfx.* this, *Alt.*: **d'iq, g'eq**

d'eq 叠 *v.* fold; pile up, *Alt.*: **d'iq**

d'eq-b'iq 特别 *adv.* especially

d'eq-daq(-li) 这儿 *prn.* here, *Alt.*: **g'eq-d'eu, g'eq-daq(-li), g'eq-daq-kuae, d'iq-daq**

d'eq-di 这些、这点 *prn.* these, *Alt.*: **g'eq-ngae, g'eq-di, d'iq-ngae**

d'eq-g'eq 这个 *prn.* this, *Alt.*: **g'eq-g'eq, g'eq-h'eq, d'iq-g'eq**

d'eq-kua 特快 *adj.* special express; ~ **dzòe-d'i** 特快专递 EMS express delivery

d'eq-shiq 现在、这会儿 *prn.* now (adv., conj., n.), *Alt.*: **g'eq-shiq, gēq-shiq, d'iq-shiq**

d'eq-seq-tsae 特色菜 *n.* specialty dishes

d'eq-zoe 突然 *adv.* suddenly

d'éu 豆 *n.* beans

d'éu 头 *n.* head

d'éu 投 *v.* put into, throw into; dive into

d'éu-dzï-pin 豆制品 *n.* bean/soybean products

d'éu-faq 头发 *n.* hair (on the head)

d'éu-gu 头箍 *n.* headband

d'éu-h'u-b'i 豆腐皮 *n.* sheets of bean curd, skin of soy milk

d'éu-h'u 豆腐 *n.* bean curd, tofu, *Alt.*: **d'éu-vu**

d'éu-jiã 豆浆 *n.* soy milk

d'éu-jin 脖子 *n.* neck

d'éu-jin 头巾 *n.* scarf

d'éu-jiq 豆荚 *n.* pod, bean or pea pod, *Alt.*: **jīq** 荚

d'éu-naw-koq 脑壳 *n.* skull

d'éu-nga 豆芽 *n.* bean sprouts

d'éu-tae 投胎 *v.o.* reincarnate

d'éu•huèn 头晕 *ph.* be dizzy

d'éu•tóng 头痛 *ph.* have a headache

d'éu-dzï 色子 *n.* dice

d'í 甜 *adj.* sweet

d'í 电 *n.* electricity; *attr.* electric *(adj.)*; ~ **-biaw** 电表 electric meter; ~ **-den** 电灯 electric light; ~ **-den-paw** 电灯泡 light bulb; ~ **-fong-soe** 电风扇 electric fan; ~ **-niq-h'u** 电热壶 electric kettle; ~ **-niq-tae** 电热毯 electric blanket; ~ **-shi** 电线 electric cord

d'í 田 *n.* farmland, crop field

d'í 第 *pfx. (ordinal prefix)*; ~ **yiq** first; ~ **ni** second; ~ **sae** third

d'í 填 *v.* fill, fill in, stuff

d'í 垫 *v.* place under *(as a pad or cushion)*

d'í-b'i 土地 *n.* land

d'í-b'in-tsuo 电瓶车 *n.* electric battery bicycle

d'í-bae 地板 *n.* floor, floorboards

d'í-d'i 弟弟 *n.* younger brother, *Alt.*: **āq-d'i**

d'í-dzï 垫子 *n.* cushion, pad, mat

d'í-fãw 地方 *n.* place, *Alt.*: **zǎ-huo, h'ú-d'ãw**

d'í-h'uo 电话 *n.* telephone

d'í-h'uo(-d'eu) 地下 *l.n.* underground, *Alt.*: **d'í-di-h'uo**

d'í•hú 提货 *v.o.* take delivery of goods

d'í-jin 田径 *n.* track and field

d'í-kuae-ji 提款机 *n.* ATM, automatic teller machine, *Alt.*: **chǔ-kuoe-ji**

d'í-men-shiã 电蚊香 *n.* plug-in mosquito-repellent incense

d'í-naw 电脑 *n.* computer

d'í-naw-yeu-shi 电脑游戏 *n.* computer game, video game, *Alt.*: **d'í-d'ong-yeu-shi** 电动游戏

d'í-pã 蹄膀 *n.* pork hock

d'í-shin-vu 弟媳 *n.* sister-in-law *(younger brother's wife)*

d'í-tae 地毯 *n.* carpet

d'í-tae 地摊 *n.* street vendor's stand, *Alt.*: **tàe-d'eu** 摊子

d'í-ti 电梯 *n.* elevator

d'í-tiq 地铁 *n.* subway; **~ -zae** 地铁站 subway station

d'í-tsuo 电车 *n.* electric tram

d'í-vae-b'aw 电饭煲 *n.* electric rice cooker

d'í-'yã 地 *n.* ground, the ground

d'í-yin 电影 *n.* movie

d'í-yin-'yüoe 电影院 *n.* movie theater

d'í-yin-min-shin 电影明星 *n.* movie star

d'í-yin-piaw 电影票 *n.* movie ticket

d'í-zen 橙子 *n.* orange *(fruit)*

d'í-zï 电池 *n.* battery

d'í-zï(-ji) 电视机 *n.* television

d'í-zoe 传真 *n.* fax, *Alt.*: **fà-kaq-sï; fãq•~** 发传真 *v.o.* send a fax

d'iáw 条 *m.w. for fish, ropes, towels, pants, skirts*

d'iáw 换、调 *v.* change; adjust; exchange

d'iáw 搅拌 *v.* stir, mix, *Alt.*: **b'óe**

d'iáw-b'i 调皮 *adj.* mischievous, naughty

d'iáw-goe 身材 *n.* figure, physique

d'iáw-h'in-mo 条形码 *n.* UPC symbol

d'iáw-gã 汤匙 *n.* soup spoon

d'iáw-ven 条文 *n.* clause *(as in a contract)*

d'ín 亭 *n.* kiosk

d'ín 停 *v.* stop

d'ín-dãw 停当 *adj.* ready and in order, suitably prepared

d'ín-jin 定金 *n.* down payment, deposit, *Alt.*: **d'ín-h'iã**

d'ín•tsuò 停车 *n.* park a car

d'iq 这 *prn. pfx.* this, *Alt.*: **d'eq, g'eq**

d'iq-daq 这儿 *prn.* here, *Alt.*: **g'eq-d'eu, g'eq-daq(-li), g'eq-daq-kuae, d'eq-daq(-li)**

d'iq-dzï 碟子 *n.* small plate, saucer

d'iq-g'eq 这个 *prn.* this, *Alt.*: **g'eq-g'eq, g'eq-h'eq, d'eq-g'eq**

d'iq-ku 迪斯科舞 *n.* disco

d'iq-ngae 这些、这点 *prn.* these, *Alt.*: **g'eq-ngae, g'eq-di, d'eq-di**

d'iq-shiq 现在、这会儿 *prn.* now, *Alt.*: **g'eq-shiq, gēq-shiq, d'eq-shiq**

d'iq-tin 迪斯科舞厅 *n.* discothèque

d'iq-'wae 故意 *adv.* intentionally, on purpose, *Alt.*: **d'eq-'wae**

d'óe-dãw 断档 *v.o.* sold out, discontinued

d'óe•ná 断奶 *v.o.* wean, *Alt.*: **gāq•ná**

d'óe-teq 断掉 *v.c.* end, break off, cut off

d'óng 铜 *n.* copper

d'óng 动 *v.* move

d'óng-chi 生气 *v.o.* get angry, take offense; *adj.* mad, angry

d'óng-d'i 钱 *n.* money, *Alt.*: **'yǎ-d'i**

d'óng-d'ong-ngae 洞 *n.* cave, hole

d'óng-h'oq 同学 *n.* classmate

d'óng-jü 同居 *v.* cohabit

d'óng-tsuo 动车 *n.* high-speed rail train

d'óng-vã 洞房 *n.* nuptial chamber, *Alt.*: **shìn-vã**

d'óng-veq-'yüoe 动物园 *n.* zoo

d'óng-(veq-)d'ong 动不动 *adv.* inevitably, usually, *Alt.*: **b'ǎ-(veq-)b'ã** 经常

d'oq 毒、残忍 *adj.* ruthless, cruel

d'oq 读 *v.* read, study; ~•sï 读书 *v.o.* study, attend school

d'ú 大 *adj.* big, large; bigger

d'ú 度 *m.w.* degree *(unit of measure or scale)*

d'ú 背负 *v.* carry on one's back

d'ú-b'i 肚子、腹部 *n.* belly, abdomen

d'ú-b'i-ngae *n.* navel, belly button, *Alt.*: **d'ú-zyi** 肚脐

d'ú-b'i-za 泻肚子 *ph.* have diarrhea, *Alt.*: **d'ú-li-za**

d'ú-bae 驼背 *n.* hunched back, *Alt.*: **hèu-bae**

d'ú-din 图钉 *n.* thumbtack, *Alt.*: **chín-din**

d'ú-dzã 图章 *n.* seal, chop, stamp

d'ú-fãw 大方 *adj.* generous, *Alt.*: **d'ú-pa**

d'ú-fãw-b'oe 大放盘 *v.o.* sell at drastically reduced prices, dump on the market

d'ú-jiaq-pãw 大腿 *n.* thigh, *Alt.*: **d'ú-pãw**

d'ú-jüoe-huo 杜鹃花 *n.* azalea

d'ú-m̀-dzï 大拇指 *n.* thumb, *Alt.*: **d'á-mu-dzï**

d'ú-ni-tsu-yiq 大年初一 *n.* Chinese New Year's Day *(the 1st day of the 1st lunar month)*, *Alt.*: **ní-tsu-yiq**

d'ú-zã 肠子 *n.* intestines

D

dá 戴 *v.* wear, put on *(clothing accessories)*

dá-ñg 带鱼 *n.* ribbonfish

dǎ 打 *v.* hit, strike; play

dǎ•b'á 打牌 *v.o.* play cards, *Alt.*: **déu•b'á**

dǎ-bae 打扮 *v.* dress up, put on makeup

dǎ-baw 打包 *v.o.* wrap up

dǎ•bú-din 打补丁 *v.o.* patch, put on a patch

dǎ•d'í-h'uo 打电话 *v.o.* make a phone call

dǎ•d'í-pu 打地铺 *v.o.* sleep on the floor or ground

dǎ•d'óng 打洞 *v.o.* pierce, put a hole in

dǎ-di 打点 (贿赂) *v.* bribe

dǎ•dzèn 打针 *v.o.* give or get an injection

dǎ•dzēq-d'eu 打折 *v.o.* give a discount

dǎ•g'áe 打嗝儿 *v.o.* belch, burp

dǎ•h'uaq-d'aq 打滑 *v.o.* slip *(on a slippery surface)*

dǎ•huèn-d'u 打呼噜 *v.o.* snore

dǎ•huò-shi 打哈欠 *v.o.* yawn

dǎ•j'iéu 打球 *v.o.* play ball

dǎ•jìn-dzen 行针灸 *v.o.* get or give acupuncture

dǎ•kàe-sǐ 接吻 *v.o.* kiss, *Alt.*: **shiǎ•mí-kong, shiǎ•dzǐ-bo**

dǎ•kēq-tsong 打瞌睡 *v.o.* take a nap, doze off

dǎ•láe 打雷 *v.o.* thunder, *Alt.*: **láe-shiǎ**

dǎ•mó-jiǎ 打麻将 *v.o.* play mahjongg, *Alt.*: **tsuò•mó-jiǎ(-b'a)**

dǎ•ōq-shin 恶心 *v.o. (feel)* nauseous *(adj.)*

dǎ-pen-ti 打喷嚏 *v.o.* sneeze

dǎ-saw 打扫 *v.* clean up

dǎ•táe 打胎 *v.o.* induce abortion

dǎ•'yǎ 打烊 *v.o.* close shop *(for the day)*

dǎ•'yéu-shi-ji 打游戏机 *v.o.* play video games

dǎ-yin-ji 打印机 *n.* printer *(for a computer)*

dǎ-zaw 打搅 *v.* disturb

dáe 对 *adj.* right, correct; *prep.* to, toward, facing *(someone)*; *m.w.* pairs, *Alt.*: **sǎw** 双

dáe•d'ú 胆大 *n.adj.* bold, audacious *(adj.)*

dáe-mi 对面 *l.n.* opposite *(side)*, across from, *Alt.*: **dàe-gu, dáe-mi-zyi**

dáe•shiáw 胆小 *n.adj.* timid, cowardly, *(adj.)* *Alt.*: **sōq**

dáe-veq-chi 对不起 *interj.* pardon me; sorry, *Alt.*: **dáe-veq-zï!**

dáe-zeq 直、直着 *adv., adj.* straight, direct

dáe-zï 但是 *conj.* but

dàe 堆 *m.w. for piles of things*

dàe-h'in-d'aw 单行道 *n.* one-way street, *Alt.*: **dàe-h'âw-d'aw**

dàe-sen-hoe 单身汉 *n.* bachelor

dàe-shin 担心 *v.o.* worry, feel anxious

dàe-'wae 单位 *n.* work unit

dàe-yeu 担忧 *adj.* apprehensive

dàe-zen 单程 *n.* one-way *(not round-trip) (adj.)*

dāq 答 *v.* answer, reply

dāq 搭 *v.* erect, put up, support

dāq-dāw 搭档 *v.* team up; *n.* partner

dāq•dzḯ 插嘴 *v.o.* interrupt *(in a conversation)*, break in, *Alt.*: **tsāq•dzḯ**

dāq-teq 耽误、浪费 *v.* delay, waste

dáw 到 *v.* arrive at, reach; *prep.* to

dáw 倒 *v.* fall down; pour; turn over

dáw-bi 倒闭 *v.* go bankrupt

dáw-di 到底 *adv.* after all, in the end, *Alt.*: **dáw-jieu**

dáw-gu-lae 倒过来 *v.c.* turn over

dáw-loe 捣乱、捣蛋 *v.o.* make trouble, cause a disturbance, *Alt.*: **dáw-d'ae**

dáw•máe 倒霉 *adj.* unlucky, out of luck, *Alt.*: **huàe-chi** 晦气

dáw 挡 *v.* hold back, ward off

dáw 当 *v.* pawn

dáw-di 当铺 *n.* pawn shop

dáw-dzong-'yüoe 中间人 *n.* middle-man, *Alt.*: **dzòng-nin**

dàw-dzong 中间 *l.n.* middle, center, *Alt.*: **dàw-dzong-h'uã-li**

dàw-shin 小心 *adj.* careful

dàw-shin 当心 *interj.* be careful, take care, look out

dàw-ti 当天 *t.n.* same day

dàw-zï(-h'eu) 当时 *t.n.* at that time, in those days

dàw-zoe 当然 *adv.* of course, naturally, *Alt.*: **zḯ-zoe** 自然

dén 太饱 *adj.* too full *(after eating)*, surfeited

dén 顿 *m.w. for meals, beatings, scoldings*

dén 炖 *v.* steam *(in a pot)*, heat or cook by steaming

dén 等 *v.* wait, wait for, await, *Alt.*: **h'éu** 侯

dén(-dzǐ) 凳子 *n.* stool, bench

dén-nga-pin 等外品 *n.* substandard product

dèn 灯 *n.* light, lamp

dèn 蹲 *v.* squat

dèn-dzaw 灯罩 *n.* lampshade

dèn-long 灯笼 *n.* lantern *(usually decorative)*

dèn•jì 登机 *v.o.* board a flight

dēq 和、跟 *prep.* with; and *(conj.)*, *Alt.*: **dēq-dzǐ, tēq, tēq-dzǐ, gàw, gáw, bǎw**

dēq 得 *ptl.* *(marks verb complements)*

dēq 端、掇 *v.* pick up and carry with both hands, *Alt.*: **dòe**

dēq 粘 *v.* stick on, paste, glue, *Alt.*: **tīq** 贴

Dēq-goq 德国 *n.* Germany

Dēq-nü 德语 *n.* German *(language)*

dèu-b'ong 斗篷 *n.* cloak, cape, *Alt.*: **pì-fong** 披风

dèu•fòng 兜风 *v.o.* go for a leisurely drive

dí 点 *v.* pick out, order *(from a selection)*; *m.w.* little bit, small amount, *Alt.*: **ngáe**

dí-bae-ga 基价、最底价 *n.* base price, lowest price, *Alt.*: **chí-bae-ga**

dí•d'éu 点头 *v.o.* nod one's head

dí(-dzǐ) 点儿 *n.* dot, spot, point

dí-dzong 点钟 *m.w.* hours; o'clock

dí-ga 商店 *n.* store, shop, *Alt.*: **sǎw-di**

dí-h'uo(-d'eu) 底下 *l.n.* bottom

dí-shi 底细 *n.* background detail

dí-shiaw 抵消 *v.* offset, cancel out

dí-shin 点心 *n.* pastry snacks, dim sum

dí•tsáe 点菜 *v.o.* order food *(from a menu)*

dí-'yüoe 店员 *n.* shop clerk, sales assistant, *Alt.*: **zéu-hu-'yüoe** 售货员

dì 低 *adj.* low

diá 嗲 *adj.* charming, splendid, simply wonderful, "dear"

diá-sen-dia-chi 嗲声嗲气 *adj.* coy, coquettish

dià-dia 爹爹 *n.* father, *Alt.*: **bà-ba** 爸爸, **láw-ba**

diáw 鸟 *n.* bird, *Alt.*: **niáw**

diáw 吊 *v.* hang

diáw-da-j'ün 吊带裙 *n.* sundress

diáw-dzï 吊子 *n.* kettle

diáw-ku 鸟窝 *n.* bird's nest, *Alt.*: **niáw-ku**

diáw•ñǵ 钓鱼 *v.o.* angle, go fishing

diáw•'yí-sï 输液 *v.o.* get an intravenous drip

diàw 吝啬、刁 *adj* selfish, picky

dín 最、顶 *adv.* most, *Alt.*: **dzóe** 最

dín 顶 *m.w. for hats, bridges*

dín 钉 *v.* nail, tack on

dín 订 *v.* purchase in advance, reserve

dín 沉淀 *v.* settle, allow sediment to settle

dín 顶 *v.* support; butt into; ~ **-nong** 顶你 *v.o.* support you

dín-b'ä 天棚 *n.* awning, canopy

dín-ga 顶价 *n.* price ceiling

dín-guaq 平整质量好 *adj.* trim and fine, high quality

dín•hú 订货 *v.o.* order goods

dín•huèn 订婚 *v.o.* betrothed, engaged, *Alt.*: **páe-chin**

dín-sï-din 钉书钉 *n.* staple

dín-sï-ji 钉书机 *n.* stapler

dìn 钉子 *n.* nail *(metal)*, *Alt.*: **'yǎ-din**

dìn 盯 *v.* stare at

dìn-daw 颠倒 *adj.* topsy-turvy, disordered, upside down

dìn-h'a 钉鞋 *n.* cleated shoes

dīq 捏 *v.* pinch (and pull)

dīq•páe 捶背 *v.o.* beat lightly on one's back *(as a massage)*, *Alt.*: **kàw•báe**

dīq-chüeq 的确 *adv.* indeed, certainly, *Alt.*: **dīq-chioq**

dīq-gaw 跌跤、摔跤 *v.o.* tumble, fall down, *Alt.*: **g'uáe-gaw**

dīq-sï 的士 *n.* taxi, *Alt.*: **tsà-d'eu, tsēq-dzu-chi-tsuo** 出租汽车

dóe 短 *adj.* short *(not long)*

dóe 段 *m.w.* lengths of things

dóe-li sèn-ti 锻炼身体 *v.o.* exercise

dóe-shin(-shiq) 短信息 *n.* text message

dóe-soq 简括 *adj.* brief but comprehensive

dòe 端、掇 *v.* pick up and carry with both hands, *Alt.*: **dēq**

dóng 懂 *v.* understand

dóng-zï-dzä 董事长 *n.* chairman of the board

dòng 东 *l.n.* east, east side, *Alt.*: **dòng-mi, dòng-d'eu** 东边

dòng-fāw 东方 *n.* Orient, the East

dòng-guo 冬瓜 *n.* winter melon

dòng-ti 冬天 *n.* winter, *Alt.*: **lǎ-ti**

dōq *adj.* confident and assured, *Alt.*: **dōq-d'in** 笃定

dōq 滴 *v.* shower, rain upon, drench; *n.* drip; *m.w. for drips*

dōq 熬 *v.* stew, boil

dōq 扔、丢 *v.* toss, throw

dōq-tae 笃坦 *adj.* calm, unruffled

dōq•'yǔ 淋雨 *v.o.* get wet or drenched in the rain, rained upon, *Alt.*: **lín•'yǔ**

dú 朵 *m.w. for flowers*

dú•d'óng-d'i 赌钱 *v.o.* gamble *(for money)*

dú-dzï 猪肚 *n.* pork tripe

dú-j'i 忌妒 *v.* jealous of

dù 多 *adj.* many

dù•dzǐ 多嘴 *v.o.* say more than is necessary

dù-saw 多少 *prn.* how many, *Alt.*: **jí-huo**

dù•shìn 多心 *adj.* oversensitive, overly wary

DZ

dzá-li 笊篱 *n.* straining spatula

dzà 嗓子尖 *adj.* shrill

dzǎ 胀 *adj.* swollen

dzǎ-bae 长辈 *n.* elder generation

dzǎ-h'u 账户 *n.* account

dzǎ 张 *m.w. for pictures, stamps, flat things*

dzǎ 争吵 *v.* argue about, quarrel, *Alt.*: **dzǎ•dzǐ**

dzáe 盏 *m.w. for lamps*

dzáe-h'uae! 再见！ *interj.* good-bye!

dzàe 再 *adv.* again *(in the future)*

dzàe 剁 *v.* chop

dzàe-'yeu 还有 *adv.* still have

dzāq 只 *m.w. for animals, furniture, fruit, etc.*

dzāq 扎 *v.* prick, pierce

dzāq 穿 *v.* wear, *Alt.*: **tsòe**

dzāq•j'í 下棋 *v.o.* play chess

dzāq•jín 刺激而有趣 *adj.* stimulating

dzāq-ngā 坚硬 *adj.* solid

dzāq•zyí-da 绞脐带 *v.o.* cut the umbilical cord

dzáw 早 *adj.* early

dzáw 找 *v.* make change, give change *(in a purchase)*

dzáw 罩 *v.* shade, cover

dzáw 照 *v.* shine, reflect

dzáw 按照 *prep.* do according to, *Alt.:* **dzáw-dzï** 照着, **òe-dzaw**

dzáw-ae 早晚 *adv.* sooner or later

dzáw-d'eu 零钱、找头 *n.* change *(from money paid)*

dzáw-d'eu 灶 *n.* stove

dzáw-dzï 枣子 *n.* jujube, date

dzáw-ga-b'u-saq 灶家菩萨 *n.* stove-god

dzáw-lāw 早上 *t.n.* morning, a.m.

dzáw-pi 照片 *n.* photograph

dzáw-seq *n.* flea, *Alt.:* **tiáw-seq, tiáw-dzaw** 跳蚤

dzáw-shiā-guoe 照相馆 *n.* photo studio

dzáw-shiā-ji 相机 *n.* camera

dzáw-tsae 早产 *n.* premature birth

dzáw-vae 早饭 *n.* breakfast, *Alt.:* **dzáw-di**

dzáw-zen(-d'eu) 早晨 *t.n.* early morning, *Alt.:* **dzáw-lāw(-shiā)**

dzàw-b'a 招牌 *n.* shop sign

dzàw-d'ae-su 招待所 *n.* hostel

dzàw-gu 照顾 *v.* look after, care for

dzàw-h'uae 照会 *n.* license *(obtained upon payment of tax, duty, etc.)*

dzàw•'yǎ 搔痒 *v.o.* scratch an itch

dzǎw 肥 *adj.* fat

dzǎw-b'ong 帐篷 *n.* tent

dzǎw 桩 *m.w. for matters of business*

dzǎw 装 *v.* install; assemble; load, pack; pretend, play a part, *Alt.:* **gá-dzǎw** 假装

dzǎw-h'uāw 装潢 *v.* decorate

dzǎw-lāw 蟑螂 *n.* cockroach

dzǎw-shieu 装修 *v.* renovate

dzén 准 *adj.* accurate, precise, *Alt.:* **dzén-dzoq**

dzén 正 *adj.* straight, correct, right side up

dzén 镇 *n.* town

dzén-b'ae 准备 *v.* plan, prepare to

dzén-chüeq 正确 *adj.* correct, right, proper, *Alt.:*

dzén-chioq

dzén-d'eu 枕头 *n.* pillow

dzén-d'eu-taw 枕头套 *n.* pillow case

dzén-dzï 镇纸 *n.* paperweight

dzén-dzong 正宗 *adj.* genuine

dzén-dzong-hu 正品 *n.* quality products

dzén-haw 正好 *adv.* just right; just by chance, as it happened, *Alt.*: **kāq-kaq-jiaw** 恰恰地

dzén-nin 证人 *n.* witness

dzén-niq *n.* whole day, *Alt.*: **dzén-ti** 整天

dzén-seq 正式 *adj.* formal, official

dzén-zã 正常 *adj.* normal

dzén-zyi 整齐 *adj.* neat, tidy, orderly

dzèn 真 *adj.* real, genuine, true

dzèn 针 *n.* needle, pin

dzèn 挤压 *v.* squeeze

dzèn 蒸 *v.* steam *(in a steaming tray)*

dzèn-d'eu 针 *n.* injection; syringe

dzèn-den(-bae) 砧板 *n.* cutting board

dzèn-dzï 珍珠 *n.* pearl

dzèn-dzï-mi 玉米 *n.* corn

dzèn-jieu 针灸 *n.* acupuncture and moxibustion

dzèn-long 蒸笼 *n.* steamer for food

dzèn-sï 真丝 *n.* silk, *Alt.*: **sï** 丝

dzèn-zï 真是 *adv.* truly, really

dzēq-zen 挚诚 *adj.* sincere

dzēq 只 *adv.* only

dzēq(-d'eu) 折扣 *n.* discount

dzéu 走 *v.* leave; walk

dzéu•fòng 走风、泄密 *v.o.* leak a secret

dzéu•háw! 走好！ *interj.* Take care as you go!, *Alt.*: **máe-dzéu!** 慢走！

dzèu-meq 周末 *n.* weekend

dzḯ 紫 *adj.* purple

dzḯ 嘴 *n.* mouth, *Alt.*: **dzḯ-bo** 嘴巴

dzḯ 子 *n.* seeds

dzḯ-bae-shiã 纸箱 *n.* cardboard box

dzḯ-d'eu 纸 *n.* paper

dzḯ•gòe 口渴 *n.adj.* thirsty *(adj.)*

dzḯ-jiaw 指教 *v.* give advice and comments

dzḯ-jin 纸巾 *n.* facial tissue

dzí-kaq-j'i 指甲刀 *n.* nail clipper, *Alt.:* **g'aq-dzï-j'i**

dzí-nin-ga 主人 *n.* host

dzí-nü 子女 *n.* children, sons and daughters

dzí-saw 至少 *adv.* at least

dzí-seq 紫色 *n.* purple

dzí-shi 仔细 *adj.* attentive to detail, *Alt.:* **bó-shi**

dzí-yaw 主要 *attr.* main, chief, principal *(adj.)*

dzí-zen 主任 *n.* director, head

dzí-zen-gaw 唇膏 *n.* lipstick

dzí-zen(-b'i) 嘴唇 *n.* lips

dzí-zeq 主食 *n.* staple food

dzì 支 *m.w. for incense sticks, candlesticks, Alt.:* **gèn** 根

dzì 枝 *m.w. for pens, pencils, sticks*

dzì-dzï 珠珠 *n.* beads

dzì-dzï 蜘蛛 *n.* spider, *Alt.:* **jīq-dzï**

dzì-baw-di 珠宝店 *n.* jewelry store

dzì-dzoe 锥子 *n.* awl

dzì-fen 脂粉 *n.* cosmetics

dzì-jiaq-dzaw 猪爪 *n.* pig's foot

dzì-liaw 蝉 *n.* cicada

dzì-lu 猪 *n.* pig

dzì-lu-b'ã *n.* pigsty, *Alt.:* **dzì-chüoe** 猪圈

dzì-mi 滋味 *n.* flavor, taste, *Alt.:* **chīq-keu**

dzì-mo 芝麻 *n.* sesame

dzì-mo-jiã 芝麻酱 *n.* sesame paste

dzì-nioq 猪肉 *n.* pork

dzì-pa 派 *v.* send *(someone on a task)*, dispatch

dzì-piaw 支票 *n.* check

dzì-tseq 支出 *n.* expenditure, disbursement, *Alt.:* **tsēq-dzã** 出账

dzì-zoe 孜然 *n.* cumin

dzóe 最 *adv.* most, *Alt.:* **dín** 顶

dzóe 簪子 *n.* hair clasp, hair pin, *Alt.:* **d'éu-faq-dzoe**

dzóe 绕、兜 *v.* walk around

dzóe•b'í-ni 占便宜 *v.o.* profit at another's expense

dzóe-boq 占卜 *n.* divination

dzóe-di-ga 最低价 *n.* lowest price

dzóe•h'eu 最后 *adv.* in the end, *Alt.:* **(zaq-)meq-jiaq, āq-meq, laq-meq**

dzóe•j'ín, 最近、近来 *adv.* recently, lately, *Alt.:* **shìn-j'in**

dzóe-lae 回来 *v.* come back, return, *Alt.*: **h'uáe-lae**

dzóe-wae 转弯 *v.o.* turn (a corner)

dzòe 钻 *v.* drill

dzòe-d'eu 砖 *n.* brick, *Alt.*: **loq-dzoe**

dzòe-dzï 钻 *n.* drill

dzòe-ma-di 专卖店 *n.* speciality shop, name brand store

dzòe-men 专门 *adv.* expressly

dzóng 种 *n.*, *m.w.* kind, kinds

dzóng-dzï 种子 *n.* seed

dzóng-dzï 粽子 *n.* *zòngzi*, sticky rice dumpling steamed in reed leaves

dzóng•fòng 中风 *v.o.* have a stroke

dzóng-g'ong 总共 *adv.* altogether, *Alt.*: **yīq-g'ong** 一共, **g'óng-dzong, lóng-dzong, yīq-taq-guaq-dzï, hǎ-baq-lā-dā**

dzóng-guae 总是 *adv.* always, *Alt.*: **dzōq-guae**

dzóng-lieu 肿瘤 *n.* tumor

dzòng 中 *adj.* medium

dzòng 钟 *n.* clock; bell

dzòng-'wu 中午 *t.n.* noon, midday, *Alt.*: **dzòng-lǎ(-shiǎ), niq-dzong-shin(-li)**

dzòng-'yaq-di 中药店 *n.* Chinese medicine shop

dzòng-d'eu 钟头 *n.*, *m.w.* hour

dzòng-di-gong 钟点工 *n.* hourly labor

Dzòng-goq 中国 *n.* China; ~ **gòng-fu** ~功夫 *n.* Chinese *kungfu*

Dzòng-goq-nin 中国人 *n.* Chinese *(person)*

dzòng-h'oq 中学 *n.* middle school

dzòng-jia 中介 *n.* intermediary

dzòng-shin-seq-'yǎ 中性式样 *n.* unisex

dzòng-'yü 终于 *adv.* finally, *Alt.*: **dzóng, 'yü**

dzōq 满 *adj.* full, *Alt.*: **móe**

dzōq 聚集 *v.* assemble, get together

dzòng-vae 午饭 *n.* lunch

dzòng-yi 满意 *adj.* satisfied, *Alt.*: **dzóng-yi**

dzòng•sï 中暑 *v.o.* suffer heatstroke or sunstroke, *Alt.*: **fāq•suò**

dzōq 烛 *n.* candle, *Alt.*: **'yǎ-laq-dzoq** 蜡烛

dzōq 粥 *n.* congee, rice porridge

dzōq 捉 *v.* catch, capture

dzōq-b'ae 竹片 *n.* bamboo strips

dzōq-d'ae 烛台 *n.* candlestick *(holder)*

dzōq-d'eu 竹子 *n.* bamboo

dzōq-geu 足够 *adj.* enough, sufficient, *Alt.*: **géu-zï, gèu-zï**

dzōq-h'u 祝贺 *v.* congratulate

dzōq-j'ieu 足球 *n.* soccer; soccer ball

dzōq-liaw 作料 *n.* ingredients

dzōq-moq-niaw 啄木鸟 *n.* woodpecker

dzōq-sen 竹笋 *n.* bamboo shoots, *Alt.*: **sén** 笋

dzōq•sí 找死 *v.o.* court death, *Alt.*: **bí-sï**

dzōq-shin 可能 *adv.* perhaps, possibly, maybe, *Alt.*: **'yáe-shü** 也许

dzōq-zyiq 竹席 *n.* bamboo mat

dzōq•ńǵ-g'eq 渔夫 *n.* fisherman

dzú 做 *v.* do, make, produce

dzú-dzã 组长 *n.* section chief, *Alt.*: **kù-dzã** 科长

dzú-dzoq 做作 *adj.* affected, artificial

dzú•lí-ba 做礼拜 *v.o.* worship, attend church

dzú-mi 左边 *l.n.* left side

dzú-mu 祖母 *n.* grandmother *(paternal)*, *Alt.*: **ńǵ-na, āq-na**

dzú•nín 做人 *v.o.* behave, conduct oneself

dzú-sã-h'ueq 干活 *v.o.* work on a job

dzú-seu 左手 *n.* left hand, *Alt.*: **jí-seu**

dzú-vu 祖父 *n.* grandfather *(paternal)*, *Alt.*: **'yá-'ya, láw-dia**

dzú-'yeu 左右 *num.* about, around, more or less

dzú•shìn-vu 做媳妇 *v.o.* become a daughter-in-law

dzuó 炸 *v.* deep fry, *Alt.*: **tén**

dzuó•nín 敲诈 *v.* extort, blackmail

dzuò 遮 *v.* cover, block, conceal

dzuò 抓 *v.* grab *(with hands)*, *Alt.*: **wò**

E

'ér 二 *num.* two, *Alt.*: **ní**

'ér-du 耳朵 *n.* ear, *Alt.*: **ní-du**

'ér-dzï 儿子 *n.* son, *Alt.*: **ní-dzï, nóe-shiaw-noe**

'ér-g'uae 耳环 *n.* earring, *Alt.*: **ní-du-g'uae**

'ér-ji 耳机 *n.* headphone, earphone

ēq 覆盖 *v.* cover

èu 低头、曲背 *v.* stoop, duck

Èu-dzeu 欧洲 *n.* Europe

F

fáe 反 *adj.* reverse, inside out, topside down

fáe-gu-lae 反过来 *v.c.* turn over

fáe-'er 反而 *adv.* unexpectedly

fáe•'wáe 反胃 *v.o.* upset one's stomach

fàe-g'a 西红柿 *n.* tomato

fàe•kèn-deu 翻跟斗 *v.o.* somersault

fāq•b'í-chi 发脾气 *v.o.* get angry, flare up, *Alt.*: fāq•gāq

fāq•d'ú-sï 发大水 *v.o.* flood

fāq•déu 发抖、哆嗦 *v.* shiver, tremble, *Alt.*: déu 抖, j'ín

fāq•diá(-jin) 撒娇 *v.o.* act spoiled or coquettish

fāq-dzï 办法、法子 *n.* way, method, solution

fāq•fòng 发疯 *v.o.* go crazy, go mad, *Alt.*: fāq•tsï̀

Fāq-goq 法国 *n.* France

fāq•h'óe-niq 发烧 *v.o.* have a fever, *Alt.*: fāq•niq, fāq•gàw-saw

fāq•hú 发火、发怒 *v.o.* lose one's temper, get angry, *Alt.*: kuǎ•hú, fāq•máw, fāq•hèu

fāq•j'ín 发寒颤 *v.o.* have the chills

Fāq-nü 法语 *n.* French *(language)*

fāq-piaw 发票 *n.* invoice, bill of sale, receipt

fǎw•gá 放假 *v.o.* be on vacation, *Alt.*: fǎw•jiá

fǎw•shin 放心 *v.o.* relieved, assured, put at ease

fǎw 方 *adj.* square

fǎw-b'i 方便 *adj.* convenient, easy, *Alt.*: b'í-dǎw 便当

fǎw-dzï 方子 *n.* prescription, *Alt.*: 'yaq-fǎw 药方

fǎw-shiã 方向 *n.* direction; orientation, goal

fǎw-'yi 方言 *n.* dialect

fén-bin 粉饼 *n.* makeup powder cake

fén-biq 粉笔 *n.* chalk *(for writing)*

fén-h'ong-seq 粉红色 *n.* pink

fèn 分 *n., m.w.* minute; cent, one tenth of one *yuán*, *Alt.*: fèn-d'eu

fèn-kae 分开 *v.c.* separate, part

fèn-su 分数 *n.* grade *(of achievement)*

fí 肺 *n.* lungs

fí-shin 费心 *v.o.* make an effort, go to trouble

fì 飞 *v.* fly

Fì-dzeu 非洲 *n.* Africa

fì-h'in 飞行 *n.* flying, flight; *v.* fly

fì-ji 飞机 *n.* airplane

fì-ji-zã 飞机场 *n.* airport, *Alt.:* **kòng-gãw** 空港

fì-tsoe 翡翠 *n.* jadeite

fì-zã(-dzï) 非常 *adv.* extraordinarily, *Alt.:* **hãq, lae-deq(-g'eq)**

fòng 封 *v.* seal; *m.w. for letters*

fòng 风 *n.* wind

fòng-dzï 疯子 *n.* lunatic, *Alt.:* **tsï̀-dzï**

fòng-guãw 风光 *n.* sight, view

fòng-j'in 风琴 *n.* organ

fòng-jin-chü 风景区 *n.* scenic area

fòng-ku 蜂窝 *n.* hive, beehive, wasp's nest

fòng-liã 凉快 *adj.* cool, pleasantly cool, *Alt.:* **liã̀-sãw**

fòng-liã-h'a 凉鞋 *n.* sandals

fòng-shiã 风箱 *n.* bellows

fòng-sï 风水 *n.* geomancy, feng-shui

fòng-yi 风衣 *n.* windbreaker

fōq-chi 福气 *n.* good fortune, happy luck, *Alt.:* **fōq-ven**

fōq-zyiq 复习 *v.* review

fú 付 *v.o.* pay

fú-deu 斧头 *n.* axe

fù-chi 夫妻 *n.* husband and wife

fù-nin 夫人 *n.* wife *(polite)*

fù-'yi 敷衍 *v.* do perfunctorily

G'

g'á 解开 *v.* untie, loosen

g'á-dzï 茄子 *n.* eggplant, *Alt.:* **loq-su**

g'á-meq 芥末 *n.* wasabi, mustard

g'áe 嗝儿 *n.* burp

g'áe 斜靠 *v.* lean against

g'aq 挤 *v.* squeeze, cram, crowd, jostle; **g'aq-jin** 挤进 *v.c.* squeeze into

g'aq•b'ã́-'yeu 交朋友 *v.o.* make friends

g'aq•b'ín 结好〔账〕 *v.c.* reconcile *(an account)*; **g'aq-veq-b'in** 结不了〔账〕 cannot reconcile *(an account)*, *Alt.*: **g'aq-veq-long**

g'aq-d'eu 夹子 *n.* clip

g'aq•dzǎ 结账 *v.o.* settle an account

g'aq-laq 肯定 *adv.* positively, definitely

g'aq•náw-mǎ 凑热闹 *v.o.* join in the fun, join in the trouble, *Alt.*: **tséu•niq-naw**

g'aq•piáw 剪票 *v.o.* punch ticket

g'aq•pìn-d'eu 轧姘头 *v.o.* have an extramarital affair

g'aq-tsuo 发夹 *n.* hairpin, bobby pin

g'áw 搞 *v.* do, *Alt.*: **nòng** 弄

g'ǎ̌w 戆 *adj.* dumb, dull, stupid

g'én 倔 *adj.* headstrong, unbending, stubborn, *Alt.*: **j'üeq, j'üeq-j'iǎ** 倔强, **j'ioq-jiǎ, ngǎ̌-j'iǎ**

g'eq 个 *m.w.* for people (general usage), places, *Alt.*: **h'eq**

g'eq 这 *prn. pfx.* this, *Alt.*: **d'iq, d'eq**

g'eq 的、地 *ptl.* (particle marking attributives before nouns and verbs), *Alt.*: **h'eq**

g'eq 孵 *v.* hug, hold in arms

g'eq-d'eu 这儿 *prn.* here, *Alt.*: **g'eq-daq(-li), g'eq-daq-kuae, d'iq-daq, d'eq-daq(-li)**

g'eq-g'eq 这个 *prn.* this, *Alt.*: **g'eq-h'eq, d'iq-g'eq, d'eq-g'eq**

g'eq-ngae 这些、这点 *prn.* these, *Alt.*: **g'eq-di, d'iq-ngae, d'eq-di**

g'eq-shiq 现在、这会儿 *prn.* now *(adv.)*, *Alt.*: **gēq-shiq, d'iq-shiq, d'eq-shiq**

g'óng-dzong 总共 *adv.* altogether, *Alt.*: **yīq-g'ong** 一共, **dzóng-g'ong, lóng-dzong, yīq-taq-guaq-dzǐ, hǎ̌-baq-lǎ-dǎ**

g'uáe 扔 *v.* throw, toss

g'uáe-gaw, 摔跤 *v.o.* tumble, fall down, *Alt.*: **dīq-gaw** 跌跤

g'uáe-teq 仍掉 *v.c.* throw away, toss out

G

gá 假 *adj.* false, fake, *Alt.*: **jiá**

gá 锯 *v.* saw, *Alt.*: **g'á, sà**

gá 假 *n.* vacation, leave; **fǎw•~** 放假 have a vacation, *Alt.*: **jiá**

gá-d'eu 假货 *n.* fake goods, *Alt.*: **d'á-ka**

gá-d'i 价钱 *n.* price, *Alt.*: **gá-'wae** 价位

gá-dzāw 嫁妆 *n.* dowry, *Alt.*: **b'áe-ga**

gá-dzï 戒指 *n.* ring *(for a finger)*

gá-faq 假发 *n.* wig

gá•nóe-nin 嫁男人 *v.o.* marry *(of a woman)*, *Alt.*: **tsēq•gá** 出嫁

gá-sï-'yüoe 驾驶员 *n.* driver, pilot, *Alt.*: **jiá-sï-'yüoe**

gà 街 *n.* street, *Alt.*: **gà-d'aw** 街道, **gà-lu**

gà 这么 *adv.* in this way, so, as (+ *adj.*)... as this; **~ - shü•dù** 这么多 as many as this

gà 家 *n.* family; *m.w. for families, companies*

gà-dǎw 家当 *n.* family property

gà•gòng-d'i 加工资 *v.o.* raise wages

gà-jü 家具 *n.* furniture, *Alt.*: **jià-jü**

gà-li 咖喱 *n.* curry

Gà-na-da 加拿大 *n.* Canada

gà•'yéu! 加油！ *interj.* go!, do your best! *(lit. 'add gas')*

gǎ 梗、阻塞 *v.* clog, obstruct, *Alt.*: **zaq**

gǎ 鲠 *v.* stick in one's throat *(of fish bones, etc.)*

gǎ-b'i 港币 *n.* Hong Kong dollars

gǎ 犟 *adj.* stubborn, obstinate, *Alt.*: **jiǎ**

gáe 裥 *n.* pleat, crease *(in clothing)*

gáe 挑选 *v.* select, pick out, choose, *Alt.*: **d'áw**

gáe-d'eu 盖子 *n.* cover, lid, top, cap

gáe-dzï 锯子 *n.* saw, *Alt.*: **g'á-dzï**

gáe-lae 橄榄 *n.* olive

gáe-niq 改天 *v.o.* another day, some other day *(n.)*

gàe 间 *m.w. for rooms*

gàe 拥有 *v.* possess, own

gàe-diaw 小气 *adj.* stingy, cheap, *Alt.*: **shiáw-chi**

gàe-ga 尴尬 *adj.* awkward, embarrassing *(of a situation)*

gàe-gong 监工 *n.* supervisor, overseer

gàe-jiā 尴僵 *adj.* in an awkward fix

gāq 眨 *v.* blink, wink, *Alt.*: **sāq**

gāq 隔 *v.* separate, keep apart, cut off

gāq-biq(-d'eu) 隔壁 *n.* next door

gāq-li 里子 *n.* lining (in clothing)

gáw 醒 *v.* wake up, awaken, *Alt.*: **shín, gáw-dzoe-lae** 醒来

gáw-huo-dzï 叫花子 *n.* beggar, *Alt.*: **chīq-gae** 乞丐

gàw 高 *adj.* high, tall

gàw 糕 *n.* cake, pudding

gàw 和、跟 *prep.* with; and *(conj.)*, *Alt.*: **gáw, bǎw, tēq, tēq-dzï, dēq, dēq-dzï**

gàw 交 *v.* hand over, pay, *Alt.*: **jiàw**

gàw-chiaw 高跷 *n.* stilts

gàw-d'eu 上头 *l.n.* top, above, *Alt.*: **zǎw-d'eu, zǎw-mi** 上面

gàw-'er-fu-j'ieu 高尔夫球 *n.* golf

gàw-ga 高架 *n.* elevated roadway

gàw-gen-h'a 高跟鞋 *n.* high-heel shoes

gàw-shin 高兴 *adj.* happy; *v.* happy to *(do something)*

gàw-sï 胶水 *n.* glue

gàw-su 告诉 *v.* tell, inform

gàw-tiq 高铁 *n.* high-speed rail

gàw-'yaq 膏药 *n.* medicated bandage

gǎw 讲 *v.* speak, say, tell

gǎw-d'ae 讲台 *n.* podium

gǎw-dzā 聊天 *v.* chat, have an informal conversation

gǎw•h'áe-h'uo 讲话 *v.o.* talk, speak

gǎw-ni 讲义 *n.* class handouts

gàw 缸 *n.* crock, jar

gàw 江 *n.* river, *Alt.*: **h'ú** 河

gàw 扛 *v.* carry on the shoulder, *Alt.*: **ǎw**

gǎw(-gāw) 刚刚 *adv.* just

gǎw-biq 钢笔 *n.* pen, fountain pen

gǎw-noe sǐ-shiā 江南水乡 *n.* watertown of southern Yangtze region

gén-ga 更加 *adv.* even more, *Alt.*: **gà-ni**

gèn 根 *m.w. for incense sticks, candlesticks*, *Alt.*: **dzǐ** 支

gèn 树根 *n.* root, *Alt.*: **zǐ-gen**

gēq 割 *v.* cut apart, sever, *Alt.*: **guēq**

gēq-dzï 口吃 *n.* stutter

gēq-dzï 鸽子 *n.* pigeon, dove

gēq-dzï-wu 腋窝 *n.* armpit, *Alt.*: **gēq-leq-dzoq**

gēq-dzu-sā-yi 合伙做买卖 *ph.* operate a partnership business

gēq•hu 合伙 *v.o.* form a partnership

gēq-law 所以 *conj.* so, therefore

gēq-li 蛤蜊 *n.* clam

gēq-mǎ 蚱蜢 *n.* grasshopper

gēq-meq 那么 *conj.* well, then, well then, in that case

gēq-shiq 现在、这会儿 *prn.* now, *Alt.:* **g'eq-shiq, d'iq-shiq, d'eq-shiq**

gēq-soe 合算 *adj.* worthwhile

géu 狗 *n.* dog

gèu•bó 个把 *num.* some, one or two, a few, *Alt.:* **gú•bó**

góe 敢 *aux.* dare to

góe-b'u 干部 *n.* cadre

góe-jin 赶紧 *adv.* quickly, lose no time, hurry, *Alt.:* **h'áw-saw**

gòe 干 *adj.* dry, *Alt.:* **gòe-saw** 干燥

gòe 肝 *n.* liver

gòe•bàe 干杯 *v.o.* drink a toast, make a toast; *interj.* Cheers!, Bottoms up!

gòe-dzuo 甘蔗 *n.* sugarcane

gòe-tsoe 干脆 *adj.* right to the point, clear cut, outright

gòe-zin 干净 *adj.* clean

gòng-b'u 公婆 *n.* in-laws *(husband's parents)*

gòng-d'eu 工头 *n.* foreman

gòng-d'i 工资 *n.* wages, *Alt.:* **gòng-dzï**

gòng-dzoq 工作 *v.* work *(at a job)*

gòng-fu 功夫 *n.* kungfu; great effort or time *(spent working on or learning something)*

gòng-g'ong-chi-tsuo 公共汽车 *n.* bus, public bus

gòng-gong 公公 *n.* father-in-law *(husband's father)*, *Alt.:* **āq-gong**

gòng-guae jìn-li 公关经理 *n.* public relations manager

gòng-jiaw 公共交通 *n.* public transportation

gòng-jin 公斤 *n.* kilogram

gòng-kae 公开 *adv.* openly, publicly; *v.* make public

gòng-ku 功课 *n.* homework

gòng-ni 工艺 *n.* handicraft

gòng-nin 工人 *n.* worker, laborer

gòng-nü 公寓 *n.* apartment, flat, *Alt.:* **gòng-'yü**

gòng-shi 恭喜 *v.* congratulate; *interj.* Congratulations!

gòng-shiaw-ku 供销科 *n.* marketing division

gòng-sï 公司 *n.* company

gòng-zǎ 工场 *n.* workshop, *Alt.*: **tsuò-gae** 车间

gòng-zen-sï 工程师 *n.* engineer

gòng-'yüoe 公园 *n.* park

gòng•yàw 弓腰 *v.o.* bend at the waist, stoop, *Alt.*:
　　wàe•yàw 弯腰

gōq 角 *m.w.* ten *fēn*, one tenth of one *yuán*

gōq 谷 *n.* grain

gōq 各 *prn.* each, each one, *Alt.*: **gōq-g'eq** 各个

gōq•dzí 漱口 *v.o.* rinse one's mouth

gōq-jia 国家 *n.* country, nation, state, *Alt.*: **gōq-d'u**

gōq-lǎw 角上 *l.n.* in the corner, *Alt.*: **gōq-goq-lǎw-shiǎ**

gōq-leu 阁楼 *n.* loft

gōq-loq(-d'eu) 角落 *n.* corner, nook

gōq-zaq 觉得 *v.* feel

gu 过 *ptl.* (marks experiental aspect), *Alt.*: **shiq, gu-
　　shiq, shiq-gu**

gú 鼓 *adj.* bulging, swelling

gú 过 *v.* pass, go by, cross, exceed

gú 裹 *v.* wrap

gú-b'i 果皮 *n.* peel

gú•bó 个把 *num.* some, one or two, a few, *Alt.*: **gèu•bó**

gú-chi 过去 *t.n.* formerly, in the past (*adv.*), *Alt.*:
　　zóng-zyi 从前

gú-ji 估计 *v.* estimate, appraise

gú-kaq 顾客 *n.* customer

gú-nieu 蜗牛 *n.* snail (*dry land type*)

gú-piaw 股票 *n.* share certificate, stock

gú-ven 顾问 *n.* consultant, advisor

gú-'woe sǎw-di 古玩商店 *n.* antique store

gú-zï 故事 *n.* story

gú-zoe 果然 *adv.* as expected, sure enough it turns out
　　that

gù 歌 *n.* song

gù-dzï 锅子 *n.* wok, pot, pan, *Alt.*: **h'oq-dzï**

gù-fu 姑父 *n.* uncle (*husband of father's sister*)

gù-gu 哥哥 *n.* brother (elder), *Alt.*: **āq-gu**

gù-ma 姑妈 *n.* aunt (*father's younger sister*)

gù-mu-aq-jia 姑母阿姐 *n.* aunt (*father's elder sister*)

gù-niang 姑娘 *n.* girl, young woman (*unmarried*)

gù-tiq 锅贴 *n.* pot stickers (*fried dumplings*)

guá 怪 *v.* blame

guá-dzï 拐子 *n.* kidnapper, abductor

guá-vu 寡妇 *n.* widow, *Alt.*: **gù-sã**

guà 乖 *adj.* well-behaved, obedient

guǎ-kae 胀大裂开 *v.c.* burst

guáe-d'aw 轨道 *n.* track, railway, *Alt.*: **guàe-d'aw**

guáe-huo 桂花 *n.* osmanthus

guáe-ji 会计 *n.* accountant, bookkeeper, *Alt.*: **kuáe-ji**

guáe-'yüoe 桂圆 *n.* longan

guàe 关 *v.* close

guàe-dzaw 关照、照顾 *v.* look after; 嘱咐 *v.* notify by word of mouth

guàe-jiq 关节 *n.* joint *(in limbs and fingers)*, *Alt.*: **g'aq-jiq(-gueq-loq)**

guàe-jü 规矩 *adj.* well-behaved, acting properly

guāq 搁 *v.* slap, smack

guāq•fòng 刮风 *v.o.* windy *(adj.)*, the wind blows *(ph.)*, *Alt.*: **fāq•fòng, chí•fòng**

guǎw-bu 广播 *v., n.* broadcast

Guǎw-dzeu 广州 *n.* Canton

Guǎw-dzeu-h'ae-h'uo 广州话 *n.* Cantonese *(language)*

guǎw-gaw 广告 *n.* advertisement

guǎw-guen 光棍 *n.* bachelor

guǎw-h'uaq 光滑 *adj.* smooth, glossy, sleek

guǎw•jiāq 光脚 *v.o.* be barefoot, be barefooted, *Alt.*: **tsāq•jiāq** 赤脚

guǎw-lāw-d'eu 光头 *n.* bald head, *Alt.*: **h'ú-zāw-d'eu**

guǎw-shi 光线 *n.* light, *Alt.*: **liǎ-guāw**

guǎw-'yong 光荣 *n., adj.* honor, glory

guén 滚 *v.* roll; boil

guēq-d'eu 骨头 *n.* bone

guēq-huae 骨灰 *n.* ashes of the dead

guó-h'aw-shin 挂号信 *n.* registered mail, registered letter

guò-b'aw 瓜刨 *n.* vegetable peeler

guò-b'i-maw 瓜皮帽 *n.* skullcap

guóe-d'eu 罐子 *n.* can, jar

guóe-ga 管家 *n.* steward, *Alt.*: **guóe-jia**

guòe-yin-b'u-saq 观音菩萨 *n.* Guanyin *(a Bodhisattva)*

guòe-zae 棺材 *n.* coffin

H'

h'á-d'i 鞋垫 *n.* insole, shoe pad

h'á-di 鞋底 *n.* sole *(of a shoe)*

h'á-dzï 鞋子 *n.* shoes

h'á-li 哪 *prn.pfx.* which *(used with measure words)*; ~ -(yiq-)g'eq 哪个 which one, *Alt.*: **h'á-li-(yiq-)h'eq**

h'á-li 哪儿 *prn.* where, *Alt.*: **h'á-li-daq**

h'ǎ́ 风行 *v.* be in fashion

h'ǎ́-dzï 杏子 *n.* apricot

h'ǎ́-li 行李 *n.* luggage

h'ǎ́-li-piaw 行李票 *n.* baggage check

hǎ̌-baq-lǎ-dǎ 总共 *adv.* altogether, *Alt.*: **yīq-g'ong** 一共, **g'óng-dzong, lóng-dzong, yīq-taq-guaq-dzï, dzóng-g'ong**

h'áe 闲 *adj.* idle, not busy, free

h'áe 咸 *adj.* salty; salt-perserved

h'áe-(aq-)d'ae 咸（鸭）蛋 *n.* salt-preserved duck egg

h'áe-h'uo 话 *n.* talk; speech, language

h'aq 窄 *adj.* narrow

h'aq 盒 *m.w. for boxes of things*

h'aq-dzï 盒子 *n.* box, case

h'aq-vae 盒饭 *n.* boxed meal, *Alt.*: **b'í-dāw**

h'áw 号 *n.* number; size; *m.w.* size, day of the month, date

h'áw-h'uo 豪华 *adj.* luxurious

h'áw-saw 赶紧 *adv.* quickly, lose no time, hurry, *Alt.*: **góe-jin**

h'ǎ́w 缝 *v.* sew

h'ǎ́w-hu 行货 *n.* legitimate goods

h'ǎ́w-ga 行家 *n.* expert, connoisseur, *Alt.*: **h'ǎ́w-jia, náe-h'ǎw** 内行

h'ǎ́w-kong-shin 航空信 *n.* airmail letter

h'ǎ́w-li 项链 *n.* necklace, *Alt.*: **lí-d'iaw**

h'ǎ́w-veq-loq 吃不消 *v.c.* unable to stand, cannot bear, *Alt.*: **chīq-veq-shiaw**

h'én 恨 *v.* hate

h'eq 个 *m.w. for people (general usage), places, Alt.*: **g'eq**

h'eq 的、地 *ptl. (particle marking attributives before nouns and verbs), Alt.*: **g'eq**

h'eq-tsãw 合唱 *v.* sing in a chorus

h'éu 厚 *adj.* thick

h'éu 侯 *v.* wait, wait for, await, *Alt.:* **dén** 等

h'éu-d'ae 后台 *n.* backstage, behind-the-scene

h'éu-d'eu 后头 *l.n.* back, behind, *Alt.:* **h'éu-mi** 后面, **h'éu-di(-d'eu)**

h'éu-d'eu-lae 后来 *t.n.* afterward, later on *(adv.)*, *Alt.:* **h'éu-lae, h'éu-seu-lae**

h'éu-huae 后悔

h'éu-men 后门 *n.* back door

h'éu-niq 后天 *t.n.* day after tomorrow, *Alt.:* **h'éu-ti-dzï**

h'éu-sã 年轻 *adj.* young, *Alt.:* **ní-chin**

h'í 嫌 *v.* dislike, be averse to, repelled by, *Alt.:* **h'í-bi, yì-dzï**

h'í-ni-vae 嫌疑犯 *n.* criminal suspect

h'í-tsaw 现钞 *n.* cash, *Alt.:* **h'í-jin** 现金, **kàe-shü**

h'í-zae 现在 *t.n.* now, *Alt.:* **náe**

h'iá-du-li 斜的 *n.* diagonal

h'iáw-dzã 校长 *n.* principal, president *(of a school)*

h'ín-kuae 幸亏 *adv.* fortunately, *Alt.:* **chǜ-deq, kuàe-deq** 亏得

h'ióng 熊 *n.* bear

h'ióng-ji 公鸡 *n.* rooster, cock

h'ióng-maw 熊猫 *n.* panda

h'ióng-nieu 公牛 *n.* bull

h'óe 汗 *n.* sweat

h'óe 含 *v.* hold in the mouth

h'óe-d'eu 蚕豆 *n.* broad beans, *Alt.:* **zóe-d'eu**

h'óe-ga 寒假 *n.* winter vacation, *Alt.:* **h'óe-jia**

H'óe-goq 韩国 *n.* Korea

h'óe-j'in 寒噤 *n.* chill, shiver

h'óe-ku 汗裤 *n.* knit cotton underpants

h'óe-maw 汗毛 *n.* body hair *(on people)*

h'óe-niq 发烧 *n.* fever

H'óe-nü 韩语 *n.* Korean *(language)*

h'óe-sae 汗衫 *n.* undershirt

h'óng 红 *adj.* red

h'óng 彩虹 *n.* rainbow, *Alt.:* **héu** 鲎

h'óng-loq-den 红绿灯 *n.* traffic light

h'óng-seq 红色 *n.* red

h'óng-sï 洪水 *n.* flood

h'óng-'yaq-sï 红药水 *n.* mercurochrome

h'óng-zuo 红茶 *n.* black tea

h'oq-d'u 学徒 *n.* apprentice, trainee

h'oq-dzï 锅 *n.* wok, pot, pan, *Alt.*: **gù-dzï**

h'oq-gae 锅盖 *n.* pot cover, wok lid, *Alt.*: **gù-gae**

h'oq-h'iaw 学校 *n.* school, *Alt.*: **h'oq-d'âw** 学堂

h'oq-jiaw 锅巴 *n.* rice crust *(at the bottom of a pot of cooked rice)*, *Alt.*: **váe-zï**

h'oq-sã 学生 *n.* student

h'oq-tsae 锅铲 *n.* spatula *(for cooking)*, *Alt.*: **tsáe-daw**

h'ú 糊 *adj.* overcooked and mushy

h'ú 湖 *n.* lake, *Alt.*: **h'ú-paq** 湖泊

h'ú 河 *n.* river, *Alt.*: **gầw** 江

h'ú-baw-d'ae 荷包蛋 *n.* fried egg

h'ú-chi 和气 *adj.* polite and amiable, *Alt.*: **táe-h'u**

h'ú-d'en-ñg 河豚鱼 *n.* pufferfish

h'ú-d'eu 户头 *n.* bank account; client, buyer

h'ú-d'iq 蝴蝶 *n.* butterfly

h'ú-d'iq-jiq 蝴蝶结 *n.* bow knot

h'ú-diaw 胡闹、乱来 *v.* act foolishly or recklessly

h'ú-d'u 糊涂 *adj.* muddled, confused, bewildered, *Alt.*: **móng-tsong, mắw-tsong**

h'ú-dzaw 护照 *n.* passport

h'ú-faq-su 护发素 *n.* hair conditioner

h'ú-fong 蚂蜂 *n.* wasp

h'ú-huo 荷花 *n.* lotus flower

h'ú-j'in 胡琴、二胡 *n.* Chinese fiddle

h'ú-j'iq 沪剧 *n.* Shanghai opera

h'ú-jiaw 胡椒 *n.* pepper

h'ú-lae-d'eu 荷兰豆 *n.* snow peas, pea pod

h'ú-law-b'oq 胡萝卜 *n.* carrot

h'ú-li 狐狸 *n.* fox

h'ú-long 喉咙 *n.* throat, *Alt.*: **h'éu-long**

h'ú-b'in 和平 *n.* peace

h'ú-chi 和气 *n.* kind

h'ú-seu-sãw 护手霜 *n.* hand lotion

h'ú-su, 胡须 *n.* beard, whiskers, moustache, *Alt.*: **ngá-su, h'ú-dzï** 胡子

h'ú-ti 楼梯 *n.* stairs

h'ú-zãw 和尚 *n.* Buddhist monk

h'ú-zï 护士 *n.* nurse

h'uá 坏 *adj.* bad, broken, spoiled

h'uá-ti-chi 坏天气 *n.* bad weather

h'uá•'yǔn 怀孕 *v.o.* be pregnant, get pregnant *(adj., v.)*, *Alt.:* **h'uá•yóng, d'ú-d'u-b'i, 'yéu-shi** 有喜

h'uǎ-d'aw-shi 人行横道 *n.* crosswalk, *Alt.:* **bàe-mo-shi**

h'uǎ-li-shiã 横的 *n., attr.* horizontal *(adj., n.)*

h'uǎ•sì-'yin 打赌 *v.o.* bet, wager

h'uǎ-zaq-goq 斜对面 *l.n.* diagonally opposite, *Alt.:* **chiá-dae-gu, zyiá-dae-mi**

h'uǎ 蛮横 *adj.* unreasonable, arbitrary, *Alt.:* **h'uǎ-bã**

h'uáe 会 *aux.* can, know how to, *Alt.:* **wáe, wáe-deq, h'uáe-deq**

h'uáe 会 *n.* meeting, *Alt.:* **wáe**

h'uáe 还 *v.* return, give back

h'uáe-baw 回报 *v.* reciprocate, repay

h'uáe-d'eu-kaq 回头客 *n.* return customer

h'uáe-daq 回答 *n., v.* answer

h'uáe-(dzoe-)chi 回去 *v.c.* return, go back

h'uáe-h'in-b'iq-dzen 回形针 *n.* paperclip

h'uáe-jiaw 回教 *n.* Islamism

h'uáe-kuoe 汇款 *v.o.* remit money

h'uáe-kuoe-dae 汇款单 *n.* money order

h'uáe-lae 回来 *v.* come back, return, *Alt.:* **dzóe-lae**

h'uáe-shiã 茴香 *n.* anise, fennel

h'uáe-shin 彗星 *n.* comet, *Alt.:* **sáw-tseu-shin** 扫帚星

h'uáe-wãw-shin 后悔心 *n.* regret

h'uáe-yin 回音 *n.* reply

h'uaq 滑 *adj.* slippery

h'uaq-d'eu 滑头 *adj.* shifty, cunning

h'uaq-h'u-ti 滑梯 *n.* slide

h'uaq-ji 滑稽 *adj.* funny, amusing, *Alt.:* **shüēq, shiōq, fãq•shüēq, fãq•shiōq**

h'uaq-ji-shi 滑稽戏 *n.* comic opera

h'uǎw 黄 *adj.* yellow

h'uǎw-d'eu 黄豆 *n.* soybeans

h'uǎw-guo 黄瓜 *n.* cucumber

h'uǎw-huen-d'eu 黄昏 *n.* dusk, *Alt.:* **'yá-kua-d'eu**

h'uǎw-liq 黄历 *n.* almanac

h'uǎw-mae-'yü 黄梅雨 *n.* springtime rainy season

h'uắw-nieu 黄牛 *n.* scalper *(black market reseller of theater tickets)*

h'uắw-seq 黄色 *n.* yellow

h'uắw-suo 沙子 *n.* sand

h'uắw-yin 黄莺 *n.* oriole

h'uắw-zoe 鳝鱼 *n.* ricefield eel

h'uén 浑浊 *adj.* muddy, turbid

h'uén 混 *v.* mix up, pass off as, muddle along

h'ueq 核儿 *n.* kernel, pit, fruit stone

h'ueq 活 *v.* live, be alive

h'ueq-d'ong 活动 *n.* activity; ~ -gae 活动间 *n.* activity room, family room, den

h'uén-lin(-d'eu) 灵魂 *n.* soul, spirit, *Alt.*: **lín-h'uen**

h'ueq-fae 活泼、伶俐 *adj.* lively and quickwitted

h'ueq-len 囫囵 *adj.* whole, entire

h'ueq-loq 活络 *adj.* noncommittal, loose, clever

h'ueq-paq 活泼 *adj.* lively, vivacious

h'ueq-sen 猴子 *n.* monkey

h'uó 下 *v.o.* get off, get out of, *Alt.*: **loq**

h'uó-b'oq 下巴 *n.* chin, *Alt.*: **h'uó-b'o**

h'uó-boe-ti 下午 *t.n.* afternoon, *Alt.*: **h'uó-boe-niq, h'éu-boe-niq**

h'uó-chi 下去 *v.* descend, go down

h'uó-d'eu 下头 *l.n.* below, underside, *Alt.*: **h'uó-mi** 下面, **h'uó-di(-d'eu)**

h'uó-dzoe 下次 *t.n.* next time

h'uó-dzoq 下流 *adj.* obscene, degenerate, *Alt.*: **ōq-h'in**

h'uó-g'eq-'yüeq 下个月 *t.n.* next month

h'uó-j'iaw 华侨 *n.* overseas Chinese

h'uó-j'iq 话剧 *n.* play *(in theater)*

h'uó-li-ba 下礼拜 *t.n.* next week

h'uó-ti 夏天 *n.* summer, *Alt.*: **niq-ti**

h'uó•mí 下面 *v.o.* cook noodles

h'uóe 换 *v.* change, switch, exchange

h'üóe 悬 *v.* hang, suspend *(literally and figuratively)*

h'üóe-guae 玄关 *n.* vestibule, antechamber, mud room

H

há 蟹 *n.* crab, *Alt.*: **b'áw-ha** 螃蟹

hǎ 气喘喘 *adj.* breathless, panting

háe 海 *n.* sea, ocean

háe-baw 海豹 *n.* seal *(animal)*

háe-da 海带 *n.* seaweed, kelp

háe-sen 海参 *n.* sea cucumber, sea slug

háe-shi 海鲜 *n.* seafood

háe-zeq 海蜇 *n.* jellyfish, *Alt.*: **b'aq-b'i-dzï**

hàe 肿 *v.* swell up, *Alt.*: **shín**

hàe-d'eu 那儿 *prn.* there, *Alt.*: **yì-mi**

hāq 吓 *v.* frighten, scare

hāq-ngae 瞎眼 *v.o.* blind

hāq-yiq-tiaw 吓一跳 *v.o.* startle, take a fright

haw-lae 好了 *ptl. (marks suggestive tone)*, *Alt.*: **law-loq**

háw 好 *adj.* good

háw 好、可以、容易 *aux., adv.* can; easy

háw-chiq 好吃 *adj.* tasty, tastes good, delicious; 可以吃 edible

háw-koe 好看 *adj.* good looking, pretty

háw-zae 好在 *adv.* luckily, *Alt.*: **háw-deq**

háw-zyiā 好象 *adv.* seem like, seems that, *Alt.*: **zyiǎ-saq**

hàw 哈喇 *adj.* rancid

hàw-chi 哈喇气味 *n.* rancid odor

hǎw-zyin 行情 *n.* current market conditions

hēq 黑 *adj.* black

hēq-bae 黑板 *n.* blackboard

hēq-seq 黑色 *n.* black

hén 狠 *adj.* cruel, heartless

hén•b'iq-ti 擤鼻涕 *v.o.* blow one's nose

hóe-baw-baw 汉堡包 *n.* hamburger

hòng 烘 *v.* toast, roast

hōq-shi 打闪 *v.o.* lightning flashes

hú-ga 货架 *n.* goods rack, store shelf

hú-gu 火锅 *n.* hotpot, firepot, *shabu-shabu*

hú-seq 货色 *n.* quality of goods, specifications

hú-tae 火腿 *n.* ham

hú-tsuo 火车 *n.* train

hú-tsuo-zae 火车站 *n.* railway station, train station

hú-zaq 着火 *v.o.* catch on fire

hù 呼 *v.* suck in, inhale, *Alt.*: **shīq** 吸

huà 歪 *adj.* crooked, askew, *Alt.*: **wàe, chiá**

huàe 灰 *adj.* gray; *n.* ash

huàe-seq 灰色 *n.* gray

huàe-zen 灰尘 *n.* dust, *Alt.*: **b'óng-zen**

huāq 舍弃 *v.* give up, abandon

huāq•kàe 裂 *v.* split, crack, *Alt.*: **tsāq, kàe•tsāq**

huāq-huaq 裂缝 *n.* crack, crevice, *Alt.*: **tsāq-tsaq, liq-vong**

huǎw 晃 *adj.* shaky; 摇晃 *v.* sway, rock

huèn-suo 婚纱 *n.* wedding dress

huèn-tsae 荤菜 *n.* meat dish

huèn-yin 婚姻 *n.* marriage

huó-dzāw-pin 化妆品 *n.* makeup

huò 花 *n.* flower; ~ **-b'ae** 花瓣 petals; ~ **-b'en** 花盆 flowerpot

huò 虾 *n.* shrimp, *Alt.*: **hòe**

huò-b'in 花瓶 *n.* vase

huò-di 花店 *n.* flower shop, florist

huò-dzā 假账 *n.* padded accounts, fake accounting

huò-mi 虾米 *n.* dried shrimp, *Alt.*: **hòe-mi**

huò-nin 虾仁 *n.* shelled shrimp, *Alt.*: **hòe-nin**

huò-sen 花生 *n.* peanut

huò-sen-jiā 花生酱 *n.* peanut butter

huò-shi 哈欠 *n.* yawn

huò-tsae 花椰菜 *n.* cauliflower

huò-'yā, 花样 *n.* variations, variety of design or conception, *Alt.*: **huò-d'eu** 花头

huòe-nin 欢迎 *v.* welcome, greet; *interj.* Welcome!

huòe-shi 喜欢 *v.* like, love

J'

j'í 健 *adj.* strong and healthy

j'í 件 *m.w. for shirts, blouses*

j'í 骑 *v.* ride *(a bicycle, horse, etc.)*

j'í-b'aw 旗袍 *n.* cheongsam

j'í-gua 奇怪 *adj.* weird, strange, *Alt.*: **'yéu-jin**

j'í-j'ieu 期盼 *v.c.* expect, hope for

j'í-kā 健康 *adj.* healthy

j'í-sen-vãw 健身房 *n.* exercise room

j'í-zeq 其实 *adv.* in fact, actually

j'í-zeq gú-ven 技术顾问 *n.* technical advisor

j'í-zeq-(zen-)'yüoe 技术人员 *n.* technical personnel

j'iá 强健、能干 *adj.* strong and capable

j'iá-keq(-sae) 夹克 *n.* jacket

j'iǎ 强 *adj.* strong, *Alt.:* **j'iǎ-dzãw** 强壮

j'iǎ-d'aw 强盗 *n.* robber, bandit

j'iáw 桥 *n.* bridge

j'iáw 撬 *v.* pry open

j'iáw-b'a 桥牌 *n.* bridge *(card game)*

j'iáw-maq-mi 荞麦面 *n.* buckwheat noodles

j'iéu 旧 *adj.* old *(not new)*

j'iéu 就 *adv.* then, right away, *Alt.:* **zyiéu**

j'iéu 束 (毬) *m.w. for* bouquet

j'iéu-d'ae 球队 *n.* sports team

j'iéu-h'a 球鞋 *n.* athletic shoes

j'iéu-j'ieu 舅舅 *n.* uncle *(mother's brother)*, *Alt.:*
  niǎ-j'ieu

j'iéu-ma 舅母 *n.* aunt *(wife of mother's brother)*

j'iéu-sae 球赛 *n.* ball game

j'iéu-zã 球场 *n.* ball field, ball court

j'ín 近 *adj.* near

j'ín-j'i 勤俭 *adj.* hardworking and thrifty, *Alt.:* **bò-jiq**

j'ín-j'in 仅仅、才 *adv.* only, *Alt.:* **dzèn-dzen**

j'ín-kua 勤快 *adj.* diligent and conscientious

j'ín-ñg 鲸鱼 *n.* whale

j'ín-tsae 芹菜 *n.* celery

j'ín-zï 近视 *adj.* nearsighted

j'ín-zï-ngae 近视眼 *n.* nearsightedness

j'ióng 穷 *adj.* poor

j'ióng 尽力地 *adv.* with all one's effort

j'iq 极了、透 *d.c.* extremely, very, *Alt.:* **sãq** 煞, **sãq-
  deq, téu**

j'iq-zã 剧场 *n.* theater, *Alt.:* **j'ĭq-'yüoe** 剧院

j'ǔ-d'ae 柜台 *n.* front desk, shop counter, *Alt.:* **g'uáe-
  d'ae**

j'ǔ-loq-b'u 俱乐部 *n.* club

j'üeq 倔 *adj.* headstrong, unbending, stubborn, *Alt.:*
  j'üeq-j'iǎ 倔强, **j'ioq-jiǎ, ngǎ-j'iǎ, g'én**

j'üeq-tsoq 局促 *adj.* narrow and cramped, *Alt.*: **j'ioq-tsoq**

j'ün-dzï 裙子 *n.* skirt, *Alt.*: **j'ióng-dzï**

J

jí 茧 *n.* cocoon; **jīq- ~** 结茧 spin a cocoon

jí 几 *num.* how many

jí 剪 *v.* cut *(with scissors)*, clip, trim

jí 寄 *v.* mail

jí•d'éu-faq 剪头发 *v.o.* cut one's hair, *Alt.*: **tí•d'éu(-faq)**, **lí•fāq** 理发

jí-d'i 多少钱 *n.m.* how much does it cost

jí-daw 剪刀 *n.* scissors, shears

jí-dia 后父 *n.* stepfather, *Alt.*: **gú-vãw-'ya**

jí-dzae 记者 *n.* journalist, reporter

jí•dzǎ 记账 *v.o.* record on account, *Alt.*: **dzú•dzǎ**

jí-dzï 茧子 *n.* cocoon

jí-dzï 毽子 *n.* shuttlecock

jí-dzoq 建筑 *n.* architecture

jí-dzoq-sï 建筑师 *n.* architect

jí-g'eq 几个 *n.m.* how many, a few, some, *Alt.*: **jí-eq**

jí-huo *prn.* how many, *Alt.*: **dù-saw** 多少

jí-kaq 翅膀 *n.* wing, *Alt.*: **tsï̀-bãw**

jí-loq 记录 *v.* make note of, write down, record

jí-mae 姐妹 *n.* sisters *(elder and younger)*

jí•mí 见面 *v.o.* meet, see

jí-ni-'yüoe 检验员、检货员 *n.* inspector, *Alt.*: **jí-hu-'yüoe**

jí-shin 记忆力 *n.* memory *(faculty)*

jí-seu *n.* left hand, *Alt.*: **dzú-seu** 左手

jí-teq 记得 *v.* remember

jí-ti-zï 简体字 *n.* simplified characters, *Alt.*: **shiáw-shia-zï**

jí-zï 多少时间 *prn.* how long, *Alt.*: **dù-saw zén-guãw**

jí-zï 什么时候 *prn.* when

jì 尖 *adj.* sharp

jì 鸡 *n.* chicken; **~ -maw** 鸡毛 chicken feather; **~ -shin** 鸡心 chicken heart; **~ -shiong** 鸡胸 chicken breast; **~ -tae** 鸡腿 chicken leg

jì 煎 *v.* fry in shallow oil

jì 揲 v. pick up (with chopsticks), Alt.: **jīq**

jì-bãw 鸡翅 n. chicken wing

jì-bãw 肩膀 n. shoulder, Alt.: **jì-gaq**

jì-d'ae 鸡蛋 n. chicken egg

jì-doq 基督 n. Christ

jì-doq-jiaw 基督教 n. Christianity, Protestantism

jì-dzen 鸡胗 n. chicken gizzard

jì-hu 几乎 adv. almost

jì-jiaq-dzaw 鸡爪 n. chicken feet

jì-nin 记号 n. mark, sign

jì-nioq 鸡肉 n. chicken (meat)

jì-nioq 肌肉 n. muscle

jì-shiaw 讥笑 v. ridicule

jì-zã-ba-sï 机场巴士 n. airport bus

jì-zoe 居然 adv. to one's surprise, Alt.: **jín(-zoe)** 竟然

jì-zoe 既然 conj. since

jiá-fu 姐夫 n. brother-in-law (elder sister's husband)

jiá-jia 姐姐 n. sister (elder), Alt.: **āq-jia, āq-ji**

jiá-keu 借口 n. excuse, pretext, Alt.: **yìn-d'eu, tàe-d'eu**

jiá-zaw 介绍 v. introduce, Alt.: **jí** 荐

jià-d'in-yin-'yüoe 家庭影院 n. home theater

jià-pu 家谱 n. family tree, genealogy

jià-shiã 家乡 n. hometown, native place

jià-zã-vae 家常饭 n. home cooking

jià-zoq 家属 n. family members

jiá-jin 奖金 n. bonus (money)

jiá-paq 强迫 v. force (someone to do something)

jiá-'yeu 酱油 n. soy sauce

jiã 犟 adj. stubborn, obstinate, Alt.: **kǎ**

jiã 姜 n. ginger, Alt.: **sã-jiã** 生姜

jiã 掺 v. mix in, put in, Alt.: **tsàe, shiã**

jiã 浆 v. starch

jiã-h'u 浆糊 n. paste

jiã-lae 将来 n. future, in the future

jiāq 脚 n. foot (sometimes including the leg)

jiāq-d'aq-tsuo 脚踏车 n. bicycle

jiāq-d'eu 行踪 n. whereabouts

jiāq-dzãw 脚掌 n. sole (of the foot), Alt.: **jiāq-di(-bae)**

jiāq-h'eu-gen 脚跟 n. heel

jiāq-jiq-d'eu 脚趾 n. toe, Alt.: **jiāq-dzï-d'eu**

jiāq-koq-zong 甲壳虫 n. beetle

jiāq-ku-gueq 踝骨 *n.* ankle, anklebone

jiāq-li 脚链 *n.* ankle bracelet

jiāq-moe-deu 膝盖 *n.* knee

jiāq-ñg 鳖 *n.* turtle

jiāq-pǎw 腿 *n.* leg

jiāq-seq 角色 *n.* role, part

jiāq-shi 脚癣 *n* athlete's foot, *Alt.*: **jiāq-chi, shià-gǎw-jiaq**

jiáw 叫 *v.* call, shout, cry out; called, named

jiáw 教 *v.* teach

jiáw-bi 哨子 *n.* whistle, *Alt.*: **jiáw-dzï**

jiáw-d'āw 教堂 *n.* church, cathedral, mosque, temple, *Alt.*: **lí-ba-d'āw**

jiáw-gaw 叫醒 *v.c.* rouse, awaken, wake (someone) up

jiáw-gu-gu 蝈蝈 *n.* katydid

jiáw-h'uaq 狡猾 *adj.* sly, slick, scheming

jiáw•ngá-ma 叫外卖 *v.o.* order take-out (food)

jiáw-seq 教室 *n.* classroom, *Alt.*: **kú-d'āw(-gae)**

jiàw 焦 *adj.* burnt, scorched

jiàw 浇 *v.* water, irrigate

jiàw-dzï 饺子 *n. jiǎozi*, dumpling (steamed or boiled), *Alt.*: **jiáw-dzï**

jiàw-guae 很、相当多 *adv.* very, quite; *adj.* very many, much, rather a lot, a good number of

jiàw-ngaw 骄傲 *adj.* conceited, arrogant

jiàw-zyin 交情 *n.* friendship

jiéu 酒 *n.* liquor, wine

jiéu 九 *num.* nine

jiéu-ba 酒吧 *n.* bar, pub

jiéu-di 酒店 *n.* hotel

jiéu-h'u-tsuo 救护车 *n.* ambulance, *Alt.*: **jiéu-min-tsuo**

jiéu-niǎ 酒酿 *n.* fermented rice (usually served sweet)

jiéu-seq 九十 *num.* ninety

jiéu-tsae 韭菜 *n.* Chinese chives

jiéu-'yüeq 九月 *t.n.* September, *Alt.*: **jiéu-'yoq**

jiéu-yiq 酒窝 *n.* dimples, *Alt.*: **jiéu-wu**

jín 紧 *adj.* tight

jín 井 *n.* well, water well

jín 进 *v.* enter, go in, come in

jín-chiaw 俊俏 *adj.* lovely and graceful

jín-d'eu 劲头 *n.* enthusiasm, vigor

jín-di 景点 *n.* scenic spot

jín-dzã 紧张 *adj.* exciting, tense

jín-dzǐ 镜子 *n.* mirror

jín-dzï 风景 *n.* scenery, view

jín•hú 进货 *v.o.* stock with goods

jín-jiq 紧急 *adj.* urgent

jín-lae 进来 *v.* come in

jín-tsaq 警察 *n.* police

jín-tsaq-j'üeq 警察局 *n.* police station

jín(-zoe) 竟然 *adv.* to one's suprise, *Alt.*: **jì-zoe** 居然

jìn 精 *adj.* shrewd, astute, *Alt.*: **jìn-min** 精明, **jìn-guaq**

jìn 斤 *n.* catty *(a Chinese unit of weight now standardized at 500 grams)*

jìn-dzaw(-dzǐ) 今天 *t.n.* today

jìn-dzen(-tsae) 金针 *n.* day-lily flower *(dried to use as a vegetable)*

jìn-dzï 金子 *n.* gold

jìn-gu 经过 *v.* pass

jìn-gua 精明乖巧 *adj.* astute and clever

jìn•guǎw 精光 *adj.* completely used up, with nothing left

jìn-h'uãw 金黄 *n.* gold *(in color)*

jìn-ji 经济 *n.* economy

jìn-jiaw 信教 *v.o.* profess a religion

jìn-jiaw-dzae 教徒 *n.* follower of a religion

jìn-li 经理 *n.* manager

jìn-ñg 金鱼 *n.* goldfish

jìn-ni 今年 *t.n.* this year

jìn-nioq 瘦肉 *n.* lean meat, *Alt.*: **séu-nioq**

jìn-shi 京剧 *n.* Beijing opera

jìn-tsae 精彩 *n.* delightful, wonderfully entertaining

jìn-'yong 经用 *adj.* durable, wears well, lasts long

jìn-'yong 金融, *n.* finance

jiõq-huo 菊花 *n.* chrysanthemum, *Alt.*: **jüēq-huo**

jīq 荚 *n.* pod, bean pod, pea pod, *Alt.*: **d'éu-jiq** 豆荚

jīq 接 *v.* catch; receive; connect

jīq 结 *v.* tie, knot

jīq-ae-zen-bi 节哀顺变 *ph.* condolences *(n.)*

jīq-pu-tsuo 吉普车 *n.* jeep

jīq•bìn 结冰 *v.o.* freeze, ice up

jīq-d'eu-yin 指印 *n.* fingerprint *(on a surface)*

jīq-dzaq 结扎 *v.* get a vasectomy or a tubal ligation

jīq-dzen 急诊 *n.* emergency room

jīq-dzï 蜘蛛 *n.* spider, *Alt.:* **dzï̀-dzï**

jīq-dzï-lu-mãw 蜘蛛网 *n.* spiderweb

jīq-huen 结婚 *v.o.* marry, get married *(of both bride and groom)*

jīq-kaq-'yeu 指甲油 *n.* nail polish

jīq-moq 积木 *n.* blocks *(toy)*

jīq-nen-den 节能灯 *n.* energy saving lamp

jīq-sã 接生 *v.o.* deliver a child

jīq-sï … h'á 即使 … 也 *conj.* even if …, still

jīq-soq 结束 *v.* end

jīq-tsaw 急躁 *adj.* irritable, *Alt.:* **jīq-dzaw, b'áw-tsaw, b'áw-dzaw** 暴躁

jīq-vi 结尾; *n.* end

jīq-zeq 结实 *adj.* durable, solid

jīq•zeq 积食 *v.o.* have indigestion, *Alt.:* **dén•zeq**

jīq-zeu 接受 *v.* accept

jīq-zï 急事 *n.* urgent matter, emergency

jǘ 贵 *adj.* expensive

jǘ 句 *m.w. for sentences*

jǘ 鬼 *n.* ghost, *Alt.:* **guáe**

jǘ *v.* raise, hold up, *Alt.:* **j'í** 举

jǜ-li 果子冻 *n.* jello

jüēq-dzï 橘子 *n.* tangerine, *Alt.:* **jiōq-dzï**

jüēq-dzï-sï 橘子水 *n.* orange juice

jüēq-h'ong-seq 橘红色 *n.* orange *(color)*, *Alt.:* **jiōq-h'ong-seq, jüēq-h'uãw-seq** 橘黄色, **jiōq-h'uãw-seq**

jüóe 卷 *v.* roll up

jüóe-d'eu 手帕 *n.* handkerchief

jüóe-d'ong-dzï 卷筒纸 *n.* toilet paper in a roll

K

ká-la-wo-kae 卡拉OK *n.* karaoke, *Alt.:* **kàe-gu**

ká-pi 卡片 *n.* card

ká-tsuo 卡车 *n.* truck

kà 擦、揩 *v.* wipe, erase

kà-ba 咖啡吧 *n.* café, coffee shop

kà-bu 抹布 *n.* wiping cloth, dish rag, *Alt.:* **kà-d'ae-bu, meq-bu**

kà-fī 咖啡 *n.* coffee

kà-fī-seq 咖啡色 *n.* brown *(n., adj.)*

kà-tsae 芥菜 *n.* mustard greens

káe 撞 *v.* collide with, run into, *Alt.:* **zǎw**

kàe 铅 *n.* lead

kàe 开 *v.* open

kàe•b'óe 开盘 *n.* opening price *(at an exchange)*

kàe-biq 铅笔 *n.* pencil

kàe-d'eu 开始 *n.* beginning, initial stage, *Alt.:* **kàe-sï**

kàe•dàw 开刀 *v.o.* operate, perform surgery, get an operation, *Alt.:* **d'óng•séu-zeq** 动手术

kàe-faq-chü 开发区 *n.* development zone

kàe•gá 开价 *n.* opening price

kàe-guae 开关 *n.* switch

kàe-shiaw 开销 *n.* expenses

kàe-shin 开心 *adj.* happy, cheery

kàe-sï 开始 *v.* begin, start

kàe-sï 开水 *n.* boiled water

kàe•tsuò 开车 *v.o.* drive a car

kàe•'wóe-shiaw 开玩笑 *v.o.* tell a joke, *Alt.:* **dǎ•b'ǎ**

kāq-chi 客气 *adj.* polite, courteous

kāq-h'u 客户 *n.* client, customer

kāq-kaq-jiaw 恰恰地 *adv.* just by chance, as it happened, *Alt.:* **dzén-haw** 正好

kāq-moe 客满 *v.* have a full house, be sold out

kāq-nin 客人 *n.* guest, *Alt.:* **nín-kaq**

káw 靠 *v.* get near, approach

káw 烤 *v.* roast, broil

káw-jieu 考究、讲究 *adj.* fastidious, particular about

káw-jüoe 考卷 *n.* examination paper

káw-shiā 烤箱 *n.* oven

káw-sï 考试 *n.* test, examination

kàw 敲 *v.* knock

kàw•báe 敲背 *v.o.* beat lightly on one's back *(as a massage)*, *Alt.:* **dīq•páe** 捶背

kàw•d'ín 敲定 *v.c.* make a final decision, come to an agreement

kàw•jiǎ-jin 减奖金 *v.o.* cut bonus

kàw-seu-yi 靠手椅 *n.* armchair

kǎw 藏 *v.* store, put away, conceal, hide

kén 积垢 *n.* grime *(as on skin)*, *Alt.:* **láw-ken**

kén 啃 *v.* gnaw on, *Alt.*: **ngà, ngá**

kēq 刻 *m.w.* quarter hour

kēq•d'éu 磕头 *v.o.* kowtow *(the traditional gesture of touching the forehead to the ground as a sign of deference)*

kēq-seu 咳嗽 *v.* cough

kēq-tin 客厅 *n.* living room

kēq-tsong 瞌睡 *n.* nap, snooze

kēq-vāw 客房 *n.* guest room, hotel room

kéu 口 *m.w. for mouthfuls*

kéu 正好 *adj.* just right

kèu 抠 *adj.* stingy, miserly

kóe 看 *v.* look, see, watch; visit; read

kóe-deq-chi 看得起 *v.c.* think highly of, respect, *Alt.*: **kóe•zóng** 看重, **kóe-zen**

kóe-koe-koe 看看 *v.* have a look, take a try, *Alt.*: **kóe-koe-jiaw**

kóe-māw 看望 *v.* visit, call on

kóe-shiā 看中 *v.c.* take a fancy to, settle on, *Alt.*: **kóe-dae**

kóe•sì 看书 *v.o.* read *(a book)*, study

kóng 欠 *v.* owe

kóng-chiaq 孔雀 *n.* peacock

kóng-po 恐怕 *adv.* probably, *Alt.*: **kóng-vāw(-b'āw), zǎ-po**

kóng-vāw-gae 空房间 *n.* vacant room

kòng 空 *adj.* empty

kòng-chi 空气 *n.* air

kòng-d'iaw(-ji) 空调机 *n.* air-conditioner

kòng-d'iaw-tsuo 空调车 *n.* air-conditioned car or bus

kòng-d'iaw-vāw 空调房 *n.* air-conditioned room

kōq 哭 *v.* cry, weep

kōq-dzï 壳子 *n.* shell, hard case

kú 苦 *adj.* bitter

kú-naw 苦恼 *adj.* miserable, bitter

kú-naw-dzï 可怜的样子 *adj.* pitiful

kú-ben 课本 *n.* textbook

kú-li 可怜 *adj.* pitiable, pitiful

kú-nen 可能 *adv.* possibly

kú-shiq 可惜 *adj.* be a pity

kú-yi 可以 *aux.* can; be permitted to

kú-zen 课程 *n.* course, curriculum

kù 棵 *m.w. for plants, trees*

kù 窝 *n.* nest, lair

kù-dzã 科长 *n.* division chief, section chief, *Alt.*: **dzú-dzã** 组长

kù-dzï 裤子 *n.* pants, *Alt.*: **kú-dzï**

kù-jiaq 裤腿 *n.* pant leg, *Alt.*: **kú-jiaq, kú-d'ong**

kù-'yüoe 科员 *n.* division member

kuá 快 *adj.* fast; sharp; 快要 *adv.* soon, about to, will soon

kuá-d'i 快递 *n.* express mail, *Alt.*: **kuá-j'i; ~ -shin** 快递信 express mail letter

kuá-di 快点 *adv.* hurry up

kuá-h'ueq 快活 *adj.* happy, thrilled, *Alt.*: **ká-h'ueq**

kuá-loq 快乐 *adj.* happy

kuá-tsoe 快餐 *n.* fast food

kuá-tsoe váe-di 快餐饭店 *n.* fast food restaurant

kuà-dzã 夸张 *v.* exaggerate; *adj.* exaggerated, overstated

kuáe 块 *m.w. for lumps, chunks, soap, bricks*; Chinese *yuán (basic monetary unit)*, *Alt.*: **'yüóe**

kuáe 疙瘩 *n.* swelling, lump, *Alt.*: **gēq-daq**

kuáe 筷子 *n.* chopsticks, *Alt.*: **kuáe-dzï**

kuáe-d'ong 筷子筒 *n.* chopstick holder, *Alt.*: **kuáe-zï-long**

kuáe-ji 会计 *n.* accountant, bookkeeper, *Alt.*: **guáe-ji**

kuàe 傲慢 *adj.* haughty, arrogant, *Alt.*: **láw-kuae**

kuàe•bén 亏本 *v.o.* lose capital, suffer a loss in business, *Alt.*: **zeq•bén** 折本

kuén 睡觉 *v.o.* sleep, *Alt.*: **kuén•gáw, kuèn-gaw**

kuén-yi(-kuen-ku) 睡衣（睡裤）*n.* pajamas, night clothes

kuén-j'iong 睡衣 *n.* nightgown

kuèn-chüeq 昆曲 *n.* Kunqu opera, *Alt.*: **kuèn-chioq**

kuēq 宽 *adj.* wide, broad

kuó 跨 *v.* stride across, straddle, *Alt.*: **kuá**

kuòe-da-mãw 宽带网 *n.* broadband internet

kuòe-jin-da 松紧带 *n.* elastic

kuòe-kueq 宽阔 *adj.* broad and spacious

kuòe-sï 宽舒 *adj.* abundant *(space or wealth)* and comfortable, *Alt.*: **kuòe-'yü** 宽余

L

lá 诬赖 *v.* blame falsely; 抵赖 *v.* deny, repudiate, go against one's word

lá-ba 喇叭 *n.* speaker, loudspeaker

lá-geq-bo 癞蛤蟆 *n.* toad, *Alt.*: **lá-sï-geq, lá-ha-mo**

lá-shi 垃圾 *n.* garbage, refuse, *Alt.*: **leq-seq**

lá•dzǎ 赖账 *v.o.* repudiate a debt

là 拉 *v.* pull, *Alt.*: **bàe**

là•b'ín 扯平 *v.* average out, make even

là•ká 刷卡 *v.o.* swipe a credit card

là-li 拉练 *n.* zipper

là-mi 拉面 *n.* pulled-dough noodles

lá 冷 *adj.* cold

lá-d'ae 冷淡 *adj.* cold, indifferent, cheerless

lá-men-hu 冷门货 *n.* low sales item

lá-ti *n.* winter, *Alt.*: **dòng-ti** 冬天

lá-zyin 冷静 *adj.* cool, calm and collected; sober

lae 吧、呢 *ptl. (at sentence end marks assumptions, suggestions, etc.)*

lae 正在 *ptl. (after verb marks progressive aspect)*

láe 蓝 *adj.* blue

láe 懒 *adj.* lazy, *Alt.*: **láe-du** 懒惰, **láe-poq**

láe 烂 *adj.* rotten

láe 雷 *n.* thunder

láe 来 *v.* come

láe(-d'eu) 篮子 *n.* basket

láe-gae 栏杆 *n.* railing, banister

láe-huo 兰花 *n.* orchid

láe-j'ieu 篮球 *n.* basketball

láe-seq 蓝色 *n.* blue

láe-sï 蕾丝 *n.* lace

láe-wu-ni 泥巴，泥土 *n.* mud, dirt, *Alt.*: **ná-ni, ní-d'eu**

láe-zen-'yü 雷阵雨 *n.* thunderstorm

láe-zï 能干 *adj.* capable, competent, *Alt.*: **láe-sae**

laq 辣 *adj.* spicy, hot

laq 在 *v., prep.* be in, be at, be on, *Alt.*: **laq-hae, laq-laq, laq-lãw** 在里头、在那儿

laq-biq 蜡笔 *n.* crayon

laq-d'eu 猎头 *n.* headhunter

laq-dzï 蜡纸 *n.* wax paper

laq-jiaw 辣椒 *n.* chili pepper

laq-taq 脏乱 *adj.* dirty and messy

laq-'yeu 辣油 *n.* chili oil

láw 老 *adj.* old *(not young)*; tough *(not tender)*

láw 牢 *adj.* sturdy, firm, durable

láw 很 *adv.* very, *Alt.:* **zyiá-chi**

láw-b'oq 萝卜 *n.* white radish, *Alt.:* **lú-b'oq**

láw-bae 老板 *n.* boss; shopkeeper

láw-bae-niã 老板娘 *n.* boss' wife; female shopkeeper

láw-chi 老气 *adj.* old-fashioned, outdated

láw-d'eu-dzï 老头子 *n.* old man

láw-dzaw(-dzï) 老早 *t.n., adv.* very early on, long ago, quite early, *Alt.:* **láw-di-dzï**

láw-gae 监狱 *n.* jail, prison

láw-gong 老公 *n.* husband, *Alt.:* **zã́-fu** 丈夫

láw-h'uo 乌鸦 *n.* crow, *Alt.:* **wù-ya**

láw-hu 老虎 *n.* tiger

láw-hu-j'i 钳子 *n.* pliers, tongs

láw-jü 经验丰富 *adj.* experienced, *Alt.:* **jü•láw(-lae)**

láw-sï 老师 *n.* teacher, *Alt.:* **làw-sï**

láw-ta(-ta) 老太太 *n.* old woman

láw-tsï 老鼠 *n.* mouse, rat, *Alt.:* **láw-zong**

láw-yin 老鹰 *n.* hawk, eagle

láw-zeq 老实 *adj.* honest and nice

làw 捞 *v.* scoop out *(of water)*, fish out

lãw 狼 *n.* wolf

lãw 上 *sfx.* on *(locative suffix)*, *Alt.:* **zãw, lãw-shiã**

lãw 晾 *v.* air dry

lãw-d'eu 锤子 *n.* hammer

lãw-d'eu 波浪 *n.* wave

lãw-fi 浪费 *v.* waste; *adj.* wasteful

lãw•yì-zã 晾衣服 *v.o.* hang clothing to air dry

lén-b'oe 轮子 *n.* wheel

lén-zoe 轮船 *n.* passenger ship

leq 了 *ptl.* (*marks perfective aspect*), *Alt.:* **dzï, zï, teq, laq-leq**

leq 捋 *v.* stroke, smooth out

leq-b'ã-gueq 肋骨 *n.* rib

léu•chí 漏气 *v.o.* leak air

léu-deu 漏斗 *n.* funnel, strainer

léu-h'uo-d'eu 楼下 *n.* downstairs

léu-lãw 楼上 *n.* upstairs

léu-vãw 楼房 *n.* building *(usually of two or more stories)*

léu-zoq 漏勺 *n.* slotted spoon

lí 连 *prep.* even including, *Alt.*: **lí-deq**

lí 离 *prep.* from *(in distance)*

lí 练 *v.* practice, train, drill

lí 理 *v.* tidy up, put in order, straighten up

lí 沥 *v.* trickle out, drain through a strainer

lí-ba 礼拜 *n.* week

lí-ba-loq 礼拜六 *t.n.* Saturday

lí-ba-ñg 礼拜五 *t.n.* Friday

lí-ba-ni 礼拜二 *t.n.* Tuesday, *Alt.*: **lí-ba-liã**

lí-ba-niq 礼拜日 *t.n.* Sunday

lí-ba-sae 礼拜三 *t.n.* Wednesday

lí-ba-sï 礼拜四 *t.n.* Thursday

lí-ba-yiq 礼拜一 *t.n.* Monday

lí-d'ãw 礼堂 *n.* auditorium

lí-d'eu 里头 *l.n.* inside, *Alt.*: **lí-shiã(-d'eu)**

lí-dzï 帘子 *n.* curtain, hanging screen

lí-dzï 李子 *n.* plum

lí•fãq 理发 *v.o.* cut one's hair, *Alt.*: **tí•d'éu(-faq), jí•d'éu-faq**

lí-faq-di 理发店 *n.* barbershop

lí-h'ae 厉害 *adj.* formidable

lí-huen 离婚 *v.o.* divorce

lí-jiq 里脊 *n.* pork tenderloin

lí-kae 离开 *v.* leave, depart

lí-liq 利率 *n.* interest rate

lí-ñg 鲤鱼 *n.* carp

lí-sae-j'ün 连衣裙 *n.* one-piece dress, *Alt.*: **lí-sae-j'iong**

lí-shin 莲子 *n.* lotus seed

lí-shiq 利息 *n.* interest *(on investment)*, *Alt.*: **lí-d'i**

lí-'yeu 理由 *n.* reason, grounds

lí-zyiq 痢疾 *n.* dysentery

lí-zyiq-b'u 练习本 *n.* exercise book

liã́ 亮 *adj.* bright

liã́ 两 *num.* two; *n.* tael (a Chinese unit of weight now standardized at 50 grams)

liã́-b'ãw-bi 两边 *n.* both sides

liǎ-chi 气量 *n.* tolerance, *Alt.:* **chí-liã**

liǎ-maw 凉帽 *n.* summer hat, *Alt.:* **fòng-liã-maw**

liǎ-sǎw 凉快 *adj.* cool, pleasantly cool, *Alt.:* **fòng-liã**

liǎ-tsae 凉菜 *n.* cold dishes, appetizers, *Alt.:* **lǎ-b'en** 冷盘

liǎ-tsï 两次 *n.m.* twice

liǎ-'yüeq 二月 *n.* February, *Alt.:* **liǎ-'yoq**

liéu 留 *v.* remain, stay; reserve, keep

liéu•b'iq-ti 流鼻涕 *v.o.* have a runny nose

liéu•h'óe 流汗 *v.o.* sweat

liéu-h'in-gu-chüeq 流行歌曲 *n.* popular songs

liéu-h'in-shin góe-maw 流行性感冒 *n.* flu

liéu-hae 刘海 *n.* bangs, *Alt.:* **zyí-lieu-hae**

liéu•ngáe-li 流眼泪 *v.* weep, shed tears, *Alt.:* **loq•ngáe-li**

liéu-shin 流星 *n.* meteor, shooting star

lín 灵 *adj.* efficacious, *Alt.:* **lín-guǎw** 灵光

lín 菱 *n.* water caltrop, *Alt.:* **lín-goq** 菱角

lín 零 *num.* zero

lín 淋 *v.* drip, shower, rain upon, drench

lín-chiaw 灵巧 *adj.* dexterous, nimble

lín-d'ǎw 冰柱 *n.* icicle

lín-d'eu 领子 *n.* collar

lín-d'eu 零头 *n.* small change; remainder

lín-gong 零工 *n.* day laborer

lín-h'uen 灵魂 *n.* soul, spirit, *Alt.:* **h'uén-lin(-d'eu)**

lín-h'ueq 灵活 *adj.* nimble, flexible, quick-witted

lín-jü 邻居 *n.* neighbor, *Alt.:* **lín-suo**

lín-li 伶俐 *adj.* quick-witted, clever, bright

lín-ma 零售 *v.* sell by the piece, *Alt.:* **diáw-tsen**

lín-min 灵敏 *adj.* agile, keen, clever

lín-sae 零碎 *adj.* piecemeal, small and fragmentary

lín-sae 零工 *n.* odd jobs

lín-'yã 领养 *v.* adopt

lín-'yoq 淋浴 *n.* shower *(bath)*

lín-'yoq-vǎw 淋浴房 *n.* shower *(stall)*, *Alt.:* **tsòng-lin-vǎw**

lín•'yǘ 淋雨 *v.o.* get wet or drenched in the rain, be rained upon, *Alt.:* **dōq•'yǘ**

lín-zaq 临着 *adv.* prior to, just before, *Alt.:* **lín-daw**

lín-zeq 零食 *n.* snack

lín-zï-guoe 领事馆 *n.* consulate

lìn 拎 *v.* carry

liq 粒 *m.w. for pieces of candy, marbles, single grains*

liq 滴干、漏干 *v.* drip dry

liq 站、立 *v.* stand

liq 搣 *v.* twist

liq-chi 力气 *n.* strength *(physical)*, *Alt.*: **chí-liq, liq-d'aw**

liq-dzï 栗子 *n.* chestnut

liq-dzï 荔枝 *n.* lychee, *Alt.*: **mó-liq-dzï**

liq-faq 法律 *n.* law

liq-shiq 碎屑 *n.* crumbs

liq-vong 裂缝 *n.* crack, crevice, *Alt.*: **tsāq-tsaq, huāq-huaq**

lóe 乱 *adj.* chaotic

lóe-gãw 乱讲 *v.* talk nonsense, prattle on, *Alt.*: **hāq-h'uo, hāq-gãw** 胡说

lóng-b'ã 耳聋 *v.* deaf

lóng-d'ãw 弄堂、胡同 *n.* lane, alley

lóng-dzong 总共 *adv.* altogether, *Alt.*: **yīq-g'ong** 一共, **g'óng-dzong, dzóng-g'ong, yīq-taq-guaq-dzï, hã-baq-lã-dã**

lóng-huo 龙虾 *n.* lobster

lóng-jüoe-fong 龙卷风 *n.* tornado, cyclone

loq 绿 *adj.* green

loq 六 *num.* six

loq 下 *v.o.* get off of; get out of, *Alt.*: **h'uó**

loq-chi 下去 *v.* go down, fall, drop

loq-d'eu 绿豆 *n.* mung beans

loq-d'i 绿地 *n.* greenery; green area

loq•lú-sï 下露 *v.o.* dew

loq•sãw 下霜 *v.o.* frost

loq-seq 绿色 *n.* green

loq-seq 六十 *num.* sixty

loq•shīq 下雪 *v.o.* snow

loq-teq 掉 *v.* drop, fall; 丢失 *v.* lose *(something)*

loq-toq 落拓 *adj.* casual, unconventional

loq•'yü 下雨 *v.o.* rain

loq-'yü-ti 下雨天 *n.* rainy weather

loq-'yüeq 六月 *t.n.* June, *Alt.*: **loq-'yoq**

loq-yin 录音 *v.* record *(audio)*

loq-yin-ji 录音机 *n.* recorder

lú 指纹 *n.* fingerprint *(on the finger)*, *Alt.*: **vén-lu**

lú 锣 *n.* gong

lú 路 *n.* road, public road, *Alt.*: **gòng-lu** 公路, **mó-lu** 马路

lú-gu 如果 *conj.* if, *Alt.*: **zǐ-gu, yáw-zï** 要是

lú-kuǎw, 笋筐、栲栳 *n.* bamboo or wicker basket *(large)*, *Alt.*: **gēq-law**

lú-sen 芦笋 *n.* asparagus

lú-sï 露水 *n.* dew

lú-sï 螺蛳 *n.* snail *(water dwelling)*

lù-su 罗嗦 *adj.* long-winded, troublesome

lǘ-guoe 旅馆 *n.* inn, hotel

lǘ-h'in 旅行 *v.* travel, take a journey

lǘ-h'in dzǐ-piaw 旅行支票 *n.* traveler's check

lǘ-'yeu 旅游 *v., n.* tour

M

m̄-meq 没有 *adv.* did not; *v.* do not have; there is not

m̄-meq guàe-shi! 没关系! *interj.* It doesn't matter! , *Alt.*: **veq-taq gá!**

m̄-meq-leq 死了 *v.* dead *(adj.)*, *Alt.*: **gú-leq**

m̀-ma 妈妈 *n.* mother, *Alt.*: **mà-ma, láw-ma**

má 埋 *v.* bury

má 买 *v.* buy

má 卖 *v.* sell

má-dae! 埋单! *interj.* The check *(please)*!

má-dzï 买主 *n.* buyer

má-ma 买卖 *n.* business, trade

má-yüoe 埋怨 *v.* complain, grumble

mà-hu 马虎 *adj.* sloppy, careless, overly casual

mà-zã, 马上 *adv.* immediately, *Alt.*: **mó-zã, jiq-keq, zóe-jiq, shíq-shiq**

mǎ 密 *adj.* dense, tightly spaced, crowded, *Alt.*: **miq**

máe 慢 *adj.* slow

máe 煤 *n.* coal

máe-chi 煤气 *n.* gas, coal gas, *Alt.*: **gáe-sï**

máe-dzéu! 慢走! *interj.* Take care as you go!, *Alt.*: **dzéu•háw!** 走好!

máe-dzï 梅子 *n.* Japanese apricot, *ume*

máe-fu 妹夫 *n.* brother-in-law *(younger sister's husband)*

Máe-goq 美国 *n.* America

Máe-goq-nin 美国人 *n.* American

máe-guae 玫瑰 *n.* rose, *Alt.*: **zyiǎ-b'i, zyiǎ-vi** 薔薇

máe-h'ong-'yüoe 美容院 *n.* beauty parlor

máe-huo 梅花 *n.* plum blossom

máe-mae 妹妹 *n.* younger sister, *Alt.*: **āq-mae**

máe-niã 后母 *n.* stepmother

máe-nin 媒人 *n.* matchmaker, *Alt.*: **jiá-zaw-nin** 介绍人

máe-'yeu 漫游 *v.* roam

máe-'yüoe 美元 *n.* U.S. dollars, *Alt.*: **máe-jin** 美金

màe 很、蛮 *adv.* very, quite, rather

màe 每 *num.* every, *Alt.*: **máe**

maq-dzï 袜子 *n.* socks, *Alt.*: **maq**

maq-keq-fong 麦克风 *n.* microphone

maq-sã-nin 陌生人 *n.* stranger

maq-zoe 短袜 *n.* anklet socks

máw 毛 *n.* fur; feather

máw 锚 *n.* anchor

máw 猫 *n.* cat, *Alt.*: **máw-mi**

máw-biq 毛笔 *n.* writing brush, *Alt.*: **meq-biq**

máw-d'eu 毛豆 *n.* tender soybeans, edamame

máw-d'eu-yin 猫头鹰 *n.* owl

máw-dzï 帽子 *n.* hat

máw-hu 毛料 *n.* woolen fabric

máw-jin 毛巾 *n.* towel

máw-jin-ga 毛巾架 *n.* towel rack

máw-maw-'yü 毛毛雨 *n.* drizzle, misty rain

máw-maw-zong 毛毛虫 *n.* caterpillar

máw-ngae 猫眼 *n.* peephole *(in a door)*

máw-'yi 帽檐 *n.* hat brim

mǎw 忙 *adj.* busy

mǎw 望 *v.* 远看 look into the distance; *prep.* toward, facing, *Alt.*: **záw** 朝, **'wǎw** 往

mǎw-ba 网吧 *n.* internet café

mǎw-gu 芒果 *n.* mango

mǎw-huen 网婚 *n.* internet marriage, cyber marriage

mǎw-ji 忘记 *v.* forget

mǎw-lǎw 网上 *l.n.* online

mǎw-loq 网络 *n.* the Internet, the web

mǎw-shi 网线 *n.* Ethernet cable

mǎw-tsong 糊涂 *adj.* muddled, confused, bewildered,

Alt.: **h'ú-d'u, móng-tsong**

mén 门 *n.* door, gate

mén 问 *v.* ask

mén 闻 *v.* smell, *Alt.*: **'wén, tèn**

mén-dzã 蚊帐 *n.* mosquito net, *Alt.*: **dzã̌-dzï**

mén-dzen 门诊 *n.* outpatient office

mén-kae *n.* 门槛 threshold, doorstep

mén-lu 门路 *n.* associations and contacts

mén-mi 门面 *n.* shop front, facade

mén-piaw 门票 *n.* admission ticket

mén-d'i 问题 *n.* question, problem

mén-zen(-b'u-saq) 门神 (菩萨) *n.* door-god

mén-zong 蚊子 *n.* mosquito

mén-zong-shiã 蚊香 *n.* mosquito-repellent incense

mèn 焖 *v.* braise

mèn-niq 闷热 *adj.* sultry, muggy

meq 么 *ptl. (marks pauses for thought, etc.)*

meq 墨 *n.* inkstick

meq 没 *v.* sink; overflow

meq-bu 抹布 *n.* wiping cloth, dish rag, *Alt.*: **kà-bu, kà-d'ae-bu**

meq-li-huo 茉莉花 *n.* jasmine

meq-sï 墨水 *n.* ink

meq-zï 东西 *n.* thing

méu 某 *prn.* certain, a certain

méu-dae-huo 牡丹花 *n.* peony, tree peony, *Alt.*: **máw-dae-huo**

mí 面 *m.w. for mirrors, flags*

mí 面 *n.* noodles *(made of wheat)*, *Alt.*: **mí-d'iaw** 面条

mí-aw 棉袄 *n.* cotton padded jacket

mí-b'en 脸盆 *n.* washbasin

mí-baw 面包 *n.* bread

mí-baw-tsuo 面包车 *n.* van, minibus

mí-baw-vãw 面包房 *n.* bakery

mí-bo 尾巴 *n.* tail, *Alt.*: **ní-bo**

mí(-d'aw) 味道 *n.* smell

mí-dzï-su 味精 *n.* monosodium glutamate, MSG, *Alt.*: **ví-dzï-su**

mí-fen 面粉 *n.* wheat flour

mí-h'eu-d'aw 猕猴桃 *n.* kiwi *(fruit)*, Chinese gooseberry

mí-h'uāw 米黄 *attr.* beige, straw-colored *(n., adj.)*

mí-huo 棉花 *n.* cotton

mí-jin 面筋 *n.* wheat gluten

mí-kong 脸 *n.* face

mí-ku 棉裤 *n.* cotton padded pants

mí-maw 眉毛 *n.* eyebrow

mí-maw-sae 棉毛衫 *n.* cotton jersey

mí-seq 米色 *n.* beige *(n., adj.)*

mí-shi 苋菜 *n.* amaranth

mí-sï 秘书 *n.* secretary, *Alt.:* **mì-sï**

mí-vae 米饭 *n.* cooked rice

mí-'yā 绵羊 *n.* sheep

mí•zï 面市 *n.* go on the market

mí•zoq 面熟 *adj.* familiar, familiar-looking, *Alt.:* **zoq**
熟

miáw 庙 *n.* temple

miáw-h'uae 庙会 *n.* fair at a temple

mín-b'a 名牌 *n.* name brand

mín-chi 名气 *n.* reputation, fame, name

mín-dzaw(-dzï) 明天 *t.n.* tomorrow, *Alt.:* **mén-dzaw**
(-dzï)

mín-gong 民工 *n.* migrant laborer *(from the countryside)*

mín-gu 民歌 *n.* folk song

mín-min(-jiaw) 明明 *adv.* obviously, plainly, *Alt.:*
mín-min-dzï

mín-ni(-dzï) 明年 *t.n.* next year, *Alt.:* **kàe-ni(-dzï)**

mín-pi 名片 *n.* name card

mín-shi 明显 *adj.* obvious

mín-shin-pi 明信片 *n.* postcard

mín-zï 名字 *n.* name

miq 密 *adj.* dense, tightly spaced, crowded, *Alt.:* **mấ**

miq-d'āw 蜂蜜 *n.* honey

miq-fong 蜜蜂 *n.* bee

mó 沫子 *n.* foam, froth

mó 麻 *n.* hemp

mó 马 *n.* horse

mó 磨 *v.* grind, rub, polish, *Alt.:* **mú, nì, ní** 研

mó 骂 *v.* scold, curse

mó-bu, h'uó-bu 麻布 *n.* burlap

mó-chiaq 麻雀 *n.* sparrow, *Alt.:* **mó-jiaq**

mó-d'a 马达 *n.* motor

mó-d'eu 码头 *n.* pier

mó-d'ong 马桶 *n.* toilet, commode, night soil bucket;
  tsèu-sï-mo-d'ong 抽水马桶 flush toilet

mó-deng 摩登 *adj.* modern, fashionable

mó-dzï 模子 *n.* mold, die

mó-gaq-j'ün 马夹裙 *n.* halter dress, *Alt.:* **mó-gaq-**
  j'ióng

mó-gaw-ñg 鲅鱼 *n.* mackerel

mó-gu 蘑菇 *n.* mushroom

mó-jiã 麻将 *n.* mahjongg

mó-jiã-b'a 麻将牌 *n.* mahjongg tile

mó-keq-biq 马克笔 *n.* marker

mó-lae-d'eu 马兰头 *n.* aster greens

mó-lu 马路 *n.* street

mó-naw 玛瑙 *n.* agate

mó-ni 蚂蚁 *n.* ant

mó-sï 慕司、摩丝 *n.* mousse

mó-toq-tsuo 摩托车 *n.* motorcycle

mó-tsaq 磨擦 *v.* chafe, grind at, rub against, *Alt.:*
  mú-tsaq

mó-vae 麻烦 *adj.* troublesome, inconvenient

mó-'yeu 麻油 *n.* sesame oil

móe 满 *adj.* full, *Alt.:* **dzōq**

móe 鳗鱼 *n.* eel, *Alt.:* **máe-ñg**

móe 瞒、隐瞒 *v.* conceal the facts, hide the truth,
  Alt.: **yín-moe**

móe-d'eu 包子、馒头 *n.* steamed bun *(stuffed or
  unstuffed)*

móe-yi 满意 *adj.* satisfied

móe-'yüeq 满月 *v.o.* be one month old *(of babies)*,
  Alt.: **móe-'yoq**

móng-tsong 糊涂 *adj.* muddled, confused, bewildered,
  Alt.: **h'ú-d'u, mãw-tsong**

moq 摸 *v.* feel, stroke

moq-d'eu 木头 *n.* wood

moq-'er 木耳 *n.* wood ear edible fungus

moq-g'oq 麻木(因冷所致) *adj.* numb *(from the cold)*

moq-gong 木工 *n.* woodworking; woodworker

moq-guo 木瓜 *n.* papaya

moq-ngeu 木偶 *n.* puppet

moq-ngeu-shi 木偶戏 *n.* puppet show

moq-sï 梳子 *n.* comb

moq-tae 木炭 *n.* charcoal

moq-zyiã 木匠 *n.* carpenter

N

ná 乳房 *n.* breast *(of a woman)*, *Alt.*: **ná-na**

ná 你们 *prn.* you *(plural)*

ná-dzaw 胸罩 *n.* bra, brassière, *Alt.*: **vén-shiong**

ná-fen 奶粉 *n.* powdered milk

ná-g'eq 你们的 *prn.* yours *(plural)*, *Alt.*: **ná-eq**

ná-ma 奶妈 *n.* wet nurse

ná-na-d'eu 乳头 *n.* nipple, *Alt.*: **ná-d'eu**

ná-nen 怎么、怎么样 *adv.* how, *Alt.*: **ná-nen-ga**

ná-seu 拿手 *adj.* adept, good at

náe 难 *adj.* difficult

náe 二十（廿）*num.* twenty, *Alt.*: **niáe**

náe-gu 难过 *adj.* sick, unwell; feel sorry, feel badly

náe-gua 难怪 *adv.* no wonder

náe-koe 难看 *adj.* ugly

náe-shin 耐心 *n.* patience

náe-'wae 为难 *n.* put in a bind, be in an awkward situation

náe-'wae-zyin 难为情 *adj.* embarrassed, shy

náe-yi 内衣 *n.* underwear

náe-zã 内脏 *n.* organs, viscera

náe-zen 内存 *n.* memory *(in a computer)*

náw-d'ae 脑袋 *n.* head, brains

náw-dzï 脑子 *n.* brains, mind, *Alt.*: **náw-jin** 脑筋, **d'éu-naw-dzï**

náw-mã 热闹 *adj.* lively, buzzing with excitement, *Alt.*: **niq-naw, náw-niq**

nàw 拿 *v.* hold, take in the hand, *Alt.*: **nàe, nuò, nuó**

nén 嫩 *adj.* tender

nén-geu 能够 *aux.* can, able to

neq 呢 *ptl. (marks questioning tone)*, *Alt.*: **ni**

ni 呢 *ptl. (marks questioning tone)*, *Alt.*: **neq**

ní 年 *n., m.w.* year

ní 二 *num.* two, *Alt.*: **'ér**

ní 染 *v.* dye

ní-bo 尾巴 *n.* tail, *Alt.*: **mí-bo**

ní-chin 年轻 *adj.* young, *Alt.*: **h'éu-sã**

ní-d'ae 砚台 *n.* inkstone

ní-d'eu 瘾 *n.* addiction

ní-d'eu-lãw 年初 *t.n.* beginning of the year

ní-du 耳朵 *n.* ear, *Alt.*: **'ér-du**

ní-du-taw 耳朵套 *n.* earmuff

ní-dzï 儿子 *n.* son, *Alt.*: **'ér-dzï, nóe-shiaw-noe**

ní-gaw 年糕 *n.* New Year's cake *(made of sticky rice)*

ní-gu 尼姑 *n.* Buddhist nun

ní-gu-oe 尼姑庵 *n.* Buddhist nunnery, *Alt.*: **òe-d'ãw**

ní-jiaq-bi 年底 *t.n.* end of the year, *Alt.*: **ní-'ya-jiaq-bi, ní-di**

ní•jìn 念经 *v.o.* chant *(Buddhist)* scriptures

ní-(lu-)'wãw 阎王 *n.* Yama, King of Hell

ní-maw 呢帽 *n.* wool hat, felt hat

ní-shin 怀疑 *v.* suspect

ní-shin-b'in 疑心病 *n.* paranoia

ní-sï-gong 泥瓦工 *n.* mason, tileworker

nì 拖沓 *adj.* dilatory, sluggish

nì 磨、研 *v.* grind, rub, polish, *Alt.*: **mó, mú, ní**

nì 捻 *v.* screw off, screw on, twist *(with the fingers)*

nì-jieu 研究 *v.* research, study in depth; *n.* research, study

nì-zoq 螺丝刀 *n.* screwdriver

niã̌ 馅儿 *n.* stuffing, filling

niã̌ 让 *v.* allow, let

niã̌-niã-chiã 娘娘腔 *n.* effeminate manner

niã̀-niã 姑母 *n.* aunt *(father's sister)*

niáe 二十 (廿) *num.* twenty, *Alt.*: **náe**

niaq 握、持 *v.* grasp, hold in hand

niáw 鸟 *n.* bird, *Alt.*: **diáw**

niáw 饶 *v.* spare *(from harsh treatment)*

niáw-d'eu 饶头 *n.* extra paid for good measure

niéu 牛 *n.* ox, cow, bull

niéu-dzae-ku 牛仔裤 *n.* jeans

niéu-dzï 纽扣 *n.* button

niéu-na 牛奶 *n.* cow's milk

niéu-nioq 牛肉 *n.* beef

niéu-nioq-goe 牛肉干 *n.* beef jerky, dried beef

nièu 扭 *v.* sway, twist, turn

nín 有韧性、黏性大 *adj.* chewy and sticky; tough but pliable; 稠 viscous

nín 人 *n.* person

nín 认 *v.* recognize, know, *Alt.*: **nín-deq** 认得

nín-dzen 认真 *adj.* serious, earnest, *Alt.*: **dín-dzen**

nín-dzǐ 银子 *n.* silver

nín-ga 人家 *prn.* those people, others

nín-gong 人工 *n.* worker, laborer

nín-h'ãw 银行 *n.* bank

nín-h'u 银河 *n.* milky way, *Alt.*: **tì-h'u**

nín-ku 宁可 *adv.* would rather, *Alt.*: **nín-ken**

nín-mong-sï 柠檬汁 *n.* lemonade

nín-pin 人品 *n.* quality of one's character

nín-'yüeq 闰月 *n.* intercalary month *(a month added when necessary to allow the lunar calendar to match up with solar time)*, *Alt.*: **nín-'yoq**

nióng 浓 *adj.* concentrated, dense

nióng 绒 *n.* velvet

nióng-shi-sae 毛线衣 *n.* sweater

nióng-tãw 浓汤 *n.* thick soup, chowder

nioq 玉 *n.* jade

nioq 肉 *n.* meat

nioq 揉 *v.* knead, rub

nioq-b'i 肉皮 *n.* pork skin

nioq-dong 肉冻 *n.* meat jelly, aspic

nioq-dzǐ 褥子 *n.* cotton mattress *(or any non-spring mattress or padding)*, *Alt.*: **b'í-nioq**

nioq-lae-huo 玉兰花 *n.* magnolia, *Alt.*: **nüeq-lae-huo**

nioq-mo 肉麻 *adj.* creepy, disturbing, discomfiting

nioq-tong 心疼 *adj.* cherish, loath to part with, *Alt.*: **shìn-tong**

nioq-'yüoe 肉圆 *n.* meatball

niq 热 *adj.* hot

niq 日 *n., m.w.* day, *Alt.*: **tì** 天

niq-chi 热气, *n.* heat, hot air

niq-d'eu-niq-jiaq 日期 *n.* date

niq-dzǐ-j'i 镊子 *n.* tweezers

niq-fong 逆风 *v.o.* go against the wind

niq-guãw 太阳光 *n.* sunshine

niq-jiaq 日子 *n.* days

niq-li-d'eu 白天 *n.* daytime, *Alt.*: **niq-li(-shiã), b'aq-ti**

niq-men 热门 *adj.* in demand, hot, popular

niq-men-hu 热门货 *n.* hot sales item

niq-naw 热闹 *adj.* lively, buzzing with excitement, *Alt.*: **náw-mã, náw-niq**

niq-niq 天天 *adv.* every day, *Alt.*: **tì-ti, màe-niq** 每天

niq-shin 热心 *adj.* enthusiastic, ardent

nóe 暖 *adj.* warm, pleasantly warm, *Alt.*: **nóe-niq**

nóe 南 *l.n.* south, south side, *Alt.*: **nóe-mi** 南边

nóe 小孩 *n.* child, *Alt.*: **shiáw-noe, shiáw-nin**

nóe-chi 暖气 *n.* heat, heating

nóe-guo 南瓜 *n.* pumpkin *(or similar yellow squash variety)*, *Alt.*: **váe-guo**

nóe-ñg 女儿 *n.* daughter, *Alt.*: **nǔ-er, nǔ-shiaw-noe**

nóe-nin(-ga) 男人、男的 *n.* man, *Alt.*: **nóe-g'eq**

nóng 你 *prn.* you *(singular)*

nóng-g'eq 你的 *prn.* yours *(singular)*, *Alt.*: **nóng-eq**

nóng háw! 你好！ *interj.* Hello!

nóng-min 农民 *n.* peasant, farmer

nóng-tsen 农村 *n.* countryside, rural area, *Alt.*: **shiǎ-h'uo** 乡下

nóng záw! 你早！ *interj.* Good morning!

nòng 弄 *v.* do, *Alt.*: **g'áw** 搞

nú 柔软 *adj.* tender and silky

nú-mi 糯米 *n.* glutinous rice

nuò 拿 *v.* hold, take in the hand, *Alt.*: **nuó, nàw, nàe**

nǔ-er 女儿 *n.* daughter, *Alt.*: **nǔ-shiaw-noe, nóe-ñg**

nǔ-loq 娱乐 *n.* entertainment, *Alt.*: **'yǔ-loq**

nǔ-nin(-ga) 女人（家）*n.* woman, *Alt.*: **nǔ-g'eq** 女的

nǔ-shi 女婿 *n.* son-in-law, *Alt.*: **nǔ-shü**

nǔ-zï 女士 *n.* Ms.

nüóe 软 *adj.* soft

nüóe-lae 原来 *adv.* originally, *Alt.*: **bén-lae** 本来, **bén-sã**

nüóe-shiaw-jiq 元宵节 *n.* Lantern Festival *(the 15th day of the 1st lunar month)*

nüóe-yin 原因 *n.* cause, reason

nüóe-zoq 软熟 *adj.* soft and comfy

NG

ńǵ 鱼 *n.* fish; ~ **-nioq** 鱼肉 fish *(meat)*; ~ **-'yüoe** 鱼丸子 fish ball; ~ **-dzï** 鱼卵 fish eggs; ~ **-gueq-d'eu** 鱼刺 fish bone; ~ **-lin-b'ae** 鱼鳞 fish scales; ~ **-paw-paw** 鱼鳔 fish air bladder; ~ **-tsï** 鱼翅 fish fin

ńǵ 五 *num.* five

ńǵ-'yüeq 五月 *t.n.* May, *Alt.:* **ńǵ-'yoq**

ńǵ-geq-sae 鳃 *n.* gill, *Alt.:* **gēq-sae**

ńǵ-huo-nioq 五花肉 *n.* pork belly meat

ńǵ-seq 五十 *num.* fifty

ngá 拖延 *v.* delay, put off, *Alt.:* **d'á**

ngá-b'i 外币 *n.* foreign currency

ngá-d'eu 外头 *l.n.* outside, *Alt.:* **ngá-mi** 外面, **ngá-di'd'eu**

ngá-dzu-mu 外祖母 *n.* grandmother *(maternal)*, *Alt.:* **ngá-b'u** 外婆

ngá-dzu-vu 外祖父 *n.* grandfather *(maternal)*, *Alt.:* **ngá-gong** 外公

ngá-gaw 牙膏 *n.* toothpaste

ngá-goq-nin 外国人 *n.* foreigner, *Alt.:* **'yǎ-nin** 洋人

ngá-h'âw 外行 *n.* layman, nonprofessional

ngá-kua 外快 *n.* extra income

ngá-ma 外卖 *n.* take-out *(food)*

ngá-maw 外贸 *n.* overseas trade

ngá-nin 牙龈 *n.* gums *(in the mouth)*, *Alt.:* **ngá-nioq**

ngá-sã 外孙 *n.* grandson *(daughter's son)*

ngá-sã 外甥 *n.* nephew *(sister's son)*

ngá-sã-noe 外孙女 *n.* granddaughter *(daughter's daughter)*

ngá-sã-noe 外甥女 *n.* niece *(sister's daughter)*

ngá-seq 牙刷 *n.* toothbrush

Ngá-tae 外滩 *n.* the Bund

ngá-taw 外套 *n.* jacket, coat, *Alt.:* **zǎw-dzâw** 上衣

ngá-tsï 牙齿 *n.* tooth, *Alt.:* **ngá-dzï**

ngǎ 硬 *adj.* hard *(not soft)*, stiff

ngǎ-dzaq 强健 *adj.* strong and healthy

ngǎ-j'iã 倔 *adj.* headstrong, unbending, stubborn, *Alt.:* **j'üeq, j'üeq-j'iã** 倔强, **j'ioq-jiã, g'én**

ngǎ-jin 硬(要)、非得 *adv.* have got to, insist upon

ngǎ-tin 硬挺 *adj.* rigid, stiff

ngáe 点 *m.w.* little bit, small amount, *Alt.*: **dí**

ngáe 癌 *n.* cancer

ngáe 碍 *v.* obstruct, be in the way of

ngáe-bae 呆板 *adj.* inflexible, rigid, obdurate

ngáe-b'i 眼皮 *n.* eyelid

ngáe-b'ong 艾 *n.* artemesia, mugwort *(fragrant herb used in moxibustion)*

ngáe-ji-maw 睫毛 *n.* eyelash

ngáe-jin 眼睛 *n.* eye

ngáe-jin 眼镜 *n.* eyeglasses

ngáe-li(-sï) 眼泪 *n.* tears

ngáe-niq 眼热 *adj.* envious, covetous, *Alt.*: **ngáe-'yă, ngáe-h'ong** 眼红

ngáe-seq 颜色 *n.* color, *Alt.*: **sēq**

ngáe-wu-dzï 眼珠 *n.* eyeball

ngáe-zï 碍事 *v.o.* hinder; bother

ngaq-dzï 名额 *n.* quota *(of people)*

ngaq-goq-d'eu 额头 *n.* forehead

ngaq(-deq) 缺，弄个缺口 *v.* chip

ngáw 咬 *v.* bite

ngáw 熬 *v.* endure, hold out

ngéu 藕 *n.* lotus root

ngéu-fen 藕粉 *n.* lotus root flour

ngó-pi 瓦片 *n.* tiles, *Alt.*: **ngó-b'ae**

ngóe 岸、河岸 *n.* riverbank, *Alt.*: **h'ú-tae-bi**

ngoq-mu 岳母 *n.* mother-in-law *(wife's mother)*, *Alt.*: **zǎ-m̂(-niâ)** 丈母娘

ngoq-vu 岳父 *n.* father-in-law *(wife's father)*, *Alt.*: **zǎ-nin** 丈人

ngú 饿 *adj.* hungry, *Alt.*: **d'ú-b'i-ngu** 肚子饿

ngú 鹅 *n.* goose

ngú 我 *prn.* I, me, *Alt.*: **'wú**

ngú-d'ong(-zï) 梧桐(树) *n.* Chinese parasol tree

ngú-g'eq 我的 *prn.* my, mine, *Alt.*: **ngú-eq**

Ngú-goq 俄国 *n.* Russia

Ngú-nü 俄语 *n.* Russian *(language)*

ngú-seq 卧室 *n.* bedroom

O

óe 暗 *adj.* dark *(little light)*

òe 遮掩 *v.* cover up with the hands, *Alt.:* **yīq**

òe-d'in 安定 *adj.* stable, settled, *Alt.:* **òe-sã**

òe-dzaw 按照 *prep.* do according to, *Alt.:* **dzáw, dzáw-dzï** 照着

òe-dzãw 安葬 *v.o.* bury *(the dead)*, *Alt.:* **loq•dzãw**

òe-jin 安静、清静 *adj.* quiet, *Alt.:* **chìn-jin**

òe-mo 按摩 *v.* massage

òe-yiq 安逸 *adj.* safe and sound; at ease, easy

òe-zen 鹌鹑 *n.* quail

òe-zyi 安全 *adj.* safe

óng 腐臭味 *adj.* rotton *(smell)*, putrid

óng-b'iq-d'eu 齆鼻 *n.* stuffed nose, *Alt.:* **óng-b'eq-d'eu**

óng-dzong 懊丧 *adj.* despondent, dejected, *Alt.:* **àw-sãw**

óng-tsae 空心菜 *n* water spinach, *Alt.:* **òng-tsae**

ōq 非常非常 *adv.* extremely

ōq 恶 *adj.* fiendish, hateful, vicious

ōq-din 屋顶 *n.* roof, *Alt.:* **vǎw-din**

ōq-li 家里 *n.* home, *Alt.:* **ōq-li-shiã**

ōq-shin 恶心 *adj.* nauseous, nauseating, gross

ōq-tsoq 肮脏 *adj.* dirty, filthy

P

pá-d'eu 派头 *n.* style *(usually bold)*, manner *(usually grand)*

pá-la 破、破烂 *adj.* ragged, tattered, worn out

pá-tseq-su 派出所 *n.* police substation, precinct office

pà-dae 派对 *n.* party

pà-keq 派克 *n.* parka

pà-sï 出入证 *n.* pass

pāq 拍 *v.* pat, clap

pāq-dãw 合作伙伴 *n.* collaborator, collaborative partner

pāq•dzáw(-shiã) 拍照 *v.o.* take pictures, photograph

pāq•séu 拍手 *v.* clap one's hands

páw 泡 *v.* soak

páw 泡 *n.* bubble, blister, *Alt.*: **sǐ-paw** 水泡
pàw-paw 泡儿 *n.* bubbles
pàw-zã 炮长 *n.* firecrackers, *Alt.*: **bì-paw** 鞭炮
pǎw 胖 *adj.* fat *(of people)*
pèn 喷 *v.* spurt, spray, gush
pèn-d'eu 喷头 *n.* shower head
pèn-ti 喷嚏 *n.* sneeze
pí 片 *m.w.* slices
pí-dzï 骗子 *n.* swindler
pí-zï 譬如 *n.* example; *adv.* for example, *Alt.*: **bí-fãw**
   比方
pì 批 *m.w.* groups, batches, *Alt.*: **pēq**
pì-b'in 批评 *v.* criticize
pì-faq 批发 *n.* wholesale
pì-fong 披风 *n.* cloak, cape, *Alt.*: **dèu-b'ong** 斗篷
pì-gu(-d'eu) 屁股 *n.* buttocks, rump
pì-ji 披肩 *n.* shawl
pì-piq 偏僻 *adj.* remote, out-of-the-way
pì-shin 偏心 *adj.* partial, biased
piáw 票 *n.* ticket, *Alt.*: **piàw-dzï**
piáw-liã 漂亮 *adj.* beautiful
pín-'wae 品位 *n.* grade, value, quality
pìn-b'en 拼盘 *n.* assorted cold appetizers
pìn-pã(-j'ieu) 乒乓球 *n.* ping-pong; ping-pong ball
pó 怕 *v.* fear, be afraid of
póng 捧 *v.* hold or carry with both hands, *Alt.*: **hóng**
pōq-den-zong 灯蛾 *n.* moth
pōq-keq-b'a 扑克牌 *n.* poker cards; poker *(game)*
pōq-nin 仆人 *n.* servant, *Alt.*: **'yóng-nin** 佣人
pù 坡 *n.* slope
pù 铺 *v.* pave, lay out
pù 沸溢 *v.* boil over
pú-tong 普通 *adj.* ordinary, common
Pú-tong-h'uo 普通话 *n.* Pǔtōnghuà, Mandarin

S

sá 什么 *prn.* what, *Alt.*: **sá-g'e, sá-h'eq**
sà•d'í-fãw 什么地方 *prn.* where
sá•gãw-jieu 什么原因 *prn.* why, what reason
sá-nin 谁 *prn.* who

sá-nin-g'eq 谁的 *prn.* whose, *Alt.:* **sá-nin-h'eq**

sá•zén-guãw 什么时候、什么时间 *prn.* what time, when, *Alt.:* **sá-g'eq•zén-guãw**

sà-du 劳累、疲惫 *adj.* exhausted, worn-out

sǎ 生 *adj.* raw

sǎ-b'in-nin 病人 *n.* patient, invalid

sǎ-baw-tae 双胞胎 *n.* twins

sǎ•fòng 感冒 *v.o.* catch a cold

sǎ-h'ueq 工作 *n.* work, job

sǎ-ji-moe-d'eu 生煎馒头 *n.* fried meat buns

sǎ-li 梨 *n.* pear

sǎ•máw-b'in 生病 *v.o.* get sick, fall ill, *Alt.:* **sǎ•b'ín**

sǎ-ñg-pi 生鱼片 *n.* sashimi, *Alt.:* **sǎ-shi-mi**

sǎ•shìn 伤心 *adj.* grieved, sad

sǎ-tsae 生菜 *n.* lettuce

sǎ-'yiq 桑叶 *n.* mulberry leaves

sǎ-yi 生意 *n.* business, trading

sáe 散 *adj.* scattered, loose

sáe 碎 *adj.* shattered, fragmentary

sáe 雨伞 *n.* umbrella, *Alt.:* **'yǎ-sae**

sáe-b'aw 赛跑 *n., v.* race *(running)*

sáe-b'u 散步 *v.o.* take a walk

sáe-gu 帅哥 *n.* handsome fellow

sáe-song 松弛、松散 *adj.* lax, inattentive

sàe 山 *n.* mountain

sàe 三 *num.* three

sàe-d'ong 山洞 *n.* mountain cave

sàe-fen-dzï-yiq 三分之一 *num.* third *(1/3)*

sàe-goq 山谷 *n.* mountain valley, ravine

sàe-goq-ku 三角裤 *n.* panties

sàe-h'u-tu 混凝土 *n.* concrete

sàe-jiaq-ga 三脚架 *n.* tripod

sàe-len-tsuo 三轮车 *n.* tricycle pedicab

sàe-len-tsuo-fu 三轮车夫 *n.* pedicab driver

sàe-men-ñg 三文鱼 *n.* salmon

sàe-min-zï 三明治 *n.* sandwich

sàe-seq 三十 *num.* thirty

sàe-'yã 山羊 *n.* goat

sàe-'yü 甘薯 *n.* sweet potato

sàe-'yüeq 三月 *t.n.* March, *Alt.:* **sàe-'yoq**

sàe-zï 杉树 *n.* cedar tree

sāq 煞 *adv.* very, *Alt.*: **sāq-deq, téu, j'iq**

sāq 湿 *adj.* wet

sāq 眨 *v.* blink, wink, *Alt.*: **gāq**

sāq 涮 *v.* quick-boil, parboil

sāq-gen-ga 煞根价 *n.* extremely low price

sāq-la 色拉 *n.* salad

sāq-laq 狠毒 *adj.* ruthless, tricky

sāq•gèn 过瘾 *adj.* enjoyable to the fullest, completely satisfying

sáw 少 *adj.* few

sáw 扫 *v.* sweep

sáw-dzeu 扫帚 *n.* broom

sáw-saw 嫂嫂 *n.* sister-in-law *(elder brother's wife)*, *Alt.*: **āq-saw**

sàw 烧、煮 *v.* boil; cook; ~ •**váe** 做饭 *v.o.* cook *(a meal)*

sàw-kaw 烧烤 *n.* barbecue

sàw-ma 烧卖 *n.* stuffed and steamed open-topped dumpling

sàw-'wae 稍微 *adv.* slightly

sắw 爽 *adj.* refreshing, bracing, gratifying, *Alt.*: **sắw-kua** 爽快

sắw-chi 爽快 *adj.* straightforward, no-nonsense

sắw-shin *adj.* content 爽心

sầw 费 *adj.* wasted, suffered a damaging loss

sầw 双 *m.w.* pairs, *Alt.*: **dáe** 对

sầw 霜 *n.* frost

sầw-biaw 商标 *n.* trademark

sầw-pin-vãw 商品房 *n.* commercial housing, condominium

sầw-di 商店 *n.* store, shop, *Alt.*: **dí-ga**

sầw-liã 商量 *v.* talk over, discuss, consult

sầw-nin 商人 *n.* businessman, merchant, *Alt.*: **sầ-yi-nin** 生意人

sầw-niq 商业 *n.* commerce, trade

sầw-zã 商场 *n.* market, mall

sén 笋 *n.* bamboo shoots, *Alt.*: **dzōq-sen** 竹笋

sén-sen 婶母 *n.* aunt *(wife of father's younger brother)*, *Alt.*: **sén-niã**

sèn 深 *adj.* deep; dark *(color)*

sèn-baw 申报 *v.* declare *(dutiable goods)*

sèn-dzï 孙子 *n.* grandson *(son's son)*

sèn-lin 森林 *n.* forest

sèn-nü 孙女 *n.* granddaughter *(son's daughter)*, *Alt.:*
  sèn-noe(-ñg)

sèn-ti 身体 *n.* body; health

sèn-'yeu 花生油 *n.* peanut oil

sèn-yin 声音 *n.* sound, tone, voice, *Alt.:* **sà-chi**

sēq 塞 *adj* clogged, blocked up; *v.* stop up, stuff, cork

sēq 涩 *adj.* puckery, astringent

sēq 湿 *adj.* wet, damp, *Alt.:* **sāq**

sēq 色 *n.* color, *Alt.:* **ngáe-seq** 颜色

sēq 刷 *v.* brush, scrub, paint

sēq-dzï 虱子 *n.* louse, *Alt.:* **láw-b'aq-seq**

sēq•hú 识货 *v.o.* see the quality of the goods, know
  the value of the merchandise

sēq•ká 刷卡 *v.o.* pay with a credit card

sēq-shiã 识相 *v.o.* sensible, tactful

sēq•sï̀ 说书 *v.o.* storytelling *(traditional)*

sēq•tsuò 堵车 *v.o.* traffic jam

sēq-yi 适意 *adj.* agreeable, comfortable

sēq•zḯ 识字 *v.o.* be literate

séu 瘦 *adj.* thin *(not fat)*, lean, skinny

séu 手 *n.* hand

séu-b'a-dãw 手排挡 *n.* manual transmission

séu-biaw 手表 *n.* wristwatch, *Alt.:* **biáw**

séu-d'i-d'ong 手电筒 *n.* flashlight, *Alt.:* **d'í-d'ong**

séu-dzãw 手掌 *n.* palm *(of hand)*

séu-ji 手机 *n.* cell phone, mobile phone

séu-ji-ka 手机卡 *n.* SIM card, *Alt.:* **SIM ká** SIM卡

séu-jiq-d'eu 手指头 *n.* finger, *Alt.:* **séu-dzï-d'eu**

séu-jiq-kaq 手指甲 *n.* fingernail, *Alt.:* **séu-dzï-kaq**

séu-ni-nin 手艺人 *n.* craftsman

séu-seq 首饰 *n.* jewelry

séu-taw 手套 *n.* gloves

séu-ven 手纹 *n.* handprint; lines on the palm

séu-wae 手腕 *n.* wrist

séu-zoq 手镯 *n.* bracelet, *Alt.:* **zoq-d'eu**

séu-zoq-fi 手续费 *n.* service fee, commission

sèu 馊 *adj.* spoiled *(of food)*; ~ **-teq** 馊了 gone bad,
  spoiled *(of food)*

sèu 收 *v.* receive; accept; gather; harvest

sèu-b'oe 收盘 *n.* closing price *(at an exchange)*

sèu-d'iaw 收条 *n.* receipt, *Alt.*: **sèu-jü** 收据, **fāq-piaw** 发票

sèu-daw 收到 *v.* receive

sèu•dzǎ 收账 *v.o.* collect payment

sèu•dzǐ 收支 *n.* revenue and expenditures, *Alt.*: **sèu•fú**

sèu-dzoq 收拾 *v.* tidy up, put in order

sèu-yin-ji 收音机 *n.* radio

sèu-zeq 收入 *n.* revenue, income, receipts, *Alt.*: **jín-dzã** 进账

sǐ 水 *n.* water

sǐ 四 *num.* four

sǐ-b'iaw 瓢 *n.* ladle made from a gourd

sǐ-d'ong 水桶 *n.* water bucket

sǐ-fen-dzǐ-yiq 四分之一 *num.* quarter

sǐ-ga 暑假 *n.* summer vacation, *Alt.*: **sǐ-jia**

sǐ-geu 水沟 *n.* ditch, gully

sǐ-gu 水果 *n.* fruit

sǐ-hu 水货 *n.* smuggled goods

sǐ-huen 试婚 *v.o.* trial marriage

sǐ-ji-d'eu 四季豆 *n.* string beans

sǐ-jiaq-zuo 蜥蜴 *n.* lizard

sǐ-jiaw 水饺 *n.* boiled dumpling

sǐ-long-d'eu 水龙头 *n.* faucet

sǐ-ni 水泥 *n.* cement, *Alt.*: **sǐ-men-tin, 'yǎ-huae**

sǐ-nieu 水牛 *n.* water buffalo

sǐ-seq 四十 *num.* forty

sǐ-sǐ-koe 试试看 *v.* try

sǐ-'yüeq 四月 *t.n.* April, *Alt.*: **sǐ-'yoq**

sǐ-zǐ-dzǐ 水池子 *n.* sink, *Alt.*: **sǐ-zaw** 水槽

sǐ-zoq 舀子 *n.* ladle, scoop *(for liquids)*

sǐ 书 *n.* book

sǐ 丝 *n.* silk, *Alt.*: **dzèn-sǐ** 真丝

sǐ 尿水 *n.* urine

sǐ 输 *v.* lose *(not win)*

sǐ-baw 书包 *n.* book bag, satchel

sǐ-baw-d'in 书报亭 *n.* newsstand

sǐ-boq-h'uae 世博会 *n.* Expo, world's fair

sǐ-bu 尿布 *n.* diaper

sǐ-chi 书签 *n.* bookmark

sǐ-d'eu 情势 *n.* situation, circumstances

sï•d'éu 梳头 *v.o.* comb one's hair

sï-di 书店 *n.* bookstore

sï-dzï 狮子 *n.* lion

sï-dzï-d'eu 狮子头 *n.* large meatball *("lion's head")*

sï-dzoq 书桌 *n.* desk, *Alt.:* **shiá-zï-d'ae**

sï-ga 世界 *n.* world

sï-guo 丝瓜 *n.* loofah gourd; 丝瓜 **-jin** ~筋 loofah sponge

sï-ji 世纪 *n.* century

sï-ji 司机 *n.* chauffeur, driver

sï-nin 私人 *attr.* private *(adj.)*, *Alt.:* **sï-zen**

sï-'yeu 私有 *attr.* be privately owned *(adj.)*

sï-vãw 书房 *n.* study

sï-vu 师傅 *n.* master, teacher, driver *(term of respect)*

sï-zï 书橱 *n.* bookcase

sóe 扇 *m.w. for doors, windows*

sóe-b'oe 算盘 *n.* abacus

sóe-d'i 闪电 *v.o.* lightning

sóe-dzï 扇子 *n.* fan, *Alt.:* **sòe-dzï**

sóe-miaw 蒜苗 *n.* garlic shoots

sóe-min 算命 *v.o.* tell one's fortune

sóe-min-shi-sã 算命先生 *n.* fortune-teller

sòe 酸 *adj.* sour

sòe 扇 *v.* fan

sòe-laq 酸辣 *adj.* hot and sour

sòe-na 酸奶 *n.* yogurt

sòe-zoe 虽然 *conj.* although

sóng•lí 送礼 *v.o.* give a present, give gifts, *Alt.:*
    sóng•nín-zyin 送人情

sòng 松 *adj.* loose

sòng 搉 *v.* punch

sòng-tsï 松鼠 *n.* squirrel

sõq 不新鲜 *adj.* stale

sõq 胆小 *adj.* timid, cowardly, *Alt.:* **dáe•shiáw**

sõq 缩 *v.* shrink *(in size or value)*, *Alt.:* **sõq•sí** 缩水

sõq 吮 *v.* suck on

sõq-liaw 塑料 *n.* plastic

sõq-soq 叔叔 *n.* uncle *(father's younger brother)*, *Alt.:*
    sõq-vu

sõq-suo 宿舍 *n.* dormitory, hostel, *Alt.:* **sõq-sae**

sú 锁 *n., v.* lock

sú-d'iaw 薯条 *n.* French fries

sú-mo-shiã-ji 数码相机 *n.* digital camera

sú-moq 数目 *n.* number

sú-tsae 素菜 *n.* vegetable dish, vegetarian food

sú-zï-dzong 数字钟 *n.* digital clock

sù 酥 *adj.* flaky and soft

sù-dã-sï 苏打水 *n.* soda water, *Alt.*: **h'ú-lae-sï** 荷兰水

sù-tsae 蔬菜 *n.* vegetables

suó 晒 *v.* sun, sun-dry

suò-chi 赊欠 *v.* buy or sell on credit

suò-d'ãw 砂糖 *n.* granulated sugar

suò-din-ñg 沙丁鱼 *n.* sardine

suò-faq 沙发 *n.* sofa, *Alt.*: **suò-faq-yi**

suò-gu 沙锅 *n.* clay cooking pot

suò-ñg 鲨鱼 *n.* shark

suò-tsãw 纱窗 *n.* window screens

SH

shí 显：颜色明亮 *adj.* bright *(of colors)*

shí 细 *adj.* fine *(not coarse)*, thin

shí 线 *n.* line *(subway)*; thread, string, cord

shí 戏 *n.* traditional opera

shí 选 *v.* choose, elect

shí 死 *v.* die

shí-chiaq 喜鹊 *n.* magpie

shí-d'ae 戏台 *n.* stage

shí-jiq-jin 洗洁精 *n.* liquid detergent

shí-seu-gae 洗手间 *n.* restroom

shí-shi-jiaw 差点儿(不、没) *adv.* almost *(didn't)*

shí-yi-di 洗衣店 *n.* laundry, *Alt.*: **shí-yi-vãw** 洗衣房

shì 鲜 *adj.* fresh and delicious

shì 稀 *adj.* sparse, scattered; rare

shì 先 *adv.* first

shì 西 *l.n.* west, west side, *Alt.*: **shì-mi** 西边, **shì-d'eu**

Shì-bae-nga 西班牙 *n.* Spain

shì-dzãw 西装 *n.* suit, dress suit

shì-fen 粉丝 *n.* mung bean vermicelli

shì-guo 西瓜 *n.* watermelon

shì-h'uãw 希望 *v.* hope, wish

shì-j'i 稀奇 *adj.* rare, strange, curious

shì-nin-dzãw 仙人掌 *n.* cactus

shì-sā 先生 *n.* Mr., mister

shì-tsoe 西餐 *n.* Western food

shì-vae 稀饭 *n.* thin rice porridge

Shì-zā 西藏 *n.* Tibet

shiá 滑 *v.* slide

shiá 写 *v.* write, *Alt.*: **shiá•zí** 写字

shiá-yi 舒服 *adj.* comfortable

shiá-zǐ-leu 办公楼 *n.* office building

shiǎ 想 *aux.* want to *(do something)*, feel like *(doing something)*

shiǎ 香 *adj.* fragrant; *n.* incense

shiǎ 掺 *v.* mix in, put in, *Alt.*: **tsàe, jiǎ**

shiǎ-bāw 帮助 *v.* help, assist

shiǎ-dā 相当 *adv.* fairly, considerably, *Alt.*: **jiàw-guae**

shiǎ-dzï 箱子 *n.* box, chest, trunk

shiǎ-dzï 箱子 *n.* suitcase, chest, trunk, *Alt.*: **h'ǎ-li-shiǎ** 行李箱

Shiǎ-gā 香港 *n.* Hong Kong

shiǎ-gu 香菇 *n.* shiitake mushroom

shiǎ-guo-dzï 葵花子 *n.* sunflower seeds

shiǎ-h'uo 乡下 *n.* countryside, rural area, *Alt.*: **nóng-tsen** 农村

shiǎ-jiaw 香蕉 *n.* banana

shiǎ-liaw 香料 *n.* spices

shiǎ-lu 香炉 *n.* incense burner

shiǎ•mí-kong 接吻 *v.o.* kiss, *Alt.*: **shiǎ•dzí-bo, dǎ•kàe-sï**

shiǎ-shin 相信 *v.* believe, trust

shiǎ-tsae 香菜 *n.* cilantro

shiǎ-yi 香烟 *n.* cigarette

shiǎ-zā 香肠 *n.* sausage

shiāq 削 *v.* peel *(with a knife)*, *Alt.*: **chì**

shīaq•gòng-d'i 减工资 *v.o.* cut wages, *Alt.*: **gáe•gòng-d'i**

shiáw 小 *adj.* little, small

shiáw 笑 *v.* smile, laugh

shiáw-b'i 小便 *v.o.* urinate, *Alt.*: **tsāq•sǐ, zá•sǐ**

shiáw-bae 晚辈 *n.* younger generation

shiáw-chi 小气 *adj.* stingy, cheap, *Alt.*: **gàe-diaw**

shiáw-chiq 小吃 *n.* pastries, snacks, dim sum

shiáw-d'i-j'in 小提琴 *n.* violin, *Alt.*: **váe-ou-lin**

shiáw-deq 知道、晓得 *v.* know, realize, be aware of

shiáw-dzï 孝子 *n.* filial son, dutiful son

shiáw-dzï 小资 *n.* yuppie-like petty bourgeoisie

shiáw-fae 小贩 *n.* peddler

shiáw-fi 小费 *n.* tip

shiáw-gu-dzï 小姑子 *n.* sister-in-law *(husband's younger sister)*

shiáw-h'oq 小学 *n.* elementary school

shiáw-j'iaw-tsuo 小轿车 *n.* sedan

shiáw-j'ieu-dzï 小舅子 *n.* brother-in-law *(wife's younger brother)*

shiáw-ji 小鸡 *n.* chick

shiáw-jia 小姐 *n.* Miss., young lady

shiáw-law-b'u 妾 *n.* mistress, kept woman

shiáw-long-baw-dzï 小笼包子 *n.* steamed soup buns

shiáw-long-huo 小龙虾 *n.* crayfish

shiáw-maq 小麦 *n.* wheat

shiáw-maw-d'eu 婴儿 *n.* infant, *Alt.*: **shiáw-shiaw-noe, yìn-'er**

shiáw-noe-yi-zãw 童装 *n.* children's wear, *Alt.*: **d'óng-dzãw**

shiáw-soq 小叔子 *n.* brother-in-law *(husband's younger brother)*

shiáw-teu 小偷 *n.* petty thief

shiáw-'yi-dzï 小姨子 *n.* sister-in-law *(wife's younger sister)*

shiàw 揭起 *v.* lift up, turn open

shiàw-dzï 插销 *n.* latch, door bolt, *Alt.*: **tsãq-shiaw**

shiàw-'ya 熬夜 *v.* stay up all night *(working)*

shiàw-zeu 销售 *attr.* marketing, selling

shiàw-zeu-liã 销售量 *n.* volume of sales

shiéu-huo 绣花 *v.o.* embroider

shièu-d'aw-'yüoe 修道院 *n.* monastery, convent

shièu-dzen-'yiq 修正液 *n.* correction fluid

shièu-h'ae-dzãw 休闲装 *n.* leisure clothing

shièu•mí 刮脸 *v.o.* shave *(a beard)*

shín 信 *n.* letter; mail

shín 姓 *n.* surname, family name

shín 肿 *v.* swell up, *Alt.*: **hàe**

shín 醒、醒来 *v.* wake up, awaken, *Alt.*: **gáw, gáw-dzoe-lae**

shín-dzï 兴致 *n.* mood, *Alt.*: **zyín-zyü** 情绪

shín-dzï 性格 *n.* disposition, temperament, *Alt.*:
  b'í-chi 脾气

shín-dzï 信纸 *n.* stationery

shín-koq 信封 *n.* envelope, *Alt.*: **shín-fong**

shìn 新 *adj.* new

shìn 心 *n.* heart; mind

shìn 星 *n.* star, stars, *Alt.*: **shìn-shin** 星星

shìn-d'in 蜻蜓 *n.* dragonfly, *Alt.*: **chìn-d'in**

shìn•jīq 心急 *adj.* impatient, short-tempered, *Alt.*:
  shín•jīq 性急

shìn-ku 辛苦 *adj.* laborious, hard

shìn-lãw 新郎 *n.* groom, *Alt.*: **shìn-lãw-guoe, shìn-
  guoe-nin**

shìn-niã(-dzï) 新娘 *n.* bride

shìn-shi 新鲜 *adj.* fresh

shìn-tong 心疼 *adj., v.* cherish, loath to part with,
  Alt.: **nioq-tong**

shìn-ven 新闻 *n.* news

shìn-vu 媳妇 *n.* daughter-in-law

shìn-zã 心脏 *n.* heart

shiòng 胸 *n.* chest, *Alt.*: **shiòng-pu** 胸脯

shiòng-d'i 兄弟 *n.* brothers *(elder and younger)*

shīq 雪 *n.* snow

shīq 掀 *v.* lift *(a cover, etc)*

shīq 吸 *v.* suck in, inhale, *Alt.*: **hù** 呼

shīq-ga-yi 雪茄烟 *n.* cigar

shīq-guoe 吸管 *n.* drinking straw

shīq-huo 雪花 *n.* snowflakes

shīq-li-hong 雪里红 *n.* potherb mustard

shīq•niq 歇业 *v.o.* go out of business, *Alt.*: **guàe•dí**
  关店

shīq-tiq-zaq 磁石 *n.* magnet, magnetite

shú 许 *v.* allow, permit

shú-du 许多 *adj.* many, much, a lot of, quite a few

shǔ-shin 虚心 *adj.* modest, open-minded

shǔ-yaw 需要 *adv.* need

shüēq 血 *n.* blood, *Alt.*: **shiōq**

shüēq 蓄 *v.* save up *(money)*, *Alt.*: **shiōq**

shüēq-aq gàw 高血压 *ph.* have high blood pressure,
  Alt.: **shiōq-aq gàw**

shüēq-guoe 血管 *n.* blood vessel, *Alt.*: **shiōq-guoe**

shǘn 训 *v.* admonish, lecture

T

tá-j'iq-j'üoe 太极拳 *n.* tai chi
tá-'yã 太阳 *n.* sun
tá-'yã-ngae-jin 太阳眼镜 *n.* sunglasses
tà 拖 *v.* drag
tà-ta 太太 *n.* Mrs.
tǎ 烫 *adj.* burning hot to the touch, scalding
tǎ•yì-zã 熨衣服 *v.o.* iron clothing
táe 疲乏 *adj.* weary
táe-h'u 和气 *adj.* polite and amiable, *Alt.*: **h'ú-chi**
táe•hú 退货 *v.o.* return merchandise
tàe 推 *v.* push
tàe 摊 *v.* spread out
tàe-bae 相差 *v.* differ, *Alt.*: **tàe-wae**
tàe-d'eu 摊子 *n.* street vendor's stand, *Alt.*: **d'í-tae** 地摊
tàe-d'eu-shiaw-chiq 大排挡 *n.* food vending stalls
tàe-dzï 毯子 *n.* blanket
tàe-fae 摊贩 *n.* street vendor
tàe-huoe 瘫痪 *n.* paralysis, *Alt.*: **fòng-tae**
tàe-wae 差 *adj.* inferior, no good
tāq 抹、涂 *v.* smear on, apply, spread onto; ~ •'yaq-gaw ~药 apply ointment
táw 套 *m.w.* sets
táw 讨 *v.* ask for
táw-dzï 套子 *n.* sheath, case, cover, condom
táw•dzǎ 讨债 *v.o.* demand repayment
táw•gá 要价 *n.* asking price
táw•gá•h'uáe-ga 讨价还价 *v.o.* bargaining, to bargain
táw•láw-b'u 讨老婆 *v.o.* marry *(of a man)*, *Alt.*: **táw•shìn-h'u**
táw-len 讨论 *v.* discuss
táw-vãw 套房 *n.* suite
táw-yi 讨厌 *v.* detest, loath, abhor, despise
tàw-h'a 雨鞋 *n.* galoshes, *Alt.*: **táw-h'a**
tǎw 烫 *adj.* scalding; *v.* scald, burn; iron; warm
tǎw 趟 *m.w. for trips*
tǎw 躺 *v.* lie down, recline
tǎw 滑跌 *v.* slip

tắw•d'éu-faq 烫头发 *v.o.* get a perm

tắw-zoq 汤勺 *n.* serving spoon

tăw 汤 *n.* soup, *Alt.*: **tắw-sï**

tăw-d'oe 汤团 *n.* rice flower balls *(usually stuffed)*,
  Alt.: **'yüóe-dzï** 圆子

tèn 吞 *v.* swallow

tēq 太 *adv.* too, *Alt.*: **tēq-saq**

tēq 和、跟 *prep.* with; and *(conj.)*, *Alt.*: **tēq-dzï, dēq,
  dēq-dzï, gàw, gáw, bằw**

tēq 脱 *v.* take off, undress

tēq•kòng 落空 *v.o.* fail, fall through, come to nothing

téu 透、极了 *d.c.* extremely, very, *Alt.*: **sāq** 煞, **sāq-deq,
  j'iq**

tèu 偷 *v.* steal; ~ •**meq-zï** 偷东西 steal things

tèu-b'oe(-dzï) 偷偷地 *adv.* secretly

tí 舔 *v.* lick

tí•d'éu(-faq) 剃头发 *v.o.* get a haircut, *Alt.*: **lí•fāq,
  jí•d'éu-faq**

tí-daw 剃刀 *n.* razor

tí-mi 体面 *adj.* dignified, honorable

tí-tsaw 体操 *n.* gymnastics

tí-'yüeq 体育 *n.* physical education, sports, *Alt.*:
  tí-'yoq

tí-'yüeq-zã 体育场 *n.* stadium, gym, *Alt.*: **tí-'yoq-zã**

tì 天 *n.* sky, the heavens; day; *m.w. for days*, *Alt.*: **niq** 日

tì 添 *v.* add, increase

tì-chi 天气 *n.* weather

tì-dzï 天主 *n.* God *(Catholic)*

tì-dzï-jiaw 天主教 *n.* Catholicism

tì-huo-pae 天花板 *n.* ceiling, *Alt.*: **b'ín-din**

tì-loq-sï 雨水 *n.* rainwater

tì-sã 天生 *adj.* inherent, innate, inborn

tì-ta 脏乱 *adj.* unkempt, disheveled, scruffy

tiáw 跳 *v.* jump

tiáw-dzaw 跳蚤 *n.* flea, *Alt.*: **tiáw-seq, dzáw-seq**

tiáw•sí 大幅降价 ("跳水") *v.o.* dramatic fall in price

tiáw•'wú 跳舞 *v.o.* dance

tiàw-fu 挑夫 *n.* porter *(who uses a shoulder pole)*

tín-dzã 付钱 *v.o.* pay the bill/check

tín-guaq 挺括 *adj.* stiff and smooth *(as good paper)*;
  well-pressed *(of clothing)*

tín•yàw 挺腰 *v.o.* straighten one's back

tìn 听 *m.w. for cans of things*

tìn 听 *v.* listen

tìn-shia 听写 *v.o.* do dictation

tīq 铁 *n.* iron

tīq 踢 *v.* kick

tīq 贴 *v.* stick on, paste, glue, *Alt.:* **dēq** 粘

tīq-bae-saw 铁板烧 *n.* teppanyaki

tīq-bu 补贴 *v.* subsidize

tīq-dzï 帖子 *n.* card, notepaper, small notebook

tóe 松 *v.* loosen, slacken, slip off

tóe 撑 *v.* remove *(from a hook, etc.)*

tóng 痛 *adj.* painful, sore

tóng 挪 *v.* shift *(something)*, slide *(something)* across, *Alt.:* **'yí** 移

tóng-kua 痛快 *adj.* joyful, elated, gratified

tòng 通 *adj.* open and clear, unobstructed

tòng-shin-fen 通心粉 *n.* macaroni

tōq 托 *v.* hold in the palm

tōq-'er-su 托儿所 *n.* nursery, child-care center

tú-dzï 兔子 *n.* rabbit, *Alt.:* **tù-dzï**

tù•dzǎ 拖账 *v.o.* delinquent, be late in repayment

tù-fen 拖把 *n.* mop

tù-h'a 拖鞋 *n.* slippers, flip-flops

TS

tsá 扯、撕 *v.* tear

tsà-veq-du 差不多 *ph.* more or less

tsǎ 厂 *n.* factory, plant, *Alt.:* **tsǎ-ga** 工厂

tsǎ 掌 *v.* brace, support

tsǎ-zǎ 厂长 *n.* factory director/manager

tsáe 菜 *n.* vegetables; dish of prepared food; non-staple food

tsáe-da 彩带 *n.* ribbon

tsáe-dae 菜单 *n.* menu

tsáe-geu-'yüoe 采购员 *n.* buyer, purchasing agent

tsáe-'yeu 菜油 *n.* vegetable oil

tsàe 掺 *v.* mix in, put in, *Alt.:* **shiǎ, jiǎ**

tsāq 尺 *n.* ruler

tsāq 插 *v.* insert, stick into

tsāq 裂 v. split, crack, *Alt.*: **kàe•tsāq, huāq•kàe**

tsāq 拆 v. take apart, dismantle

tsāq-d'eu 插头 n. plug

tsāq-d'eu 赤豆 n. red beans *(small)*

tsāq•dzí 插嘴 v.o. interrupt *(in a conversation)*, break in, *Alt.*: **dāq•dzí**

tsāq-gueq-loq 裸体、赤裸裸 *adj.* naked, stark naked

tsāq•jiāq 赤脚 v.o. be barefoot, *Alt.*: **guăw•jiāq** 光脚

tsāq-boq 赤膊 *adj.* bare to the waist

tsāq-pi-gu 光屁股 *adj.* stark naked

tsāq-shiaw 插销 n. latch, door bolt, *Alt.*: **shiàw-dzï**

tsāq-shiq 拆息 n. daily interest rate

tsāq-tsoe 拆穿 v. unmask, expose

tsāq•wú 大便 v.o. defecate, *Alt.*: **d'á-b'i, zá•wú**

tsáw 吵 *adj.* noisy; v. quarrel, wrangle

tsáw 炒 v. stir-fry

tsáw-d'eu 苜蓿 n. alfalfa greens

tsáw-ji 草鸡 n. free-range chicken

tsáw-maw 草帽 n. straw hat

tsáw-mi-huo 米花 n. puffed rice

tsáw-piaw 钞票 n. paper money, bank note

tsáw-shiā-mo 吵架 v. argue, fight, *Alt.*: **zyín-shiā-mo**

tsáw-zyiq 草席 n. straw mat

tsàw 抄 v. copy, transcribe, plagerize

tsàw-dzï 手纸 n. toilet paper

tsǎw 闯 v. rush, charge, dash

tsǎw 唱 v. sing

tsǎw•h'ú 闯祸 v.o. cause a disaster

tsǎw-kae-su 卡拉OK／唱K所 n. karaoke bar

tsǎw•shí 唱戏 v.o. perform in traditional opera

tsǎw 窗子 n. window, *Alt.*: **tsǎw-men**

tsǎw-d'ae 窗台 n. windowsill, *Alt.*: **tsǎw-b'oe**

tsǎw-keu 窗口 n. window *(ticket, teller's, etc.)*

tsǎw-li 窗帘 n. window curtain

tsǎw-yin 苍蝇 n. fly

tsén 秤 n. scales, balance scale

tsén (tsuò-dzï) 乘(车) v.o. ride, take *(a bus or train)*

tsén-sae 衬衫 n. shirt

tsèn 皲 *adj.* chapped

tsèn-dzā 村庄 n. village

tsèn-dzï 蛏子 n. razor clam

tsèn-jiq 春节 *n.* Spring Festival, Chinese *(Lunar)* New Year

tsèn-jüoe 春卷 *n.* spring rolls

tsèn-ti 春天 *n.* spring *(season)*

tsēq-naq-'yüoe 出纳员 *n.* cashier, teller

tsēq•bìn 出殡 *v.o.* have a funeral, hold a burial ceremony, *Alt.:* **tsēq•sǎw**

tsēq•d'éu 出面 *v.o.* appear personally, show up, *Alt.:* **tsēq•zǎ** 出场

tsēq•jìn 到极点 *d.c.* extremely *(adv.)*

tsēq-ni 测验 *n* quiz, test

tsēq-tǎw 上桌面、见过世面 *adj.* outgoing and sophisticated

tsēq•tsà 出差 *v.o.* go on a business trip

tsēq•tsà-tsuo 出差错 *v.* slip up, err, fumble

tsēq-tsae 出产 *v.* manufacture, produce

tséu 臭 *adj.* stinky

tséu 凑 *v.* gather together, pool

tséu•niq-naw 凑热闹 *v.o.* join in the fun, join in the trouble, *Alt.:* **g'aq•náw-mā**

tséu-zong 臭虫 *n* bedbug

tsèu 抽 *v.* pull out, draw out, take out *(from in between)*

tsèu-d'eu 抽屉 *n.* drawer, *Alt.:* **tsèu-ti**

tsèu•jin 抽筋 *v.o.* get cramps, pull a tendon

tsǐ 次 *m.w. for times (one does something)*, *Alt.:* **d'á**

tsǐ-hu 次货 *n.* inferior goods, *Alt.:* **tsǐ-pin** 次品

tsǐ•niéu-b'i 吹牛 *v.o.* brag, boast, *Alt.:* **tsǐ•niéu-sae**

tsǐ-su(-gae) 厕所 (间) *n.* toilet, watercloset, lavatory

tsǐ 痴 *adj.* silly, idiotic

tsǐ 吹 *v.* blow

tsǐ•d'éu-faq 吹头发 *v.o.* blow-dry hair

tsǐ-dzï 疯子 *n.* lunatic, *Alt.:* **fòng-dzï**

tsǐ•fòng 着凉 *v.o.* catch a chill

tsǐ-fong-ji 吹风机 *n.* hair dryer

tsǐ-ji 母鸡 *n.* hen

tsǐ-nieu 母牛 *n.* cow

tsóe 脆 *adj.* fragile; crisp

tsóe 惨、糟糕 *adj.* messed up, gone bad, suffering a turn of bad luck

tsóe 串 *m.w. for bunches, clusters, things strung together*

tsóe-tin 餐厅 *n.* dining hall, dining room

tsòe 猜 *v.* guess, *Alt.:* **ní**

tsòe 催 *v.* hurry, urge to hasten

tsòe 穿 *v.* wear, *Alt.:* **dzāq**

tsòe-ga 参加 *v.* participate in

tsòe-gu 穿过 *v.* cross

tsòe-jìn-dzï 餐巾纸 *n.* paper napkin

tsòng 葱 *n.* scallion

tsòng-di 充电 *v.o.* charge, recharge *(a battery)*

tsòng-min 聪明 *adj.* smart

tsòng-zeq 充值 *v.o.* add minutes *(to a mobile plan)*

tsōq 戳 *v.* jab, stab, poke, *Alt.:* **zoq**

tsōq-sā 畜生 *n.* beast

tsú 醋 *n.* vinegar

tsú-daw 锉刀 *n.* file *(metal)*

tsù 粗 *adj.* thick; coarse; rough; stout

tsù 错 *adj.* wrong, incorrect, mistaken, *Alt.:* **tsuò**

tsù-lu 粗鲁 *adj.* rude, crude

tsù-shin 粗心 *adj.* thoughtless, careless

tsù-su 粗俗 *adj.* vulgar

tsuó•yīq-jiaq 插手 *v.o.* get involved in, meddle in, *Alt.:* **dāq-yiq-jiaq**

tsùo 搓 *v.* rub with the hands, *Alt.:* **tsù**

tsuò-dzï 车 *n.* car, vehicle; cart

tsuò-gae dzḯ-zen 车间主任 *n.* factory floor manager

tsuò-lu 岔路 *n.* branch road

tsuò•mó-jiā(-b'a) *v.o.* play mahjongg, *Alt.:* **dā́•mó-jiā** 打麻将

tsuò-piaw 车票 *n.* bus ticket

tsuò-shiā 车厢 *n.* subway car, railway car

tsuò-tae 车胎 *n.* tire

tsuò-veq-du, 差不多 *adj.* almost the same, not much different; *adv.* almost, *Alt.:* **tsà-veq-du**

tsuò-zae 车站 *n.* bus stop, *Alt.:* **záe-d'eu**

V

va 吗 *ptl. marks questions*

váe 饭 *n.* cooked rice, food, meal

váe 帆 *n.* sail

váe 万 *num.* ten thousand

váe-di 饭店 *n.* restaurant, *Alt.*: **váe-guoe** 饭馆, **jiéu-ga** 酒家, **tsáe-guoe** 菜馆

váe-guae 犯规 *v.o.* break the rules, violate a taboo

váe-guo 南瓜 *n.* pumpkin *(or similar yellow squash variety)*, *Alt.*: **nóe-guo**

váe-nae 烦难 *adj.* hard to tackle, troublesome

váe-naw 烦恼 *adj.* vexed, worried

váe-nin 犯人 *n.* criminal

váe-ti-zï 繁体字 *n.* traditional *(non-simplified)* Chinese characters, *Alt.*: **d'ú-shia-zï** 大写字

váe-tsaw 饭勺 *n.* rice serving spatula, *Alt.*: **váe-zoq (-dzï)**

váe-zï 锅巴 *n.* rice crust *(at the bottom of a pot of cooked rice)*, *Alt.*: **h'oq-jiaw**

váe-zoe 帆船 *n.* sailboat, *Alt.*: **tsà-b'ong-zoe**

vaq-d'ong-d'i 罚款 *v.o.* fine, impose a fine

vaq•dzéu 赌咒、发誓 *v.o.* swear

vǎw-d'ae 房贷 *n.* mortgage, loan to purchase a house

vǎw-dong 房东 *n.* landlord

vǎw-dzï 房子 *n.* house, building

vǎw-fong-jin 风镜 *n.* goggles, *Alt.*: **bǎw-fong-jin**

vǎw-gae 房间、屋子 *n.* room, *Alt.*: **vǎw-dzï** 房子

vǎw-h'ae 妨碍 *v.* hinder, hamper

vǎw-ka 房卡 *n.* key card *(for a hotel room)*

vǎw-kaq 房客 *n.* tenant

vǎw-suo-sǎw 防晒霜 *n.* sunscreen

vén 坟 *n.* grave, *Alt.*: **vén-mo, vén-mu** 坟墓

vén-b'in 文凭 *n.* diploma

vén-chi 文气、娴静 *adj.* gentle and refined

vén-dae 柚子 *n.* pomelo

vén-huo 文化 *n.* culture, civilization

vén-j'ü-di 文具店 *n.* stationery shop

vén-liǎ 重量 *n.* weight

veq 不 *adv.* no, not

veq 佛 *n.* Buddha, *Alt.*: **zḯ-lae-veq** 如来佛

veq•dàe-dae 不只 *adv.* not only

veq-deq 不得 *p.c.* cannot, not able to

veq-dzae-gu 不粘锅 *n.* non-stick pan, *Alt.*: **veq-tiq-gu**

veq-dzï 不止 *adv.* not limited to, not just

veq-fǎw 不妨 *adv.* might as well, can't hurt to, *Alt.*: **bēq-fǎw**

veq-guae 不习惯 *adj.* not used to, not accustomed to

veq-haw-yi-sï 不好意思 *adj.* embarrassed

veq-jiaw 佛教 *n.* Buddhism

veq-lae 不来 *p.c.* cannot, not know how to

veq-len 不论 *conj.* no matter *(who, what, when, etc.)*, regardless

veq-seq-yi 不舒服 *adj.* feel ill, not well

veq-shiaw 不需要 *adv.* don't need

veq-shiaw-huo 消化不良 *v.* indigestion, suffer from poor digestion

veq-shü 不许 *v.* not allow, not permit

veq-sï-voq 不舒服 *adj.* uncomfortable, ill-at-ease, *Alt.*: **wēq**

veq-tsen-shin 不满意 *adj.* dissatisfied

veq-yaw 别、不要 *adv.* don't, *Alt.*: **viáw**

veq-yiq-'yā 不一样 *adj.* different

veq-zoe-ga 不然的话 *adv.* otherwise

véu 浮 *v.* float, *Alt.*: **vú**

ví-bu-lu 微波炉 *n.* microwave oven

ví-dzï-su 味精 *n.* monosodium glutamate, MSG, *Alt.*: **mí-dzï-su**

viáw zyiá 不谢, *interj.* You're welcome!, *Alt.*: **viáw kāq-chi** 别客气

voq-dzāw-di 服装店 *n.* clothing shop

voq-h'u-'yüoe 服务员 *n.* attendant, waiter, waitress

voq-tiq 服从 *v.* obey, submit to

vú 扶 *v.* support with the hands

vú-j'in 附近 *l.n.* nearby, vicinity, *Alt.*: **b'ā̆w-b'i-hae-d'eu**

'W

'wáe 为 *prep.* for, for the sake of , in order to, *Alt.*: **'wáe-leq** 为了, **'wáe-dzï**

'wáe 位 *m.w. for people (polite)*

'wáe 胃 *n.* stomach

'wáe-dzï 位子 *n.* seat

'wáe-sa 为什么 *prn.* why *(adv., conj.)*

'wáe-sen-gae 卫生间 *n.* toilet, washroom, restroom

'wáe-shi 危险 *adj.* dangerous

'wā̆w 往 *prep.* toward, facing, *Alt.*: **záw** 朝, **mā̆w** 望

'wén-d'en 馄饨 *n.* wonton

'wóe-b'i 顽皮 *adj.* naughty, mischievous, *Alt.*: **b'í** 皮, **lá-b'i**

'wóe-'yaq 药丸 *n.* pill

'wú 我 *prn.* I, me, *Alt.*: **ngú**

'wú 雾 *n.* fog, *Alt.*: **mí-'wu**

'wú(-d'aw) 舞蹈 *n.* dance

'wú-gong 蜈蚣 *n.* centipede

'wú-min-dzï 无名指 *n.* ring finger, third finger

W

wáe 会 *aux.* can, know how to, *Alt.*: **h'uáe, wáe-deq, h'uáe-deq**

wáe 会 *n.* meeting, *Alt.*: **h'uáe**

wàe 歪 *adj.* crooked, askew, *Alt.*: **huà, chiá**

wàe 弯 *v.* bend, flex

wāq 挖 *v.* dig

wǎw-fae 往返 *v.* go and return, travel round-trip

wén-dǎw 稳当 *adj.* reliable, stable, steady, *Alt.*: **bó•wén**

wèn-d'u-ji 温度计 *n.* thermometer

wēq 烦闷 *adj.* uncomfortable; edgy, *Alt.*: **wēq-seq**

wó-dzï 哑巴 *n.* mute, dumb person

wò-d'eu 丫头 *n.* girl

wóe 碗 *n.* bowl

wóe-d'eu 豌豆 *n.* peas, *Alt.*: **wòe-d'eu**

wù 陷入 *v.* fall into, get bogged in

wù 捂 *v.* muffle, cover, seal

wù-chin-kuae 血晕 *n.* bruise

wù-deu 得意（含贬义）*adj.* smug, complacent

wù-jü 乌龟 *n.* tortoise

wù-shin 得意 *adj.* complacent

wù-su 乌苏 *adj.* grimy, grubby

wù-ya 乌鸦 *n.* crow, *Alt.*: **láw-h'uo**

'Y

'yá 也 *adv.* also, *Alt.*: **'yáe, dù**

'yá 夜 *t.n.* night; 晚上 evening, *Alt.*: **'yá-daw**

'yá-li(-shiã), 'yá-d'eu-di, tì•hēq 夜里 *n.* nighttime

'yá-h'iaw 夜校 *n.* night school

'yá-mae 野蛮 *adj.* wild, savage, barbarous

'yá-vae 晚饭 *n.* dinner

'yá-niã 父母 *n.* parents

'yá-zï-mi 夜市 *n.* night market

'yǎ 痒 *adj.* itchy

'yǎ 羊 *n.* sheep, goat

'yǎ 生 *v.* give birth; ~ •**shiáw-noe** 生小孩 *v.o.* bear a child; 养 *v.* raise, rear, nuture

'yǎ 化 *v.* melt, dissolve

'yǎ-d'ae 阳台 *n.* balcony, terrace, deck

'yǎ-d'i 钱 *n.* money, *Alt.:* **d'óng-d'i**

'yǎ-dzï 养子 *n.* adopted son

'yǎ-dzï 样子 *n.* appearance, manner

'yǎ-mae 杨梅 *n.* red bayberry

'yǎ-nin 洋人 *n.* foreigner, *Alt.:* **ngá-goq-nin** 外国人

'yǎ-nioq 羊肉 *n.* mutton, goat meat, lamb meat

'yǎ-sae-'yü 土豆 *n.* potato

'yǎ-tsong-d'eu 洋葱 *n.* onion

'yǎ-vãw 洋房 *n.* Western-style house with a yard, *Alt.:* **huò-'yüoe-'yǎ-vãw** 花园洋房

'yǎ-wa-wa 洋娃娃 *n.* doll, *Alt.:* **'yǎ-noe-noe**

'yáe-shü 也许、可能 *adv.* perhaps, possibly, maybe, *Alt.:* **dzōq-shin**

'yaq 药 *n.* medicine

'yaq-di 药店 *n.* drugstore

'yaq-fen 药粉 *n.* medicinal powder

'yaq-gaw 药膏 *n.* ointment, salve

'yaq-pi 药片 *n.* medicinal tablet, pill

'yaq-sï 药水 *n.* liquid medicine

'yaq-zï 钥匙 *n.* key

'yáw 舀 *v.* ladle out, scoop up *(with a dipper)*

'yáw 摇 *v.* shake

'yǎw 旺 *adj.* vigorous *(as a flame or plants)*, fiercely hot or growing, *Alt.:* **'wǎw**

'yéu 又 *adv.* again *(in the past)*, *Alt.:* **'yí**

'yéu 油 *n.* oil

'yéu 有 *v.* have, there is

'yéu 游 *v.* travel, rove around, tour

'yéu-baw 邮包 *n.* postal parcel

'yéu-chiq-gong 油漆工 *n.* painter *(of buildings)*

'yéu-d'i-'yüoe 邮递员 *n.* mailman, letter carrier, *Alt.:* **'yéu-tsa** 邮差

'yeu-d'iaw 油条 *n.* Chinese cruller

'yéu-d'ong 邮筒 *n.* mailbox, postbox, *Alt.:* **'yéu-shiã** 邮箱

'yéu•dǎw-tsï 有档次 *adj.* have class

'yéu-dzen bì-mo 邮政编码 *n.* postal code, zip code

'yéu•dzóng 有种 *adj.* gutsy

'yéu-h'in 游行 *n.* parade; *v.* march

'yéu-j'üeq 邮局 *n.* post office

'yéu-mi 右边 *n.* right side

'yéu-min 有名 *adj.* famous

'yéu-ñg 鱿鱼 *n.* squid

'yéu-nioq 肥肉 *n.* fatty meat

'yéu-piaw 邮票 *n.* postage stamp

'yéu•pín(-'wae) 有品位、格调高 *adj.* tasteful, stylish, elegant

'yéu-seu 右手 *n.* right hand

'yéu•sú 有数 *v.o.* know how things stand, aware of the real situation

'yéu-ta-jiaw 犹太教 *n.* Judaism

'yéu-tsae 油菜 *n.* rapeseed, canola

'yéu•tsáw-piaw 有钱 *adj.* rich

'yéu-'yong 游泳 *v.o.* swim, *Alt.:* **'yéu•sï** 游水

'yéu-'yong-zï 游泳池 *n.* swimming pool

'yéu•yì-sï 有意思 *adj.* interesting

'yéu-zen-guãw 有时候 *adv.* sometimes, *Alt.:* **'yéu-zã-zï**

'yéu-zoe 游船 *n.* sightseeing boat

'yí 又 *adv.* again *(in the past)*, *Alt.:* **'yéu**

'yí 沿 *prep.* following, follow along, *Alt.:* **'yí-leq, 'yí-dzï** 沿着

'yí 他、她 *prn.* he, she, him, her

'yí 盐 *n.* salt

'yí 移 *v.* shift, *Alt.:* **tóng** 挪

'yí-fu 姨夫 *n.* uncle *(husband of mother's sister)*

'yí-jin 已经 *adv.* already, *Alt.:* **yí-jin**

'yí-laq 他们 *prn.* they, them, *Alt.:* **'yí-la**

'yí-laq-g'eq 他们的 *prn.* their, theirs, *Alt.:* **'yí-la-eq**

'yí-ma, à-'yi 姨妈 *n.* aunt *(mother's sister)*

'yí-'yeu 蛞蝓 *n.* slug, *Alt.:* **sǐ-'yi-'yeu, b'iq-ti-zong**

'yín 引 *v.* lead, guide, draw, pull

'yín 赢 *v.* win

'yín-hu-zong 萤火虫 *n.* firefly

'yín-niq 营业 *v.o.* do business

'yín-niq-dzong 营业中 *ph.* open for business

'yín-seq-pin 印刷品 *n.* printed matter

'yín-shiaw-ku 营销科 *n.* marketing division

'yiq 页 *m.w. for pages, Alt.:* **báe**

'yiq-dzï 叶子 *n.* leaf

'yiq-jin-b'in 液晶屏 *n.* liquid crystal display, LCD screen

'yóng 用 *v., prep.* use, employ, apply

'yóng-d'eu 用处 *n.* use, utility, application

'yóng-gong 用功 *adj.* studious

'yóng-kong 超支 *v.c.* overspend, exceed credit limit

'yóng-nin 佣人 *n.* servant, *Alt.:* **pōq-nin** 仆人

'yóng-shin 用心 *adj.* attentive, focused; *v.o.* put effort into

'yóng-yi 容易 *adj., adv.* easy, *Alt.:* **b'í-dǎw**

'yoq-gae 洗澡间 *n.* bathroom, *Alt.:* **d'á-'yoq-gae**

'yoq-jin 浴巾 *n.* bath towel

'yoq-kǎw 浴缸 *n.* bathtub

'yoq-li 浴帘 *n.* shower curtain

'yoq-maw 浴帽 *n.* shower cap

'yoq-zã 浴场 *n.* bathing area, swimming beach

'yǔ 雨 *n.* rain

'yǔ-d'ae-d'ae 围嘴 *n.* bib, *Alt.:* **tsuò-shiong-d'ae**

'yǔ-di-dzï 雨点子 *n.* raindrops

'yǔ-j'ün 围裙 *n.* apron, *Alt.:* **'wáe-j'iong, váe-dae**

'yǔ-jin 围巾 *n.* muffler, scarf

'yǔ-maw-j'ieu 羽毛球 *n.* badminton; shuttlecock

'yǔ-na 芋艿 *n.* taro, *Alt.:* **'yǔ-d'eu, 'yǔ-na-d'eu**

'yǔ-niong-sae 羽绒衫 *n.* down coat

'yǔ-shi 预先 *adv.* in advance

'yǔ-yi 雨衣 *n.* raincoat

'yüeq 月 *n.* month, *Alt.:* **'yoq**

'yüeq-bin 月饼 *n.* moon cake, *Alt.:* **'yoq-bin**

'yüeq-d'ae 月台 *n.* platform at a rail station, *Alt.:* **'yoq-d'ae**

'yüeq-di 月底 *t.n.* end of the month, *Alt.:* **'yoq-di**

'yüeq-jin 月经 *n.* menstrual period, *Alt.:* **'yoq-jin**

'yüeq-liã 月亮 *n.* moon, *Alt.*: **'yoq-liã**

'yüeq-liã-guãw 月光 *n.* moonlight, *Alt.*: **'yoq-liã-guãw**

'yüeq-liq 月历 *n.* calendar *(monthly)*, *Alt.*: **'yoq-liq**

'yüeq-nga-nga 月牙 *n.* crescent moon

'Yüeq-noe 越南 *n.* Vietnam

'yüeq-tsu 月初 *t.n.* beginning of the month, *Alt.*: **'yoq-tsu, 'yüeq-d'eu**

'yüeq-zeq 月食 *n.* eclipse of the moon, *Alt.*: **'yoq-zeq**

'yǔn 云 *n.* clouds, *Alt.*: **'yóng**

'yǔn-chi 运气 *n.* luck, fortune, *Alt.*: **'yóng-chi, 'yǔn-d'aw**

'yǔn-d'ong 运动 *n.* sports, athletics

'yǔn-d'ong-'yüoe 运动员 *n.* athlete

'yǔn-d'ong-zã 运动场 *n.* athletic field, *Alt.*: **'yóng-d'ong-zã**

'yǔn-vu 孕妇 *n.* pregnant woman, expectant mother, *Alt.*: **yóng-vu, tsáe-vu** 产妇

'yüóe 远 *adj.* far

'yüóe 圆 *adj.* round

'yüóe 元 *m.w. yuán (basic unit of Chinese money)*, *Alt.*: **kuáe** 块

'yüóe-dzï 圆子 *n.* rice flower balls *(usually stuffed)*, *Alt.*: **tãw-d'oe** 汤团

'yüóe-guae 圆规 *n.* compass *(for math and drafting)*

'yüóe-zï 远视 *adj.* farsighted

'yüóe-zï-ngae 远视眼 *n.* farsightedness

Y

Yá-dzeu 亚洲 *n.* Asia

yà-su 耶稣 *n.* Jesus

yǎ 求 *v.* entreat, beg of

yãq-haw 约好 *v.c.* agree on *(a time to meet)*

yáw 要 *v., aux.* want; want to, intend to, will

yáw-haw 要好 *adj.* close *(in friendship)*, on very good terms

yáw-jin 要紧 *adj.* critical, crucial, important

yáw-zï 要是 *conj.* if, *Alt.*: **zǐ-gu, lú-gu** 如果

yàw 腰 *n.* waist

yàw-da 腰带 *n.* belt, *Alt.*: **kú-yaw-da** 裤腰带

yàw-dzï 肾 *n.* kidney

yàw-j'ieu 要求 *v., n.* request, demand

yéu-'er-'yüoe 幼儿园 *n.* kindergarten, *Alt.*: **yéu-zï-'yüoe**

yí 比长度 *v.* compare length

Yí-d'a-li 意大利 *n.* Italy

Yí-d'a-li-nü 意大利语 *n.* Italian *(language)*

yí-dzï 燕子 *n.* swallow *(a bird)*

yí-dzï 椅子 *n.* chair, *Alt.*: **yǔ-dzï**

yí-jin 已经 *adv.* already, *Alt.*: **'yí-jin**

yí-mi 意大利面 *n.* spaghetti

yí•shí 演戏 *v.o.* perform *(in a play)*, *Alt.*: **dzú•shí**

yí-tseq 演出 *v.* perform; *n.* performance

yí-'wae 以为 *adv.* think erroneously

yí-'yüoe 演员 *n.* actor, actress, performer

yì 疮痂 *n.* scab

yì 依 *v.* comply with

yì 烟 *n.* tobacco; cigarette, *Alt.*: **shiǎ-yi** 香烟

yì-dzï 胭脂 *n.* rouge

yì-g'eq 那个 *prn.* that, *Alt.*: **yì-eq, àe-g'eq, àe-eq**

yì•h'éu 以后 *n.* after, afterwards, later

yì•h'uó 以下 *n.* under, below, less than *(adv.)*

yì•máw-b'in 治病 *v.o.* cure

yì-mi 那儿 *prn.* there, *Alt.*: **àe-d'eu**

yì-sã 医生 *n.* doctor

yì-'yüoe 医院 *n.* hospital

yì•zǎ 以上 *n.* above, over, more than *(adv.)*

yì-zãw 衣裳 *n.* clothing, clothes

yì-zãw-ga 衣架 *n.* clothes hanger, coat rack

yì-zï 衣橱 *n.* closet, wardrobe

yì•zyí 以前 *t.n.* before, in the past

yín 凉爽 *adj.* chilly, brisk

yín-h'in-ngae-jin 隐形眼镜 *n.* contact lenses

yín-liaw 饮料 *n.* drink

yín-sï-chi 饮水器 *n.* drinking fountain

yín-dzong 影踪 *n.* trace, tracks, sign

yìn-bãw 英镑 *n.* pounds sterling

yìn-d'eu-li 阴凉处 *n.* shade

yìn-'er 婴儿 *n.* infant, *Alt.*: **shiáw-shiaw-noe, shiáw-maw-d'eu**

yìn-gae 应该 *aux.* should

Yìn-goq 英国 *n.* Britain

Yìn-goq-nin 英国人 *n.* Briton

yìn-liã 阴凉 *adj.* shady and cool

yìn-liã-ti 阴凉天 *n.* cold and cloudy day

Yìn-nü 英语 *n.* English, *Alt.:* **Yìn-ven** 英文

yìn-ti 阴天 *n.* cloudy weather

yīq 一 *num.* one

yīq 噎 *v.* choke, *Alt.:* **dǎ•yīq**

yīq-d'aw 一起 *adv.* together

yīq-d'in 一定 *adv.* definitely, certainly, *Alt.:* **dzén-d'in, báe**

yīq-g'ong 一共 *adv.* altogether, *Alt.:* **dzóng-g'ong** 总共, **g'óng-dzong, lóng-dzong, yīq-taq-guaq-dzï, hǎbaq-lã-dǎ**

yīq-shiá(-dzï), 一下 *n.m.* once, briefly *(adv.)*, *Alt.:* **yīq-ji-d'eu**

yīq-shiã, 一向 *adv.* all along, up to now, consistently, *Alt.:* **yīq-jiaq, yīq-zeq, yīq-jin**

yīq-tsï 一次 *n.m.* once

yīq-tsï-shin 一次性 *attr.* disposable *(adj.)*

yīq-'yã 一样 *adj.* same

yīq-'yüeq 一月 *t.n.* January, *Alt.:* **yīq-'yoq**

yīq-zeq-'yeu 一日游 *n.* one-day tour

yóng-deu 熨斗 *n.* iron *(for pressing fabric)*, *Alt.:* **'yǔn-deu**

yóng-'yüoe 永远 *adv.* forever

yǔ-dzï 椅子 *n.* chair, *Alt.:* **yí-dzï**

yǔ•ná 喂奶 *v.* breast-feed, nurse

yüòe-wãw 冤枉 *v., adj.* wrong, treat unjustly

yüòe-yã-diaw 鸳鸯 *n.* mandarin ducks

Z

zá-hu 惹火 *v.* inflame, provoke, incite

zá-wú 大便 *v.o.* defecate, *Alt.:* **tsãq•wú, d'á-b'i**

zǎ 长 *adj.* long

zǎ 高 *adj.* tall *(of people)*

zá 剩 *v.* left over, remain

zá 惹 *v.* provoke, incite, *Alt.:* **zá-nin** 惹人

zǎ-d'u 高大（身材）*adj.* big and tall *(of stature)*

zǎ-d'u-d'i-h'uo 长途电话 *n.* long-distance call

zǎ-fu 丈夫 *n.* husband, *Alt.:* **láw-gong** 老公

zǎ-guen 长棍 *n.* baguette *(French bread)*

zǎ-hu 剩货 *n.* remnants, leftover goods

zǎ-shin 恒心 *n.* perseverance

zǎ-tong-maq 长袜 *n.* long stockings

zǎ-zā 常常 *adv.* often, frequently, *Alt.:* **zǎ-dzāw**

záe 饱满 *adj.* full, plump

záe 全 *adv.* all, *Alt.:* **zyí-bu**

záe 裁 *v.* cut cloth or paper

záe 溅 *v.* splash, splatter

záe 站 *v.* station

záe-d'eu 车站 *n.* bus stop, *Alt.:* **tsuò-zae**

záe-d'eu 利润 *n.* profit

záe-d'in 暂停 *v.* suspend *(an activity temporarily)*

záe-dzen 财政 *n.* finance

záe-jiq 蟋蟀 *n.* cricket

záe-law 嘴馋 *adj.* gluttonous, fond of eating

záe•tsàw-piaw 赚钱 *v.o.* make money, earn a living, *Alt.:* **záe•d'óng-d'i**

záe-tu(-sǐ) 口水 *n.* saliva

záe-vong 裁缝 *n.* tailor

záe-vong-di 裁缝店 *n.* tailor shop, *Alt.:* **zén-yi-di**

záe-wu-ku 财务科 *n.* financial division

záe-zen(-b'u-saq) 财神 *n.* god of wealth

zaq 弱 *adj.* weak

zaq 宅 *m.w.* for houses, apartments, condos

zaq 掷、投 *v.* cast, hurl

zaq 阻塞 *v.* clog, obstruct, *Alt.:* **gǎ** 梗

zaq 跺 *v.* stamp, stomp *(one's foot)*

zaq-d'eu 石头 *n.* rock, stone

zaq-d'i 住宅 *n.* residence, *Alt.:* **zǐ-zaq**

zaq-dzǐ 碎石头 *n.* pebble, gravel

zaq-goq 对角 *n.* opposite corner

zaq-hu-di 杂货店 *n.* general store

zaq•lǎ 着凉 *v.o.* get chilled

zaq-lieu 石榴 *n.* pomegranate

zaq-zaq 撞见 *v.* discover by chance, meet by happenstance

zaq-zeq 踏实 *adj.* practical, realistic

zǎw 胃酸多不舒服 *adj.* dyspepsic, have a feeling like dyspepsia

zǎw 朝 *prep.* toward, facing, *Alt.:* **mǎw** 望, **'wǎw** 往

záw-fae 造反 *v.* revolt, rebel

záw-ga 造价 *n.* cost of building

záw-h'eu 往后 *t.n.* in the future

záw•nín 嘲讽别人 *v.o.* taunt, mock, sneer at others

záw-seq 潮湿 *adj.* humid

záw-sï 潮水 *n.* tide

zắw 床 *n.* bed

zắw 幢 *m.w. for buildings*

zắw 上 *sfx.* on (locative suffix), *Alt.*: **lắw, lắw-shiã**

zắw 撞 *v.* collide with, run into, *Alt.*: **káe**

zắw 上 *v.* get on, get into

zắw-bae 上班 *v.o.* go to work

zắw-boe-niq 上午 *t.n.* morning, forenoon, *Alt.*: **zắw-dzeu**

zắw-chi 上去 *v.* ascend, go up

zắw-d'eu 上头 *l.n.* top, above, *Alt.*: **zắw-mi** 上面, **gàw-d'eu**

zắw-dae 床单 *n.* bedsheets, *Alt.*: **b'í-dae** 被单

zắw-di 上帝 *n.* God (Protestant)

zắw•dzáw 上照 *adj.* photogenic

zắw-dzãw 上衣 *n.* coat, jacket, *Alt.*: **ngá-taw** 外套

zắw-g'eq-'yüeq 上个月 *t.n.* last month

zắw-h'uo 上下 *num.* about, around, more or less, *Alt.*: **zắw-shia**

Zắw-hae 上海 *n.* Shànghǎi

Zắw-hae-h'ae-h'uo 上海话 *n.* Shanghainese (language)

Zắw-hae-nin 上海人 *n.* Shanghainese (person)

zắw•kú 上课 *v.o.* go to class, attend class

zắw-li-ba 上礼拜 *t.n.* last week

zắw•mắw 上网 *v.o.* go online (on the Internet)

zãw-sï 上司 *n.* superior, supervisor

zắw•tsáe 上菜 *v.o.* serve food

zắw•vén 上坟扫墓 *v.o.* visit a grave

zén 层 *m.w. for layers*

zén 阵 *m.w. for spells of wind or rain*

zén 城 *n.* city, *Alt.*: **zén-zï** 城市

zén 顺 *prep.* along, in the same direction as; *adj.* effortless, trouble-free

zén 沉 *v.* sink

zén-chi 神气 *adj.* cocky

zén-(da-)bi 顺便 *adv.* in passing

zén-dzeq 存折 *n.* deposit book

zén-dzï 绳子 *n.* rope, string

zén-fong-liã 乘凉 *v.o.* cool off in the shade or a breeze, *Alt.*: **tsï-fong-liã**

zén-guãw 时候、时间 *n.* time, time when

zén-hu 陈货 *n.* old stock, shopworn goods

zén-jiaw 成交 *v.o.* close a deal

zén-jin-b'in 神经病 *n.* mental disorder

zén-jiq-dae 成绩单 *n.* report card

zén-ka 正宗货物 *n.* genuine products

zén-kuoe 存款 *n.* deposit; savings in the bank

zén-leu 楼层 *n.* floor, level

zén-li 顺利 *adj.* smooth, successful, without a hitch

zén-min-b'i 人民币 *n.* RMB, *Rénmínbì (the Chinese currency)*

zén-saq 淹死 *v.c.* drown

zén-tsae 莼菜 *n.* water shield *(a vegetable)*

zén•tsáw-piaw 存钱 *v.o.* deposit money

zén-sï 精力 *n.* vigor, energy

zén-vu 神父 *n.* priest *(Catholic)*

zén-zyiã 神像 *n.* idol

zeq 直 *adj.* straight

zeq 贼、小偷 *n.* thief, *Alt.*: **zeq-kueq-d'eu**

zeq 十 *num.* ten

zeq 值 *v.* worth; ~ •**d'óng-d'i** 值钱 *adj.* valuable

zeq-baq 十八 *num.* eighteen

zeq•bén 折本 *v.o.* lose capital, suffer a loss in business, *Alt.*: **kuàe•bén** 亏本

Zeq-ben 日本 *n.* Japan

zeq-chiq 十七 *num.* seventeen

zeq-d'ãw 食堂 *n.* cafeteria, canteen

zeq-d'eu 舌头 *n.* tongue

zeq-deq 值得 *adj., aux.* worthwhile

zeq-dzï 食指 *n.* forefinger, index finger

zeq-dzï 侄子 *n.* nephew *(brother's son)*, *Alt.*: **ãq-zeq**

zeq-h'uae 实惠 *adj.* economical, substantial, practical

zeq-j'in-'yüoe 值勤员 *n.* on-duty personnel

zeq-jieu 十九 *num.* nineteenth

zeq-kuae 直快 *adj.* non-stop

zeq-liq 日历 *n.* calendar *(daily)*

zeq-loq 十六 *num.* sixteen

zeq-ñg 十五 *num.* fifteen
zeq-ni 十二 *num.* twelve
zeq-ni-'yüeq 十二月 *t.n.* December, *Alt.*: **zeq-ni-'yoq**
zeq-noe(-ñg) 侄女 *n.* niece *(brother's daughter)*
Zeq-nü 日语 *n.* Japanese *(language)*
zeq-pin 食品 *n.* foodstuff, food
zeq-sae 十三 *num.* thirteen
zeq-sãw 直爽 *adj.* candid, forthright
zeq-sen-fi-ji 直升机 *n.* helicopter
zeq-sï 十四 *num.* fourteen
zeq-teu 偷窃 *v.* steal, *Alt.*: **tèu** 偷
zeq-'yüeq 十月 *t.n.* October, *Alt.*: **zeq-'yoq**
zeq-'yüoe 日元 *n.* Japanese *yen*
zeq-yiq 十一 *num.* eleven
zeq-yiq-'yüeq 十一月 *t.n.* November, *Alt.*: **zeq-yiq-'yoq**
zeq-zae 实在 *adv.* really, honestly
zeq-zeq 日食 *n.* eclipse of the sun
zéu-bu-di 绸布店 *n.* silk shop
zéu-d'oe 绸缎 *n.* silks and satins
zéu-hu-'yüoe 售货员 *n.* sales assistant, *Alt.*: **dí-'yüoe** 店员
zéu-piaw-'yüoe 售票员 *n.* ticket seller, *Alt.*: **má-piaw-'yüoe**
zḯ 橱 *n.* cabinet
zḯ 寺 *n.* temple
zḯ 树 *n.* tree
zḯ 是 *v.* be, is, are
zḯ 住 *v.* live, live at, stay at
zḯ-b'i 树皮 *n.* bark *(of a tree)*
zḯ-chi 瓷器店 *n.* china
zḯ-chi-di 瓷器店 *n.* china shop
zḯ-d'ãw 祠堂 *n.* ancestral hall
zḯ-d'ãw 池塘、小池 *n.* pond, pool, *Alt.*: **h'ú-d'ãw**
zḯ-d'ong-dãw 自动排挡 *n.* automatic transmission
zḯ-daw 迟到 *v.* be tardy, be late to arrive
zḯ-dzï 柿子 *n.* persimmon
zḯ-dzï 柱子 *n.* pillar, post
zḯ-dzoe 瓷砖 *n.* tile
zḯ-fi 除非 *prep.* unless
zḯ-ga 自己 *prn.* oneself, selves

zí-gã-dzï 树枝 *n.* branch

zí-gen 树根 *n.* root, *Alt.*: **gèn** 根

zí-gu 如果 *conj.* if, *Alt.*: **lú-gu, yáw-zï** 要是

zí-ka 磁卡 *n.* ATM card

zí-keu 市口 *n.* market district, shopping center

zí-lae-hu 火柴 *n.* match, matchstick

zí-leq 除了 *prep.* except for, excluding, *Alt.*: **zí-teq, zí-tseq**

zí-liq 视力 *n.* eyesight

zí-maw 时髦 *adj.* fashionable, in vogue, *Alt.*: **zí-shin**

zí-min-h'u 自鸣壶 *n.* whistling kettle

zí-shüeq 储蓄 *n.* savings

zí-sï 厨师 *n.* chef, cook

zí-ti 事情 *n.* matter, business, affair

zí-tsãw 橱窗 *n.* display window, showcase

zí-vãw(-gae) 厨房 *n.* kitchen

zí-veu-tsuo 磁浮车 *n.* maglev *(magnetic levitation)* train

zí-'yeu 自由 *adj.* free

zí-'yeu-zï-zã 自由市场 *n.* free market, open market

zí-zã 市场 *n.* market

zí-zaq 住宅 *n.* residence, *Alt.*: **zaq-d'i**

zí-zu-tsoe 自助餐 *n.* buffet, cafeteria

zí-zyiq 除夕 *n.* Chinese New Year's Eve

zín-ti 晴天 *n.* clear weather, clear sky

zóe 船 *n.* boat, ship

zóe 随 *prep.* follow, *Alt.*: **zóe-leq**

zóe 传 *v.* pass on, transmit

zóe 纠缠 *v.* pester, bother, nag

zóe-b'i 随便 *adj.* casual, random, careless, willful

zóe-baw-baw 蚕宝宝 *n.* silkworm

zóe-d'aw 隧道 *n.* tunnel

zóe-h'u 随和 *adj.* amiable, easy going

zóe-piaw 船票 *n.* boat ticket

zóe-zoe 传染 *n.* infect, spread *(of disease)*

zóng 重 *adj.* heavy

zóng 从 *prep.* from

zóng-dzï 虫子 *n.* bug, insect

zóng-zyi 从前 *n.* formerly, in the past, *Alt.*: **gú-chi** 过去

zoq 熟 *adj.* familiar, familiar-looking, *Alt.*: **mí•zoq** 面熟

zoq 熟 *adj.* ripe; cooked; processed

zoq 凿 *v.* chisel at
zoq-d'eu 凿子 *n.* chisel, *Alt.*: **zoq-dzï**
zoq-h'i 续弦 *v.o.* remarry *(of a widower)*
zoq-niq 昨天 *t.n.* yesterday, *Alt.*: **zuó-niq, zoq-ti, zuó-ti**
zú 座 *m.w. for bridges, mountains*
zú 坐 *v.* sit
zú-tsae-zï 助产士 *n.* midwife
zuó 蛇 *n.* snake
zuó 茶 *n.* tea
zuó 查 *v.* examine
zuó-bae 茶杯 *n.* teacup
zuó-d'i 茶垫 *n.* coaster for teacups
zuó•dzǎ 查账 *v.o.* audit account
zuó-h'u 茶壶 *n.* teapot
zuó-ji 茶几 *n.* tea table, coffee table, side table
zuó-'yiq 茶叶 *n.* tea leaf

ZY

zyí 全 *adj.* entire, complete
zyí 齐 *adj.* even, neat, straight
zyí-bu 全部 *adv.* all, *Alt.*: **záe**
zyí-chiaw 恰巧 *adv.* concidentially
zyí-d'eu 前头 *l.n.* front, *Alt.*: **zyí-mi** 前面
zyí-da 脐带 *n.* umbilical cord
zyí-fong 旋风 *n.* whirlwind
zyí-g'uae 脐环 *n.* belly button ring
zyí-maq-mi-baw 全麦面包 *n.* whole wheat bread
zyí-niq(-dzï) 前天 *t.n.* day before yesterday, *Alt.*: **zyí-ti(-dzï)**
zyí-tsae 荠菜 *n.* shepherd's purse
zyiá 斜 *adj.* slanting, oblique, *Alt.*: **chiá**
zyiá 谢 *v.* thank, *Alt.*: **zyiá-zyia** 谢谢; ~ **-nong!** 谢谢你
   ! *interj.* thank you!
zyiá-chi 很 *adv.* very, *Alt.*: **láw**
zyiá-dae-mi 斜对面 *l.n.* diagonally opposite, *Alt.*:
   chiá-dae-gu, h'uǎ-zaq-goq
zyiǎ 象 *n.* elephant
zyiǎ 像 *v.* like, resemble; *adj.* similar
zyiǎ-b'i 橡皮 *n.* eraser
zyiǎ-biq 墙壁 *n.* wall, *Alt.*: **zyiǎ-d'eu**

zyiǎ-gaw 橡胶 *n.* rubber

zyiǎ-j'í 象棋 *n.* chess *(Chinese style)*

zyiǎ-vi 蔷薇 *n.* rose, *Alt.*: **zyiǎ-b'i, máe-guae** 玫瑰

zyiǎ•'yǎ 像样 *adj.* presentable, decent

zyiaq 嚼 *v.* chew

zyiéu 就 *adv.* then, right away, *Alt.*: **j'iéu**

zyiéu-dzï(-guoe) 袖子 *n.* sleeve

zyiéu-keu 袖口 *n.* cuff *(of a sleeve)*

zyiéu-soe 就算 *conj.* even if, *Alt.*: **zyiéu-zï** 就是

zyiéu-zï 就是 *adv.* is precisely, quite exactly; *conj.* even if

zyín 找 *v.* look for, seek

zyín•dáe-zyiã 找对象 *v.o.* seek a marriage partner, *Alt.*: **dzáw•dáe-zyiã**

zyín-d'ãw 饴糖 *n.* malt sugar, *Alt.*: **maq-nga-d'ãw** 麦芽糖

zyín-nin 情人 *n.* lover

zyín-nüoe 情愿 *v.* would rather

zyín-zyü 情绪 *n.* mood, *Alt.*: **shín-dzï** 兴致

zyiq-dzï 席子 *n.* mat *(usually of woven bamboo or fiber)*

zyiq-zï 集市 *n.* local market, county fair

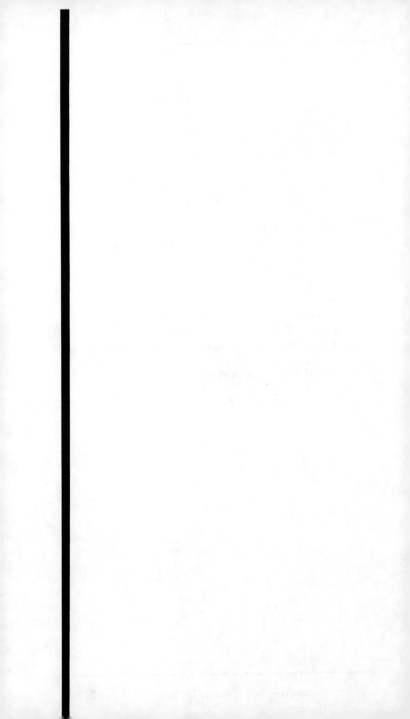

SHANGHAINESE PHRASEBOOK

with Mandarin glosses in Chinese Characters

INTRODUCTIONS

Greetings

Good morning!	**Nóng záw!** 你早！
Hello!	**Nóng háw!** 你好！

Response: **Nóng háw!** 你好！

How are you?	Is your health good?
Nóng háw va?	**Nóng sèn-ti háw va?**
你好吗？	你身体好吗？

Response: Fine. And you?
Màe háw. Nóng-neq?
很好。你呢？

Have [you] eaten?
Váe chīq-gu-leq va? 吃饭了吗？

Response: [Yes, I've] eaten.
Chīq-gu-leq. 吃过了。

Are you busy?
Nóng mǎw va? 你忙吗？

Response: I'm not too busy.
Ngú veq-d'a mǎw. 我不太忙。

I'm quite busy.
Ngú láw mǎw h'eq. 我很忙的。

Good-bye! / See you later!	See you tomorrow!
Dzáe-h'uae!	**Mén-dzaw-h'uae!**
再见！	明天见！

Basic Etiquette

Welcome!　　**Huòe-nin!** 欢迎！

Please …　　**Chín** … 请 …
　　enter. / come in. **jín.** / **jín-lae.** 进。 / 进来。
　　sit down. **zú!** 坐！
　　drink/have some tea. **chīq•zuó.** 喝茶。
　　have some coffee. **chīq•kà-fì.** 喝咖啡。

You may hear ...

the following courteous phrases in situations where favors are exchanged or requests are made:

Chín•mén ... 请问...
Excuse me, may I ask ...

> **Mó-vae-nong-leq!** 麻烦你了！
> Thanks for taking the trouble!

Dǎ-zaw-nong-leq! 打搅你了！
Sorry to disturb you!

> **Shìn-ku-leq!** 辛苦了！
> You've been working hard!

Gú-yi-veq-chi! 过意不去！
(I) feel badly for the imposition!

> **'Wú-su-'wae!** 无所谓！
> Whatever is fine!

Jiàw-guae b'áw-chi! 很抱歉！
I'm really sorry!

> **Chín nüóe-liã!** 请原谅！
> Please forgive me!

Veq-haw-yi-sï. 不好意思。
I'm rather embarrassed.

> **Tēq kāq-chi!** 太客气！
> Too polite!

Ḿ-meq guàe-shi! 没关系！
It doesn't matter!

> **Veq-yaw-jin!** 不要紧！
> It's not important!

Veq-ngae-zï! 不碍事！
It's not a problem!

> **Bá-toq-nong!** 拜托你！
> I beg of you!

Niǎ-nong fí-shin! 让你费心！
I've put you to a lot of trouble!

> **Tì-nong mó-vae!** 给你添麻烦！
> I've burdened you!

Dáe-veq-chi! / Dáe-veq-zï! 对不起！
(I'm) sorry and ashamed!

| Thanks! | **Zyiá-zyia!** 谢谢！ |
| Thank you! | **Zyiá-zyia-nong!** 谢谢你！ |

You are welcome. / No need for formality.
Viáw zyiá. / Viáw kāq-chi. 不谢。 / 别客气。

Take care as you go! / Be at ease on your way!
Dzéu•háw! / Máe-dzeu! 慢走！

See you later!	See you tomorrow!
Dzáe-h'uae!	**Mén-dzaw-h'uae!**
再见！	明天见！

Introducing Oneself and Others

What is your family name?*
Nóng guáe-shin? / Dzèn-shin? 您贵姓？

> *Response*: My family name is …
> **Ngú shín** … 我姓 …

What's your name?
Nóng jiáw sá-h'eq-min-zï? 你叫什么名字？

> *Response*: My name is …
> **Ngú jiáw** … 我叫…

Who is/are …?
… sá-nin a? / … zǐ sá-nin? …是谁？

he / she	**'Yí** 他 / 她
they	**'Yí-laq** 他们
this *man*	**G'eq-'wae** *shì-sã* 这位先生
that *woman*	**Àe-'wae** *nǘ-zï* 那位女士

I don't know him/her.
Ngú veq nín-deq 'yí. 我不认识他 / 她。

I'll introduce you.
Ngú láe bǎw-na jiá-zaw. 我来给你们介绍。

This is …	**G'eq-h'eq zǐ** … 这个是 …
Mr. …	**… shì-sã** …先生
Mrs. …	**… tà-ta** …太太
Miss …	**… shiáw-jia** …小姐

You may hear . . .

one of the following common family names if you ask this question of someone:

Chièu	Qiū	邱	**Lú**	Luó	罗
D'ǎw	Táng	唐	**Lǚ**	Lǚ	吕
D'én	Dèng	邓	**Mǎ**	Mèng	孟
D'í	Tián	田	**Máw**	Máo	毛
Dìn	Dīng	丁	**Mó**	Mǎ	马
Dóng	Dǒng	董	**Nín**	Nìng	宁
Dzǎ	Zhāng	张	**Nüóe**	Yuán	元
Dzèng	Zēng	曾	**Póe**	Pān	潘
Dzèu	Zhōu	周	**Sén**	Shēn	深
Dzǐ	Zhū	朱	**Sèn**	Sūn	孙
Èu-'yā	Ōuyáng	欧阳	**Shīq**	Xuē	薛
Fú	Fù	傅	**Shǔ**	Xǔ	许
Gǎw	Jiāng	江	**Sí**	Shǐ	史
Gēq	Gě	葛	**Sì-mo/a**	Sīmǎ	司马
Gōq	Guō	郭	**Sóng**	Sòng	宋
Gú	Gù	顾	**Sù**	Sū	苏
H'óng	Hóng	洪	**Tsàe/**	Cuī	崔
H'ú	Hé	何	**Tsòe**		
H'ú	Hú	胡	**Váe**	Fàn	范
H'uǎ	Huáng	黄	**Vóng**	Féng	冯
H'uó	Huà	华	**'Wǎw**	Wáng	王
Hóe	Hán	韩	**'Wǎw**	Wāng	汪
Jí	Jì	季	**'Wú**	Wú	吴
Jiá	Jiǎ	贾	**'Yìq**	Yè	叶
Jiá	Jiǎng	蒋	**'Yǔ**	Yú	余
Jià	Jiāng	姜	**'Yǔ**	Yú	俞
Kǎw	Kāng	康	**'Yüóe**	Yuán	袁
Kóng	Kǒng	孔	**Záw**	Cáo	曹
Kù	Kē	柯	**Záw**	Shào	邵
Lí	Lí	黎	**Záw**	Zhào	赵
Lí	Lǐ	李	**Zén**	Chén	陈
Liǎ	Liáng	梁	**Zén**	Chéng	程
Liáw	Liào	廖	**Zén**	Zhèng	郑
Lièu	Liú	刘	**Zyí**	Qí	齐
Lín	Lín	林	**Zyí**	Qián	钱
Loq	Lù	陆	**Zyiá**	Xiè	谢
Lú	Lǔ	鲁	**Zyín**	Qín	秦

Response: How do you do!
Nóng háw! / Nóng háw!
你好！/ 你好！

Is this …? **G'eq-'wae āq-zï …? /**
G'eq-'wae zí …va?
这位是…吗？

Mr. … … **shì-sã** …先生
Mrs. … … **tà-ta** …太太
Miss … … **shiáw-jia** …小姐

We have (not) met before.
Āq-laq (m̀-meq) jí-gu-mi.
我们见过面 / 没见过面。

This is my name card.
G'eq-h'eq zí ngú-h'eq mín-pi.
这是我的名片。

Meeting you has been a pleasure.
Nín-deq-nong ngú láw gàw-shin h'eq.
认识你，我很高兴。

You may hear …

the following terms, which can also serve as forms
of address just like Mr., Mrs., and Miss:

jìn-li 经理 Manager
  for example, *Lí-jin-li* 李经理 (Manager Lǐ)

láw-sï 老师 Teacher
  for example, *Lú-law-sï* 罗老师 (Teacher/Professor
  Luó)

sï̀-vu 师傅 Master/Driver
  for example, *Dóng-sï-vu* 董师傅 (Driver Dǒng)

à-'yi 阿姨 Auntie
  for example, *Póe-a-'yi* 潘阿姨 (Auntie Pān)

> **Note...**
> Just as in standard Chinese, all the various forms of
> address follow the surname in Shanghainese:
>
> | | | | |
> |---|---|---|---|
> | **Sī-miq-sī *shì-sā*** | 史密斯先生 | *Mr.* Smith |
> | **Zhàng-*nü-zī*** | 张女士 | *Ms.* Zhāng |
> | **'Wú-*ta-ta*** | 吴太太 | *Mrs.* Wú |
> | **Zén-*shiaw-jia*** | 陈小姐 | *Miss* Chén |

Nationalities, Countries, and Places of Origin

Where are you from?
Nóng sá-d'i-fāw nín? 你是那里人？

I am (a/an) ...　　**Ngú zī** ... 我是...

American	**Máe-goq-nin**	美国人
Australian	**Áw-d'a-li-ya-nin**	澳大利亚人
British	**Yìn-goq-nin**	英国人
Canadian	**Gà-na-da-nin**	加拿大人
Cantonese	**Guǎw-dong-nin**	广东人
Chinese	**Dzòng-goq-nin**	中国人
French	**Fāq-goq-nin**	法国人
German	**Dĕq-goq-nin**	德国人
Italian	**Yí-d'a-li-nin**	意大利人
Japanese	**Zeq-ben-nin**	日本人
Korean	**H'óe-goq-nin**	韩国人
Russian	**Ngú-goq-nin**	俄国人
Shanghainese	**Zǎw-hae-nin**	上海人
Spanish	**Shì-bae-nga-nin**	西班牙人

Where did ... come from?
... sá-d'i-fāw láe h'eq. ....是什么地方来的。

you (singular)	**Nóng**	你
you (plural)	**Ná**	你们
he / she	**'Yí**	他 / 她
they	**'Yí-laq**	他们
this *man/woman*	**G'eq-'wae *shì-sā/nü-zī***	
	这位先生 / 女士	

I/*We* am/are from …
Ngú / Āq-laq zí̈ … **láe h'eq.** 我 / 我们是 … 来的。

Countries

America / United States	**Máe-goq** 美国
Australia	**Áw-d'a-li-ya** 澳大利亚
Britain	**Yìn-goq** 英国
Brazil	**Bò-shi** 巴西
Canada	**Gà-na-da** 加拿大
China	**Dzòng-goq** 中国
France	**Fāq-goq** 法国
Germany	**Dēq-goq** 德国
Italy	**Yí-d'a-li** 意大利
Japan	**Zeq-ben** 日本
Korea	**H'óe-goq** 韩国
Russia	**Ngú-goq** 俄国
Spain	**Shì-bae-nga** 西班牙
Vietnam	**'Yüeq-noe** 越南

Continents

Africa	**Fì-dzeu** 非洲
Asia	**Yá-dzeu** 亚洲
Antarctica	**Nóe-j'iq-dzeu** 南极洲
Australia	**Áw-d'a-li-ya-dzeu** 澳大利亚洲
Europe	**Èu-dzeu** 欧洲
North America	**Bōq Máe-dzeu** 北美洲
South America	**Nóe Máe-dzeu** 南美洲

Chinese Cities

Běijīng	**Bōq-jin** 北京
Canton/ Guǎngzhōu	**Guǎw-dzeu** 广州
Hángzhōu	**H'ǎw-dzeu** 杭州
Hong Kong	**Shiǎ-gā** 香港
Nánjīng	**Nóe-jin** 南京
Níngbō	**Nín-bu/Nín-boq** 宁波
Shànghǎi	**Zǎw-hae** 上海
Sūzhōu	**Sù-dzeu** 苏州
Táiběi	**D'áe-bōq** 台北
Tiānjīn	**Tì-jin** 天津
Wúxī	**Vú-shiq** 无锡
Yángzhōu	**'Yǎ-dzeu** 扬州

Chinese Provinces and Regions

Ānhuī	**Òe-huae**	安徽
Fújiàn	**Fōq-ji**	福建
Guǎngdōng	**Guǎw-dong**	广东
Jiāngsū	**Gǎw-su**	江苏
Shāndōng	**Sàe-dong**	山东
Sìchuān	**Sǐ-tsoe**	四川
Táiwān	**D'áe-'wae**	台湾
Tibet	**Shì-zā**	西藏
Zhèjiāng	**Dzēq-gā**	浙江

Languages

Do you speak …?
Nóng … gǎw-deq láe va?　你会讲 … 吗？

Cantonese	**Guǎw-dzeu-h'ae-h'uo**	广州话
Chinese	**Dzòng-men / Dzòng-ven**	中文
English	**Yìn-nü / Yìn-ven**	英语 / 英文
Japanese	**Zeq-nü**	日语
Korean	**H'óe-nü**	韩语
French	**Fāq-nü**	法语
German	**Dēq-nü**	德语
Pǔtōnghuà / Mandarin	**Pú-tong-h'uo**	普通话
Russian	**Ngú-nü**	俄语
Shanghainese	**Zǎw-hae-h'ae-h'uo**	上海话

Yes, I can speak it.
Ngú gǎw-deq-lae. 我会讲。

I can understand a little.
Tìn-deq-dong yīq-ngae-ngae. 听得懂一点儿。

No, I cannot speak it.
Ngú gǎw-veq-lae h'eq. 我不会讲。

I cannot speak …
Ngú … gǎw-veq-lae h'eq. 我不会讲…。

What language(s) do you know how to speak?
Nóng h'uáe-deq gǎw sá-g'eq h'ae-h'uo?
你会讲什么话？

WEATHER

What's the weather like to today?
Jìn-dzaw tì-chi ná-nen? 今天天气怎么样？

Today it is …	**Jìn-dzaw …** 今天…
clear	**zín-ti** 晴天
warm	**nóe-niq-ti** 暖天
cloudy	**yìn-ti** 阴天
rainy	**loq-'yü-ti** 下雨天
cold and cloudy	**yìn-liã-ti** 阴凉天

What will the weather be like tomorrow?
Mín-dzaw tì-chi ná-nen? 明天天气怎么样？

Tomorrow it will …
Mín-dzaw yáw … 明天要…

snow	**loq•shīq** 下雪
be windy	**chí•fòng** 刮风
have thunder showers	**láe-zen-'yü** 雷阵雨

It seems it's about to …
Háw-zyiã yáw … leq. 好象要…了。

rain	**loq•'yǘ** 下雨
flood	**fāq•d'ú-sǐ** 发大水
snow	**loq•shīq** 下雪
get windy	**chí•fòng** 刮风

What is the temperature now?
G'eq-shiq jí-d'u? 现在几度？

Now it's …	**G'eq-shiq …** 现在…
15°	**zeq-ñg-d'u** 十五度
20°	**niáe-d'u** 二十度
25°	**niáe-ñg-d'u** 二十五度
30°	**sàe-seq-d'u** 三十度
32°	**sàe-zeq ní-d'u** 三十二度

Weather Vocabulary

bad weather	**h'uá-ti-chi** 坏天气
clouds	**'yǔn / 'yóng** 云
cold	**lǎ** 冷

catch a chill	**tsì•fòng** 着凉
cool and comfortable weather	**liǎ-sǎw-ti-chi** 凉爽天气
dark and rainy day	**yìn-'yü-ti** 阴雨天
dew *n.*	**lú-sï** 露水
dew *v.*	**loq•lú-sï** 下露
drizzle *n.*	**máw-maw-'yü** 毛毛雨
dry	**gòe-saw** 干燥
fine weather	**háw-ti** 好天
flood *n.*	**h'óng-sï** 洪水
fog	**'wú** 雾
fog arises	**chí••'wú** 起雾
freeze / ice up	**jīq•bìn** 结冰
frost *n.*	**sǎw** 霜
frost *v.*	**loq•sǎw** 下霜
get wet in the rain	**lín••'yú** 淋雨
hailstone	**bìn-b'aw** 冰雹
hot	**niq** 热
humid	**záw-seq** 潮湿
ice	**bìn** 冰
icicle	**lín-d'ǎw** 冰柱
lightning flashes	**hōq-shi** 打闪
melt	**'yǎ** 化
neither hot nor cold	**veq lǎ veq niq** 不冷不热
rain *n.*	**'yú** 雨
rain *v.*	**loq•'yú** 下雨
rainbow	**h'óng / héu** 彩虹
raindrops	**'yú-di-dzï** 雨点子
rainwater	**tì-loq-sï** 雨水
snow *n.*	**shīq** 雪
snow *v.*	**loq•shīq** 下雪
snowflakes	**shīq-huo** 雪花
thunder sounds	**láe-shiǎ** 打雷
tide	**záw-sï** 潮水
tide goes out	**táe•záw / loq•záw** 退潮
tide rises	**dzǎ•záw / chí•záw** 涨潮
tornado / cyclone	**lóng-jüoe-fong** 龙卷风
torrential rain	**b'áw-'yü** 暴雨
typhoon	**d'áe-fong** 台风
weather	**tì-chi** 天气
whirlwind	**zyí-fong** 旋风
wind	**fòng** 风

Note . . .

The temperature is a frequent topic of conversation regarding Shanghai weather. The basic unit is always Celsius (C), which is easy to manage by keeping in mind the following rough Fahrenheit (F) equivalents as a guide:

0° C = 32° F	22° C = 72° F
5° C = 41° F	25° C = 77° F
10° C = 50° F	30° C = 86° F
15° C = 59° F	32° C = 90° F
20° C = 68° F	

wind blows	**chí•fòng**	刮风
with the wind	**zén-fong**	顺风
against the wind	**niq-fong**	逆风

The Sky

sky	**tì**	天
sun	**tá-'yã**	太阳
sunshine	**niq-guãw**	太阳光
shade	**yìn-d'eu-li**	阴凉处
moon	**'yüeq-liã / 'yoq-liã**	月亮
moonlight	**'yüeq-liã-guãw /**	
	'yoq-liã-guãw	月光
crescent moon	**'yüeq-nga-nga**	月牙
star(s)	**shìn-shin**	星星
big dipper	**bōq-deu-shin**	北斗星
comet	**h'uáe-shin /**	
	sáw-tseu-shin	彗星
meteor, shooting star	**liéu-shin**	流星
milky way	**nín-h'u / tì-h'u**	银河

The Seasons

spring	**tsèn-ti**	春天
summer	**h'uó-ti / niq-ti**	夏天
autumn, fall	**chièu-ti**	秋天
winter	**dòng-ti / lǎ-ti**	冬天
springtime rainy season	**h'uǎw-mae-'yü**	黄梅雨
hot autumn weather	**chièu-law-hu**	秋老虎

TRANSPORTATION & ASKING DIRECTIONS

On Foot

Excuse me, may I ask …
Chín•mén … 请问…

How can I get to …?
Dáw … ná-nen-ga dzéu-faq? 到…怎么走？

Yùyuán Garden	**'Yǘ-'yüoe** 豫园
Peace Hotel	**H'ú-b'in-vae-di** 和平饭店
Shànghǎi Grand Theater	**Zǎw-hae d'á-j'iq-'yüoe** 上海大剧院
Jade Buddha Temple	**Nioq-veq-zï** 玉佛寺
the U.S. consulate	**Máe-goq lín-zï-guoe** 美国领事馆

Where is the …?
… leq sá-d'i-fǎw? … 在哪儿？

restroom	**shí-seu-gae** 洗手间
toilet / watercloset	**tsǐ-su** 厕所
ticket kiosk	**má-piaw-d'in** 买票亭
bus stop	**tsuò-zae / záe-d'eu** 车站
airport bus stop	**jì-zǎ-ba-sï záe-d'eu** 机场巴士车站
subway station	**d'í-tiq-zae** 地铁站

Is there a/an … nearby?
G'eq-daq vú-j'in 'yéu … va? 这附近有 … 吗？

bank	**nín-h'ǎw** 银行
café / coffee shop	**kà-ba** 咖啡吧
convenience store	**b'í-li-di** 便利店
inn / hotel	**lǚ-guoe** 旅馆
internet café	**mǎw-ba** 网吧
post office	**'yéu-j'üeq** 邮局
Starbucks	**shìn-ba-keq** 星巴克
restaurant	**váe-guoe / tsáe-guoe** 饭馆 / 菜馆

You may hear . . .

the following in response to your request for directions:

bīq-zeq (záw-zyi) b'áw 一直（往前）走
go straight (ahead)

> **dzéu-daw h'óng-loq-den** 走到红绿灯
> walk to the traffic light

tsòe-gu mó-lu 穿过马路
cross the street

> **dzú-dzoe-wae** 左传
> turn left

'yéu-dzoe-wae 右转
turn right

> **gú-leq h'óng-loq-den** 过了红绿灯
> after passing through the light

j'iéu-daw-leq 就到了
(you will) be there

Note that you will hear both *dzéu* 走 and *b'áw* 跑 meaning 'walk' or 'go' in Shanghainese.

Bus and Subway

Pardon me, ...
Dáe-veq-chi, ... 对不起，...

Which bus should I take to ...?
Dáw ... tsén sá tsuò-dzï? 到 ... 坐什么车?

Which (subway) line should I take to ...?
Dáw ... tsén jí-h'aw-shi? 到 ... 坐记号线?

the Bund	**Ngá-tae** 外滩	
People's Square	**Zén-min-guăw-zã** 人民广场	
Pǔdōng	**Pú-dong** 浦东	
Xújiāhuì (District)	**Zyí-ga-h'uae** 徐家汇	
Yán'ān Road	**'Yí-oe-lu** 延安路	
Xīzàng Road	**Shì-zã-lu** 西藏路	
Sìchuān Road	**Sĭ-tsoe-lu** 四川路	

Note ...

Bus and subway lines are all identified by numbers:

...-lu ... 路车 Bus number ...

as in:

Yīq-liã loq-lu 一二六路车 Bus number 126

...-h'aw-shi ... 号线 Line number ...

as in:

Bāq-h'aw-shi 八号线 Line number 8

Does this bus/train go to ...?
G'eq-g'eq tsuò-dzï dáw ... va? 这个车到 ... 吗?

Shànghǎi Rail Station	**Zǎw-hae hú-tsuo-zae** 上海火车站
Xīntiāndì (Leisure Street)	**Shìn-ti-d'i** 新天地
Hóngqiáo Airport	**H'óng-j'iaw jì-zã** 虹桥机场
Temple of the City God	**Zén-h'uãw-miaw** 城隍庙
Huáihái Road	**H'uá-hae-lu** 淮海路

Are we at the stop/station for ... ?
Dáw ... záe leq va? 到 ... 站了吗?

Which is the stop/station to get off for ...?
Dáw ... laq h'á-li-zae h'uó•tsuò?
到 ... 在哪个站下车?

Jìng'ān Temple	**Zyín-oe-zï** 静安寺
Nánjīng Road	**Nóe-jin-lu** 南京路
Dàshìjiè (Great World Amusement Center)	**D'á-sï-ga** 大世界
Lǎoxīmén	**Láw-shi-men** 老西门

I will get off here.
Ngú laq g'eq-d'eu h'uó•tsuò. 我在这儿下车。

You may hear . . .
the taxi driver ask you:

Nóng fú h'í-jin h'uáe-zï là•ká?
你付现金还是刷卡？
Will you pay cash or by [prepaid metro] card?

You can respond:
Pay cash. **Fú h'í-jin.** 付现金。
or By card. **Là•ká.** 刷卡。

By Taxi

I want to hail a taxi.
Ngú yáw jiáw dīq-sï. 我要叫的士。

Driver, we want to go to …
Sï-vu, āq-laq yáw dáw … 师傅，我们要到…

Pǔdōng Airport	**Pú-dong jì-zã** 浦东机场
Pearl of the Orient Tower	**Dòng-fāw mín-dzï-taq** 东方明珠塔
Jīnmào Mansion	**Jìn-maw d'á-sa** 金茂大厦

We will get off just in front there.
Āq-laq laq zyí-mi hàe-d'eu h'uó•tsuò.
我在前面那儿下车。

Please give me the receipt.
Chìn bāq ngú fāq-piaw. 请给我发票。

Train Station and Airport

Where is the ticket window?
Má piáw-h'eq tsǎw-keu laq-laq h'á-li?
买票的窗口在哪儿？

Should tickets be purchased in advance?
Piáw yáw 'yǔ-shi dín va? 票要预先订吗？

Can tickets be bought the same day?
Kú-yi dầw-ti má piáw va? 可以当天买票吗?

Are there still *train/air* tickets to Canton?
Chí Guẳw-dzeu-h'eq *hú-tsuo/fì-ji* piáw àe 'yéu va?
去广州的火车／飞机票还有吗?

Reserve a ... ticket for me.
Gáw ngú d'ín yīq-dzã ... piáw. 给我定一张 ... 票。

non-stop	**zeq-kua**	直快
special express	**d'eq-kua**	特快
airplane	**fì-ji**	飞机

I'll buy a ... ticket.
Ngú má yīq-dzã ... piáw. 我买一张 ... 票。

one-way	**dàe-zen**	单程
round-trip	**wẳw-fae**	往返
high speed rail	**d'óng-tsuo**	动车

What time does this train leave?
G'eq-bae hú-tsuo jí-di-dzong kàe?
这班火车几点开?

Can I/we ... now?
Kú-yi ... leq va? 可以 ... 了吗?

board the flight	**dèn•jì**	登机
get on the bus/train	**zẳw•tsuò**	上车
get off the bus/train	**h'uó•tsuò / loq•tsuò**	下车

You may be asked ...

when you arrive in Shanghai:

Chín nóng nàw h'ú-dzaw bēq ngú kóe-koe.
请拿护照给我看看。
Please show me your passport.

Nóng laq Sẳw-hae yáw dù-saw zén-guãw?
你在上海要多长时间?
How long will you be in Shanghai?

'Yéu sá-h'eq meq-zǐ yáw sèn-baw va?
有什么东西要申报吗?
Do [you] have anything to declare?

Transportation and Places to Go

Transportation Activities

check a/one's ticket	**zuó•piáw** 查票
drive a car	**kàe•tsuò** 开车
get off or out of a car/bus/train	**h'uó•tsuò / loq•tsuò** 下车
get on or into a car/bus/train	**zắw•tsuò** 上车
go on a business trip	**tsēq•tsà** 出差
park a car	**d'ín•tsuò** 停车
punch a/one's ticket	**g'aq•piáw** 剪票
take (a bus or train)	**tsén (tsuò-dzǐ)** 乘（车）
traffic is jammed	**sēq•tsuò** 堵车
travel / take a journey	**lǘ-h'in** 旅行
go for a leisurely drive	**dèu•fòng** 兜风
turn left / left turn	**dzú-dzoe-wae** 左转弯
turn right / right turn	**'yéu-dzoe-wae** 右转弯

Means of Getting There

air-conditioned car/bus	**kòng-d'iaw-tsuo** 空调车
airplane	**fì-ji** 飞机
airport	**fì-ji-zã** 飞机场
airport bus	**jì-zã-ba-sï** 机场巴士
ambulance	**jiéu-h'u-tsuo** 救护车
baggage check	**h'ắ-li-piaw** 行李票
bicycle	**jiãq-d'aq-tsuo** 自行车
boat / ship	**zóe** 船
bus stop	**záe-d'eu / tsuò-zae** 车站
bus ticket	**tsuò-piaw** 车票
bus / public bus	**chí-tsuo / gòng-g'ong-chi-tsuo** 公共汽车
car / vehicle	**tsuò-dzǐ** 车
crosswalk	**h'uắ-d'aw-shi** 人行横道
electric battery bicycle	**d'í-b'in-tsuo** 电瓶车
electric tram	**d'í-tsuo** 电车
elevated roadway	**gàw-ga** 高架
ferryboat	**bá-d'u-zoe** 渡船
flight or train number	**bàe-d'eu** 班次
large bus / coach	**d'á-ba** 大巴
light rail	**chìn-guae** 轻轨

maglev (magnetic levitation) train	**zí-veu-tsuo** 磁浮车
motorcycle	**mó-toq-tsuo** 摩托车
one-way street	**dàe-h'in-d'aw** 单行道
passenger ship	**lén-zoe** 轮船
pedestrian street	**b'ú-h'in-ga** 步行街
platform at a rail station	**'yüeq-d'ae** 月台
subway	**d'í-tiq** 地铁
subway or railway car	**tsuò-shiã** 车厢
taxi	**dīq-sï / tsà-d'eu** 出租汽车 / 的士
track / railway	**guáe-d'aw** 轨道
train	**hú-tsuo** 火车
tricycle pedicab	**sàe-len-tsuo** 三轮车
truck	**ká-tsuo** 卡车
tunnel	**zóe-d'aw** 隧道
van / minibus	**mí-baw-tsuo** 面包车

Places to Go

antique store	**gú-'woe sǎw-di** 古玩商店
bakery	**mí-baw-vãw** 面包房
bar / pub	**jiéu-ba** 酒吧
barbershop	**lí-faq-di** 理发店
beauty parlor	**máe-h'ong-'yüoe** 美容院
bookstore	**sǐ-di** 书店
candy shop	**d'ǎw-gu-di** 糖果店
Chinese medicine shop	**dzòng-'yaq-di** 中药店
clothing shop	**voq-dzǎw-di** 服装店
development zone	**kàe-faq-chü** 开发区
dining hall	**tsóe-tin** 餐厅
discothèque	**d'iq-tin** 迪斯科舞厅
drugstore	**'yaq-di** 药店
fabric store	**bú-di** 布店
flower shop	**huò-di** 花店
fruit store	**sí-gu-di** 水果店
furniture store	**gà-j'ü-di / jià-j'ü-di** 家具店
general store	**zaq-hu-di** 杂货店
home	**õq-li-shiã** 家中
hospital	**yì-'yüoe** 医院
jewelry store	**dzì-baw-di** 珠宝店
jiaozi restaurant	**sí-jiaw-di** 饺子馆

karaoke bar	**tsắw-kae-su** 卡拉OK / 唱K所
laundry	**shí-yi-di** 洗衣店
market	**sầw-zã** 商场
newsstand	**sì-baw-d'in** 书报亭
pawn shop	**dắw-di** 当铺
photo studio	**dzáw-shiã-guoe** 照相馆
police substation / precinct office	**pá-tseq-su** 派出所
silk shop	**zéu-bu-di** 绸布店
speciality shop	**dzòe-ma-di** 专卖店
stationery shop	**vén-j'ü-di** 文具店
steamed bun shop	**móe-d'eu-di** 馒头店
store / shop	**sầw-di / dí-ga** 商店
tailor shop	**záe-vong-di / zén-yi-di** 裁缝店
tea room	**zuó-tsoe-tin** 茶餐厅
tea store	**zuó-'yiq-di** 茶叶店
underground mall	**d'í-h'uo sầw-zã** 地下商场

Directions & Positions

east	**dòng** 东
east side	**dòng-mi / dòng-d'eu** 东边
south	**nóe** 南
south side	**nóe-mi** 南边
west	**shì** 西
west side	**shì-mi / shì-d'eu** 西边
north	**bōq** 北
north side	**bōq-mi** 北边
left	**dzú-mi** 左边
right	**'yéu-mi** 右边
top / above	**zắw-d'eu / zắw-mi** 上头
below / underside	**h'uó-d'eu / h'uó-mi** 下头
bottom	**dí-h'uo** 底下
front	**zyí-d'eu / zyí-mi** 前头
back / behind	**h'éu-d'eu / h'éu-mi** 后头
inside	**lí-d'eu / lí-shiã(-d'eu)** 里头
outside	**ngá-d'eu / ngá-mi** 外头
middle / center	**dắw-dzong** 中间
side / beside	**b'ắw-b'i / bì-d'eu** 旁边
both sides	**liắ-b'ầw-bi** 两边

here	**g'eq-d'eu / g'eq-daq(-li)** 这儿
there	**hàe-d'eu** 那儿
nearby / vicinity	**vú-j'in** 附近
in the corner	**gōq-lāw** 角上
in the room	**ōq-li-shiā** 房里
opposite (side)	**dáe-mi** 对面
opposite corner	**zaq-goq** 对角
diagonally opposite	**zyiá-dae-mi / chiá-dae-gu** 斜对面
across from	**dàe-gu** 对面
next door	**gāq-biq(-d'eu)** 隔壁
toward / facing	**záw** 朝
floor / on the ground	**d'í-lāw-shiā / d'í-gaw-d'eu** 地上
underground	**d'í-h'uo-d'eu / d'í-di-h'uo** 地下

ACCOMMODATIONS & HOTELS

Are there any … nearby?
Vú-j'in 'yéu-sa … va? 附近有什么 … 吗？

> inexpensive hotels **b'í-ni-di-h'eq lǘ-guoe** 便宜一点
> 的旅馆
> better inns **hàw-di-h'eq jiéu-di** 好一点的酒店
> three star hotels **sàe-shin-jiq lǘ-guoe** 三星级旅馆
> hostels **dzàw-d'ae-su** 招待所
> guesthouses **bìn-guoe** 宾馆

Do you have any vacant rooms?
'Yéu kóng-vǎw-gae va? 有空房间吗？

We want to stay in a …
Āq-laq yáw zǐ … 我们要住…

> standard room **biàw-vǎw** 标准房间
> ordinary room **pú-tong kēq-vǎw** 普通客房
> luxury room **h'áw-h'uo kēq-vǎw** 豪华客房
> air conditioned room **kòng-d'iaw-vǎw** 空调房
> suite **táw-vǎw** 套房
> room with one queen bed **d'ú-zǎw-gae** 大床间
> room with two beds **sǎw-zǎw-vǎw** 双床房

How many days will you (*plural*) stay?
Ná zǐ jí-niq? 你们住几天？

How much per night?
Jí-d'i yīq-'ya? 多少钱一个晚上？

Does that include breakfast?
Bàw-gua dzáw-di va? 包括早点吗？

Is broadband Internet available?
'Yéu kuòe-da-mǎw va? 有宽带网吗？

Where is the …?
… laq sá-d'i-fǎw? …在哪儿？

> dining room **tsóe-tin** 餐厅
> exercise room **j'í-sen-vǎw** 健身房

swimming pool   **'yéu-'yong-zï** 游泳池
laundry room   **shí-yi-vāw** 洗衣房

When is the dining room open …?
… tsóe-tin jí-di-dzong kàe váe?
…餐厅几点钟开饭？

in the morning	**dzáw-lāw**	早上
at noon	**dzòng-wu**	中午
in the evening	**'yá-li**	晚上

This bed is too …
G'eq-dzaq zǎw tēq … 这个床太…

hard	**ngǎ**	硬
soft	**nüóe**	软
small	**shiáw**	小
big	**d'ú**	大

The room is too …
G'eq-gae vǎw-gae tēq … 这间房间太…

cold	**lǎ**	冷
hot	**niq**	热
dark	**óe**	暗
damp	**sēq**	湿
noisy	**tsáw**	吵
dirty	**ōq-tsoq**	肮脏

There isn't/aren't enough …
… veq-geu. …不够。

bath towels	**'yoq-jin**	浴巾
facial tissue	**dzǐ-jin**	纸巾
hair conditioner	**h'ú-faq-su**	护发素
hand lotion	**h'ú-seu-sāw**	护手霜
shampoo	**d'á-d'eu-gaw**	洗发乳
soap	**b'í-zaw / shiǎ-zaw**	肥皂 / 香皂
toothpaste	**ngá-gaw**	牙膏

Please give me …
Chín bēq … ngú. 请给我…

a hair dryer	**yīq-g'eq tsǐ-fong-ji**	一个吹风机

a comb	**yīq-g'eq moq-sï**	一个梳子
a pillow	**yīq-g'eq dzén-d'eu**	一个枕头
a quilt	**yīq-d'iáw b'í-d'eu**	一条被子
toilet paper	**dí tsàw-dzï**	一点手纸
a toothbrush	**yīq-dzāq ngá-seq**	一只牙刷
a towel	**yīq-d'iáw máw-jin**	一条毛巾

Inside the Hotel

balcony	**'yǎ-d'ae**	阳台
bath towel	**'yoq-jin**	浴巾
bathroom	**d'á-'yoq-gae / 'yoq-gae**	洗澡间
bathtub	**'yoq-kāw**	浴缸
bed	**zǎw**	床
bedsheets	**zǎw-dae / b'í-dae**	床单 / 被单
bench / stool	**báe-den**	板凳
blanket	**tàe-dzï**	毯子
bookcase	**sì-zï**	书橱
cabinet	**zí' 橱**	
carpet	**d'í-tae**	地毯
chair	**yǔ-dzï / yí-dzï**	椅子
closet / wardrobe	**yì-zï**	衣橱
clothes hanger / coat rack	**yì-zǎw-ga**	衣架
comb	**moq-sï**	梳子
desk	**sì-dzoq / shiá-zï-d'ae**	书桌
door / gate	**mén**	门
downstairs	**léu-h'uo-d'eu**	楼下
drawer	**tsèu-d'eu / tsèu-ti**	抽屉
elevator	**d'í-ti**	电梯
facial tissue	**dzï-jin**	纸巾
floor	**d'í-bae**	地板
glass window	**bù-li-tsāw**	玻璃窗
hair conditioner	**h'ú-faq-su**	护发素
hair dryer	**tsǐ-fong-ji**	吹风机
hand lotion	**h'ú-seu-sāw**	护手霜
hot water heater	**niq-sï-chi**	热水器
key	**'yaq-zï**	钥匙
key card	**vǎw-ka**	房卡
laundry soap/ detergent	**b'í-zaw-fen / d'á-yi-zǎw-fen** 洗衣粉	
lock	**sú**	锁

main door/gate	**d'ú-men**	大门
mirror	**jín-dzï**	镜子
mosquito net	**mén-dzā / dzã́-dzï**	蚊帐
paper napkin	**tsòe-jin-dzï**	餐巾纸
peephole (*in a door*)	**máw-ngae**	猫眼
pillow	**dzén-d'eu**	枕头
pillowcase	**dzén-d'eu-taw**	枕头套
quilt	**b'í-d'eu**	被子
quilt cover	**b'í-taw**	被套
room	**vã́w-gae**	房间
shampoo	**d'á-d'eu-gaw**	洗发乳
shower	**lín-'yoq-vãw**	淋浴房
shower curtain	**'yoq-li**	浴帘
shower head	**pèn-d'eu**	喷头
shower cap	**'yoq-maw**	浴帽
soap	**b'í-zaw / shiã̀-zaw**	肥皂 / 香皂
stairs	**h'ú-ti**	楼梯
steps	**d'áe-ga**	台阶
suitcase / chest / trunk	**shiã̀-dzï**	箱子
sunscreen	**vã́w-suo-sãw**	防晒霜
table	**d'áe-dzï**	桌子
toilet / flush toilet	**mó-d'ong / tsèu-sï-mo-d'ong**	马桶 / 抽水马桶
toilet / washroom	**'wáe-sen-gae**	卫生间
toilet / watercloset	**tsḯ-su-gae**	厕所
toilet paper	**tsàw-dzï**	手纸
toothbrush	**ngá-seq**	牙刷
toothpaste	**ngá-gaw**	牙膏
towel	**máw-jin**	毛巾
towel rack	**máw-jin-ga**	毛巾架
upstairs	**léu-lãw**	楼上
washcloth	**kà-mi-maw-jin**	洗脸毛巾
window	**tsãw / tsã̀w-men**	窗子
window curtain	**tsã̀w-li**	窗帘
window screens	**suò-tsãw**	纱窗
windowsill	**tsã̀w-d'ae / tsã̀w-b'oe**	窗台

FOOD & DRINK

Meals

breakfast   **dzáw-vae / dzáw-di** 早饭
lunch   **dzòng-vae** 午饭
dinner   **'yá-vae** 晚饭
midnight snack   **b'óe-'ya-vae** 夜宵

Feeling Hungry

I am hungry.
Ngú d'ú-b'i-ngu leq. 我饿了。

I am thirsty.
Ngú dzǐ•gòe leq. 我口渴了。

Have you eaten?
Váe chīq-gu-leq va? 吃饭了吗？

Is there a … nearby?
G'eq-daq vú-j'in 'yéu … va? 这附近有…吗？

    good restaurant
    háw-chiq-di-eq váe-di 好吃点的饭店

    clean restaurant
    chìn-sǎw-di-eq váe-di 干净点的饭店

    tea restaurant
    zuó-tsoe-tin 茶餐厅

    fast food restaurant
    kuá-tsoe váe-di 快餐饭店

    buffet / cafeteria
    zǐ-zu-tsoe 自助餐

    food vending stall
    tàe-d'eu-shiaw-chiq 大排挡

What kind of food do you want to eat?
Nóng yáw chīq sá-h'eq tsáe? 你要吃什么菜？

I want to eat…
Ngú shiǎ chīq… 我想吃…

Chinese food	**Dzòng-goq-tsae** 中国菜	
French food	**Fāq-goq-tsae** 法国菜	
Italian food	**Yí-d'a-li-tsae** 意大利菜	
Japanese food	**Zeq-ben-tsae** 日本菜	
Korean food	**H'óe-goq-tsae** 韩国菜	
noodles	**mí** 面	
Shanghai food	**Zǎw-hae-tsae** 上海菜	
Shanghai-style snacks	**Zǎw-hae shiáw-chiq** 上海小吃	
vegetarian food	**sú-tsae / b'aq-zeq** 素菜	
Western food	**Shì-tsoe** 西餐	

At the Restaurant

Do you have seats (at a table for us)?
Yéu 'wáe-dzï va? 有位子吗？

How many in your party?
Jí-'wae? 几位？

There are … of us.
Āq-la 'yéu … nín. 我们有…人。

two	**liǎ-g'eq** 两个	
three	**sàe-g'eq** 三个	
four	**sǐ-g'eq** 四个	
five	**ñǵ-g'eq** 五个	

Can I see the menu please?
Tsáe-dae bēq ngú kóe-koe háw va?
菜单给我看看好吗？

I'll order the food.
Ngú láe dí tsáe háw lae. 我来点菜吧。

What do (you) want to eat?
Shiǎ chīq dí sá? 想吃点什么？

I am a vegetarian.
Ngú chīq sú. 我吃素。

I don't eat meat.
Ngú veq chīq nioq. 我不吃肉。

I don't eat *chicken/fish*.
Ngú veq chīq *jì-nioq/ñg-nioq*. 我不吃鸡肉 / 鱼肉。

What do you want to drink?
Chīq sá yín-liaw? 喝什么饮料？

I don't drink alcohol.
Ngú veq chīq•jiéu. 我不喝酒。

I don't smoke.
Ngú veq chīq•yì.

What specialties do you have?
Ná 'yéu sá d'eq-seq-tsae? 你们有什么特色菜？

What dish is this?
G'eq-g'eq zï sá-g'eq-tsae? 这是什么菜？

Is it …? **… va?** … 吗？

bitter	**Kú** 苦	spicy	**Laq** 辣
sweet	**D'í** 甜	salty	**H'áe** 咸
sour	**Sòe** 酸		

It's not hot.   It's rather sweet.
Veq laq. 不辣。   **Màe d'í h'eq.** 很甜的。

It tastes good!   It doesn't taste good!
Háw-chiq! 好吃！   **Veq háw-chiq!** 不好吃！

Is it a meat dish?
Zï huèn-tsae va? 是荤菜吗？

It is a vegetable dish.
Zï sú-tsae. 是素菜。

I would like to have/eat some …
Ngú yáw chīq di … 我要吃点 …

I would like to have/drink some …
Ngú yáw chīq di … 我要喝点…

Do you have …?
'Yéu … va? 有…吗？

We don't have …
Ḿ-meq … 没有…

Please don't use any MSG.
Chín viáw fǎw mí-dzï-su. 请别放味精。

Please hurry and serve the food.
Chín kuá-di zǎw•tsáe. 请快点上菜。

Where is the restroom?
Shí-seu-gae laq sá•d'í-fãw? 洗手间在哪儿？

Please bring some more …
Chín dzàe nàw dí … láe. 请再拿点…来。

That's about enough.
Tsà-veq-du leq. 差不多了。

I am full!
Ngú chīq báw leq! 我吃饱了！

Please wrap this up for us.
Chín dēq āq-la dǎ-baw. 请给我们打包。

The check (please)!
Má-dae! 埋单！

Please give me a receipt.
Chín gàw-ngu kàe-dzã fãq-piaw. 请给我开张发票。

urge (a guest) to drink (wine or spirits)
chüóe•jiéu 劝酒

go dutch / share the cost equally (as of a meal)
àe-ae-dzï AA制

Cheers! / Bottoms up!	**Góe•bàe!** 干杯！
dinner engagement	**chīq-j'ioq** 饭局
drink a toast	**góe•bàe** 干杯
serve the food	**zǎw•tsáe** 上菜

Note...

Chinese and Shanghainese meals are usually eaten family-style, with all guests serving themselves from common dishes. This is the case at even the most formal gatherings. Consequently, one person often takes responsibility for ordering for the entire group at restaurants.

The Menu

Some local dishes that may be recommended or that you might see on a Shanghainese menu include:

så-ji-moe-d'eu 生煎馒头 fried meat buns
shiáw-long-baw-dzï 小笼包子 steamed soup buns
ñg-shiā-nioq-sï 鱼香肉丝 shredded pork in fish sauce
gòng-baw-ji-din 宫爆鸡丁 spicy fried chicken cubes
mó-b'u-d'eu-h'u 麻婆豆腐 tofu in hot sauce
bāq-baw-aq 八宝鸭 eight precious duck
jiàw-yi b'áe-gueq 椒盐排骨 salt and pepper pork ribs
gú-law-nioq 咕唠肉 sweet and sour pork
gà-li 'yǎ-sae-'yü 咖喱洋山芋 curried potato
dzèn sǐ-d'ae 蒸水蛋 steamed eggs
h'óng-saw sǐ-dzï-d'eu 红烧狮子头 red-cooked "lion's head" meatball

As food and eating are a big and important part of Shanghai culture, Shanghai cuisine is endlessly rich and varied. There will be far more on most restaurant menus than can be summed up in a short list. But restaurant menus often have photos of the offerings, which provide a helpful guide to what is available to order. Some restaurants also have samples of the dishes in displays that guests can browse to make their selections.

Beverages

beer	**b'í-jieu** 啤酒	
black tea	**h'óng-zuo** 红茶	
cappuccino	**ká-bu-j'i-nuo** 卡布其诺	
coffee	**kà-fi** 咖啡	

green tea	**loq-zuo** 绿茶
hot water	**niq-sï** 热水
ice cream	**bìn-j'ĭ-lin** 冰淇淋
lemonade	**nín-mong-sï** 柠檬汁
liquor / wine	**jiéu** 酒
milk	**niéu-na** 牛奶
orange juice	**jüēq-dzĭ-sï** 橘子水
plain boiled water	**b'aq-kae-sï** 白开水
popsicle / ice pop	**b'áw-bin** 冰棍儿
shaved ice	**b'áw-bin** 刨冰
soda water	**sù-dã-sï** 苏打水
soft drink	**chí-sï** 汽水
sundae	**sén-d'ae** 圣代
tea	**zuó** 茶
wine (*from grapes*)	**b'ú-d'aw-jieu** 葡萄酒
yogurt	**sòe-na** 酸奶

Foods and Condiments

apple pie	**b'ín-gu-pa** 苹果派
assorted cold appetizers	**pìn-b'en** 拼盘
bacon	**b'áe-gen** 培根
bamboo shoot, dried	**sén-goe** 干笋
bean curd / tofu	**d'éu-h'u / d'éu-vu** 豆腐
bean curd sheets / skin of soy milk	**d'éu-h'u-b'i** 豆腐皮
bean curd, dried	**d'éu-h'u-goe** 豆腐干
bean curd, dried layered sheets of	**bāq-'yiq** 百页
bean/soybean products	**d'éu-dzĭ-pin** 豆制品
beef	**niéu-nioq** 牛肉
beef jerky / dried beef	**niéu-nioq-goe** 牛肉干
boxed meal	**h'aq-vae / b'í-dãw** 盒饭
bread	**mí-baw** 面包
whole wheat bread	**zyí-maq-mi-baw** 全麦面包
broth	**chìn-(sï-)tãw** 清汤
buckwheat noodles	**j'iáw-maq-mi** 荞麦面
bun (*steamed, stuffed or unstuffed*)	**móe-d'eu** 包子 / 馒头
buns, soup (*soup-filled steamed buns*)	**tãw-baw** 汤包
butter	**b'aq-teq(-'yeu)** 黄油

cake (*Western-style*)	**d'áe-gaw**	蛋糕
cake / pudding	**gàw**	糕
candy	**d'ǎw**	糖
cheese	**chì-sï / ná-loq**	奶酪
chicken (meat)	**jì-nioq**	鸡肉
chicken breast	**jì-shiong**	鸡胸
chicken egg	**jì-d'ae**	鸡蛋
chicken feet	**jì-jiaq-dzaw**	鸡爪
chicken gizzard	**jì-dzen**	鸡胗
chicken heart	**jì-shin**	鸡心
chicken leg	**jì-tae**	鸡腿
chicken wing	**jì-bãw**	鸡翅
chili oil	**laq-'yeu**	辣油
Chinese cruller	**'yeu-d'iaw**	油条
chocolate	**chiàw-keq-liq**	巧克力
cold appetizers	**lǎ-b'en**	冷盘
cold dishes	**liǎ-tsae**	凉菜
congee / rice porridge	**dzōq**	粥
cookie	**bín-goe**	饼干
cracker	**bín-goe**	饼干
cracker (*thin, crispy*)	**kēq-liq-ka**	克力架
cumin	**dzï-zoe**	孜然
curry	**gà-li**	咖喱
dim sum	**shiáw-chiq / dí-shin**	小吃 / 点心
duck egg	**āq-d'ae**	鸭蛋
duck egg, salt-preserved	**h'áe-(aq-)d'ae**	咸 (鸭) 蛋
duck gizzard	**āq-dzen**	鸭胗
duck wing	**āq-bãw**	鸭翅
dumpling (*boiled*)	**sḯ-jiaw**	水饺
dumpling (*boiled or steamed*)	**jiàw-dzï / jiáw-dzï**	饺子
dumplings (*fried*) / pot stickers	**gù-tiq**	锅贴
dumpling (*stuffed and steamed open-topped*)	**sàw-ma**	烧卖
egg custard tart	**d'áe-ta**	蛋挞
egg, fried	**h'ú-baw-d'ae**	荷包蛋
fermented rice (*usually served sweet*)	**jiéu-niã**	酒酿
fish	**ñg̃-nioq**	鱼肉
fish ball	**ñg̃-'yüoe**	鱼丸子
French fries	**sú-d'iaw**	薯条

fried noodles	**tsáw-mi** 炒面
fried rice with egg	**d'áe-tsaw-vae** 蛋炒饭
ginger	**jiǎ / sǎ-jiā** 姜
granulated sugar	**suò-d'āw** 砂糖
ham	**hú-tae** 火腿
hamburger	**hóe-baw-baw** 汉堡包
home cooking	**jià-zā-vae** 家常饭
honey	**miq-d'āw** 蜂蜜
hot dog	**niq-geu** 热狗
jello	**jǔ-li** 果子冻
jellyfish	**háe-zeq / b'aq-b'i-dzï** 海蜇
jiǎozi / dumpling (*steamed or boiled*)	**jiàw-dzï / jiáw-dzï** 饺子
lotus root flour	**ngéu-fen** 藕粉
macaroni	**tòng-shin-fen** 通心粉
malt sugar	**zyín-d'āw / maq-nga-d'āw** 饴糖
meat (*usually pork*)	**nioq** 肉
meat, fatty	**'yéu-nioq** 肥肉
meat, lean	**jìn-nioq / séu-nioq** 瘦肉
meat dish	**huèn-tsae** 荤菜
meat jelly / aspic	**nioq-dong** 肉冻
meatball	**nioq-'yüoe** 肉圆
moon cake	**'yüeq-bin** 月饼
mousse	**mó-sï** 慕司
MSG	**ví-dzï-su / mí-dzï-su** 味精
mung bean sprouts	**loq-d'eu-nga** 绿豆芽
mung bean vermicelli	**shì-fen** 粉丝
mutton / goat meat / lamb	**'yǎ-nioq** 羊肉
New Year's cake (*made of sticky rice*)	**ní-gaw** 年糕
noodles, wheat	**mí / mí-d'iaw** 面条
oil	**'yéu** 油
pancake / crepe	**bín** 饼
pastry snacks / dim sum	**shiáw-chiq / dí-shin** 小吃 / 点心
peanut butter	**huò-sen-jiā** 花生酱
peanut oil	**sèn-'yeu** 花生油
pepper	**h'ú-jiaw** 胡椒
pig's foot	**dzǐ-jiaq-dzaw** 猪爪
pork	**dzǐ-nioq** 猪肉
pork belly meat	**ñǧ-huo-nioq** 五花肉
pork hock	**d'í-pā** 蹄膀

pork lard	**dzï-'yeu** 猪油
pork liver	**dzï-goe** 猪肝
pork ribs	**b'áe-gueq** 排骨
pork skin	**nioq-b'i** 肉皮
pork tenderloin	**lí-jiq** 里脊
pork tripe	**dú-dzï** 猪肚
pot stickers	**gù-tiq** 锅贴
(fried dumplings)	
powdered milk	**ná-fen** 奶粉
preserved egg	**b'í-d'ae** 松花蛋
pudding	**bú-din** 布丁
puffed rice	**tsáw-mi-huo** 米花
pulled-dough noodles	**là-mi** 拉面
pumpkin seeds	**nóe-guo-dzï** 南瓜子
rice *(cooked)*	**váe** 饭
rice, plain cooked	**b'aq-mi-vae** 米饭
rice dumpling / *zòngzi*	**dzóng-dzï** 粽子
(sticky rice steamed	
in reed leaves)	
rice crust *(from the*	**váe-zï / h'oq-jiaw** 锅巴
bottom of a pot of	
cooked rice)	
rice flower balls	**yüóe-dzï / tầw-d'oe**
(usually stuffed)	圆子 / 汤团
rice porridge *(thin)*	**shì-vae** 稀饭
rock sugar / sugar crystals	**bìn-d'ãw** 冰糖
salad	**sāq-la** 色拉
salt	**'yí** 盐
salt fish	**h'áe-ñg** 咸鱼
sandwich	**sàe-min-zï** 三明治
sashimi	**sẵ-ñg-pi / sẵ-shi-mi** 生鱼片
sausage	**shiẵ-zã** 香肠
sea cucumber / slug	**háe-sen** 海参
seafood	**háe-shi** 海鲜
seaweed / kelp	**háe-da** 海带
sesame oil	**mó-'yeu** 麻油
sesame paste	**dzï-mo-jiã** 芝麻酱
shrimp, dried	**huò-mi / hòe-mi** 虾米
shrimp, fresh shelled	**huò-nin / hòe-nin** 虾仁
simple meal	**b'í-vae** 便饭
snacks	**lín-zeq** 零食
soup	**tầw / tầw-sï** 汤

soup, thick	**nióng-tǎw** 浓汤
soup buns (*soup-filled steamed buns*)	**tǎw-baw** 汤包
soup noodles	**tǎw-mi** 汤面
soy milk	**d'éu-jiā** 豆浆
skin of soy milk	**d'éu-h'u-b'i** 豆腐皮
soy sauce	**jiǎ-'yeu** 酱油
spaghetti	**yí-mi** 意大利面
spring rolls	**tsèn-jüoe** 春卷
stuffing / filling	**niǎ** 馅儿
sugar / candy	**d'ǎw** 糖
sunflower seeds	**shiǎ-guo-dzï** 葵花子
tea eggs	**zuó-'yiq-d'ae** 茶叶蛋
teppanyaki	**tīq-bae-saw** 铁板烧
tiramisu	**d'í-la-mi-su** 提拉米苏
vegetable dish	**sú-tsae** 素菜
vegetable oil	**tsáe-'yeu** 菜油
vegetables	**tsáe** 菜
vegetables, dried	**tsáe-goe** 干菜
vegetarian food	**b'aq-zeq / sú-tsae** 素食
vinegar	**tsú** 醋
wasabi / mustard	**g'á-meq** 芥末
watermelon seeds	**shì-guo-dzï** 西瓜子
wheat flour	**mí-fen** 面粉
wheat gluten	**mí-jin** 面筋
wonton	**'wén-d'en** 馄饨
zòngzi (*sticky rice dumpling steamed in reed leaves*)	**dzóng-dzï** 粽子

Fruit and Nuts

apple	**b'ín-gu** 苹果
apricot	**h'ǎ-dzï** 杏子
banana	**shiǎ-jiaw** 香蕉
cherry	**ǎ-d'aw / yìn-d'aw** 樱桃
chestnut	**liq-dzï** 栗子
date / jujube	**dzáw-dzï** 枣子
fruit	**sǐ-gu** 水果
grape	**b'eq-d'aw / b'u-d'aw** 葡萄
Japanese apricot (*ume*)	**máe-dzï** 梅子
kiwi	**mí-h'eu-d'aw** 猕猴桃
longan	**guáe-'yüoe** 桂圆
loquat	**b'iq-b'oq** 枇杷

lychee	**liq-dzï / mó-liq-dzï** 荔枝
mango	**mǎw-gu** 芒果
olive	**gáe-lae** 橄榄
orange	**d'í-zen** 橙子
papaya	**moq-guo** 木瓜
peach	**d'áw-dzï** 桃子
peanut	**huò-sen** 花生
pear	**sà-li** 梨
persimmon	**zí-dzï** 柿子
pineapple	**bù-lu-miq** 菠萝
plum	**lí-dzï** 李子
pomegranate	**zaq-lieu** 石榴
pomelo	**vén-dae** 柚子
red bayberry	**'yǎ-mae** 杨梅
sugarcane	**gòe-dzuo** 甘蔗
tangerine	**jüēq-dzï / jiōq-dzï** 橘子
walnut	**b'ú-d'aw** 核桃
water chestnut	**b'eq-zyi / b'iq-zyi / d'í-liq** 荸荠
watermelon	**shì-guo** 西瓜

Vegetables

alfalfa greens	**tsáw-d'eu** 苜蓿
amaranth	**mí-shi** 苋菜
asparagus	**lú-sen** 芦笋
aster greens	**mó-lae-d'eu** 马兰头
bamboo shoots	**sén / dzōq-sen** 笋 / 竹笋
beans	**d'éu** 豆
broad beans	**h'óe-d'eu / zóe-d'eu** 蚕豆
green beans	**bí-d'eu** 扁豆
mung beans	**loq-d'eu** 绿豆
red beans (*small*)	**tsāq-d'eu** 赤豆
cabbage	**b'aq-tsae** 白菜
carrot	**h'ú-law-b'oq** 胡萝卜
cauliflower	**huò-tsae** 花椰菜
celery	**j'ín-tsae** 芹菜
chili pepper	**laq-jiaw** 辣椒
Chinese chives	**jiéu-tsae** 韭菜
chrysanthemum greens	**b'óng-haw-tsae** 茼蒿
cilantro	**shiǎ-tsae** 香菜
cucumber	**h'uǎw-guo** 黄瓜
day-lily flower (*dried and used as a vegetable*)	**jìn-dzen(-tsae)** 金针

eggplant	g'á-dzï / loq-su	茄子
garlic	d'á-soe	大蒜
garlic shoots	sóe-miaw	蒜苗
green (hot) pepper	chìn-laq-jiaw	青椒
green beans	bí-d'eu	扁豆
green vegetables	chìn-tsae	青菜
lettuce	sǎ-tsae	生菜
lily bulbs	bāq-h'eq	百合
loofah gourd	sǐ-guo	丝瓜
lotus root	ngéu	藕
lotus seed	lí-shin	莲子
mung beans	loq-d'eu	绿豆
mushroom	mó-gu	蘑菇
mustard greens	kà-tsae	芥菜
onion	'yǎ-tsong-d'eu	洋葱
peas	wóe-d'eu	豌豆
potato	'yǎ-sae-'yü	土豆
potherb mustard	shīq-li-hong	雪里红
pumpkin (or similar yellow squash variety)	nóe-guo / váe-guo	南瓜
red beans (small)	tsāq-d'eu	赤豆
scallion	tsòng	葱
sesame	dzǐ-mo	芝麻
shepherd's purse	zyí-tsae	荠菜
shiitake mushroom	shiǎ-gu	香菇
snow peas, pea pods	h'ú-lae-d'eu	荷兰豆
soybeans	h'uǎw-d'eu	黄豆
tender soybeans	máw-d'eu	毛豆
spinach	bù-tsae	菠菜
string beans	sǐ-ji-d'eu	四季豆
sweet potato	sàe-'yü	甘薯
taro	'yǔ-na / 'yǔ-d'eu / 'yǔ-na-d'eu	芋艿
tomato	fàe-g'a	西红柿
vegetables	sù-tsae	蔬菜
water caltrop	lín	菱角
water shield	zén-tsae	莼菜
water spinach	óng-tsae / òng-tsae	空心菜
white radish	láw-b'oq / lú-b'oq	萝卜
winter melon	dòng-guo	冬瓜
wood ear (edible fungus)	moq-'er	木耳

Cooking Methods and Eating

barbecue	**sàw-kaw** 烧烤
boil	**sàw** 煮; (*stew*) **dōq** 熬
braise	**mèn** 焖
brew tea	**chí•zuó / páw•zuó** 沏茶
broil	**káw** 烤
chop meat	**dzáe•nioq** 剁肉
cook	**sàw** 煮
cook a meal	**sàw•váe** 做饭
cook noodles	**h'uó•mí** 下面
deep fry	**dzuó / tén** 炸
drink	**chīq** 吃
eat	**chīq** 吃
flavor / taste	**dzì-mi / chīq-keu** 滋味
fry in oil	**jì** 煎
knead dough	**nioq•mí** 揉面
ladle out / scoop up (*in a dipper*)	**'yáw** 舀
order take-out food	**jiáw•ngá-ma** 叫外卖
pick up (*with chopsticks*)	**jì / jīq** 搛
pour	**dáw** 倒
pour tea	**dáw•zuó** 倒茶
quick-boil	**sāq** 涮
roast	**káw** 烤; **hòng** 烘
steam in a pot / heat or cook by steaming	**dén** 炖
steam in a steaming tray	**dzèn** 蒸
stew	**dōq** 熬
stir-fry	**tsáw** 炒
stir-fry vegetables	**tsáw•tsáe** 炒菜
take-out food	**ngá-ma** 外卖
toast	**hòng** 烘
wrap wonton	**kú•'wén-den** 包馄饨

KITCHEN UTENSILS

basin	**b'én-dzï** 盆子	
basket	**láe(-d'eu)** 篮子	
bottle	**b'ín(-dzï)** 瓶子	
bowl	**wóe** 碗	
can / jar	**guóe-d'eu** 罐子	
chopstick holder	**kuáe-d'ong / kuáe-zï- long** 筷子筒	
chopsticks	**kuáe / kuáe-dzï** 筷子	
disposable chopsticks	**yīq-tsï-shin kuáe-dzï** 一次性筷子	
clay cooking pot	**suò-gu** 沙锅	
coaster for teacups	**zuó-d'i** 茶垫	
crock / jar	**gǎw** 缸	
cup / mug / glass	**bàe-dzï** 杯子	
cutting board	**dzèn-den(-bae)** 砧板	
dish detergent	**shí-jiq-jin** 洗洁精	
dish rag	**meq-bu / kà-bu / kà-d'ae-bu** 抹布	
dishwasher	**d'á-woe-ji** 洗碗机	
drinking fountain	**yín-sï-chi** 饮水器	
drinking straw	**shīq-guoe** 吸管	
earthen jar	**b'ǎ** 坛子	
egg beater	**dǎ-d'ae-chi** 打蛋器	
electric kettle	**d'í-niq-h'u** 电热壶	
electric rice cooker	**d'í-vae-b'aw** 电饭煲	
flat-bottomed pot	**b'ín-di-gu** 平底锅	
frying pan	**b'ín-di-gu** 平底锅	
funnel	**léu-deu** 漏斗	
glass (for drinking)	**bù-li-bae** 玻璃杯	
long-stem glass	**gàw-jiaq-bae** 高脚杯	
hotpot / firepot	**hú-gu** 火锅	
jar	**guóe-d'eu** 罐子 / **gǎw** 缸	
jar (earthen)	**b'ǎ** 坛子	
kettle	**diáw-dzï** 吊子	
ladle / scoop (*for liquids*)	**sǐ-zoq** 舀子	
ladle made from a gourd	**sǐ-b'iaw** 瓢	
microwave oven	**ví-bu-lu** 微波炉	
non-stick pan	**veq-dzae-gu / veq-tiq-gu** 不粘锅	
oven	**káw-shiã** 烤箱	

platter / tray	**b'óe(-dzĭ)** 盘子
pot / pan	**h'oq-dzï / gù-dzï** 锅
pot cover	**h'oq-gae / gù-gae** 锅盖
rice bowl	**váe-woe** 饭碗
rice cooking pot	**váe-h'oq(-dzĭ) /** **váe-gu(-dzĭ)** 饭锅
rice serving spatula	**váe-tsaw / váe-zoq(-dzĭ)** 饭勺
serving spoon	**tǎw-zoq** 汤勺
slotted spoon	**léu-zoq** 漏勺
small bowl	**bēq-d'eu** 钵儿
small plate / saucer	**d'iq-dzï** 碟子
soup bowl	**tǎw-woe** 汤碗
soup spoon	**d'iáw-kã** 汤匙
spatula (for cooking)	**h'oq-tsae / tsáe-daw** 锅铲
steamer for food	**dzèn-long** 蒸笼
strainer	**léu-deu** 漏斗
straining spatula	**dzá-li** 笊篱
teacup	**zuó-bae** 茶杯
teapot	**zuó-h'u** 茶壶
vase	**huò-b'in** 花瓶
vegetable knife	**b'oq-daw / chīq-tsae-daw** **/ tsáe-daw** 菜刀
vegetable peeler	**guò-b'aw** 瓜刨
water pot	**sǐ-h'u** 水壶
whistling kettle	**zǐ-min-h'u** 自鸣壶
wine glass	**jiéu-bae** 酒杯
wiping cloth / dish rag	**meq-bu / kà-bu /** **kà-d'ae-bu** 抹布
wok / pot / pan	**h'oq-dzï / gù-dzï** 锅
wok lid	**h'oq-gae / gù-gae** 锅盖

JOBS & BUSINESS

What business are you in?
Nóng dzú sá zǐ-ti? 你做什么事情？

What kind of work do you do?
Nóng dzú sá gòng-dzoq? 你做什么工作？

I am a/an … in an overseas trade company.
Ngú zǐ ngá-maw-gong-sï h'eq …
我是外贸公司的…

>　accountant / bookkeeper **guáe-ji / kuáe-ji** 会计
>　architectural consultant **jí-dzoq gú-ven** 建筑顾问
>　chairman of the board **dóng-zǐ-dzã** 董事长
>　chief officer in the financial division
>　　**záe-wu-ku kù-dzã** 财务科科长
>　buyer **tsáe-geu-'yüoe** 采购员
>　engineer **gòng-zen-sï** 工程师
>　public relations manager **gòng-guae jìn-li** 公关经理
>　member of the marketing division
>　　**gòng-shiaw-ku kù-'yüoe** 供销科科员
>　technical advisor **j'í-zeq gú-ven** 技术顾问

What is the name of your company's manager?
Ná gòng-sï-g'eq jìn-li jiáw sá-g'eq mín-dzï?
你们公司的经理叫什么名字？

What is the name of the boss of your unit?
Ná dàe-'wae-g'eq láw-bae jiáw sá?
你们单位的老板叫什么？

Where do you work?
Nóng laq sá•d'í-fãw gòng-dzoq? 你做什么工作？

I work at/in …
Ngú laq … gòng-dzoq. 我在 … 工作。

Workplaces

bank　　　　　　　　　**nín-h'ãw** 银行
child-care center　　　**tōq-'er-su** 托儿所

college / university	d'á-h'oq 大学
factory / plant	tsǎ / tsǎ-ga 厂 / 工厂
hospital	yì-'yüoe 医院
kindergarten	yéu-'er-'yüoe / yéu-zï-'yüoe 幼儿园
nursery / child-care center	tōq-'er-su 托儿所
office	báe-gong-seq 办公室
office building	shiá-zï-leu 办公楼
school	h'oq-h'iaw / h'oq-d'ǎw 学校
elementary school	shiáw-h'oq 小学
middle school	dzòng-h'oq 中学
night school	'yá-h'iaw 夜校
university	d'á-h'oq 大学
workshop	gòng-zã / tsuò-gae 工场 / 车间

Jobs and Professions

accountant / bookkeeper	guáe-ji / kuáe-ji 会计
actor / actress / performer	yí-'yüoe 演员
architect	jí-dzoq-sï 建筑师
assistant	bǎw-seu / tí-seu 帮手
bodyguard	báw-biaw 保镖 / jín-'wae-'yüoe 警卫员
boss	láw-bae 老板
boss' wife	láw-bae-niã 老板娘
businessman / merchant	sǎw-nin / sǎ-yi-nin 商人 / 生意人
buyer / purchasing agent	tsáe-geu-'yüoe 采购员
cadre	góe-b'u 干部
carpenter	moq-zyiã 木匠
cashier / teller	tsēq-naq-'yüoe 出纳员
chauffeur / driver	sì-ji 司机
chef / cook	zǐ-sï 厨师
child-care worker	báw-'yüeq-'yüoe 保育员
consultant / advisor	gú-ven 顾问
craftsman	séu-ni-nin 手艺人
custodian	chìn-jiq-gong 清洁工
day laborer	lín-gong 零工
director / head	dzǐ-zen 主任
doctor	yì-sã 医生

driver (chauffeur)	**sì-ji** 司机
driver (pedicab)	**sàe-len-tsuo-fu** 三轮车夫
driver (pilot)	**gá-sï-'yüoe / jiá-sï-'yüoe** 驾驶员
engineer	**gòng-zen-sï** 工程师
factory manager	**tsã-zã** 厂长
factory floor manager	**tsuò-gae dzï-zen** 车间主任
farmer	**nóng-min** 农民
fisherman	**dzōq•ñǵ-g'eq** 渔夫
foreman	**gòng-d'eu** 工头
head-hunter	**laq-d'eu** 猎头
hourly labor	**dzòng-di-gong** 钟点工
housekeeper	**báw-mu** 保姆
inspector	**jí-ni-'yüoe / jí-hu-'yüoe** 检验员 / 检货员
intermediary	**dzòng-jia** 中介
journalist / reporter	**jí-dzae** 记者
mailman / letter carrier	**'yéu-d'i-'yüoe / 'yéu-tsa** 邮递员 / 邮差
manager	**jìn-li** 经理
mason / tileworker	**ní-sï-gong** 泥瓦工
middle-man	**dãw-dzong-'yüoe / dzòng-nin** 中间人
midwife	**zú-tsae-zï** 助产士
migrant laborer (*from the countryside*)	**mín-gong** 民工
movie star	**d'í-yin-min-shin** 电影明星
nurse	**h'ú-zï** 护士
on-duty personnel	**zeq-j'in-'yüoe** 值勤员
painter (*of buildings*)	**'yéu-chiq-gong** 油漆工
peasant	**nóng-min** 农民
pedicab driver	**sàe-len-tsuo-fu** 三轮车夫
pilot	**gá-sï-'yüoe / jiá-sï-'yüoe** 驾驶员
police	**jín-tsaq** 警察
porter (*who uses a shoulder pole*)	**tiàw-fu** 挑夫
principal / president (*of a school*)	**h'iáw-dzã** 校长
sales assistant	**zéu-hu-'yüoe** 售货员
secretary	**mì-sï** 秘书
section chief	**dzú-dzã / kù-dzã** 组长 / 科长

servant	'yóng-nin / pōq-nin
	佣人 / 仆人
shop clerk	dí-'yüoe 店员
shopkeeper (*male*)	láw-bae 老板
shopkeeper (*female*)	láw-bae-niã 老板娘
steward	guóe-ga / guóe-jia 管家
street cleaner	chìn-jiq-gong 清洁工
student	h'oq-sã 学生
supervisor / overseer	gàe-gong 监工
supervisor / superior	zǎw-sï 上司
teacher	làw-sï / láw-sï 老师
technical personnel	j'í-zeq-(zen-)'yüoe
	技术人员
ticket seller	zéu-piaw-'yüoe /
	má-piaw-'yüoe 售票员
wet nurse	ná-ma 奶妈
witness	dzén-nin 证人
woodworker	moq-gong 木工
work odd jobs	dzú•lín-sae 打零工
worker	gòng-nin 工人

Employment

cut bonus	kàw•jiǎ-jin 减奖金
cut wages	shīaq•gòng-d'i /
	gáe•gòng-d'i 减工资
earnings made on the side	b'ó-fen 赚钱（额外的）
extra income	ngá-kua 外快
look for a job	zyín•sǎ-yi 找工作
make money /	záe•tsàw-piaw /
earn a living	záe•d'óng-d'i 赚钱
wages	gòng-d'i / gòng-dzï 工资
worker / laborer	nín-gong 人工

Commercial Trade

advertisement	guǎw-gaw 广告
asking price	táw•gá 要价
base/lowest price	dí-bae-ga / chí-bae-ga
	基价 / 最底价
business / trading	sǎ-yi 生意
buyer	má-dzï 买主
ceiling price	dín-ga 顶价

client / buyer	**h'ú-d'eu** 户头
client / customer	**kāq-h'u** 客户
close a deal	**zén-jiaw** 成交
commerce / trade	**sāw-niq** 商业
customer	**gú-kaq** 顾客
go out of business	**shīq•niq / guàe•dí** 歇业 / 关店
grade / value	**pín-'wae** 品位
license (*obtained upon payment of tax, duty, etc.*)	**dzàw-h'uae** 照会
low sales item	**lǎ-men-hu** 冷门货
lowest acceptable price	**bàe•gá** 扳价
manufacture / produce	**tsēq-tsae** 出产
opening price	**kàe•gá** 开价
operate a partnership business	**gēq-dzu-sǎ-yi** 合伙做买卖
order goods	**dín•hú** 订货
price	**gá-d'i / gá-'wae** 价钱 / 价位
profit	**záe-d'eu** 利润
quality of goods / specifications	**hú-seq** 货色
quality products	**dzén-dzong-hu** 正品
return customer	**h'uáe-d'eu-kaq** 回头客
return merchandise	**táe•hú** 退货
run a business / engage in trade	**dzú•sǎ-yi / dzú•má-ma / chīq•sǎ-yi-vae** 做生意 / 做买卖 / 经商
run a store	**kàe•dí** 开店
sell at drastically reduced prices / dump on the market	**d'ú-fāw-b'oe** 大放盘
sell by the piece	**lín-ma / diáw-tsen** 零售
stock with goods	**jín•hú** 进货
substandard product	**tén-nga-pin** 等外品
take delivery of goods	**d'í•hú** 提货
take inventory	**b'óe•hú** 盘货
wholesale	**pì-faq** 批发

Finance

account statement / detailed list	**chìn-dae** 清单
audit the account	**zuó•dzǎ** 查账
bank account	**h'ú-d'eu** 户头

be in debt	**kóng•d'óng-d'i / chí** 欠债 / 欠账
be late in repayment	**tù•dzǎ** 拖账
bonus (money)	**jiǎ-jin** 奖金
buy and resell for profit	**má-jin-ma-tseq** 倒卖
cannot reconcile (the account)	**g'aq-veq-long / g'aq-veq-b'in** 结不了 （账）
capital / principal (*original sum invested*)	**bén-d'i** 本钱
closing price (*at an exchange*)	**sèu-b'oe** 收盘
collect payment	**sèu•dzǎ** 收账
cost of building	**záw-ga** 造价
current market conditions	**hǎw-zyin** 行情
daily interest rate	**tsāq-shiq** 拆息
demand repayment	**táw•dzǎ** 讨债
down payment / deposit	**d'ín-jin / d'ín-h'iǎ** 定金
dramatic fall in price	**tiáw•sǐ** 大幅降价 （"跳水"）
expenditure / disbursement	**dzǐ-tseq / tsēq-dzǎ** 支出 / 出账
expenses	**kàe-shiaw** 开销
extra paid for good measure	**niáw-d'eu** 饶头
foot the entire bill (*at a business meal*)	**zyí-tin-dzā** 全挺张
free/open market	**zǐ-'yeu-zǐ-zā** 自由市场
go bankrupt	**dáw-bi** 倒闭
go on the market	**mí•zǐ** 面市
interest (*on investment*)	**lí-d'i** 利钱
lose capital / suffer a loss in business	**zeq•bén / kuàe•bén** 亏本 / 折本
opening price (*at an exchange*)	**kàe•b'óe** 开盘
overspend / exceed credit limit	**'yóng-kong** 超支
padded accounts / fake accounting	**huò-dzā** 假账
raise wages	**gà•gòng-d'i** 加工资
reconciled (*the account*)	**g'aq•b'ín** 结好（账）
record on account	**jí•dzā / dzú•dzǎ** 记账

repudiate a debt	**lá•dzǎ** 赖账
revenue / income / receipts	**sèu-zeq / jín-dzã** 收入 / 进账
revenue and expenditure	**sèu•dzǐ / sèu•fú** 收支
settle accounts	**g'aq•dzǎ** 结账
share certificate / stock	**gú-piaw** 股票
shrink (*in size or value*)	**sōq•sǐ** 缩水
trademark	**sǎw-biaw** 商标

Note...

The exchange of **business cards** is an important and useful aspect of Shanghai business etiquette. One should always have a plentiful supply on hand. When handing out your business card present it formally with the card facing the recipient and held between the thumb and forefinger of both hands.

In the process you may hear, and may also say:

G'eq-h'eq zǐ ngú-h'eq mín-pi. 这是我的名片。
This is my name card.

Chín dù-du dzǐ-jiaw. 请多多指教。
Please frequently give me your advice.

SHOPPING

bargain *v*	**táw•gá•h'uáe-ga**	讨价还价
brand	**b'á-dzï**	牌子
buy	**má**	买
cash	**kàe-shü / h'í-tsaw /**	
	h'í-jin	现金 / 现钱
change (*from money paid*)	**dzáw-d'eu**	零钱 / 找头
close shop (*for the day*)	**dǎ•'yǎ**	打烊
county fair	**zyiq-zï**	集市
credit (buy or sell on ~)	**suò-chi**	赊欠
discontinued	**d'óe-dǎw**	断档
discount by 50 percent	**dǎ•dáe-dzeq**	打对折
display window / showcase	**zǐ-tsãw**	橱窗
do business	**'yín-niq**	营业
front desk	**j'ǔ-d'ae / g'uáe-d'ae**	柜台
goods/products		
fake goods	**ká-d'eu / d'á-ka**	假货
genuine products	**zén-ka**	正宗货物
inferior goods	**tsǐ-hu / tsǐ-pin**	次货 / 次品
imitation goods / pirated products	**d'á-shin-hu / máw-b'a-hu**	冒牌货
legitimate goods	**h'ǎw-hu**	行货
leftover goods	**zǎ-hu**	剩货
old stock / shopworn goods	**zén-hu**	陈货
smuggled goods	**sǐ-hu**	水货
goods rack / store shelf	**hú-ga**	货架
hot sales item	**niq-men-hu**	热门货
how much?	**jí-d'i?**	多少钱？
invoice / bill of sale	**fāq-piaw**	发票
label	**b'á-dzï**	牌子
market	**zǐ-zã**	市场
local market / county fair	**zyiq-zï**	集市
night market	**'yá-zǐ-mi**	夜市
market district	**zǐ-keu**	市口
newly out on the market	**shìn-den-zã**	新登场
old stock	**zén-hu**	陈货
open for business	**'yín-niq-dzong**	营业中
payee / recipient (of check)	**d'áe-d'eu**	台头

price	**gá-d'i** 价钱 / **gá-'wae** 价位	
asking price	**táw•gá** 要价	
extremely low price	**sãq-gen-ga** 煞根价	
sky-high price	**tì-ga** 天价	
products. *See* goods/products		
receipt	**sèu-d'iaw** / **sèu-jü** 收条，收据	
remnants	**zã-hu** 剩货	
sell	**má** 卖	
shop counter	**j'ü-d'ae** / **g'uáe-d'ae** 柜台	
shop front/facade	**mén-mi** 门面	
shop sign	**dzàw-b'a** 招牌	
shopping center	**zǐ-keu** 市口	
sold out	**d'óe-dãw** 断档	
tag	**b'á-dzï** 牌子	
UPC symbol	**d'iáw-h'in-mo** 条形码	
valuable	**zeq•d'óng-d'i** 值钱	
weight	**vén-liã** <u>重量</u>	

Asking Prices and Bargaining

What would you like to buy?
Nóng yáw má sá? 你要买什么？

I'm just looking.
Ngú kóe-koe. 我看看。

I would like to buy …
Ngú shiǎ má … 我想买…

How much is this?
G'eq-h'eq jí-d'i? 这个多少钱？

How much?
Jí-d'i a? 多少钱啊？

Oh, it's that expensive?
Gà jǖ a? 那么贵啊？

That's too expensive!
Tēq jǖ leq! 太贵了！

That's the lowest price.
Dzóe-di-ga. 最低价.

You may hear . . .

Bāq•nóng … háw-lae. 给你 … 吧。
(I'll) give you …

dǎ•jiéu-dzeq	打九折	10% off
dǎ•bāq-dzeq	打八折	20% off
dǎ•chīq-dzeq	打七折	30% off
dǎ•loq-dzeq	打六折	40% off
dǎ•ńǵ-dzeq /	打五折 /	50% off
dǎ•dáe-dzeq	打对折	

How about a little cheaper?
Háw j'iǎ-yiq-ngae va? / Kú-yi b'í-ni-di va?
便宜一点好吗？

Nothing higher than …
B'ǎ-din … 最高…

Please give me a different one.
Chín h'uóe yīq-dzeq. 请换一只。

Shopping for Clothing and Accessories

Where can I buy (a) …?
… leq sá-d'i-fǎw má? … 在哪儿买？

children's wear	**shiáw-noe-yi-zǎw / d'óng-dzǎw** 童装
men's clothing	**nóe-nin-g'eq yì-zǎw** 男人的衣裳
pants	**kù-dzï / kú-dzï** 裤子
shirts	**tsén-sae** 衬衫
shoes	**h'á-dzï** 鞋子
skirt	**j'ǔn-dzï / j'ióng-dzï** 裙子
women's clothing	**nǘ-nin-g'eq yì-zǎw** 女人的衣裳

I'd like to buy a suit.
Ngú shiǎ má yīq-j'í shì-dzǎw.
我想买一件西装。

Go to the 5th floor to buy that.
Dáw ñǵ-zen-leu-chi má. 到五楼去买。

How much for …?
Jí-d'i …? 多少钱…?

one skirt / pair of pants	**yīq-d'iaw**	一条
one shirt/blouse/jacket	**yīq-j'í**	一件
one pair of shoes/socks	**yīq-sǎw**	一双
¥98.00 a pair	**jiéu-zeq-baq-kuae**	
	yīq-sǎw 九十八块一双	

Clothing

anklet socks	**maq-zoe** 短袜
apron	**'yǘ-j'ün** 围裙
bikini	**bí-ji-ni** 比基尼
bra / brassière	**ná-dzaw / vén-shiong** 胸罩
cashmere sweater	**'yǎ-niong-sae** 羊绒衫
cheongsam	**j'í-b'aw** 旗袍
clothing	**yì-zǎw** 衣裳
coat / jacket	**z'ǎw-dzǎw / ngá-taw** 上衣 / 外套
collar	**lín-d'eu** 领子
cotton jersey	**mí-maw-sae** 棉毛衫
cotton padded jacket	**mí-aw** 棉袄
cotton padded pants	**mí-ku** 棉裤
down coat	**'yǘ-niong-sae** 羽绒衫
fur coat	**máw-b'i-d'a-i** 毛皮大衣
halter dress	**mó-gaq-j'ün / mó-gaq-j'ióng** 马夹裙
jacket	**j'iá-keq(-sae)** 夹克
jeans	**niéu-dzae-ku** 牛仔裤
leisure clothing	**shièu-h'ae-dzǎw** 休闲装
lining (*in clothing*)	**gāq-li** 里子
long pants	**zǎ-ku** 长裤
long sleeve	**zǎ-zyieu** 长袖
long stockings	**zǎ-tong-maq** 长袜
name brand	**mín-b'a** 名牌
nightgown	**kuén-j'iong** 睡衣
one-piece dress	**lí-sae-j'ün / lí-sae-j'iong** 连衣裙
overcoat	**d'á-yi** 大衣

pajamas	**kuén-i(-kuen-ku)** 睡衣（睡裤）
pant leg	**kù-jiaq / kú-jiaq / kú-d'ong** 裤腿
panties	**sàe-goq-ku** 三角裤
pants	**kù-dzï / kú-dzï** 裤子
parka	**pà-keq** 派克
shawl	**pì-ji** 披肩
shirt	**tsén-sae** 衬衫
short pants	**dóe-ku** 短裤
short sleeve	**dóe-zyieu** 短袖
silk stockings/hose	**sì-maq** 丝袜
skirt	**j'ǔn-dzï / j'ióng-dzï** 裙子
sleeve	**zyiéu-dzï(-guoe)** 袖子
socks	**maq-dzï / maq** 袜子
sundress	**diáw-da-j'ün** 吊带裙
sweater	**nióng-shi-sae** 毛线衣
T-shirt	**tì-shüeq-sae** T恤衫
underpants (knit cotton)	**h'óe-ku** 汗裤
undershirt	**h'óe-sae** 汗衫
underwear, lace	**láe-sï náe-yi** 蕾丝内衣
unisex	**dzòng-shin-seq-'yã** 中性式样
v-neck collar	**ví-zï-lin** V字领
vest	**báe-shin / mó-gaq** 背心
wear clothing	**tsòe•ì-zãw / dzãq•ì-zãw** 穿衣服
wedding dress	**huèn-suo** 婚纱
Western-style suit	**shì-dzãw** 西装
windbreaker	**fòng-yi** 风衣

Hats and Shoes

athletic shoes	**j'iéu-h'a** 球鞋
baseball cap	**b'ǎ́w-j'ieu-maw** 棒球帽
cleated shoes	**dìn-h'a** 钉鞋
cloth shoes	**bú-h'a(-dzï)** 布鞋
earmuff	**ní-du-taw** 耳朵套
flat cap	**āq-zeq-d'éu máw-dzï** 鸭舌帽
flip-flops	**tù-h'a** 拖鞋
galoshes	**tàw-h'a / táw-h'a** 雨鞋
hat	**máw-dzï** 帽子
hat brim	**máw-'yi** 帽檐
headband	**d'éu-gu** 头箍
high-heel shoes	**gàw-gen-h'a** 高跟鞋

insole / shoe pad	h'á-d'i	鞋垫
leather shoes	b'í-h'a	皮鞋
running shoes	b'áw-h'a	跑鞋
sandals	fòng-liã-h'a	凉鞋
shoes	h'á-dzï	鞋子
skullcap	guò-b'i-maw	瓜皮帽
slippers	tù-h'a	拖鞋
sole (of a shoe)	h'á-ti	鞋底
straw hat	tsáw-maw	草帽
summer hat	liã-maw / fòng-liã-maw	凉帽
sun hat	tá-'yã-maw	太阳帽
wool/felt hat	ní-maw	呢帽

Accessories, Jewelry, and Makeup

beads	dzï̀-dzï	珠珠
belt	yàw-da / kú-yaw-da	腰带 / 裤腰带
bracelet	séu-zoq / zoq-d'eu	手镯
button	niéu-dzï	纽扣
cosmetics	dzï̀-fen	脂粉
earrings	'ér-g'uae / ní-du-g'uae	耳环
gloves	séu-taw	手套
gold ring	jìn-ga-dzï	金戒指
hair clasp / hair pin	dzóe / d'éu-faq-dzoe	簪子
handkerchief	jüóe-d'eu	手帕
jewelry	séu-seq	首饰
leather belt	b'í-da	皮带
lipstick	dzï̃-zen-gaw	唇膏
make-up powder cake	fén-bin	粉饼
muffler / scarf	'yü̃-jin	围巾
nail polish	jīq-kaq-'yeu	指甲油
necklace	h'ã́w-li / lí-d'iaw	项链
pearl	dzèn-dzï	珍珠
ring	gá-dzï	戒指
rouge	yì-dzï	胭脂
scarf	d'éu-jin	头巾
silk scarf	sì-jin	丝巾
suspenders	bàe-da	背带
wristwatch	séu-biaw / biáw	手表
wig	gá-faq	假发

SHOPPING

Sizes

What size do you *wear*?
Nóng *tsòe/dzāq* jí-huo d'ú a? 你穿多大的啊?

I *wear* … **Ngú *tsòe/dzāq* …** 我穿…

size 4	**sī́-h'aw**	四号
size 5	**ñǵ-h'aw**	五号
size 6	**loq-h'aw**	六号
size 7	**chīq-h'aw**	七号
size 8	**bāq-h'aw**	八号
size 9	**jiéu-h'aw**	九号
size 10	**zeq-h'aw**	十号
size 11	**zeq-yiq-h'aw**	十一号
size 12	**zeq-ni-h'aw**	十二号

I would like to try it on.
Ngú shiǎ dzāq-dzaq-koe. 我想穿穿看。

It's a little …
'Yéu ngáe-ngae … 有点…

It's too …
Tēq … leq. 太…了。

big	**d'ú** 大		small	**shiáw** 小
long	**zǎ** 长		short	**dóe** 短

This one is not as … as that one.
G'eq-j'í m̄-meq àe-j'í … 这件没有那件…

nice looking	**háw-koe**	好看
high quality	**dín-guaq**	平整质量好
inexpensive	**b'í-niq**	便宜
expensive	**jǘ**	贵

This … is just right.
G'eq-… dzén-haw. 这 … 正好。

pair (of shoes)	**sǎw**	双
one (shirt, blouse)	**j'í**	件
pair (of pants) / one (skirt)	**d'iáw**	条

Shopping for Food

How much are the ...?
... jí-d'i? ...多少钱？

How much are the ... per *jīn*?
... jí-d'i yīq-jin a? ...几块一斤？

See Food & Drink section for names of foods.

¥4 *yuán* per *jīn*.
Sí-kuae yīq-jin. 四块一斤

¥1.50 *yuán* per *jīn*.
yīq-kuae ńǵ yīq-jin. 四块五一斤

> ### *You may hear ...*
> the common units for weight in Shanghai,
> *jìn*—which in markets is 500 grams, and
> *liǎ*—which in markets is 50 grams. Because
> the latter is homophonous with the word for
> two, when speaking of "two *liǎ*" the alter-
> nate word for 'two'—*ní*—is used with it:
>
> | | | |
> |---|---|---|
> | **liǎ-jin** | 两斤 | two *jìn* |
> | **ní-liǎ** | 二两 | two *liǎ* |

COLORS

beige	**mí-h'uã**	米黄
black	**hēq**	黑
blue	**láe**	蓝
brown	**kà-fi-seq**	咖啡色
gold	**jìn-h'uã**	金黄
gray	**huàe**	灰
green	**loq**	绿
orange	**jüēq-h'ong**	橘红
peach	**d'áw-h'ong**	桃红
pink	**fén-h'ong**	粉红
purple	**dzí̆**	紫
red	**h'óng**	红
sky-blue	**tì-lae**	天蓝
snow-white	**shīq-b'aq**	雪白
white	**b'aq**	白
yellow	**h'uắw**	黄

MONEY

How much is this?
G'eq-h'eq jí-d'i? 这个多少钱？

¥10.50	**zeq-kuae ñg** 十块
¥22.40	**náe-ni-kuae sǐ-goq** 二十二块四毛
¥125.00	**yīq-baq náe-ñǵ-kuáe** 一百二十五块
¥409.00	**sǐ-baq lín-jieu kuáe** 四百零九块

money	**d'óng-d'i / 'yǎ-d'i** 钱
cash	**kàe-shü / h'í-tsaw / h'í-jin** 现金
paper money / bank note	**tsáw-piaw** 钞票
rénmínbì	**zén-min-b'i** 人民币
foreign currency	**ngá-b'i** 外币
pay the bill/check	**tín-dzã** 付钱
pay (cash)	**fú•tsáw-piaw** 付现钞
pay with a credit card	**sēq•ká** 刷卡
tip *n.*	**shiáw-fī** 小费

At the Bank

I want to change money.
Ngú yáw h'uóe d'óng-di. 我要换钱。

I want to exchange … for *rénminbì*.
Ngú yáw nàw … d'iáw zén-min-b'i.
我要用 … 换人民币。

U.S. dollars	**máe-'yüoe / máe-jin** 美元
Hong Kong dollars	**gǎ-b'i** 港币
pounds sterling	**yìn-bãw** 英镑
Japanese *yen*	**zeq-'yüoe** 日元

What is the exchange rate?
D'áe-h'uoe-liq zǐ dù-saw? 兑换率？

Can I exchange a traveller's check?
Kú-yi h'uóe lǘ-h'in dzǐ-piaw va?
可以换旅行支票吗？

Note...

The basic monetary unit of China, *rénmínbì*, in Shanghai is the *yuán* (¥), which is colloquially called *kuáe* in Shanghainese. One *kuáe* can be further divided into *gōq*—one tenth of one *kuáe*—and *fèn*—one one-hundredth of one *kuáe*. Prices and sums of money are given in these units, from largest to smallest:

náe-baq-kuae ñǵ-goq sàe-fen
二十八块五毛三分
¥28.53

The words *gōq* and *fèn* do not have to be said if they are last after a larger unit:

loq-zeq-sae kuáe chǐq
六十三块七
¥63.70

basic monetary unit, *yuán*	**kuáe** 块
fēn (one hundredth of one *yuán*)	**fèn / fèn-d'eu** 分
ten *fēn* (one tenth of one *yuán*)	**gōq** 角
small change / remainder	**lín-d'eu** 零头

Change this into smaller bills for me.
Chín bǎw ngú h'uóe lín-sae-tsaw-piaw.
请帮我换零的。

I want to make a deposit.
Ngú yáw zén tsáw-piaw. 我要存钱。

Is there a bank nearby?
Vú-j'in 'yéu nín-h'ãw va?
附近有提款机吗？

Is there an ATM nearby?
Vú-j'in 'yéu d'í-kuae-ji va? 附近有提款机吗？

account	**dzǎ-h'u** 账户
ATM	**d'í-kuae-ji / chǘ-kuoe-ji / ATM** 提款机
ATM card	**zí-ka** 磁卡
deposit	**zén-kuoe** 存款
deposit book	**zén-dzeq** 存折
exchange rate	**d'áe-h'uoe-liq** 兑换率
interest	**lí-shiq** 利息
interest rate	**lí-liq** 利率
money order	**h'uáe-kuoe-dae** 汇款单
remit money	**h'uáe-kuoe** 汇款
savings	**zí-shüeq** 储蓄
service fee	**séu-zoq-fi** 手续费

You may hear . . .

Hú-dzaw dá-lae va? 护照带了吗？
Did you bring your passport?

Nóng yáw máe-jin àe-zï zén-min-b'i? 你要
美金还是人民币？
Do you want U.S. dollars or *rénmínbì*?

Chín chí-zï. 请签字。
Please sign your name.

CALENDAR & TIME

Year, Seasons, and Festivals

year	**ní** 年
one year	**yīq-ni** 一年
this year	**jìn-ni** 今年
last year	**chǘ-ni / j'iéu-ni** 去年
year before last year	**zyí-ni** 前年
next year	**mín-ni / kàe-ni** 明年
year after next year	**h'éu-ni** 后年
end of the year	**ní-di / ní-jiaq-bi** 年底
beginning of the year	**ní-d'eu-lǎw** 年初
middle of the year	**ní-dzong-shin** 年中
first half of the year	**zǎw-boe-ni / zyí-boe-ni** 上半年
second half of the year	**h'uó-boe-ni / h'éu-boe-ni** 下半年
spring	**tsèn-ti** 春天
summer	**h'uó-ti / niq-ti** 夏天
autumn / fall	**chièu-ti** 秋天
winter	**dòng-ti / lǎ-ti** 冬天
Chinese New Year's	**tsèn-jiq** 春节
Chinese New Year's Day (*the 1ˢᵗ day of the 1ˢᵗ lunar month*)	**d'ú-ni-tsu-iq / ní-tsu-iq** 大年初一
Chinese New Year's Eve	**zǐ-zyiq** 除夕
pay a New Year's visit	**bá ní** 拜年
Lantern Festival (*the 15ᵗʰ day of the 1ˢᵗ lunar month*)	**nüóe-shiaw-jiq** 元宵节
Dragon Boat Festival (*the 5ᵗʰ day of the 5ᵗʰ lunar month*)	**dòe-ñg-jiq / dòe-'wu-jiq** 端午节

Mid-Autumn Festival	**dzòng-chieu-jiq /**
(the 15th day of the 8th lunar month)	**d'óe-'yüoe-jiq** 中秋节

Months

What month is it?
H'í-zae zí jí-'yüeq a? 现在是几月？

It is …   **H'í-zae zí …** 现在是…

January	**yīq-'yüeq** 一月
February	**liǎ-'yüeq** 二月
March	**sàe-'yüeq** 三月
April	**sǐ-'yüeq** 四月
May	**ñǵ-'yüeq** 五月
June	**loq-'yüeq** 六月
July	**chiēq-'yüeq** 七月
August	**bāq-'yüeq** 八月
September	**jiéu-'yüeq** 九月
October	**zeq-'yüeq** 十月
November	**zeq-yiq-'yüeq** 十一月
December	**zeq-ni-'yüeq** 十二月

When will you go on vacation?
Nóng jí-zï fǎ̀w•gá? 你什么时候放假？

month	**'yüeq / 'yoq** 月
one month	**yīq-g'eq-'yüeq** 一个月
this month	**g'eq-g'eq 'yüeq** 这个月
beginning of the month	**'yüeq-tsu** 月初
middle of the month	**'yüeq-dzong** 月中
end of the month	**'yüeq-di** 月底
last month	**zǎ̀w-g'eq-'yüeq** 上个月
month before last	**zǎ̀w-zǎ̀w-g'eq-'yüeq** 上上个月
next month	**h'uó-g'eq-'yüeq** 下个月
month after next	**h'uó-h'uo-g'eq-'yüeq** 下下个月

Dates

What is/was the date …?
… **zǐ jí-h'aw a?** …是几号啊?

today	**jìn-dzaw**	今天
yesterday	**zoq-niq / zuó-ti**	昨天
day before yesterday	**zyí-niq / zyí-ti**	前天
tomorrow	**mín-dzaw / mén-dzaw**	
	明天	
day after tomorrow	**h'éu-niq / h'éu-ti-dzǐ**	
	后天	

Today is the … **Jìn-dzaw zǐ …** 今天是…

1st	**yīq-h'aw**	一号
2nd	**liǎ-h'aw**	两号
3rd	**sàe-h'aw**	三号
4th	**sǐ-h'aw**	四号
5th	**ńg-h'aw**	五号
6th	**loq-h'aw**	六号
7th	**chīq-h'aw**	七号
8th	**bāq-h'aw**	八号
9th	**jiéu-h'aw**	九号
10th	**zeq-h'aw**	十号
11th	**zeq-yiq-h'aw**	十一号
12th	**zeq-ni-h'aw**	十二号
13th	**zeq-sae-h'aw**	十三号
14th	**zeq-sǐ-h'aw**	十四号
15th	**zeq-ńg-h'aw**	十五号
16th	**zeq-loq-h'aw**	十六号
17th	**zeq-chiq-h'aw**	十七号
18th	**zeq-baq-h'aw**	十八号
19th	**zeq-jieu-h'aw**	十九号
20th	**náe-h'aw**	二十号
21st	**náe-yiq-h'aw**	二十一号
22nd	**náe-ni-h'aw**	二十二号
23rd	**náe-sae-h'aw**	二十三号
24th	**náe-sǐ-h'aw**	二十四号
25th	**náe-ńg-h'aw**	二十五号
26th	**náe-loq-h'aw**	二十六号
27th	**náe-chiq-h'aw**	二十七号
28th	**náe-baq-h'aw**	二十八号

29th	náe-jieu-h'aw	二十九号
30th	sàe-seq-h'aw	三十号
31st	sàe-zeq yīq-h'aw	三十一号

day	niq / tì 天
days	niq-jiaq 日子
half a day / a long time	bóe-niq / bóe-ti 半天
one day	yīq-niq / yīq-ti 一天
whole day	dzén-niq / dzén-ti 整天
entire day	zyí-niq / zyí-ti 全天
every day	niq-niq / tì-ti / màe-niq 日日 / 天天 / 每天
another day / some other day	gáe-niq 改天

Days of the Week

What day of the week is it?
Jìn-dzaw zǐ lí-ba-ji? 今天是星期几?

Today is … **Jìn-dzaw zǐ …** 今天是…

Monday	lí-ba-yiq 礼拜一
Tuesday	lí-ba-ni / lí-ba-liã 礼拜二
Wednesday	lí-ba-sae 礼拜三
Thursday	lí-ba-sï 礼拜四
Friday	lí-ba-ñg 礼拜五
Saturday	lí-ba-loq 礼拜六
Sunday	lí-ba-niq 礼拜日

week	lí-ba 礼拜
this week	g'eq-g'eq lí-ba 这个礼拜
last week	zǎw-li-ba 上礼拜
next week	h'uó-li-ba 下礼拜
two weeks	liǎ-g'eq lí-ba 两个礼拜

Telling Time

What time is it?
H'í-zae jí-di-dzong? 现在几点钟?

It is … in the morning.
H'í-zae zí dzáw-lãw … 现在是早上…

6:00	**loq-di-dzong**	六点钟
7:30	**chīq-di-boe**	七点半
8:15	**bāq-di zeq-ñg-fen**	八点十五分
9:45	**jiéu-di sàe-keq**	九点三刻
five minutes to 10:00	**zeq-di chüêq-ñg-fen**	
	差五分十点	

hour	**dzòng-d'eu**	钟头
one hour	**yīq-g'eq-dzong-d'eu**	一个钟头
two and a half hours	**liã-h'eq-boe dzong-d'eu**	
	两个半钟头	
minute	**fèn**	分
one minute	**yīq-fen(-dzong)**	一分（钟）

daybreak	**chìn-dzaw**	清晨
early morning	**dzáw-zen / dzáw-lãw**	早晨
morning / a.m.	**zắw-boe-niq / zắw-dzeu**	上午
daytime	**niq-li-d'eu / b'aq-ti**	白天
noon / midday	**dzòng-'wu / dzòng-lãw-shiã**	中午
afternoon / p.m.	**h'uó-boe-ti / h'uó-boe-niq**	下午
dusk	**h'uắw-huen-d'eu**	黄昏
evening	**'yá-d'eu**	晚上
nightfall	**b'ắw-'wae-zen-guãw**	傍晚
nighttime	**'yá-li**	夜里
midnight /	**bóe-'ya**	半夜
middle of the night		

Discussing One's Schedule

When do/will you …
Nóng sá•zén-guãw … 你什么时候…

leave	**dzéu**	走
come back	**h'uáe-lae / dzóe-lae**	回来
go to work	**zắw-bae**	上班
get off work	**h'uó-bae**	下班
have class	**zắw•kú**	上课
get out of class	**h'uó•kú**	下课
sleep	**kuén•gáw / kuèn-gaw**	睡觉
get up	**chí-lai**	起来

eat	**chīq•váe**	吃饭
go food shopping	**chí má•tsáe**	去买菜
go watch a movie	**chí kóe•d'í-yin**	去看电影
go watch the show	**chí kóe•shí**	去看戏

I will go at … in the afternoon.
Ngú h'uó-boe-niq … chí. 我下午 … 去。

1:00	**yīq-di-dzong**	一点钟
2:30	**liǎ-di-boe**	两点半
3:15	**sàe-di yīq-keq**	三点一刻
4:45	**sǐ-di sǐ-zeq ñǵ-fen**	四点四十五分
ten minutes to 5:00		
ñǵ-di chüēq-zeq-fen	差十分五点	

What time does the … begin?
… jí-di-dzong kàe-sï? …几点钟开始?

meeting	**Wáe/h'uáe**	会
movie	**D'í-yin**	电影
performance	**Yí-tseq**	演出
ball game	**J'iéu-sae**	球赛

At 8:00 in the evening
'Yá-d'eu bāq-di-dzong. 晚上八点钟.

Making an Appointment

When did you (*plural*) arrange to …?
Ná yāq-haw laq sá•zén-guǎw … h'eq?
你们约好什么时候…?

What time do you (*singular*) want to …?
Nóng shiǎ jí-di-dzong …? 我们几点钟…?

meet	**b'ǎ•d'éu**	碰头
go	**chí**	去
come	**láe**	来
wait for him/her	**dén 'yí**	等他/她
discuss (it)	**táw-len**	讨论

I'll go at …, OK?
Ngú … chí, háw va? 我…去，好吗?

noon / midday	**dzòng-'wu / dzòng-lãw-shiã**	中午
11:50	**zeq-yiq-di ñǵ-seq-fen**	
	十一点五十分	
12 o'clock	**zeq-ni-di-dzong** 十二点钟	

now	**h'í-zae / náe** 现在	
in a short while / momentarily	**áe-shiq / áe-shiq-di** 一会儿	
next time	**h'uó-dzoe** 下次	
afterwards / later	**yì•h'éu** 以后	
future	**jiǎ-lae** 将来	
in the future	**záw-h'eu** 往后	
before / in the past	**yì•zyí** 以前	
recently / lately	**dzóe•j'ín / shìn-j'in** 最近 / 近来	
time / time when	**zén-guãw** 时候 / 时间	

COMMUNICATIONS

At the Post Office

I want to mail ...
Ngú yáw jí ... 我要寄...

a letter	**shín**	信
a postcard	**mín-shin-pi**	明信片
a parcel	**bàw-gu**	包裹
by ordinary mail	**b'ín-shin**	平信
a registered letter	**guó-h'aw-shin**	挂号信
an airmail letter	**h'áw-kong-shin**	航空信
printed matter	**h'ín-seq-pin**	印刷品
an express mail letter	**kuá-d'i-shin**	快递信

How much is the postage to mail this to ...?
Jí-daw ..., 'yéu-piaw tîq dù-saw?
寄到..., 贴多少邮票?

America	**Máe-goq**	美国
San Francisco	**J'iéu-jin-sae**	旧金山
Australia	**Áw-d'a-li-ya**	澳大利亚
Britain	**Yìn-goq**	英国
Canada	**Gà-na-da**	加拿大
Europe	**Èu-dzeu**	欧洲

When will it arrive?
Sá•zén-guãw sèu-daw? 什么时候收到?

airmail letter	**h'áw-kong-shin**	航空信
EMS express delivery	**d'eq-kua dzòe-d'i**	特快专递
envelope	**shín-koq / shín-fong**	信封
express mail	**kuá-d'i / kuá-j'i**	快递
letter	**shín**	信
mail a letter	**jí•shín**	寄信
mail a parcel	**jí•bàw-gu**	寄包裹
mailbox	**'yéu-d'ong / 'yéu-shiã**	邮筒 / 邮箱
ordinary/surface mail	**b'ín-shin**	平信
package / parcel	**bàw-gu**	包裹
post office	**'yéu-j'üeq**	邮局

postage stamp	**'yéu-piaw** 邮票
postal code	**'yéu-dzen bì-mo** 邮政编码
postal parcel	**'yéu-baw** 邮包
postcard	**mín-shin-pi** 明信片
printed matter	**'yín-seq-pin** 印刷品
registered mail	**guó-h'aw-shin** 挂号信
stationery	**shín-dzï** 信纸

Phone and Electronic Communications

Where can I …?
Sá-d'i-fãw kú-yi …? 哪儿可以…?

buy a mobile phone	**má séu-ji** 买手机
buy a *cellular / SIM* card	**má *séu-ji / SIM* ká** 买手机 / SIM卡
add minutes (to my mobile plan)	**tsòng-zeq** 充值
go on-line	**zäw•mäw** 上网

What is your cell phone number?
Nóng séu-ji-h'aw dù-saw? 你手机号多少?

Can you write it down?
Kú-yi shiá-loq-lae va? 可以写下来吗?

Please call me.
Chín dä d'í-h'uo bãq ngú. 请给我打电话。

Please text me.
Chín fãq dóe-shin bãq ngú. 请给我发短信。

cell phone	**séu-ji** 手机
e-mail	**yì-mae-er** 电子邮件
Ethernet cable	**mäw-shi** 网线
fax	**d'í-zoe, fà-kaq-sï** 传真
fax machine	**zóe-dzen-ji** 传真机
headphone / earphone	**'ér-ji** 耳机
home theater	**jià-d'in-yin-'yüoe** 家庭影院
Internet / the web	**mäw-loq** 网络
Internet café	**mäw-ba** 网吧
LCD television	**'yiq-jin-d'i-zï** 液晶电视

liquid crystal display / LCD screen	**'yiq-jin-b'in** 液晶屏
long-distance call	**zǎ-d'u-d'i-h'uo** 长途电话
make a phone call	**dǎ d'í-h'uo** 打电话
microphone	**maq-keq-fong** 麦克风
on-line	**mǎw-lǎw** 网上
radio	**sèu-yin-ji** 收音机
recorder	**loq-yin-ji** 录音机
roaming	**máe-'yeu** 漫游
speaker / loudspeaker	**lá-ba** 喇叭
telephone	**d'í-h'uo** 电话
television set	**d'í-zǐ-ji** 电视机
text message	**dóe-shin(-shiq)** 短信息
wireless network	**'wú-shi-mǎw** 无线网

HAIR SALON & BARBER

I want to …
Ngú yáw … 我要…

get a haircut	**tí•d'éu-faq** 理发
have my hair trimmed	**jí d'éu-faq** 剪头发
get a perm	**tǎw•d'éu-faq** 烫头发
have my hair shampooed	**d'á d'éu-faq** 洗头发
have my hair blow-dried	**tsǐ d'éu-faq** 吹头发
get a shave	**shièu•mí** 刮脸

Please don't cut it too short.
Chín viáw jí tēq dóe. 请别剪太短。

Cut it like it was before.
Dzáw nüóe-lae-g'eq 'yǎ-dzï tí. 照原来的样子剪。

I'd like it slightly shorter.
Sàw-'wae dóe-yiq-di. 稍微短一点。

Would you like a massage?
Tēq nóng òe-mo yáw va? 给你按摩好吗？

I don't have time.
Ḿ-meq zén-guāw.

Just a light pounding on my back will be fine.
Dīq-diq-páe háw-leq. 捶捶背就好。

ENTERTAINMENT & SIGHTSEEING

Where is a fun place to go?
Chí sá•d'í-fāw háw b'eq-shiã h'eq? 去哪儿好玩儿？

What is your plan for the weekend?
Nóng dzén-b'ae ná-nen gú dzèu-meq a?
你准备怎么过周末？

How about going to …?
Chí … ná-nen? 去…怎么样？

I would like to go …
Ngú shiǎ chí … 我想去…

watch a movie	**kóe•d'í-yin** 看电影	
watch a show	**kóe•yí-tseq** 看演出	
watch Shanghai opera	**tìn h'ú-j'iq** 听沪剧	
dance	**tiáw•'wú** 跳舞	
take a sightseeing boat	**zú•'yéu-zoe** 坐游船	
sing karaoke	**tsǎw•ká-la-wo-kae /**	
	tsǎw•kàe-gu 唱卡拉OK	
window shopping	**d'ǎw•mó-lu** 逛街	
tour a watertown	**gǎw-noe sǐ-shiã lǖ-'yeu**	
	江南水乡旅游	
see the evening lights	**kóe-koe 'yá-jin** 看看夜景	
see the sights on the	**kóe-koe ngá-tae fòng-guāw**	
Bund	看看外滩风光	
to the pedestrian mall	**Nóe-jin-lu b'ú-h'in-ga**	
on Nánjīng Road	南京路步行街	

I want to take a drive to …
Ngú yáw kàe-b'u tsuò-dzǐ chí … 我要开个车去…

Sūzhōu	**Sù-dzeu** 苏州	
Zhūjiājiǎo Village	**Dzǐ-ga-goq** 朱家角	

I want to take a day tour of …
Ngú shiǎ tsòe-ga … yīq-zeq-'yeu. 我想参加…一日游。

Shànghǎi	**Zǎw-hae** 上海	
Zhōuzhuāng Village	**Dzèu-dzã** 周庄	
Yángchéng Lake	**'Yǎ-zã-h'u** 阳澄湖	

I want like to buy a/an...
Ngú yáw má... 我要买...

admission ticket	**mén-piaw**	门票
movie ticket	**d'í-yin-piaw**	电影票
show ticket	**shí-piaw**	戏票
bus ticket	**tsuò-piaw**	车票
boat ticket	**zóe-piaw**	船票

How much per ticket?
Yīq-dzã jí-d'i? 多少钱一张?

How many tickets are you buying?
Nóng má jí-dzã? 你买几张?

When does it start?
Jí-di-dzong kàe-sï? 几点中开始?

What time does it open?
Jí-di-dzong kàe•mén? 几点钟开门?

What time does it close?
Jí-di-dzong guàe•mén? 几点钟关门?

Is there an entrance fee?
Yáw mén-piaw va? 要门票吗?

Can I take pictures?
Kú-yi pāq•dzáw va? 可以拍照吗?

Any other activities (we can do)?
Àe-'yeu sá bīq-h'eq h'ueq-d'ong vaq-la?
还有别的活动吗?

It was quite interesting!
Zyiá-chi 'yéu yì-sï! 很有意思!

It is/was truly *a fine (site)* / *an enjoyable (show)*!
Dzèn háw-koe! 真好看!

What a delightful show!
Gà jìn-tsae-h'eq yí-tseq a! 真精彩的演出啊!

Performances and Amusements

ballet	**bà-lae-'wu** 芭蕾舞
Beijing opera	**jìn-shi** 京剧
comic opera	**h'uaq-ji-shi** 滑稽戏
dance	**'wú(-d'aw)** 舞蹈
evening tour	**'yá-'yeu** 夜游
folk song	**mín-gu** 民歌
full house (sold out)	**kāq-moe** 客满
Kunqu opera	**kuèn-chüeq** 昆曲
lion dance	**w'ú-sï-dzï** 舞狮子
listen to opera	**tìn-shi** 听戏
magic performance	**bí•shí-faq** 变魔术
movie	**d'í-yìn** 电影
movie theater	**d'í-yin-'yüoe** 电影院
night market	**'yá-zï-mi** 夜市
one-day tour	**yīq-zeq-'yeu** 一日游
pedestrian mall	**b'ú-h'in-ga** 步行街
perform (in a play)	**yí•shí / dzú•shí** 演戏
perform in traditional opera	**tsā́w•shí** 唱戏
performance	**yí-tseq** 演出
play *n.*	**h'uó-j'iq** 话剧
play *v.* / have fun / enjoy oneself	**b'eq-shiã(-shiã)** 玩儿
popular songs	**liéu-h'in-gu-chüeq** 流行歌曲
puppet show	**moq-ngeu-shi** 木偶戏
Shanghai opera	**h'ú-j'iq** 沪剧
sing (a song)	**tsā́w•gù** 唱歌
sing in a chorus	**h'eq-tsāw** 合唱
sold out	**kāq-moe** 客满
stage	**shí-d'ae** 戏台
stilt walking	**d'aq•gàw-chiaw** 踩高跷
storytelling (*traditional*)	**sēq•sï̀** 说书
theater	**j'iq-zā̃** 剧场
ticket	**piáw / piàw-dzï̀** 票
ticket kiosk	**má-piaw-d'in** 买票亭
ticket seller	**zéu-piaw-'yüoe / má-piaw-'yüoe** 售票员
window shopping	**d'ā́w•mó-lu** 逛街

Sights in Shanghai

Well-Known Sights

banks of the Huángpǔ River **H'uǎw-pu-gang liǎ-ngoe** 黄浦江两岸

the Bund **Ngá-tae** 外滩

Century Boulevard **sì-ji-d'a-d'aw** 世纪大道

Dàshìjiè (Great World Amusement Center) **D'á-sï-ga** 大世界

Huáihái Road **H'uá-hae-lu** 淮海路

Nánjīng Road **Nóe-jin-lu** 南京路

People's Square **Zén-min-guǎw-zǎ** 人民广场

Pǔdōng **Pú-dong** 浦东

Shanghai EXPO **Zǎw-hae sì-boq-h'uae** 上海世博会

Shanghai Old Street **Zǎw-hae láw-ga** 上海老街

Site of the First Conference of the CCP **Yīq-d'a h'uáe-dzï** 一大会址

Sūzhōu Creek **Sù-dzeu-h'u** 苏州河

Xīntiāndì (Leisure Street) **Shìn-ti-d'i** 新天地

Yùyuán Garden **'Yǔ-'yüoe** 豫园

Famous Buildings

Global Architectural Complex **Váe-goq jí-dzoq bōq-lae-j'ün** 万国建筑博览群

Jīnmào Mansion **Jìn-maw d'á-sa** 金茂大厦

Peace Hotel **H'ú-b'in-vae-di** 和平饭店

Pearl of the Orient Tower **Dòng-fǎw mín-dzï-taq** 东方明珠塔

Churches and Temples

Catholic Church in Xújiāhuì **Zyí-ga-h'uae Tì-zï-jiaw-d'ǎw** 徐家汇天主教堂

Jade Buddha Temple **Nioq-veq-zï** 玉佛寺

Jìng'ān Temple **Zyín-oe-zï** 静安寺

Lónghuá Temple **Lóng-h'uo-zï** 龙华寺

Temple of the City God **Zén-h'uǎw-miaw** 城隍庙

Parks and Outdoor Spots

Century Park	**Sǐ-ji-gong-'yüoe** 世纪公园
Chángfēng Park	**Zǎ-fong-gong-'yüoe** 长风公园
Gòngqīng Forest Park	**G'óng-chin sèn-lin-gong-'yüoe** 共青森林公园
Yán'ān Road Greenery	**'Yí-dzong loq-d'i** 延中绿地
Yángchéng Lake	**'Yǎ-zǎ-h'u** 阳澄湖

Other Places of Interest

Hóngkǒu Football (Soccer) Stadium
H'óng-keu dzōq-j'ieu-zǎ 虹口足球场

Shanghai Grand Theater
Zǎw-hae d'á-j'iq-'yüoe 上海大剧院

Shanghai History Museum
Zǎw-hae liq-sï zén-liq-guoe 上海历史陈列馆

Shanghai Museum
Zǎw-hae bōq-veq-guóe 上海博物馆

Shanghai Museum of Science and Technology
Zǎw-hae kù-j'i-guoe 上海科技馆

Shanghai Stadium
Zǎw-hae tí-'yüeq-zǎ 上海体育场

Shanghai Zoo
Zǎw-hae d'óng-veq-'yüoe 上海动物园

Places Near Shanghai

Gǔyīyuán in Nánxiáng
Nóe-zyiǎ-h'eq Gú-j'i-'yüoe 南翔的古猗园

Qiūxiá Garden in Jiādìng
Gà-d'in-h'eq Chièu-ya-pu 嘉定的秋霞圃

Qǔshuǐyuán in Qīngpǔ
Chìn-pu-h'eq Chüěq-sï-'yüoe 青浦的曲水园

Shéshān Scenic Area
Zuó-sae fòng-jin-chü 佘山风景区

Zhōuzhuāng Village
Dzèu-dzǎ 周庄

Zhūjiājiǎo Village
Dzǐ-ga-goq 朱家角

Zuìbáichí in Sōngjiāng
Sòng-gãw-h'eq Dzóe-b'aq-zï 松江的醉白池

Note ...

Buses and day tours to the above places, as well as many other interesting destinations, leave from:

Zãw-hae lí-'yéu zyiq-sae dzòng-shin
上海旅游集散中心
Shànghǎi Touring Center

which is near

Zãw-hae tí-'yüeq-zã 上海体育场
Shànghǎi Stadium

Most of these places are representative of what are fondly referred to as:

Gãw-noe sí-shiã mín-'yüoe 江南水乡名园
Famous Watertowns of the Southern Yangtze Valley

SPORTS & GAMES

What sports do you like?
Nóng huòe-shi sá-g'eq 'yǔn-d'ong?
你喜欢什么运动?

I like to *watch/play*...
Ngú huòe-shi *kòe/dǎ*... 你喜欢看/打...

badminton	**'yǔ-maw-j'ieu**	羽毛球
baseball	**b'ǎw-j'ieu**	棒球
basketball	**láe-j'ieu**	篮球
bowling	**báw-lin-j'ieu**	保龄球
golf	**gàw-'er-fu-j'ieu**	高尔夫球
ping-pong	**pìn-pǎ(-j'ieu)**	乒乓球
tai chi	**tá-j'iq-j'üoe**	太极拳
volleyball	**b'á-j'ieu**	排球

I like to play soccer.
Ngú huòe-shi tǐq dzōq-j'ieu. 你喜欢踢足球

Go! Do your best! (*lit.* "add gas")
Gà•'yéu! 加油

Did you watch the competition yesterday?
Zoq-niq-h'eq bí-sae kóe leq va?
你看了昨天的比赛吗?

I didn't watch it.
Ḿ-meq kóe. 没有看。

What competition?
Sá-h'eq bí-sae? 什么比赛?

Who played whom?
Sá-nin tēq sá-nin bí-sae? 谁跟谁比赛?

Was it exciting?
Jín-dzǎ va? 紧张吗?

Which team won?
H'á-li-g'eq d'áe 'yín leq? 哪个队赢了?

Which team lost?
H'á-li-g'eq d'áe sǐ leq? 那个队输了?

The Brazilian team won.
Bò-shi-d'ae 'yín leq. 巴西队赢了。

The French team lost.
Fāq-goq-d'áe sǐ leq. 法国队输了。

Sports Terms

athletic field	**'yǔn-d'ong-zǎ / 'yóng-d'ong-zǎ** 运动场
badminton / shuttlecock	**'yǔ-maw-j'ieu** 羽毛球
ball field/court	**j'iéu-zǎ** 球场
ball game	**j'iéu-sae** 球赛
ball team	**j'iéu-d'ae** 球队
baseball	**b'ǎw-j'ieu** 棒球
basketball	**láe-j'ieu** 篮球
bathing area / swimming beach	**'yoq-zǎ** 浴场
bowling	**báw-lin-j'ieu** 保龄球
boxing	**b'oq-keq-shiong** 拳击
bunjee jumping	**bèn•j'iq** 蹦极
Chinese *kungfu*	**Dzòng-goq gòng-fu** 中国功夫
competition	**bí-sae** 比赛
exercise	**dóe-li sèn-ti** 锻炼身体
golf	**gàw-'er-fu-j'ieu** 高尔夫球
gym	**tí-'yüeq-zǎ / tí-'yoq-zǎ** 体育场
gymnastics	**tí-tsaw** 体操
kick a shuttlecock	**tīq•jí-dzï** 踢毽子
lose	**sǐ** 输
physical education / sports	**tí-'yüeq / tí-'yoq** 体育
ping-pong / ping-pong ball	**pìn-pǎ-j'ieu** 乒乓球
play ball	**dǎ•j'iéu** 打球
play ping-pong	**dǎ•pìn-pǎ** 打乒乓
race (running)	**sáe-b'aw** 赛跑
soccer / soccer ball	**dzōq-j'ieu** 足球
somersault	**fàe•kèn-deu** 翻跟斗
sports / athletics	**'yǔn-d'ong** 运动
swim	**'yéu-'yong / 'yéu•sï** 游泳
swimming pool	**'yéu-'yong-zǐ** 游泳池
tai chi	**tá-j'iq-j'üoe** 太极拳

take a sauna bath	**d'á sà-na** 洗桑拿
take a walk	**sáe-b'u** 散步
team	**d'áe** 队
track and field	**d'í-jin** 田径
volleyball	**b'á-j'ieu** 排球
win	**'yín** 赢

Games

What card game would you like to play?
Nóng shiǎ dǎ sá-g'eq b'á? 你想打什么牌？

I don't like to play cards.
Ngú veq huòe-shi dǎ•b'á. 我不喜欢打牌。

I like to play chess.
Ngú huòe-shi dzāq•j'í. 我喜欢下棋.

Do you know how to play mahjongg?
Nóng h'uáe tsuò•mó-jiā va? 你会打麻将吗？

I don't know how to play (mahjongg).
Ngú veq h'uae tsò. 我不会打。

How do you play it?
Ná-nen dǎ? 怎么打？

Will you teach me?
Nóng jiáw ngú háw va? 你教我好吗？

play chess	**dzāq•j'í** 下棋
chess (Chinese-style)	**zyiǎ-j'í** 象棋
mahjongg	**mó-jiā** 麻将
mahjongg tile	**mó-jiā-b'a** 麻将牌
play mahjongg	**dǎ•mó-jiā / tsuò•mó-jiā(-b'a)** 打麻将
play cards	**dǎ•b'á / déu•b'á** 打牌
play poker	**dǎ•pōq-keq** 打扑克
poker cards	**pōq-keq-b'a** 扑克牌
play bridge	**dǎ•j'iáw-b'a** 打桥牌
play video games	**dǎ•'yéu-shi-ji** 打游戏机

FAMILY & KINSHIP

child	nóe / shiáw-noe / shiáw-nin 小孩
children	dzí-nü 子女
elder generation	dzǎ-bae 长辈
family	gà 家
family members	jià-zoq 家属
husband and wife	fù-chi 夫妻
in-laws (*husband's parents*)	gòng-b'u 公婆
infant	yìn-'er / shiáw-shiaw-noe shiáw-maw-d'eu 婴儿
parents	'yá-niã 父母
relatives	chìn-jüoe 亲戚
relatives by marriage	chìn-ga 亲家
younger generation	shiáw-bae 晚辈
brother (*elder*)	gù-gu / āq-gu 哥哥
brother (*younger*)	d'í-d'i / āq-d'i 弟弟
brothers (*elder and younger*)	shiòng-d'i 兄弟
cousins (*female / with a different surname*)	biáw-ji-mae 表姐妹
cousins (*male / with a different surname*)	biáw-shiong-d'i 表兄弟
cousins (*male / with the same surname*)	d'ǎw-shiong-d'i 堂兄弟
daughter	nǚ-er / nǚ-shiaw-noe / nóe-ñg 女儿
daughter-in-law	shìn-vu 媳妇
father	bà-ba / dià-dia / láw-ba 爸爸

Note...

The Shanghainese have a complex set of vocabulary for relatives that makes fine distinctions regarding relationships—distant as well as close. Here we only list the words for the more immediate family members. For aunts, uncles, specific cousins, and in-laws, consult the relevant English term in the dictionary section.

father-in-law (*husband's father*)	**gòng-gong / āq-gong** 公公
father-in-law (*wife's father*)	**ngoq-vu / zǎ-nin** 岳父
granddaughter (*daughter's daughter*)	**ngá-sã-noe** 外孙女
granddaughter (*son's daughter*)	**sèn-nü / sèn-noe(-ñg)** 孙女
grandfather (*maternal*)	**ngá-dzu-vu / ngá-gong** 外祖父
grandfather (*paternal*)	**dzú-vu / 'yá-'ya / láw-dia** 祖父
grandmother (*maternal*)	**ngá-dzu-mu / ngá-b'u** 外祖母
grandmother (*paternal*)	**dzú-mu / ñg̀-na / āq-na** 祖母
grandson (*daughter's son*)	**ngá-sã** 外孙
grandson (*son's son*)	**sèn-dzï** 孙子
husband	**zǎ-fu / láw-gong** 丈夫
mother	**mì-ma / mà-ma / láw-ma** 妈妈
mother-in-law (*husband's mother*)	**b'ú-b'u / āq-b'u** 婆婆
mother-in-law (*wife's mother*)	**ngoq-mu / zǎ-m̃(-niã)** 岳母
nephew (*brother's son*)	**zeq-dzï / āq-zeq** 侄子
nephew (*sister's son*)	**ngá-sã** 外甥
niece (*brother's daughter*)	**zeq-noe(-ñg)** 侄女
niece (*sister's daughter*)	**ngá-sã-noe** 外甥女
sister (*elder*)	**jiá-jia / āq-jia / āq-ji** 姐姐
sister (*younger*)	**máe-mae / āq-mae** 妹妹
sisters (*elder and younger*)	**jí-mae** 姐妹
son	**ní-dzï / 'ér-dzï / nóe-shiaw-noe** 儿子
son-in-law	**nǔ-shi / nǔ-shü** 女婿
wife	**chì-dzï / tà-ta / láw-b'u** 妻子 / 太太
wife (*polite*)	**fù-nin** 夫人

RELIGION

I believe in …
Ngú jìn … 我信…

Buddhism	**veq-jiaw**	佛教
Catholicism	**tì-dzï-jiaw**	天主教
Daoism	**d'áw-jiaw**	道教
Islamism	**h'uáe-jiaw**	回教
Judaism	**'yéu-ta-jiaw**	犹太教
Protestantism	**jì-doq-jiaw**	基督教

attend church	**dzú•lí-ba**	做礼拜
Buddha	**zḯ-lae-veq / veq**	如来佛
worship Buddha	**bá•veq**	拜佛
Buddhist monk	**h'ú-zãw**	和尚
Buddhist nun	**ní-gu**	尼姑
Buddhist nunnery	**ní-gu-oe / òe-d'ãw**	尼姑庵
candle	**dzõq**	烛
candlestick	**dzõq-d'ae**	烛台
chant scriptures	**ní•jìn**	念经
(*Buddhist*)		
Christ	**jì-doq**	基督
Christianity /	**jì-doq-jiaw**	基督教
Protestantism		
church / cathedral	**jiáw-d'ãw / lí-ba-d'ãw**	教堂
convent	**shièu-d'aw-'yüoe**	修道院
Daoist	**d'áw-zï**	道士
divination	**dzóe-boq**	占卜
door-god	**mén-zen(-b'u-saq)**	门神
follower of a religion	**jìn-jiaw-dzae**	教徒
fortune-teller	**sóe-min-shi-sã**	算命先生
geomancy practitioner /	**fòng-sï-shi-sã**	风水先生
feng-shui artist		
practice *feng-shui*	**kóe•fòng-sï**	看风水
ghost	**jǘ / guáe**	鬼
God (*Catholic*)	**tì-dzï**	天主
God (*Protestant*)	**zã́w-di**	上帝
god of wealth	**záe-zen(-b'u-saq)**	财神
Guanyin (a Bodhisattva)	**guòe-yin-b'u-saq**	观音菩萨
idol	**zén-zyiã**	神像
incense	**shiã̀**	香

incense burner	**shiǎ-lu** 香炉
incense sticks	**b'ǎw-shiā** 棒香
Jesus	**yà-su** 耶稣
kowtow	**kēq•d'éu** 磕头
monastery	**shièu-d'aw-'yüoe** 修道院
mosque	**jiáw-d'āw / lí-ba-d'āw** 教堂
priest (*Catholic*)	**zén-vu** 神父
profess a religion	**jìn-jiaw** 信教
reincarnate	**d'éu-tae** 投胎
stove-god	**dzáw-ga-b'u-saq** 灶家菩萨
tell one's fortune	**sóe-min** 算命
temple	**miáw** 庙; **jiáw-d'āw / lí-ba-d'āw** 教堂
temple fair	**miáw-h'uae** 庙会
vegetarian	**chīq-su-nin** 吃素的人
eat only vegetarian food	**chīq•sú** 吃素
Yama / King of Hell	**ní-(lu-)'wāw** 阎王

OCCASIONS

Birth

Congratulations!　**Gòng-shi!** 恭喜！

Health to mother and child!　**Mú-dzǐ-b'in-oe!** 母子平安！

bear a child	**'yǎ•shiáw-noe** 生小孩
breastfeed / nurse	**yǔ•ná** 喂奶
celebrate one's birthday	**dzú•sǎ-niq** 庆祝生日
cut the umbilical cord	**dzāq•zyí-da** 绞脐带
deliver a child	**jīq-sā** 接生
get a vasectomy or a tubal ligation	**jīq-dzaq** 结扎
give birth	**'yǎ** 生
induce abortion	**dǎ•táe** 打胎
one month old (*of babies*)	**móe-'yüeq / móe-'yoq** 满月
pregnant	**h'uá••'yǔn / h'uá•yóng / d'ú-d'u-b'i / 'yéu-shi** 怀孕
pregnant woman / expectant mother	**'yǔn-vu / yóng-vu / tsáe-vu** 孕妇 / 产妇
premature birth	**dzáw-tsae** 早产
twins	**sǎ-baw-tae** 双胞胎
umbilical cord	**zyí-da** 脐带
wean	**d'óe•ná / gāq•ná** 断奶

Weddings

Congratulations on your wedding!
Gòng-h'u-shin-shi! 恭贺欣喜！

Good wishes to you!
Dzōq-h'u ná! 祝贺你们！

attend a wedding banquet	**chīq•shí-jieu** 吃喜酒
become a daughter-in-law	**dzú•shìn-vu** 做媳妇
best man	**nóe-bin-shiā** 男傧相
bridesmaid	**nǔ-bin-shiā** 女傧相
betrothal gifts	**záe-li** 财礼
betrothed / engaged	**dín•huèn / páe-chin** 订婚
bride	**shìn-niā(-dzǐ)** 新娘
cohabit	**d'óng-jü** 同居

court / woo	**d'áe•lí-ae** 谈恋爱	
divorce	**lí-huen** 离婚	
dowry	**gá-dzãw / b'áe-ga** 嫁妆	
groom	**shìn-lãw / shìn-lãw-guoe** 新郎	
have an extramarital affair	**g'áq•pìn-d'eu** 轧姘头	
Internet/cyber marriage	**mǎw-huen** 网婚	
kiss	**dǎ•kàe-sï / shiǎ•mí-kong / shiǎ•dzǐ-bo** 接吻	
make love / have sexual intercourse	**tsú•áe** 做爱	
marriage	**huèn-yin** 婚姻	
marry (*of a man*)	**táw•láw-b'u / táw•shìn-h'u** 讨老婆	
marry (*of a woman*)	**gá•nóe-nin / tsēq•gá** 嫁男人 / 出嫁	
marry / get married (*of both bride and groom*)	**jīq-huen** 结婚	
matchmaker	**máe-nin / jiá-zaw-nin** 媒人 / 介绍人	
nuptial chamber	**d'óng-vã / shìn-vã** 洞房	
remarry (*of a widower*)	**zoq-h'i** 续弦	
seek a marriage partner	**zyín•dáe-zyiã / dzáw•dáe-zyiã** 找对象	
trial marriage	**sǐ-huen** 试婚	

Death and Funerals

ancestral hall	**zǐ-d'ãw** 祠堂	
ashes of the dead	**guēq-huae** 骨灰	
bury (the dead)	**òe-dzãw / loq•dzãw** 安葬	
coffin	**guòe-zae** 棺材	
Condolences.	**Jīq-ae-zen-bi.** 节哀顺变。	
be dead *v.*	**ḿ-meq-leq / gú-leq** 死了	
die	**shí** 死	
family tree / genealogy	**jià-pu** 家谱	
funeral / burial ceremony	**tsēq•bìn / tsēq•sǎw** 出殡	
funeral home	**bìn-ni-guoe** 殡仪馆	
grave	**vén / vén-mo / vén-mu** 坟 / 坟墓	
visit a grave	**zǎw•vén** 上坟扫墓	

MEDICINE & MEDICAL HELP

The Body

Body Parts

abdomen	**d'ú-b'i** 肚子 / 腹部
ankle / anklebone	**jiāq-ku-gueq** 踝骨
arm	**bí-bo / séu-bi-bo** 胳膊 / 手臂
armpit	**gēq-dzï-wu / gēq-leq-dzoq** 腋窝
backbone / spine	**báe-jiq-gueq / jīq-dzoe-gueq** 背脊骨 / 脊椎骨
beard / whiskers / moustache	**h'ú-su / ngá-su / h'ú-dzï** 胡须
belly / abdomen	**d'ú-b'i** 肚子 / 腹部
bladder	**b'ǎ̈w-guāw / sï̀-paw** 膀胱
blood	**shüēq / shiōq** 血
blood vessel	**shüēq-guoe / shiōq-guoe** 血管
body / health	**sèn-ti** 身体
body hair (*on people*)	**h'óe-maw** 汗毛
bone	**guēq-d'eu** 骨头
brains / mind	**náw-dzï / náw-jin / d'éu-naw-dzï** 脑子
breast (*of a woman*)	**ná / ná-na** 乳房
buttocks / rump	**pì-gu** 屁股
chest	**shiòng / shiòng-pu** 胸
chin	**h'uó-b'oq / h'uó-b'o** 下巴
ear	**ní-du / 'ér-du** 耳朵
elbow	**bí-tsã-dzï** 臂肘
eye	**ngáe-jin** 眼睛
eyebrows	**mí-maw** 眉毛
eyelash	**ngáe-ji-maw** 睫毛
eyelid	**ngáe-b'i** 眼皮
face	**mí-kong** 脸
figure / physical stature	**d'iáw-goe** 身材
finger	**séu-jiq-d'eu / séu-dzï-d'eu** 手指头
forefinger / index finger	**zeq-dzï** 食指
little finger	**shiáw-jiq-d'eu** 小手指
middle finger	**dzòng-dzï** 中指
ring/third finger	**'wú-min-dzï** 无名指
fingernail	**séu-jiq-kaq / séu-dzï-kaq** 手指甲

fingerprint	**lú / vén-lu**	指纹
foot (*sometimes including the leg*)	**jiāq**	脚
forehead	**ngaq-goq-d'eu**	额头
gums	**ngá-nin / ngá-nioq**	牙龈
hair (*on the head*)	**d'éu-faq**	头发
hand	**séu**	手
handprint / lines on the palm	**séu-ven**	手纹
head	**d'éu**	头
head / brains	**náw-d'ae**	脑袋
heart	**shìn / shìn-zā**	心脏
heel	**jiāq-h'eu-gen**	脚跟
intestines	**d'ú-zā**	肠子
joint (*in limbs and fingers*)	**guàe-jiq / g'aq-jiq(-gueq-loq)**	关节
kidney	**yàw-dzǐ**	肾
knee	**jiāq-moe-deu**	膝盖
left hand	**dzú-seu / jí-seu**	左手
leg	**jiāq-pāw**	腿
lips	**dzǐ-zen(-b'i)**	嘴唇
liver	**gòe**	肝
lungs	**fí**	肺
mouth	**dzǐ / dzǐ-bo**	嘴
muscle	**jì-nioq**	肌肉
navel / belly button	**d'ú-b'i-ngae / d'ú-zyi**	肚脐
neck	**d'éu-jin**	脖子
nipple	**ná-na-d'eu / ná-d'eu**	乳头
nose	**b'iq-d'eu / b'eq-d'eu**	鼻子
nostril	**b'eq-d'eu-kong / b'iq-kong**	鼻孔
organs / viscera	**náe-zā**	内脏
palm of hand	**séu-dzāw**	手掌
rib	**leq-b'ā-gueq**	肋骨
right hand	**'yéu-seu**	右手
shoulder	**jì-bāw / jì-gaq**	肩膀
skin	**b'í**	皮
skull	**d'éu-naw-koq**	脑壳
sole of the foot	**jiāq-dzāw / jiāq-di(-bae)**	脚掌
spine	**báe-jiq-gueq / jīq-dzoe-gueq**	背脊骨 / 脊椎骨
stomach	**'wáe**	胃

teeth	**ngá-tsï / ngá-dzï** 牙齿
thigh	**d'ú-jiaq-pãw / d'ú-pãw** 大腿
throat	**h'ú-long / h'éu-long** 喉咙
thumb	**d'ú-m̌-dzï / d'á-mu-dzï** 大拇指
toe	**jiāq-jiq-d'eu / jiāq-dzï-d'eu** 脚趾
tongue	**zeq-d'eu** 舌头
waist	**yàw** 腰
wrist	**séu-wae** 手腕

Body Functions

burp *n.*	**g'áe** 嗝儿
burp *v.*	**dǎ g'áe** 打嗝儿
empty stomach *n.*	**kòng-shin-d'u-li** 空肚 / 空腹
fingerprint (*on a surface*)	**jīq-d'eu-yin** 指印
grime (*on skin*)	**kén / láw-ken** 积垢
menstrual period	**'yüeq-jin / 'yoq-jin** 月经
saliva	**záe-tu(-sï)** 口水
sweat	**h'óe** 汗
tears	**ngáe-li(-sï)** 眼泪
urine	**sï̀** 尿水
yawn *n.*	**huò-shi** 哈欠
yawn *v.*	**dǎ•huò-shi** 打哈欠

Discomfort and Illness

I am not comfortable.
Ngú veq-seq-yi. 我不舒服。

I am … **Ngú … leq.** 我…了。

cold	**lǎ** 冷
hot	**niq** 热
hungry	**ngú** 饿
thirsty	**dzǐ•gòe** 口渴

I am rather tired.
Ngú màe chīq-liq leq. 我很累了。

I want to sleep.
Ngú shiǎ kuén leq. 我想睡了。

I am not feeling too well.
Ngú gōq-zaq veq-d'a sēq-yi. 我觉得不大舒服。

I want to see a doctor.
Ngú shiǎ chí kòe yì-sā. 我想去看医生。

I want to go to the hospital.
Ngú yáw dáw yì-'yüoe chí. 我要到医院去。

I have … **Ngú …** 我…

a headache	**d'éu tóng** 头痛	
a bit of a fever	**'yéu di h'óe-niq** 有点发烧	
a high fever	**fāq•gàw-saw** 发高烧	
no energy at all	**h'uén-sen ḿ-meq liq-chi** 浑身没有力气	
diarrhea	**d'ú-b'i-za** 拉肚子	

My stomach also aches.
Ngú d'ú-b'i 'yá tóng. 我肚子也痛。

I can't eat much.
Ngú váe chīq veq-d'a loq. 我不太吃得下饭。

I am a little nauseous.
Ngú 'yéu ngáe ōq-shin. 我有点恶心。

I feel like throwing up.
Ngú shiǎ tú. 我想吐。

I sometimes feel dizzy.
Ngú 'yéu zén-guāw gōq-zaq d'éu huèn.
我有时觉得头晕。

I'm much better now.
Ngú háw jiàw-guae leq. 我好多了。

Medical Problems and Illnesses

acne	**chìn-tsen-lae** 青春痘	
athlete's foot	**jiāq-shi / jiāq-chi /**	
	shiǎ-gāw-jiaq 脚癣	
belly ache	**d'ú-b'i•tóng / d'ú-li•tóng**	
	肚子疼	

You may hear . . .

from the doctor or nurse:

Nóng 'yéu-sa veq-seq-yi? 你有什么不舒服?
What discomfort are you having?

Ná-nen veq-seq-yi? 怎么样不舒服?
What's wrong?

G'eq-daq tóng va? 这儿痛吗?
Does it hurt here?

Tóng-leq jí-niq-leq? 痛了几天了?
How many days have you had the pain?

Fāq h'óe-niq va? 发烧吗?
Do you have a fever?

Jí-d'u-a? 几度啊?
How many degrees?

Kēq-seu va? 咳嗽吗?
Do you have a cough?

'Wáe-keu ná-nen? 胃口怎么样?
How's your appetite?

Shiǎ veq shiǎ tú? 想不想吐?
Do you feel like throwing up?

Niǎ ngú tìn-tin shìn-zã. 让我听听心脏。
Let me listen to your heart.

G'eq-ngae 'yaq yīq-niq chīq•sàe-tsï.
这点药一天吃三次。
Take this medicine three times a day.

blind	**hāq-ngae**	瞎眼
bruise	**wù-chin-kuae**	血晕
cancer	**ngáe**	癌
catch a cold	**sǎ•fòng**	感冒
chapped	**tsèn**	皴
chill / shiver	**h'óe-j'in**	寒噤
cough	**kēq-seu**	咳嗽
deaf	**lóng-b'ã**	耳聋
diarrhea	**d'ú-li-za / d'ú-b'i-za**	泻肚子
dizzy	**d'éu•huèn**	头晕
dysentery	**lí-zyiq**	痢疾
feeling ill / not well	**veq-seq-yi**	不舒服
flu	**liéu-h'in-shin góe-maw** 流行性感冒	
get cramps / pull a tendon	**tsèu•jin**	抽筋
get sick / fall ill	**sǎ•máw-b'in / sǎ•b'ín**	生病
have a fever	**fāq•h'óe-niq / fāq•niq**	发烧
have a headache	**d'éu•tóng**	头痛
have a high fever	**fāq•gàw-saw**	发高烧
have a runny nose	**liéu•b'iq-ti**	流鼻涕
have a stroke	**dzóng•fòng**	中风
have indigestion	**jīq•zeq / dén•zeq**	积食
have high blood pressure	**shüēq-aq gàw / shiōq-aq gàw** 高血压	
have the chills	**fāq•j'ín**	发寒颤
heart disease	**shìn-zǎ-b'in**	心脏病
high blood pressure	**gàw-shüeq-aq / gàw-shioq-aq** 高血压	
hunched back	**d'ú-bae / hèu-bae**	驼背
illness / disease	**b'ín / máw-b'in**	病
infect / spread (*of disease*)	**zóe-zoe**	传染
lame	**chiàw-jiaq**	跛足 / 瘸
mental disorder	**zén-jin-b'in**	神经病
mute / dumb person	**wó-dzï**	哑巴
nauseated	**dǎ•ōq-shin**	恶心
paralysis	**tàe-huoe / fòng-tae**	瘫痪
paranoia	**ní-shin-b'in**	疑心病
patient / invalid	**sǎ-b'in-nin**	病人
phlegm	**d'áe**	痰
prickly heat / heat rash	**b'áe-dzï**	痱子
scab	**yì**	疮痂
scar	**bò**	疤

sneeze	**pèn-ti** 喷嚏
stomachache	**'wáe-(chi-)tong** 胃痛
strain or injure one's back	**b'iq•yàw / sén•yàw** 闪腰 / 伤腰
stuffed nose	**óng-b'iq-d'eu / óng-b'eq-d'eu** 齆鼻
suffer from poor digestion	**veq-shiaw-huo** 消化不良
suffer heatstroke or sunstroke	**dzòng•sï / fāq•suò** 中暑
swelling / lump	**kuáe / gēq-daq** 疙瘩
toothache	**ngá-tsï•tóng** 牙疼
tumor	**dzóng-lieu** 肿瘤
upset one's stomach	**fáe•'wáe** 反胃

First Aid and Medicine

acupuncture and moxibustion	**dzèn-jieu** 针灸
apply a medicated bandage	**tĩq•gàw-'yaq / tĩq•'yaq-gaw** 贴膏药
apply ointment	**tãq•'yaq-gaw** 抹药
aspirin	**à-sï-pi-lin** 阿斯匹林
bandage	**bãw-da** 绑带
cure	**yì•máw-b'in** 治病
emergency room	**jĩq-dzen** 急诊
get an intravenous drip	**diáw•'yí-sï** 输液
get or give acupuncture	**dã•jìn-dzen** 行针灸
get or give an injection	**dã•dzèn** 打针
injection / syringe	**dzèn-d'eu** 针
liquid medicine	**'yaq-sï** 药水
massage	**òe-mo** 按摩
medicated bandage	**gàw-'yaq** 膏药
medicinal powder	**'yaq-fen** 药粉
medicinal tablet	**'yaq-pi** 药片
medicine	**'yaq** 药
medicine chest	**'yaq-shiã** 药箱
mercurochrome	**h'óng-'yaq-sï** 红药水
ointment / salve	**'yaq-gaw** 药膏
operate / perform surgery / get an operation	**kàe•dàw / d'óng•séu-zeq** 开刀 / 动手术
outpatient office	**mén-dzen** 门诊

pill	**'wóe-'yaq** 药丸
prescription	**fâw-dzï** 药方
see a doctor	**kóe•máw-b'in / kóe-yi-sã** 看病
take the pulse	**bó•maq / dāq•maq** 把脉
Vaseline	**váe-zï-lin** 凡士林
vitamin	**ví-ta-min** 维生素 / 维他命
write out a prescription	**kàe•'yaq-fâw / kàe•fâw-dzï** 开药方

SCHOOL & OFFICE

School and Education

auditorium	**lí-d'āw** 礼堂
blackboard	**hēq-bae** 黑板
blackboard eraser	**hēq-bae-ka** 黑板擦
class handouts	**gǎw-ni** 讲义
classmate	**d'óng-h'oq** 同学
classroom	**jiáw-seq / kú-d'ãw(-gae)** 教室
college / university	**d'á-h'oq** 大学
course / curriculum	**kú-zen** 课程
dictation	**tìn-shia** 听写
diploma	**vén-b'in** 文凭
do homework	**dzú-gong-ku** 做作业
elementary school	**shiáw-h'oq** 小学
erase the blackboard	**kà-heq-bae** 擦黑板
examination paper	**káw-jüoe** 考卷
get out of class / finish class	**h'uó•kú** 下课
go to class / attend class	**zǎw•kú** 上课
grade	**fèn-su** 分数
graduate	**bīq-niq** 毕业
kindergarten	**yéu-'er-'yüoe / yéu-zï-'yüoe** 幼儿园
law	**liq-faq** 法律
literate	**sēq•zï̀** 识字
middle school	**dzòng-h'oq** 中学
night school	**'yá-h'iaw** 夜校
nursery / child-care center	**tōq-'er-su** 托儿所
office	**báe-gong-seq** 办公室
podium	**gǎw-d'ae** 讲台
principal / president (*of a school*)	**h'iáw-dzã** 校长
quiz / test	**tsēq-ni** 测验
quota (*of people*)	**ngaq-dzï** 名额
read (a book) / study	**kòe•sï̀** 看书
read / study	**d'oq** 读
report card	**zén-jiq-dae** 成绩单
request leave	**chín•gá** 请假
research / study in depth	**nì-jieu** 研究

review	fōq-zyiq 复习
school	h'oq-d'ãw 学校
sick leave	b'ín-ga 病假
sign up	báw•mín 报名
skip class	chiáw•kú 逃课
start school / begin a school term	kàe•h'oq 开学
student	h'oq-sã 学生
studious	'yóng-gong 用功
study / attend school	d'oq•sǐ 读书
summer vacation	sǐ-ga / sǐ-jia 暑假
tardy / late to arrive	zǐ-daw 迟到
teacher	làw-sï / láw-sï 老师
test / examination	káw-sï 考试
textbook	kú-ben 课本
(be on) vacation	fãw•gá / fãw•jiá 放假
winter vacation	h'óe-ga / h'óe-jia 寒假
write	shiá 写
write (*characters/words*)	shiá•zǐ 写字

Educational and Office Tools

abacus	sóe-b'oe 算盘
book	sǐ 书
book bag / satchel	sǐ-baw 书包
bookmark	sǐ-chi 书签
card	ká-pi 卡片
card / notepaper / small notebook	tīq-dzǐ 帖子
chalk (*for writing*)	fén-biq 粉笔
charge, recharge (*a battery*)	tsòng-di 充电
clause (*as in a contract*)	d'iáw-ven 条文
compass (*for math and drafting*)	'yúoe-guae 圆规
computer	d'í-naw 电脑
correction fluid	shièu-dzen-'yiq 修正液
crayon	laq-biq 蜡笔
eraser	zyiǎ-b'i 橡皮
exercise book	lí-zyiq-b'u 练习本
glue	gàw-sï 胶水

grind ink	**mó-meq / mú-meq / ní•meq** 磨墨 / 研磨
ink	**meq-sï** 墨水
inkstick	**meq** 墨
inkstone	**ní-d'ae** 砚台
marker	**mó-keq-biq** 马克笔
memory (*in a computer*)	**náe-zen** 内存
name card	**mín-pi** 名片
news	**shìn-ven** 新闻
newspaper	**báw-dzï** 报纸
note	**b'í-d'iaw** 便条
notebook	**b'ú-dzï / bïq-ji-b'u** 本子 / 笔记本
notebook computer	**bén-ben** 笔记本电脑
notes	**bïq-ji** 笔记
paper	**dzï-d'eu** 纸
paperclip	**h'uáe-h'in-b'iq-dzen** 回形针
paperweight	**dzén-dzï** 镇纸
paste	**jiǎ-h'u** 浆糊
pen / fountain pen	**gǎw-biq** 钢笔
pen / pencil / writing brush	**bïq** 笔
pen container	**bïq-d'ong** 笔筒
pencil	**kàe-biq** 铅笔
printer (*for a computer*)	**dǎ-yin-ji** 打印机
seal / stamp	**d'ú-dzǎ** 图章
simplified characters	**jí-ti-zï / shiáw-shia-zï** 简体字
staple	**dín-sï-din** 钉书钉
stapler	**dín-sï-ji** 钉书机
strokes of Chinese characters	**bïq-h'uaq** 笔画
thumbtack	**d'ú-din / chín-din** 图钉
traditional characters (*non-simplified*)	**váe-ti-zï / d'ú-shia-zï** 繁体字
USB drive	**ièu-b'oe** U 盘
wax paper	**laq-dzï** 蜡纸
writing brush	**máw-biq / meq-biq** 毛笔

TOOLS

awl	**dzì-dzoe** 锥子
axe	**fú-deu** 斧头
carpenter's plane / grater	**b'áw** 刨
chisel	**zoq-d'eu / zoq-dzï** 凿子
drill	**dzòe-dzï** 钻
file	**tsú-daw** 锉刀
hammer	**lǎw-d'eu** 锤子
jack	**chì-jin-din / āq-veq-saq** 千斤顶
mold / die	**mó-dzï** 模子
motor	**mó-d'a** 马达
nail	**dìn / 'yǎ-din** 钉子
pliers / tongs	**láw-hu-j'i** 钳子
saw	**gáe-dzï / g'á-dzï** 锯子
screwdriver	**nì-zoq** 螺丝刀
wrench / spanner	**bàe-d'eu / bàe-seu** 扳手

WILDLIFE

Animals

bat	**bì-foq**	蝙蝠
bear	**h'ióng**	熊
beast	**tsōq-sã**	畜生
bull	**h'ióng-nieu**	公牛
cat	**máw / máw-mi**	猫
cow	**tsî-nieu**	母牛
dog	**géu**	狗
elephant	**zyiã́**	象
fox	**h'ú-li**	狐狸
goat	**sàe-'yã**	山羊
horse	**mó**	马
lion	**sî-dzï**	狮子
monkey	**h'ueq-sen**	猴子
mouse / rat	**láw-zong / láw-tsï**	老鼠
ox / cow / bull	**niéu**	牛
panda	**h'ióng-maw**	熊猫
pig	**dzî-lu**	猪
pigsty	**dzî-lu-b'ã / dzî-chüoe**	猪圈
rabbit	**tú-dzï / tù-dzï**	兔子
sheep	**mí-'yã**	绵羊
sheep / goat	**'yã́**	羊
squirrel	**sòng-tsï**	松鼠
tail	**ní-bo / mí-bo**	尾巴
tiger	**láw-hu**	老虎
water buffalo	**sĭ-nieu**	水牛
whale	**j'ín-ñg**	鲸鱼
wolf	**lã́w**	狼

Birds

bird	**niáw / diáw**	鸟
chick	**shiáw-ji**	小鸡
chicken	**jì** 鸡 / (*free range*) **tsáw-ji**	草鸡
crow	**láw-h'uo / wù-ya**	乌鸦
dove	**gēq-dzï**	鸽子
duck	**āq / āq-dzï**	鸭子
eagle	**láw-yin**	老鹰
goose	**ngú**	鹅

hawk	**láw-yin**	老鹰
hen	**tsÏ-ji**	母鸡
magpie	**shí-chiaq**	喜鹊
mandarin ducks	**yüòe-yã-diaw**	鸳鸯
myna bird	**bāq-gu**	八哥
oriole	**h'uắw-yin**	黄莺
owl	**máw-d'eu-yin**	猫头鹰
parrot	**ầ-gu**	鹦鹉
peacock	**kóng-chiaq**	孔雀
pigeon	**gēq-dzï**	鸽子
quail	**òe-zen**	鹌鹑
rooster / cock	**h'ióng-ji**	公鸡
sparrow	**mó-chiaq / mó-jiaq**	麻雀
swallow	**yí-dzï**	燕子
wild goose	**d'á-'yi**	大雁
wing	**jí-kaq, tsÏ-bāw**	翅膀
woodpecker	**dzõq-moq-niaw**	啄木鸟

Fish and Reptiles

fish	**ñg**	鱼
carp	**lí-ñg**	鲤鱼
clam	**gēq-li**	蛤蜊
clam, freshwater	**b'ầ / h'ú-b'ã**	蚌
crab	**há / b'ắw-ha**	螃蟹
crayfish	**shiáw-long-huo**	小龙虾
eel	**móe / máe-ñg**	鳗鱼
fish bone	**ñg-gueq-d'eu**	鱼刺
fish eggs	**ñg-dzï**	鱼卵
fish fin	**ñg-tsï**	鱼翅
fish scales	**ñg-lin-b'ae**	鱼鳞
flounder	**báe-ñg / niaq-taq-ñg**	比目鱼
frog	**chìn-wo / d'í-ji**	青蛙
gill	**ñg-geq-sae / gēq-sae**	鳃
goldfish	**jìn-ñg**	金鱼
lobster	**lóng-huo**	龙虾
mackerel	**mó-gaw-ñg**	鲅鱼
pufferfish	**h'ú-d'en-ñg**	河豚鱼
razor clam	**tsèn-dzï**	蛏子
ribbonfish	**dá-ñg**	带鱼
ricefield eel	**h'uắw-zoe**	鳝鱼
salmon	**sàe-men-ñg**	三文鱼

sardine	**suò-din-ñg**	沙丁鱼
shark	**suò-ñg**	鲨鱼
shrimp	**huò / hòe**	虾
snail (*water dwelling*)	**lú-sï**	螺蛳
snake	**zuó**	蛇
squid	**'yéu-ñg**	鱿鱼
toad	**lá-geq-bo / lá-sï-geq / lá-ha-mo**	癞蛤蟆
tortoise	**wù-jü**	乌龟
turtle	**jiāq-ñg**	鳖

Insects

ant	**mó-ni**	蚂蚁
bedbug	**tséu-zong**	臭虫
bee	**miq-fong**	蜜蜂
bug	**zóng-dzï**	虫子
butterfly	**h'ú-d'iq**	蝴蝶
caterpillar	**máw-maw-zong**	毛毛虫
centipede	**'wú-gong**	蜈蚣
cicada	**dzï-liaw**	蝉
cockroach	**dzăw-lāw**	蟑螂
cocoon	**jí-dzï**	茧子
cricket	**záe-jiq**	蟋蟀
dragonfly	**shìn-d'in / chìn-d'in**	蜻蜓
earthworm	**chüēq-zoe / chiõq-zoe / chiéu-h'in / bīq-shi**	蚯蚓
firefly	**'yín-hu-zong**	萤火虫
flea	**dzáw-seq / tiáw-seq / tiáw-dzaw**	跳蚤
fly	**tsăw-yin**	苍蝇
grasshopper	**gēq-mã**	蚱蜢
house lizard	**bīq-hu**	壁虎
insect	**zóng-dzï**	虫子
katydid	**jiáw-gu-gu**	蝈蝈
lizard	**sï-jiaq-zuo**	蜥蜴
louse	**sēq-dzï / láw-b'aq-seq**	虱子
maggot	**chì**	蛆
mantis	**d'ăw-lāw**	螳螂
mosquito	**mén-zong**	蚊子
moth	**pōq-den-zong**	灯蛾

silkworm	**zóe-baw-baw** 蚕
slug	**'yí-'yeu / sǐ-'yi-'yeu / b'iq-ti-zong** 蛞蝓
snail (*dry land*)	**gú-nieu** 蜗牛
spider	**dzǐ-dzï / jīq-dzï** 蜘蛛
termite	**b'aq-mo-ni** 白蚁
wasp	**h'ú-fong** 蚂蜂

Habitats

bird's nest	**diáw-ku / niáw-ku** 鸟窝
hive / beehive / wasp's nest	**fòng-ku** 蜂窝
nest / lair	**kù** 窝
spiderweb	**jīq-dzï-lu-mãw** 蜘蛛网

USEFUL ADJECTIVES & OPPOSITES

bland—salty	d'áe—h'áe	淡一咸
bright—dark	liǎ—óe	亮一暗
clean—dirty	chìn-sǎw / gòe-zin—ōq-tsoq	干净—肮脏
clear—muddy	chìn—h'uén	清一混浊
cheap—expensive	b'í-niq / j'iǎ—jǔ	便宜一贵
coarse—fine	tsù—shí	粗一细
cooked—raw	zoq—sǎ	熟一生
dark—light	sèn—d'áe	深一淡
dense—sparse	mǎ—shì	密一稀
deep—shallow	sèn—chí	深一浅
difficult—easy	náe—'yóng-yi / b'í-dǎw	难—容易
dry—wet	gòe—sāq	干一湿
early—late	dzáw—áe	早一晚
far—near	'yüóe—j'ín	远一近
fat—thin (of people)	dzǎw / pǎw—séu	胖一瘦
fragile—tough	tsóe—nín	脆一韧
fragrant—stinky	shiǎ—tséu	香一臭
full—empty	móe—kòng	满一空
hard—soft	ngǎ—nüóe	硬一软
high—low	gàw—dì	高一低
hot—cold	niq—lǎ	热一冷
humid—dry	záw-seq—gòe-saw	潮湿—干燥
large/big—small/little	d'ú—shiáw	大一小
lean meat—fatty meat	jìn-nioq—'yéu-nioq	瘦肉—肥肉
long—short	zǎ—dóe	长一短
many—few	dù—sáw	多一少
new—old	shìn—j'iéu	新一旧
old—young (of people's age)	láw—ní-chin	老—年轻
poor—rich	j'ióng—'yéu tsáw-piaw	穷—有钱
pretty—ugly	háw-koe—náe-koe	好看—难看
protruding—sunken	d'eq—àw	凸一凹

round—square   **'yüóe—fã** 圆—方

scalding—icy   **tãw—bìn** 烫—冰

sink—float   **zén—véu** 沉—浮

slow—fast   **máe—kuá** 慢—快

straight—curved   **zeq—chüëq** 直—曲

strong—weak   **j'iã-dzãw—zaq** 强壮—弱

smart—stupid   **tsòng-min—b'én** 聪明—笨

sweet—bitter   **d'í—kú** 甜—苦

sweet—sour   **d'í—sòe** 甜—酸

tall —short (*of people*)   **zã—á** 高—矮

thick—thin   **h'éu—b'oq** 厚—薄

tight—loose   **jín—sòng** 紧—松

tough—tender   **láw—nén** 老—嫩

true—false   **dzèn—gá** 真—假

wide—narrow   **kuëq—h'aq** 宽—窄

win—lose   **'yín—sì** 赢—输

NUMBERS

0	**lín** 零
1	**yīq** 一
2	**liǎ / ní / 'ér** 两 / 二
3	**sàe** 三
4	**sǐ** 四
5	**ňg** 五
6	**loq** 六
7	**chīq** 七
8	**bāq** 八
9	**jiéu** 九
10	**zeq** 十
11	**zeq-yiq** 十一
12	**zeq-ni** 十二
13	**zeq-sae** 十三
14	**zeq-sï** 十四
15	**zeq-ňg** 十五
16	**zeq-loq** 十六
17	**zeq-chiq** 十七
18	**zeq-baq** 十八
19	**zeq-jieu** 十九
20	**niáe / náe** 二十 (廿)
21	**niáe-yiq / náe-yiq** 二十一
22	**niáe-ni / náe-ni** 二十二

Note ...

In numbers between 30 and 99, the pronunciation of the whole units of 'ten' varies from that of the intermediate units, for instance 30 is **sàe-seq**, while 31 is **sàe-zeq yiq**. Further examples are included below for reference.

30	**sàe-seq** 三十
31	**sàe-zeq yīq** 三十一
32	**sàe-zeq ní** 三十二
40	**sǐ-seq** 四十
43	**sǐ-zeq sáe** 四十三

50	**ñǵ-seq** 五十
54	**ñǵ-zeq sǐ** 五十四
60	**loq-seq** 六十
65	**loq-zeq ñǵ** 六十五
70	**chīq-seq** 七十
76	**chīq-zeq loq** 七十六
80	**bāq-seq** 八十
87	**bāq-zeq chīq** 八十七
90	**jiéu-seq** 九十
98	**jiéu-zeq bāq** 九十八
99	**jiéu-zeq jiéu** 九十九
100	**yīq-baq** 一百
101	**yīq-baq lín-yiq** 一百零一
102	**yīq-baq lín-ni** 一百零二
103	**yīq-baq lín-sae** 一百零三
104	**yīq-baq lín-sï** 一百零四
105	**yīq-baq lín-ñg** 一百零五
110	**yīq-baq-zeq** 一百一十
111	**yīq-baq zeq-yiq** 一百一十一
200	**liǎ-baq** 两百
300	**sàe-baq** 三百
400	**sǐ-baq** 四百
500	**ñǵ-baq** 五百
600	**loq-baq** 六百
700	**chīq-baq** 七百
800	**bāq-baq** 八百
900	**jiéu-baq** 九百
1,000	**yīq-chi** 一千
2,000	**liǎ-chi** 两千
10,000	**yīq-vae** 一万
first	**d'í-yiq** 第一
second	**d'í-ni** 第二
third	**d'í-sae** 第三
fourth	**d'í-sï** 第四
fifth	**d'í-ñg** 第五
sixth	**d'í-loq** 第六
seventh	**d'í-chiq** 第七

eighth	**d'í-baq**	第八
ninth	**d'í-jieu**	第九
tenth	**d'í-zeq**	第十
twentieth	**d'í-niae**	第二十

once	**yīq-tsï**	一次
twice	**liǎ-tsï**	两次
three times	**sàe-tsï**	三次

one-half	**yīq-boe**	一半
one-third	**sàe-fen-dzï-yiq**	三分之一
two-thirds	**sàe-fen-dzï-'er**	三分之二
one-quarter	**sǐ-fen-dzï-yiq**	四分之一
three-quarters	**sǐ-fen-dzï-sae**	四分之三

MEASURE WORDS

In Shanghainese all nouns are counted using measure words, just as in Mandarin and other Chinese dialects. Measure words function like the word 'item' in the phrase 'six items of clothing' which in Shanghainese would be *loq j'i yì-z'āw* 六件衣裳. Note that singular and plural forms of the noun are the same in Shanghainese. There is no separate plural form. Shanghainese measure words are frequently the same as in Mandarin, but not always. For example, the measure word for 'bed' is *dzāq* 只 in Shanghainese, but *zhāng* 张 in Mandarin. Measure words are also used with the demonstrative prefixes *g'eq* (this) and *àe* (that) to form demonstrative pronouns:

g'eq-**dzāq** (zǎw) 这张（床）	*this (bed)*
àe-**j'í** (tsén-sae) 那件（衬衫）	*that (shirt)*

The most common and useful measure words are:

For:	Use:
animals / furniture / fruit / etc.	**dzāq** 只
books	**bén** 本
bottles of things	**b'ín** 瓶
bouquets	**j'iéu** 束 (毬)
boxes of things	**h'aq** 盒
bridges, mountains	**zú** 座
buildings	**zǎw** 幢
bunches, clusters, things strung together	**tsóe** 串
cans of things	**tìn** 听
cars, vehicles	**b'ú** 部
cups of things	**bàe** 杯
days	**niq** 日
degrees (temperature)	**d'ú** 度
doors, windows	**sóe** 扇
drips	**dōq** 滴
families, companies	**gà** 家
fish, ropes, towels, pants, skirts	**d'iáw** 条
flights, trains, bus trips	**bàe** 班
flowers	**dú** 朵

For:	Use:
grains	**liq** 粒
groups, batches	**pì / pēq** 批
hats, bridges	**dín** 顶
hours, o'clock	**dí-dzong** 点钟
houses, apartments, condos	**zaq** 宅
incense sticks, candlesticks	**dzǐ / gèn** 支 / 根
kinds	**dzóng** 种
knives, tools (*that are held in the hand*)	**bó** 把
lamps	**dzáe** 盏
layers	**zén** 层
letters	**fòng** 封
lumps, chunks, soap, bricks, Chinese *yuán*	**kuáe** 块
matters of business	**dzǎw** 桩
meals, beatings, scoldings	**dén** 顿
minutes, cents	**fèn** 分
mirrors, flags	**mí** 面
mouthfuls	**kéu** 口
packages of things	**bàw** 包
pages	**y'iq / báe** 页
pairs	**dáe / sǎw** 对 / 双
pens, pencils, sticks	**dzǐ** 枝
people (*general usage*), places	**g'eq / h'eq** 个
people (polite)	**'wáe** 位
pictures, stamps, flat things	**dzǎ** 张
pieces of candy, marbles, single grains	**liq** 粒
piles of things	**dàe** 堆
plants, trees	**kù** 棵
plates of things	**b'óe** 盘
pounds	**bǎw** 磅
rooms	**gàe** 间
rows	**b'á / d'á** 排
sentences	**jǘ** 句
sets	**táw** 套
shirts, blouses	**j'í** 件
shops, stores, fields	**b'áe** 爿
slices	**pí** 片
small amounts	**ngáe** 点

For:	Use:
spells of wind or rain	**zén** 阵
sums of money	**bīq** 笔
trips	**tãw** 趟
times (*one does something*)	**tsí** / **d'á** 次
times (*beginning to end, the whole way through*)	**bí** 遍

THUMBNAIL GUIDE TO BASICS

I / me	**ngú / h'ú** 我
us / we	**āq-laq / āq-la** 我们
you (*singular*)	**nóng** 你
you (*plural*)	**ná** 你们
he / she / him / her	**'yí** 他 / 她
they / them	**'yí-laq / 'yí-la** 他们
my / mine	**ngú-g'eq / ngú-eq** 我的
ours	**āq-laq-g'eq / āq-la-eq** 我们的
yours (*singular*)	**nóng-g'eq / nóng-eq** 你的
yours (*plural*)	**ná-g'eq / ná-eq** 你们的
his / hers	**'yí-g'eq / 'yí-eq** 他的 / 她的
theirs	**'yí-laq-g'eq / 'yí-la-eq** 他们的
this	**g'eq-g'eq / g'eq-h'eq** 这个
that	**yì-g'eq / yì-eq / àe-g'eq** 那个
these	**g'eq-ngae / g'eq-di** 这些
those	**àe-ngae / yì-di** 那些
here	**g'eq-d'eu** 这儿
there	**yì-mi / àe-d'eu** 那儿
what?	**sá / sá-g'eq?** 什么？
who?	**sá-nin?** 谁？
whose?	**sá-nin-g'eq?** 谁的？
what?	**sá-meq-zï?** 什么东西？
why?	**sá-zï-ti? / sà-ti?** 为什么？
where?	**sá•d'í-fāw?** 什么地方？
when?	**sá•zén-guāw? / jí-zï?** 什么时候？
what time?	**jí-di-dzong?** 几点钟？
which?	**h'á-li?** 哪？
where?	**h'á-li? / h'á-li-daq?** 哪儿？
which one?	**h'á-li-g'eq?** 哪个？
why? / what reason?	**'wáe-sa? / sá•gãw-jieu?** 为什么？/ 什么原因？
how many?	**dù-saw? / jí-huo?** 多少？
how long?	**dù-saw zén-guāw? / jí-zï?** 多少时间？

how much does it cost?	**jí-d'i?** 多少钱？
how?	**ná-nen? / ná-nen-ga?** 怎么？/ 怎么样？
what's that?	**yì-eq zí sá-meq-zï?** 那个是什么？
is/are there ...?	**'yéu ... va?** 有...吗？
where is/are ...?	**... laq sá•d'í-fãw?** ...在哪儿？
here is/are ...	**... laq g'eq-d'eu.** ...再这儿。
have	**'yéu** 有
do/did not have	**m̄-meq** 没有
What should I do?	**Ngú yìn-gai ná-nen-dzu?** 我应该怎么做？
What do you want?	**Nóng yáw dí sá?** 你要什么？
What do you want to buy?	**Nóng má dí sá?** 你买什么？
I want to buy ...	**Ngú shiá̌ má ...** 我想买...
I want to go to ...	**Ngú shiá̌ chí ...** 我想去...
be in/at/on	**laq** 在
very	**màe / jiàw-guae** 很
most	**dín** 最
and / with	**tēq** 跟
not / no	**veq** 不
or	**àe-zï** 还是
but	**dáe-zï** 但是
more or less	**tsà-veq-du** 差不多
I like ...	**Ngú huòe-shi ...** 我喜欢...
I don't like ...	**Ngú veq-huoe-shi ...** 我不喜欢...
I want ...	**Ngú yáw ...** 我要...
I don't want ...	**Ngú veq-yaw ...** 我不要...
I want to ...	**Ngú shiá̌ ...** 我想...
I don't want to ...	**Ngú veq-shiã ...** 我不想...

I know.	**Ngú shiáw-deq.** 我知道。
I don't know.	**Ngú veq shiáw-deq.** 我不知道。
Do you understand?	**Nóng dóng va?** 你懂吗？
I understand.	**Ngú dóng h'eq.** 我懂的。
I don't understand.	**Ngú veq dóng.** 我不懂。
Don't …	**Viáw …** 别…
Sorry!	**Dáe-veq-chi!** 对不起！
Sorry to disturb you!	**Dǎ-zaw-nong-leq!** 打搅你了！
Thanks for taking the trouble!	**Mó-vae-nong-leq!** 麻烦你了！
You've been working hard!	**Shìn-ku-leq!** 辛苦了！
This is important!	**G'eq-g'eq jiàw-guae yáw-jin h'eq!** 这个很要紧的！
It's not important!	**Veq-yaw-jin!** 不要紧！
It's not a problem!	**Veq-ngae-zï!** 不碍事！
It doesn't matter!	**Ḿ-meq guàe-shi!** 没关系！
Please …	**Chín …** 请…
Can I trouble you to …	**Mó-vae-nong …** 麻烦你…
Thanks!	**Zyiá-zyia!** 谢谢！
You're welcome.	**Viáw zyiá. / Viáw kǎq-chi.** 不谢。/ 别客气。
Is there a problem?	**'Yéu mén-d'i va?** 有问题吗？
Careful!, Danger!	**Dǎw-shin!, 'Wáe-shi!** 小心！危险！
Quick! Call the police!	**Góe-jin jiáw jín-tsaq!** 赶紧叫警察！
Could you please repeat (that)?	**Chín dzáe gǎw yīq-tsï?** 请再说一次？

How do you write (that)?	**Ná-nen shiá?** 怎么写？
How do you say (that)?	**Ná-nen gǎw?** 怎么说？
How do you say …?	**… ná-nen gǎw?** …怎么说？
How do you say … in Shanghainese?	**… Zǎw-hae-h'ae-h'uo ná-nen gǎw?** …上海话怎么说？

QUICK PRONUNCIATION CHART

Letter(s)	Pronunciation	Example
' or '	like the *h* in *heather*	**d'éu** [dhuh] *head*
a	like the *a* in *father*	**má** [ma] *buy*
ã	like the *o* in *tong* with nasality	**lã́** [lahⁿ] *cold*
ae	like the *a* in *fad*	**láe** [lae] *come*
aq	like *awk* in *awkward*	**bāq** [baw^k] *eight*
aw	like the *aw* in *law*	**háw** [haw] *good*
ãw	like the *aw* in *lawn* with nasality	**mã́w** [mawhⁿ] *busy*
b	like the *b* in *bar*	**bín** [bean] *pancake*
ch	like the *ch* in *cheese*	**chīq** [chi^k] *eat*
d	like the *d* in *day*	**dí** [dee] *store*
dz	like the *ds* in *fads*	**dzòng** [dsowng] *middle*
en	like the *un* in *fun*	**dén** [dun] *wait*
eq	like *uck* in *buckwheat*	**bēq** [buh^k] *give*
er	like *are* and the *ar* in *far*	**'ér** [h-are] *ear*
eu	like the *u* in *gun*	**d'éu** [dhuh] *head*
f	like th *f* in *fine*	**fèn** [fun] *minute*
g	like the *g* in *go*	**gà** [gah] *family*
h	like the *h* in *heel*	**háw** [haw] *good*
i	like *ee* in *see*	**jí** [jee] *how many*
ï	like the *zz* in *fuzz*	**sḯ** [sszz] *four*
in	like the *in* in *pink*	**nín** [neen] *person*
iq	like the *iq* in *liquid*	**chīq** [chi^k] *seven*
j	like the *j* in *jeans*	**jiéu** [jee-uh] *wine*
k	like the *k* in *key*	**kà** [kah] *wipe*
l	like the *l* in *law*	**láw** [law] *old*
m	like the *m* in *may*	**mí** [me] *noodles*
m̃	like the *mm* in *hmm*	**m̃-ma** [mm-ma] *mother*
n	like the *n* in *need*	**niéu** [nee-uh] *cow*
ng	like the *ng* in *sing*	**ngú** [ngoo] *hungry*
ñg	like the *ng* in *sung*	**ñǵ** [ng] *five*
o	like the *oo* in *foot*	**huò** [huoo] *flower*
oe	like German *ö* or French *eu*	**gòe** [gö] *dry*
ong	like *own*, but ending in *–ng*	**fòng** [fowng] *wind*

oq	like *olk* in *folkways*	**bōq** [bow^k] *north*
p	like the *p* in *pat*	**piáw** [pee-aw] *ticket*
s	like the *s* in *sea*	**sáw** [saw] *few*
sh	like the *sh* in *she*	**shìn** [sheen] *star*
t	like the *t* in *tie*	**tì** [tee] *sky*
ts	like the *ts* in *cats*	**tsáw** [tsaw] *stir-fry*
ü	like German *ü* or French *u*	**jǚ** [jü] *expensive*
u	like *oo* in *mood*	**hú** [hoo] *fire*
uo	like the *u* in *put*	**mó** [muoo] *horse*
v	like the *v* in *vine*	**veq** [vut] *not*
w	like *oo* in *mood*	**wàe** [ooae] *crooked*
y	like *ee* in *see*	**yīq** [ee-i^k] *one*
z	like the *z* in *zoo*	**zuó** [zuoo] *tea*
zy	like the *s* in *measure*	**zyiá** [jhee-ya] *thank*

Tone Marks and Tones

Rising tone mark ´

    in one and two syllable words indicates a rising tone ↗
    in words of three or more syllables indicates rising-
    falling tone ↗ ↘

Falling tone mark `

    indicates a falling tone ↘

High tone mark ¯

    in one syllable words indicates a high tone →|
    in two syllable words indicates a rising tone ↗
    in words of three or more syllables indicates rising-
    falling tone ↗ ↘

No tone mark

    indicates a low rising tone ↗|

A dot •

    means the previous syllable is a mid-level tone →

Tone marks are only on the 1st syllable of a word; but tones spread across the whole word.